Fifth Avenue Famous

Fifth Avenue Famous

The Extraordinary Story of Music at St. Patrick's Cathedral

SALVATORE BASILE

FORDHAM UNIVERSITY PRESS New York 2010

Fordham University Press has no responsibility for the persistence or accuracy of URLs for external or third-party Internet websites referred to in this publication and does not guarantee that any content on such websites is, or will remain, accurate or appropriate.

Library of Congress Cataloging-in-Publication Data

Basile, Salvatore, 1955–
    Fifth Avenue famous : the extraordinary story of music at St. Patrick's Cathedral / Salvatore Basile.—1st ed.
        p. cm.
    Includes bibliographical references and index.
    ISBN 978-0-8232-3187-4 (cloth : alk. paper) — ISBN 978-0-8232-3189-8 (ebook : alk. paper)
    1. St. Patrick's Cathedral (New York, N.Y.). Choir—History. 2. Church music—New York (State)—New York. 3. Church music—Catholic Church. I. Title.
ML33.N49B35 2010
781.71′20097471—dc22

                    2009054040

Printed in the United States of America
12 11 10   5 4 3 2 1
First edition

To my parents and my grandparents,

the first storytellers I knew

CONTENTS

FOREWORD

Mr. Salvatore Basile has done a great service to Saint Patrick's Cathedral by writing its first history of music—from its origin in Saint Patrick's Old Cathedral in lower Manhattan through the present time.

Fifth Avenue Famous is not simply a compilation of historical facts about music. It ties these facts—and there are many—together with the events of New York as early as the late 1800s.

Mr. Basile's book is also a journal of sorts, as it records how church music has been shaped and developed through such important documents as Pope Saint Pius X's *Tra le Sollecitudini* (1903) and the Second Vatican Council.

Describing in detail prominent conductors, composers, organists, and opera singers—living and deceased—*Fifth Avenue Famous* is filled with interesting stories that will enable the reader to enjoy an up-close and behind-the-scenes look at the musical life of our beloved cathedral.

In addition, accounts of ordinations, funerals, installations, and papal visits are described in such vivid detail so as to make the reader feel present for these historic events.

Fifth Avenue Famous is wonderfully written, and I thank Mr. Basile for providing us with an engaging, interesting, and entertaining account of the music at what Archbishop John Hughes proudly referred to as our "cathedral of suitable magnificence."

+ Timothy M. Dolan
Archbishop of New York

PREFACE

The critic Charles Burney referred to them as "the refuse of the opera houses." The novel *One Foot in Heaven* labeled them "a cross between the devil's grandmother and a mountain goat"; an authority on religion called them "merely clever in doing things with their fingers or their vocal cords." They are liturgical musicians, the people who conduct, play organ, and sing in church choirs—or as one priest put it, "showbiz for people who have no business being in showbiz."

Many church choirs are admittedly dreadful and deservedly anonymous. Some, however, have achieved fame. And one of the most famous in the United States is the choir of St. Patrick's Cathedral. Depending on the era, its membership has been composed of superstar singers, or rank-and-file hardworking musicians, or untutored amateurs who are continually titillated to find themselves showing up in newspapers and national magazines and on network television. They may have joined for religious reasons or musical reasons or because they think it might be fun. Fun, however, isn't exactly what it's about.

Since the Cathedral's opening in 1879, the musicians of St. Patrick's have been responsible for providing the music for more than 6,000 Solemn Pontifical Masses—not to mention the countless Vesper services, High Masses, Low Masses, special services, concerts, weddings, funerals, and other occasions when a church function needs music. It's a huge commitment both professionally and emotionally, especially considering that the musicians are providing background scores for important milestones in the lives of people whom they have often never met. Most of this work requires an ability to function with others as a unit. Much of it requires getting up early. Singers have never been known for either quality. It takes unusual people to sing at St. Patrick's.

And it takes unusual people to lead the music. Since its first days, the Cathedral has never lacked for organists, music directors, and conductors. They have been possessed of a blinding variety of levels of ability, and in their personalities they have run the gamut from exemplary human beings to grievously flawed individuals. Their reward has rarely been monetary; it never is for anyone who works for any religious institution. But they've been on the inside, contributing to a musical effort that has often been discussed in superlatives. (One story, whether or not it's actually true, proves the point: a Christmas Eve when the Duke of Windsor attended Midnight Mass at St. Patrick's. As the tale ran, he was apparently so taken with the service that he—the once-titular head of the Church of England—stepped up to receive Holy Communion.)

St. Patrick's maintains an unusual place in the history of sacred music—not only because of its fame but also because its own history coincides with that of a critical time in the history of New York itself, when the city evolved from a commercial port town into an international capital. It's only natural that the developments occurring in one of the world's most famous cities would resonate in the music made in one of the world's most famous churches.

Any history of an organization that presents its efforts to the public on a regular basis might seem at first glance somewhat skimpy and jumpy. If the organization runs at all smoothly, a large number of those performances won't necessarily be worthy of historical note. The others, whether memorable occasions or outstanding disasters, provide the markers that punctuate that flow of time. This book attempts to tell their story.

My personal introduction to the Cathedral of St. Patrick came at the age of sixteen. I was a small-town kid visiting New York with a high school group, we were to be taken to the legendary St. Pat's for the Sunday 10:15 Mass—and, excitement of excitements, we were ushered into the front row. I drank in the brilliance of the prelude music, the surroundings . . . and then a bare minute before the Mass began, I remembered that I had left every bit of my cash on the hotel nightstand before checking out. I sprinted down the center aisle and out of St. Patrick's front door, and I never did make it back for that Mass.

When I moved to New York, I was one of the thousands of people who liked to visit the Cathedral at lunchtime. However, it never occurred to me that I would actually *sing* there. So it was a strange experience when, in 1998, I found myself auditioning for a solo in an upcoming concert. Getting hired was one thing; walking onto the famous altar and trying to croak out any sound at all, I thought, would be considerably more difficult.

But here's an inside tip: There is something, either in the architecture of the place or the stones themselves or the spirit that pervades them, that made singing at the Cathedral that first night, and on all of the occasions since, a snap.

The seed for this book was planted during preparations for the 2004 concert that marked the Cathedral's 125th anniversary. While I was researching for program notes, two things became clear. First: The music department of this place has had a fascinating history. Second: That history was in danger of being obliterated, forgotten by most people, its documentation scattered in boxes, clipping files, a line here and there in books concentrating on other subjects. Just trying to find an accurate listing of the Cathedral's music directors required consulting a number of often-contradictory sources.

Now allow me to share a personal anecdote. During one rehearsal, the men of the choir were handed copies of a piece of music—"O Salutaris," dated 1899, composed for St. Patrick's by J. C. Ungerer. Its original lithograph was executed in an elaborate copperplate script, utterly unlike the computer-produced notation of today. We were told that photocopies were necessary because the original music sheets, found in a back cabinet of the music library, were too fragile to be read without literally crumbling.

Just holding the paper was a shock. Until that moment, Ungerer's name had existed only as a part of one of those and-then-we-wrote lists, *this* choirmaster preceded by *that* choirmaster and followed by another one. But the swooping handwritten notes brought him into the room as an actual presence, a man whose many tasks apparently included the job of writing to order for a given text, a given occasion, a specific group of musicians. One wonders if Mr. Ungerer had ever given a thought to the fate of this particular piece some hundred-plus years hence. I hope he would have been glad, or at least intrigued, to know that it was being performed in the twenty-first century.

One more anecdote. When one is dealing with any world-renowned institution, the fables run thick and fast, such as the oft-stated line of a friend (who to my knowledge has never so much as set foot in St. Patrick's): "Oh, you know, Caruso sang there all the time."

I had to find out if that was true.

ACKNOWLEDGMENTS

When they say, "History doesn't happen in a vacuum," they're not kidding. The precise extent to which this adage is true will promptly become evident to anyone who prepares to write any history—as that writer discovers that the good stuff isn't always down there in black and white. I was lucky enough to track down a number of people who owned, or remembered, the good stuff. I'm amazed by the powers of recall possessed by many of them, as well as by the generosity of time and imagination they offered.

Thanks to Jennifer Pascual, who first thought that this project was worth pursuing; to Monsignor Robert Ritchie, who kindly opened the Archdiocesan Archives of New York for my use; and to Sister Marguerita Smith, O.P., who managed those archives and made them not only available but easily usable. And particular thanks to Archbishop Timothy M. Dolan, who not only encouraged the project but contributed his own time and talent. John Schaeffer provided not only continual encouragement but also the material support to make the whole thing possible.

I got plenty of help from the staffs of the New York Public Library for the Performing Arts, the New-York Historical Society, Gino Francesconi and the Carnegie Hall Archives, and the Microforms Division of the New York Public Library. Steven Jaffe and Estevan Pärt gave honest assessment as well as a broad overview, and they always asked the right questions; Lucy Jaffe provided thorough and imaginative research to get the answers. Susie Boydston-White contributed the technical skills that made bad photos viewable. Donald Dumler, Dianne Rivetti, Loretta Yon Schoen, Richard Yon, and Richard Yon Jr. opened their memories as well as their scrapbooks and cheerfully endured countless questions and repeat questions. David Skoblow not only provided memorabilia and time but also shepherded the project into the hands of Sister Anne-Marie Kirmse, whose guidance was invaluable.

Many people provided interviews, documents, pictures, and above all enthusiasm: Ellen Alexander, Jonathan Bowen, Losana Boyd, Monsignor Dermot Brennan, Peggy Breslin, Daniel Brondel, Linda Catalo, Father Stephen Concordia, O.S.B., Norman Caldwell Coombs, Brendan Corrigan, Robert C. Courboin, Robert C. Courboin Jr., Stanley Cox, Chris

Cummings, Harry Danner, Alan Davis, Monsignor Francis X. Duffy, Cori Ellison, Robert Evers, Monsignor John Ferry, Donna Halper, Walter Hook, James Javore, Patricia Kelby, Steve Lawson, John McManemin, Joseph McQuade, Dolores Nolan, Cathy O'Connor, Father John O'Hara, Nancy Parish, John Peragallo III, Stephen Pinel, James Poma, McNeil Robinson, Ned Rorem, Jim Schmitz, Roberta Shea, Chris Sheridan, Father Timothy Shreenan, O.F.M., Joseph Smith, Stephen Tharp, Jessica Tranzillo, Nancy Valtos, Father Robert Verrigni, Joe Vitacco, John Calvin West, Nadja Witkowska, and Paul Zorovich. My gratitude.

"This was just like *real* music!"

Overheard after a concert at St. Patrick's Cathedral

Chapter 1

THE SUBSTITUTE CHOIRMASTER (May 25, 1879)

> It is but natural that religious music should be very greatly affected by the secular music of the day. But it is not alone that the character of sacred music has been thus influenced; it is that the Catholic Church, in its ambitious efforts to pander to the demands of the popular taste, has taken the music of the opera direct from the stage and placed it in the choir. . . . [O]pera music is nowhere so thoroughly reproduced as at mass or vespers in our largest Catholic churches. This condition of things is about as bad as that which existed in the Church in the sixteenth century.
>
> *Harper's New Monthly Magazine*, April 1879

William F. Pecher had more than enough reason to be discouraged.

For most of his life, the organist had led an existence in which careful plans had always been made, but nothing had worked out exactly as planned. Pecher had been born sometime around 1840 (he made a life-long practice of concealing his age) to an affluent Manhattan family and educated in the city's Catholic school system, and his musical aptitude had become apparent as early as his student years. Because keyboard proficiency was useful in polite society, his parents willingly organized the drawing-room musicales that stamped a home as a place of refinement. Seated at the parlor piano throughout his adolescence, young William accompanied relays of musical acquaintances: amateur string groups, instrumentalists, singers of every type and ability.

As he grew into young manhood, it was apparent that the merchant-class bearing that he should have inherited had been overtaken by a fascination with the rituals of the Church. This may have been a problem for one who had long been expected to take over the family's wines-and-spirits importing business, as it was undoubtedly a jolt when he announced his intention to make a career in sacred music. Mr. and Mrs. Pecher may have had misgivings—music as a profession has never been high on the parental wish list—but if he were to do it, they would prefer that he do it right. In America, the truly successful musician, one who could "properly" support himself, was a musician trained in Europe. They decided that their son would finish his education in Germany, with training in composition and keyboard at the Leipzig Conservatory.

Flush with academic honors (he had been singled out for particular praise by no less a musical authority than Clara Schumann), Pecher returned to New York in 1860 and began to look for work. It was instantly apparent that the studious young man had grown into an embodiment of the "native son" cliché beloved of that Horatio Alger-esque era, but reinforced with European credentials and culture. In a city that still felt itself to be second-rate where artistic status was concerned, Pecher hoped that the blend would be attractive enough to aid him in finding a distinguished position.

Unfortunately, there were only so many distinguished positions to go around. After two years, his career track had taken him as far as St. Peter's on Barclay Street, significant for nothing except its history as the first Catholic church built in Manhattan. Also anchored in the past was its musical significance; St. Peter's had once been a glamorous location, the church whose choir gave the city notable early performances of major choral works. But New York's population center had long since shifted north of Barclay Street, and St. Peter's had become a distant second to the beloved squat, ungainly structure that was a magnet for the city's Catholics, occupying an entire block between Mulberry and Mott streets—St. Patrick's Cathedral. With its congregation and finances sadly depleted, the glory days were over for music at St. Peter's. This meant that Pecher would have to pad his slight income with any musical odd jobs that might come his way.

One of those odd jobs would be memorialized in a short *New York Times* blurb entitled CONSECRATION OF BISHOP SPAULDING on April 29, 1877. The service would take place at St. Patrick's Cathedral, the article read, and it casually added: ". . . music will be rendered under the direction of the organist of St. Peter's Church, William F. Pecher."

This engagement would prove to be more than a quick fill-in.

New York's relationship to its musical life had always been a love–hate affair, or more accurately one of love-and-neglect. The aristocratic commentator Mrs. Frances Trollope had once referred to the city's (wealthiest) citizens as the "Medici of the Republic," and this appellation flattered their image of themselves as passionate consumers of culture. But while those Medici loved the idea of seeing and being seen at cultural events, they hadn't grasped the concept of supporting those events with long-term financial patronage. So, during the years when Pecher and his ilk were trying to make a mark on the city's music, most of the city's musical organizations were doomed to extinction before the first chord was struck.

There was the Philharmonic, established for the fourth time after previous efforts had foundered, but its total subscription base could fund no more than four concerts each year. Its operating budget was so meager that musicians played without salary, settling instead for a share of the box office take. At least the orchestra members could look forward to some cash; guest soloists were expected to donate their services.

Attempt after attempt had been made to establish a regular opera company—the latest at the recently built Academy of Music, with its season lasting a total of six weeks—but New York audiences got the greater share of their operatic performances from traveling companies. Besides, the game was played almost exclusively by the city's wealthy, modish Uppertens.* Most middle-class New Yorkers equated opera with theater, where stage performers were morally suspect† and even the playhouses themselves were regarded as places for sporting men to meet women of easy virtue. Theaters, opera houses included, were furiously decried in some pulpits and many drawing rooms. (The lifelong New Yorker and diarist George Templeton Strong, an uncommonly intelligent man who was passionate about music, agonized for years over the question of whether it

* Short for "Upper Ten Thousand," the term applied at the time to the members of New York high society. It was superseded by Ward McAllister's "Four Hundred."

† The attitude was so prevalent that, on a few occasions when respectable ladies gave musical performances to benefit local charities, they would perform only if hidden by a white silk drape to avoid being mistaken for "stage creatures."

would be proper for him to actually *attend* a staged opera.) Should upright citizens be curious enough to want to hear opera singers—European, exotic, and beyond the pale—concert performances were as far as they would dare to venture.

Decades before, those visiting opera singers had found that they could defuse their notoriety while expanding their concert seasons (and earnings) by making themselves available to perform with churches and choral societies, where their efforts would be "assisted" by local vocalists. In theory the idea should have worked. But New York's residents, as well as the city's many musical publications, noted innumerable fiascos in which established professionals attempted to perform next to cowering amateurs, or the efforts of well-rehearsed volunteers were sabotaged by unprepared stars who had blithely skipped in for a quick buck.

Worse, personalities could get in the way of the music. One of the earliest events of that type, and as it turned out one of the more embarrassing, was held at St. Patrick's: the 1826 "Orphans' Benefit" concert. Manuel García and his Italian Opera Company had brought the art form to New York and taken the city by storm; so had his daughter Maria García, one of the star singers. (During her stay in the city she married, becoming Maria Malibran; soon after that her career would catch fire, and she would become an operatic legend.) The public response was so enthusiastic that one newspaper editorial suggested, "Why cannot we have High Mass celebrated at St. Patrick's Cathedral with all the richness of the Garcías? Our suggestion is worth consideration." It was considered, seriously—by one of the tour's backers, himself a trustee of St. Patrick's. And he persuaded the members of the Italian Opera Company to donate their services for a concert of oratorio selections to benefit the Catholic Orphan Asylum. Music-loving New York was electrified, Catholic New York as well. And because the performance would take place at the Cathedral, the choir was invited to participate. But there was a problem on the horizon: The Cathedral choir was made up of self-styled "gentlemen," nonprofessionals who had little truck with refinements such as sight-reading and insisted that the choirmaster teach them every note they sang.

At the first rehearsal, the gentlemen discovered that their music would consist almost entirely of choruses by Handel and Haydn. That particular level of musical difficulty, they decided, was "beyond their range." Being "mere amateurs" (their own terminology, but very much appropriate), they instantly bowed out of the performance; because they withdrew, the Cathedral trustees assumed that they need not be offered free tickets to the concert. And because they were not offered tickets, the entire choir as a body resigned from St. Patrick's.

Although the performance itself was reported to be an immense success both artistically and financially, it was nearly overshadowed by public accusations of ingratitude flying between trustees and choir, the details of which New York got to read in a Catholic newspaper called *The Truth Teller*. It took a month, but finally the choirmen had been mollified enough to go back to St. Patrick's, their return "hailed." The trustees, insisting that they bore no blame for the uproar, were "exonerated." And Malibran—she had been casting about for some additional income, but the Cathedral fracas had been too much of a free-for-all for her taste. She looked elsewhere and got a job singing at Grace Church.

The "amateur" mindset, obviously, was responsible for some very sloppy noises encountered by listeners. Strong wrote, after an Easter visit to the Church of the Ascension:

> . . . a certain Miss Gibson succeeded in establishing the fact that she is unable to sing "I know that my Redeemer liveth" to the entire and total settlement of the question. . . .

And after a performance of the American Musical Institute, a local choral society, the publication *Albion* went so far as to suggest

> . . . the propriety of engaging a number of good, professional choristers; the expense would prove a profit in the end, for amateur volunteers, though their readiness to assist deserves commendation, are of little service unless they can sing.

The American Musical Institute was by no means alone in that dismal landscape. Scores of amateur vocal and instrumental groups were continually springing up, existing for one concert or fifty—the Harmonic Society, the Mendelssohn Union, the Glee and Madrigal Society, the Song Union, the Sacred Music Society—and then disappearing without a trace, their ill-disciplined members simply unable to sustain a viable performance standard.

Not that the participants had much incentive to hone their skills. "Professional" musicians in midcentury New York were poor cousins compelled to exist in the shadow of those visiting European stars, and their status guaranteed them lukewarm response, condescending reviews, and pitiful fees.* When the sensationally popular "Swedish Nightingale," Jenny Lind, visited New York for a series of concerts in 1850, she received an upfront cash guarantee of $187,500 (in today's money, well over $4 million) and completely new furnishings in her hotel suite; in contrast, tenor Anthony Reiff (sometimes heard at St. Patrick's) augmented his earnings as a hornist and as a music teacher at the Blind Institute, and oratorio soloist Marcus Colburn moonlighted as a hotelier. Conductors and choirmasters were supposedly full-time musicians, but they had to advertise for students and pick up what extra work they could. Ureli Corelli Hill was one of the minority of New York musicians who actually made a living at music, functioning as conductor of the New York Philharmonic but seen nearly everywhere else, as conductor or instrumentalist, in a grueling self-imposed schedule. Even the highly respected William R. Bristow, while he worked as organist for St. Patrick's, found it necessary to spend his weeknights playing clarinet in the pit of the Olympic Theatre.

This vocal and instrumental job-hopping was necessary not only because musicians needed to eat but also because there were comparatively few competent artists, so very many occasions at which their services were desired, and so many New Yorkers routinely putting in a staggering five or six nights a week in concert-going—and it mattered not whether those events were presented by established luminaries or church choirs or pig-in-a-poke debutantes. After all, to hear music at all in the nineteenth century meant to hear *live* music. The invention of the player piano was around the corner; the phonograph would show up decades after that; and commercially produced recorded music would have to wait even longer. Exhausting as it might have been to maintain the music habit, many gritted their teeth and did so. Otherwise they were forced to rely upon the drawing-room soirée or their own efforts on the parlor spinet.

Music-making on a high level could be not only a gamble, but a ruinously expensive one. This was painfully learned by both Ureli Corelli

* Sometimes they earned the condescension; one group presented the Beethoven *Eroica*, played by an "orchestra" of seven musicians.

Hill (before his Philharmonic days) and the trustees of St. Peter's Church, when they gave him carte blanche to conduct a series of oratorio performances to benefit the church's building fund. He used the opportunity to stake his claim for musical quality, and everyone agreed that the results were better than anything New York had yet experienced. His first concert, Mozart's *"Twelfth" Mass*, used the city's best possible singers and instrumentalists, and it packed the 600-seat edifice with a crush of 3,000 listeners. When Hill conducted the American premiere of the complete Rossini *Stabat Mater* in 1842, the *New York Herald* reported "an excitement throughout the city yesterday that was beyond all precedent," and the performance created such a frenzy that it had to be repeated twice. Nevertheless, Hill's efforts had taxed not only the church's seating capacity but its budget as well; by 1850, St. Peter's was threatened with bankruptcy.

New Yorkers hungry for musical improvement would soon notice an increase in cash outlay, if not quality. The rise in manufacturing during the 1850s, and after that the wild economy fueled by Civil War speculation, transformed New York from a small town into a boom town, and the Brownstone Decades gave way to the Gilded Age. Many cutthroat entrepreneurs, having been transformed into multimillionaires of the most questionable type, were attempting to sanitize their reputations in order to gain entree to the city's more-established society. A favored gambit was to become staunch supporters—richly, publicly staunch—of their religious institutions. For these people, church attendance was an ideal social activity, the de rigueur see-and-be-seen instinct combined with a hefty measure of what today would be called networking and overlaid with a gloss of pietistic approval. As tightfisted robber barons recast themselves as humanitarians, more and more New York parishes gained the benefit of moving into splendiferous quarters in the newly fashionable uptown neighborhoods. Because budgets and expectations were so much higher, it was assumed that the music produced in these churches was sure to keep pace.

That wasn't always the case. Periodicals of the era were riddled with outbursts against what became known as The State of Church Music. There were still the untrained choirs, striving mightily and unsuccessfully to execute the week's output, top-heavy with supposedly soprano parish ladies, "ladies who are no doubt highly respectable and delightful companions," grumped the *Albion*, "but hardly first-class artists, even in a choral point of view."

A choirmaster might try to avoid the frustration of managing an untalented group by dumping the volunteers and resorting to a professional quartet. The "quartette choir" was a New York craze for a few decades: expedient, simple, and widespread, because it presumably sidestepped vocal and sight-reading issues, as well as the eternal problem of corralling amateurs with busy schedules. But not everyone was enchanted. There were the usual complaints of unlistenable voices and unacceptable execution, and many a choirmaster arranged his quartet's material simply to dole out frequent solo passages to each singer. In many cases the result was an exhibition rather than a church service; *The New England Magazine* complained that the quartet "appropriated the entire music of the services, so that the congregation was obliged to remain silent, even in the singing of the hymns."

Whether or not he hired a quartet, a choirmaster who used paid singers at all very often had to contend with a choir committee. Such a committee comprised parishioners, usually the ones who held the music department's purse strings, and who had given themselves authority to "consult" as regarded the hiring of professional singers. These people tended to be maddeningly nonmusical, completely uninformed, and strongly opinionated. Many of them insisted on attending vocal auditions, and there were legendary horror stories of the self-gratifying caprices to which committee members subjected singers—"vocalizations" to ludicrous heights and depths of range, "determinations" of a singer's potential for volume, sight-reading "tests" of pieces that the committee members themselves could never comprehend. Singers pored over trade-journal articles advising them of the best way to survive these gladiatorial matches. (One writer spoke from long experience in the liturgical music field: "The practical thing is to provide one's self with an oratorio number, a good sacred song and what I call a piece of trash.") Choirmasters had to be accomplished diplomats to avoid antagonizing their committees or being saddled with vocalists who might be utterly unsuited for the job.

No surprise, then, that the-bigger-the-better was the order of the day in many church music departments. When the *Herald* compared the city's choirs, it singled out the seven-voice solo ensemble heading the choir at the Church of St. Francis Xavier—using language that evoked La Scala more than it did a church—for what it considered to be high virtues indeed:

> The choir of this church is undoubtedly, in point of volume and power, one of the most excellent in this city. . . . It need scarcely be observed that the Congregational style of singing is not adopted in this church. . . . There is a musical force attached to St. Francis church abundantly able and willing to give effect to the difficult compositions of some of the most elaborate masters.
>
> The first soprano (prima donna) is Mrs. Cooper, a lady of considerable personal attraction, and a fine, rich and mellow voice. . . . The primo tenore, or leading tenor, is Mr. Hubner . . . gathering green laurels whenever he appeared. . . . [T]he baritone is, beyond doubt, one of the finest singers that can be found anywhere out of the Opera. . . . [T]he power and energy with which he renders the author's music show that he is a connoisseur in the divine art. . . .
>
> The masses sung at St. Francis Xavier are not, as some suppose, selections from operas. . . .

In marked contrast was the cult of the choirboy. Because most prosperous New Yorkers were Anglican, and because they preferred to emulate English customs whenever possible, they doted on the image of the choirboy and demanded the image on a weekly basis in their own churches. St. John's Chapel, St. Chrysostom's Chapel, and the Church of the Heavenly Rest were fortunate enough to recruit and develop respectable all-boy ensembles (and Trinity Church covered all the bases, in somewhat ruthless fashion; although its music had previously been supplied by a mixed chorus along with a double quartet, the boys were "experimentally" introduced, and as soon as their performance standard had tightened up, the females were ousted). But there were plenty of other choirmasters who had no talent for training choirboys but were nonetheless required to produce them. Many an ungifted, unwilling youngster spent Sunday mornings decked out in cassock and surplice, fidgeting—or worse; one man who as a boy had sung at Calvary Episcopal Church remembered clergymen ducking out during services to hunt down AWOL choirboys, break up fistfights, haul them back into the church, and dust them off in time to sing.

The organs at these churches only compounded the annoyance factor, as they were wheezy and underpowered instruments that flattered nothing they accompanied. Those New Yorkers who had done the Grand Tour and heard impressive European organs were usually the selfsame New Yorkers who sat on church vestries and clamored for better instruments. That particular change would be slow in coming. Superior organs were major architectural installations and astronomically expensive.*

Repertoire was an additional problem because choirmasters were discouraged from being too adventurous in repertoire choices, and new works from Europe were notoriously slow to cross the Atlantic. As a result, the city's choirs leaned heavily upon Mozart, Haydn, and Handel, sometimes in watered-down "suitable" rearrangements that avoided any sort of challenge to singers or listeners and were played into the ground. (At one point during the early 1860s, someone at St. Patrick's must have had a particular fondness for Haydn's *Lord Nelson Mass*. Performed at various services by quartet or double quartet or full choir, it showed up a bewildering number of times in reports of the Cathedral's musical offerings. Even Trinity Church had purportedly gone through a phase where "Jackson's *Te Deum*" was sung, each Sunday without fail, for more than twenty years.) To relieve the monotony, choirmasters would occasionally compose their own material; such compositions were considered both utilitarian and disposable. When Trinity's new church building was dedicated in 1847, organist Edward Hodges crafted the service music for the occasion. After the event, it was promptly forgotten.

St. Patrick's was lucky enough to have its own composer, and conductor, and organist, *and* hornist and clarinetist, in the person of the dazzlingly multitalented Gustavus Schmitz. He had replaced David R. Harrison—an organist who had knocked around the city for decades, and whose given name seems not to have ever been mentioned in print; the *Times* invariably referred to him only as "Mr."—at the beginning of the

---

* In his 1908 *History of St. Patrick's Cathedral,* John Cardinal Farley remembered their sound as "old tin horn combinations." Among the various tin horns, he was presumably excluding the 1869 organ installed in St. Patrick's by the man who had held a stranglehold on organ building in New York churches for nearly fifty years, Henry Erben. At the time of its installation, the $15,000 instrument was noted in the *New York Times* to be the largest in New York or Brooklyn, "with exception of that of Trinity Church, which is twice its size."

1864–65 season, while Harrison had previously replaced Antonio Morra, who had replaced Ureli Corelli Hill, who had replaced William R. Bristow, a revolving-door shuffle of choirmasters that had taken less than twenty years and had thoroughly rattled everyone involved. Schmitz was easily up to the task, inheriting a choir of "sixty to eighty mixed voices" along with a supply of boys who came from the city's various Catholic schools, trained to sing responses. He replaced the solo quartet with singers of his own choosing, including Madame Victor Chome, former diva of the Brussels Opera; Herr Urchs, bass soloist of the New York Liederkranz; and in a burst of fortunate nepotism, Schmitz's own brother Henry. Like Gustavus he was a multitasker, not only principal horn soloist for the Philharmonic but a surprisingly good tenor as well, and able to step in as conductor on a moment's notice.

With his personnel in place, Gustavus Schmitz settled into his job, not only bumping up the quality of the product but also composing prolifically (he produced eight Mass settings specifically for Cathedral use, as well as a sheaf of incidental pieces).* With his connections in the music community, he was able to bring in well-known singers and instrumentalists for special occasions. Other than the fact that his name was continually mangled in newspaper accounts—spelled variously Schmidtz, Schmidt, and Smitz—musical activities at St. Patrick's were looking up.

A music director's career prompts him to measure time only in weekly increments: Sunday to Sunday. The concentration on the rituals of the Church year, on the effort of fitting melodies to specific occasions, can cause the outside world to recede in importance. But the savagery of the Civil War years had ripped into the consciousness of city and Cathedral alike. The Draft Riots, with the city under siege from its own citizens and men murdered only steps from the churchyard walls; the unexpected death of Archbishop John Hughes; President Lincoln's assassination; and in between, too many memorials for fallen soldiers—these events made it obvious that the high spirits of midcentury New York were gone forever. Then only eighteen months after Lincoln's funeral came the unthinkable, a fire that devastated the Cathedral in the fall of 1866. Grimly, the congregation began restoration of the structure amid some gallows-humor commentary about the "new" St. Patrick's that was waiting uptown. It was

---

* The reality that proves the legend; regrettably, not a bit of his music seems to have survived.

true that Hughes had laid the cornerstone for a new Cathedral in 1858, but construction had been halted—by lack of funds, and then by wartime shortages—only a few years after it had begun. Moreover, that Cathedral was to be at 50th Street, a location almost impossibly suburban. No one could quite believe that the structure would ever be completed; no one could venture to guess what the following years would hold. And the reality of a new St. Patrick's was a long way off, perhaps never.

Finding Someone to Play at "Hughes's Folly"

Whatever the talent might be of Gustavus Schmitz or his crew, the musical activities at St. Patrick's were those of a Catholic institution functioning in a Protestant town, and those activities were often viewed uncharitably. The attitude usually showed itself in subtle ways, such as newspaper accounts of holiday services around the city; they frequently began with long, lovingly detailed passages describing the minutiae of Trinity Church music ("Trinity, which always takes the lead in the imposing character of its services . . ."), lingering on composers and performers and interludes. The coverage of the offerings at St. Patrick's would often come later in the article, dispatched in a single brief paragraph.

This quietly patronizing viewpoint underwent a radical shift after the end of the Civil War, when Archbishop (soon to be Cardinal) John McCloskey announced that construction would resume on the new Cathedral. As the 1870s began and the edifice took shape, there was widespread amazement that it was being finished at all, and that amazement was tinged with a flavor of anger. Hughes may have gambled on a location for the new Cathedral "beyond the reach of civilization"—but exactly as he had predicted, the city seemed to be moving up to meet the Cathedral. Furthermore, and most offensively to some New Yorkers, this new St. Patrick's Cathedral was going to be the largest house of worship in America. And a Catholic one at that.

Various members of New York's Protestant base reacted with alarm, a few of them with hostility. The *Tribune* gave vent in some bad-tempered sniping at the Cathedral's architectural "platitudes," but then again the *Tribune* had never been much of a friend to the city's Catholics. It was more of a surprise when the *Times* fired its own volley in a malevolent piece entitled THE CHURCH OF AGGRESSION:

> . . . this Church, unlike others, is seeking and has gained a political power which is dangerous to our future. . . . Nothing would give the

Roman Catholic Church of the United States such power over the masses, as large possessions of land and buildings.

More tellingly, other congregations, comprising people who had once giggled at "Hughes's Folly," were feverishly erecting their own churches on this "new" stretch of Fifth Avenue. Before St. Patrick's had been completed, the Collegiate Church of St. Nicholas, Saint Thomas Church, and Fifth Avenue Presbyterian Church had built edifices within blocks of the new Cathedral's site. So intense was the fervor for congregations to move into the area that the Church of the Heavenly Rest crammed its new structure onto the only space available, a plot having a Fifth Avenue frontage of only thirty-one feet. The result was a bizarre confection of tower-*cum*-entrance in front and church sanctuary bloating out in back. Architectural critics branded it "outrageous."

In a sense, the gauntlet had been thrown and St. Patrick's Cathedral was responsible for throwing it. The new Cathedral was going to be one of the most visible symbols of the emerging New York as-cultural-capital, and along with that distinction would be a seismic change in the way that Americans viewed every event taking place within the Cathedral's walls. What had been predominantly local fame would forever after be national renown. So it was only logical that the musical director of St. Patrick's Cathedral—but had anyone given a thought as to who it would be?—would also undergo an increase in the pressure level of his job.

The fast-mounting hoopla was guaranteeing that the job would indeed be considered a plum in the world of liturgical music—far more of a plum than any other music director's job in the United States, even more than the job at proud Trinity. And everyone associated with St. Patrick's had naturally assumed that, when the time came for the Cathedral to move house, it would be Gustavus Schmitz who would move as well to continue his work in the new surroundings. Early in 1876, however, his health went into sudden and inexplicable decline. The choir continued its usual schedule, with Henry filling in as conductor for Holy Week, and the members waited optimistically for Gustavus to return.

He never did. By April of the next year he was dead of an aneurysm.

Mingled with the sadness that everyone felt was the realization that the Cathedral's painstakingly built music department was in danger of foundering. If Henry was offered his brother's position, he didn't accept it, and New York's more prominent choirmasters were otherwise engaged.

Desperate for a stopgap measure, the Cathedral resorted to John White, a London-born organist who was a recitalist by preference and not much attracted to choral music. (Many years later, a subsequent choirmaster of the Cathedral would write White's history in a single clipped line: "Represented as a free lance,—Fine performer,—Not suited for the position.") It was a bad fit and a better-than-nothing choice. Nevertheless, the musicians of St. Patrick's determined to make the best of it.

White's outside schedule was busy enough that he was sometimes unavailable—one of those dates being the consecration of Bishop John Spaulding in May 1877. The Cathedral needed a substitute for the occasion, and someone thought of asking the ever-available organist of St. Peter's, William F. Pecher, to superintend the musical end of things. In preparation and performance, his superior mastery of both the keyboard and the choir loft was embarrassing (embarrassing in comparison to the skill level of John White) and obvious to anyone paying attention (obvious to everyone except Pecher himself, who was functioning as he always had). So it was something of a jolt in the musical community, but not really a surprise, that—on the strength of that single service—he was offered the leadership of the Cathedral's music department.

As a courtesy, John White would be asked to play at the Cathedral's dedication; otherwise, he would stay at Mott Street. He may have wanted the job at the new St. Patrick's, but he wasn't going to get it.*

New Music Director, New Cathedral

The moment that a new employee enters his workspace can be either thrilling or terrifying, and Pecher's first view of the nearly finished Cathedral building would fulfill both expectations. The topmost concern was the sheer size of the place. The Old Cathedral (that was what it was beginning to be called by some, in an undertone) wasn't overwhelming, but manageably church-sized. It seated 950 people comfortably, although the press loved to write of special liturgies drawing jam-packed congregations of 3,000 or more. The choir gallery was reached by the usual short

---

* White didn't do too badly for himself. After a season or two at the Old Cathedral, he leapfrogged his way up to a position at the very Episcopal, very tony Church of the Ascension. His domestic arrangements moved up the social scale as well, from a rear-apartment address on Cherry Street to the high fashion of Central Park West and luxury digs at The Dakota.

flight of stairs and didn't swamp those who sang in it; at full capacity it was crowded to the hilt, but that added to the excitement of a large service. And in singers' parlance, the space was "grateful"; voices were easily heard, flattered by the stone-vaulted acoustics.

The "new St. Patrick's" seated 2,600, and it could theoretically hold a maximum congregation numbering more than 18,000. The gallery was reached by a spiral staircase (wooden at first, stone afterward), requiring a climb of roughly four stories. The new gallery offered munificent space, but the view was dizzying, unnerving. Any group smaller than a full choir would be lost to sight, and possibly to sound as well: Voices would not only be issuing far above the congregation's heads but would then rise to ceiling vaults (not even of stone, but acoustically less sympathetic lath-and-plaster) more than 100 feet high. Most dismaying, those voices, to reach the communion rail, would have to travel more than 150 feet—in New York terms, a block and a half. Not everyone would be able to sing at the new St. Patrick's.*

To compound the problem, there was to be a choir screen—of carved ash—installed at the front of the gallery.† "This front screen is so high that the singers will be hidden from view, which is a good thing in a church," was the double-edged comment of the *Times* a week before the opening. Such a story couldn't have made Pecher very happy. In a large space where singers might worry about projection, a choir screen can psychologically remove the temptation to push the voice; just as often the screen can be viewed as a barrier, transforming otherwise capable vocalists into paranoiacs who are obsessed with volume and unable to relax into their work. Pecher had already been forced to deal with a choir screen at St. Peter's, a white-painted confection of wooden filigree through which his younger singers would poke their fingers when they

---

* On the other hand, Pecher's old post of St. Peter's had the chronic problem, almost from its consecration, of being too small for its music. The church could accommodate its normal congregation without crowding, and its acoustics were perfectly adequate. But never could more than twenty singers squeeze into the choir loft, a claustrophobic niche perched above one side of the altar and reachable only by a set of very, very narrow stairs.

† Whether or not the screen had actually existed, it seems that it was never installed.

were bored. A choir screen was an anomaly for a New York City church. Two screens in a row was dismayingly above the average.

That *Times* article went on to describe the "great" Jardine organ, which was receiving its final touches, five manuals and fifty-eight stops (and crushing Trinity's long-vaunted size record):

> . . . at first sight it appears that the organ almost fills [the gallery] up. . . . A large and powerful choir will be necessary at all times to properly sing the services; for without it, the voices would be lost in the great space of the building. There is certainly no room here for singers and orchestra; but, possibly, it is thought that the organ will be enough, without calling in the aid of other instruments. Four stout men are required to blow the organ, who will work on a sort of treadmill arrangement behind it. There is something irresistibly ludicrous in the appearance these perspiring Irishmen present, perched up against the back of the organ, and working their treadles with such heavy labor. Most large organs are pumped by steam or hydraulic power. What the acoustic properties of the church are can scarcely be known yet; but if the sounding of the organ [during its tuning] can be taken as a test, they are very good. The choir which will sing next Sunday have [*sic*] already had one or two rehearsals in the building.

The fact that choir members could actually get there to rehearse was evidence of the fact that the Cathedral's neighborhood had been improving to catch up with its newly conferred status. Historically, the city's workforce who weren't of the wealthy class—and this included singers at the Old Cathedral—had walked to their jobs.* While uptown reaches of Manhattan were served by horse-drawn street railroads known as "up-cars" (the new Cathedral was flanked by the New York and Harlem Rail Road (NY&H) on Fourth (Park) Avenue and, on the other side, the Sixth Avenue Railroad), the upcars weren't necessarily either quick or economical. The Sixth Avenue trip cost six cents but could take more than an hour for travel from downtown to 50th Street; the NY&H was presumably quicker, because its cars were steam-powered above 42nd Street, but

---

* But a classified ad seeking professional singers for an unnamed church specified, "The location is half an hour's sail from the City"—a fine way to spend one's Sunday commute, rough water notwithstanding.

this method required riders to change trains at Grand Central Depot. Worse, that trip could total thirty-five cents in each direction, adding up to a sizeable chunk of a singer's weekly earnings.

The situation was saved less than a year before the Cathedral's opening, as the success of the new Ninth Avenue Elevated had spurred the construction of a Sixth Avenue line that opened in mid-1878. It was faster than any surface transit, there would indeed be a stop at 50th Street, and the fare would be a nickel. So that problem was solved.*

Now to the issue of the "large and powerful choir" theorized in the *Times*. It would be largely responsible for the signature sound of the new St. Patrick's—but did any church in nineteenth-century New York actually concern itself with such a concept? What indeed was contained in a church's music or that music's performers to produce a "signature sound"?

Trinity, along with its brethren, had given itself a musical signature in the rigid, cool, hands-off perfection of its boychoir. Other churches had a tradition of dainty soprano soloists cutely dubbed "cantatrices," the flip side of those stentorian cantors favored at Temple Emanu-El. Still other congregations made a virtue out of nonmusicality in their music, stating that "overly prepared, overly performed" music in a church was nothing more than sinful display. *Harper's* fanned the flames when it ran the article CHURCH MUSIC IN AMERICA barely a month before St. Patrick's was to open, expressing pointed and specific disdain at the "operatic" character of the music heard "in New York's largest Catholic churches." Indeed, some New York choirmasters had gone through a grotesque fad of appropriating operatic ensembles outright and grafting Latin texts onto them for usage during the Mass—such as a "Tantum ergo" built upon the Sextet from *Lucia di Lammermoor*. These were usually identified as Exhibit A by those who liked to point sneeringly at the excesses of the city's Papists.

As far as William F. Pecher was concerned, that was too bad. *Harper's* could say what it liked; the new Cathedral would be emblematic of the city—New York, capital of the world—and it would be imperative that the

---

* Solved . . . to some extent. With nearly all transport lines stopping at 11:00 P.M. or midnight, musicians putting in off-hours duty at St. Patrick's would have no choice but to trudge over to the 53rd Street station of the Third Avenue El, the only 24/7 line, and wait for one of the El's "Owl Trains."

music maintain and enhance that level of splendor. At the dedication on May 25, and on every subsequent occasion under his watch, St. Patrick's Cathedral was going to sing up to its size.

Getting to Opening Day

Finding singers wasn't the hard part; finding the right ones was. Even in 1879 New York's musical community had a solidly established grapevine, and word instantly shot through the ranks as soon as the appointment of the Cathedral's music director had become general knowledge. For the first time in his career, Pecher found himself besieged by vocalists, both volunteer and professional, who wanted to get in on the excitement. Scores of hopefuls made the trip to audition for him at the Church of St. John the Evangelist, literally back-door neighbor to St. Patrick's on Fourth Avenue; its temporary wood structure had served the area for twenty years, but it was now about to be deconsecrated. For Cathedral purposes, it would serve as staging area for the dedication and as Music Central in the meantime.

Because St. Patrick's was going to be a very high-profile venue, Pecher's recruiting technique would have to avoid strenuously any appearance of pilfering talent from the city's other choirs. In touchy situations, his publicly professed stance was easy to explain; all of the solo staff at the Old Cathedral, for example, were to stay downtown with John White. On the other hand, it was common knowledge (and quietly passed from singer to singer, as it had always been with every other choir in the city) that good volunteer choristers would be welcome should they wish to defect from their current situations and join the ranks.

The voices themselves were an important part of Pecher's design for music at St. Patrick's, and this design affected his choice of soloists. At St. Peter's, his own "cantatrice" had been Mrs. Louise M. Easton, an extremely light soprano. She was a gracious colleague and a dependable musician, so he had made use of her drawing-room style by programming (and composing) music that allowed her the frequent melismas and roulades in which she excelled while sidestepping her lack of vocal power. But Mrs. Easton's strengths would be lost in the Cathedral's vast cubic space. In that pre-amplification era, stronger voices—specifically, *louder* voices—were required; but the possessors of those voices would have to be musically sensitive enough to blend with the choir when not singing solo passages. And competent sight-readers, to prepare music as quickly as it was needed. And unflappable performers, because the process of fitting music into an ongoing Mass required far more thinking on one's feet than did stage or concert work. And punctual employees, and team players, and persons of sober yet amiable demeanor, and. . . . It was a tall order, the same as that desired by any choirmaster but magnified a thousandfold because of the publicity factor, and it meant that Pecher would have to conduct his auditions with an eye to the personalities of those auditioning in an effort to cull out prima donnas and whackadoodle characters.

By early spring of 1879, he had nailed down a choir of nearly 100 singers, along with an octet of professionals: four section leaders hired to reinforce the choral sound, and four soloists (including Mme. Isadore Martinez, a soprano who had first come to New York the year before in *The Bohemian Girl* with Rubens' English Opera Company). Now he could turn his attention to polishing the music for the upcoming dedication. The *Times* reported that the setting for the Mass would be "an excellent one—Hayden's [*sic*] Sixteenth, in B flat."* As had been the case at the Old Cathedral, there would be an accompanying orchestra of musicians from the Philharmonic.

But the chancel choir had posed a problem. St. Patrick's didn't have anything like the large number of singers to render the music required in the hour-and-a-quarter blessing ceremony. More to the point, that music consisted entirely of Gregorian chant, which just hadn't been the style in New York churches—unaccompanied, completely exposed, potentially embarrassing. However, the Church of St. Paul the Apostle had organized the Chorus of St. Cecilia in 1872—exclusively male, extensively Gregorian, extremely well polished. Cardinal McCloskey was impressed with their work and solved the problem in a stroke when he asked the choir's "Preceptor," Father Alfred Young, for his group's participation. The full complement of boys and men would total 106 voices, and Father

---

* Haydn hadn't written sixteen Masses, but the ordinal notation here was based upon music publisher Vincent Novello's numbering system. The *Theresienmesse* was listed as No. 16.

As to the choice of the work, no reason was given publicly. But to Pecher, it may have been a good-luck charm: The *Theresienmesse* was the very setting he had conducted for Bishop Spaulding's consecration at the Old Cathedral.

Young plunged into the task of drilling them in the music that would accompany the procession.

They were also being drilled in the finer points of logistics, because the mere effort of getting into the Cathedral to take part would be trickier than it sounded. The Lady Chapel behind the main altar had been allowed for but not yet built, and the "rear entrance" consisted of two very undersized doorways through which every single person in the procession would have to pass. (Father Young and his assistant Father Louis Brown, directing the chanters, punctuated each rehearsal with repeated admonitions against crowding.) Emerging from behind the altar, the double line of clergy and choir would continue down the center aisle to the main door, circle the Cathedral as part of the blessing ceremony, and return to the altar to begin the dedicatory Mass.

The gallery organ had been waiting for some time over at St. John's, and by mid-May it was painstakingly moved into St. Patrick's and hauled up to the gallery.* The Thursday evening before the dedication was scheduled for a test. At that time the organ was a very important instrument not only in churches but also throughout American musical life, filling the need for large-scale music in places that lacked orchestras, and "testing" a new organ had evolved into quite an event both musically and socially. Cardinal McCloskey and an additional 500 (the *Tribune* estimated 1,000) ticket-holding spectators were luxuriating in the spaciousness of the nearly ready Cathedral, the interior lit for maximum dramatic effect by its 1,800 gas jets. The program was more casually planned; builder George Jardine knew that many in the audience were less fascinated with beauty of tone than they were with the bells-and-whistles sound tricks of which a large church organ was capable, and especially with its potential for blunt force. Jardine aimed to please, himself leading off the demonstration with a snatch of Beethoven. Guest organists, John

---

* The *Boston Globe* wrote an extensive article on the Cathedral's dedication, stating that the Jardine—"The Most Powerful Musical Instrument in the World"— was actually the *second* organ to be built for St. Patrick's, that the first instrument built for the Cathedral had been moved into St. John's in 1871 and had been destroyed in a fire, after which Jardine immediately set to work and delivered an even better organ. The article went into great detail about the organ's specifications and added, "The chime of thirty-four bells is also a feature of the instrument, and will be used at marriage ceremonies."

White among them, rendered overtures from barn-burners such as *William Tell* and *Fra Diavolo*. Jardine brought in Joseph Weinlich and Johanna Rotter-Dieffenbach, opera singers both who were employed at local churches, to further illustrate the organ's punch. (For her own turn, Mme. Rotter-Dieffenbach laid into the "Inflammatus" from Rossini's *Stabat Mater*, about as punch-oriented as a piece of music can get.) The *Times* was absolutely delighted with Jardine's exhibition:

> He says, with much pride, that it is the most powerful organ in the world. When sending out its full volume of sound, if the listener will take his place at the other end of the church and hold a hat or cane lightly suspended in his hand, he will feel it vibrate in such a way as to produce the sensation of a mild electric shock. . . . Mr. Jardine, to show the mechanical effects of the instrument, imitated a thunderstorm. Usually, such imitations lie chiefly in the imagination of the performer but in this case the imitation was at once recognized by the audience; and, indeed, there was no mistaking it, for the tremendous power of the organ and the reverberation of the great building combined to produce exactly the sound of claps of thunder and the sullen rolling away of the sound into the distance. Even the hissing sound of the furious rain was reproduced. . . . There is also a peal of bells attached to the instrument. . . .

May 25, The Day, was one of those happy occasions when everything went well. The weather cooperated magnificently. Trains ran without snags. There were many published reports of the dedication, but the multi-page coverage of *Frank Leslie's Illustrated Newspaper* was particularly enthusiastic. At 10:00 A.M., the more-than-capacity congregation heard John White's organ prelude. Then the procession, with Fathers Young and Brown heading it, filed in with the well-drilled order that they had worked to attain.

> The procession moved down the central aisle of the building, in full view of the congregation, while six priests intoned the "Psalms of the Blessing." When the Fifth Avenue entrance was reached, the procession passed out into the street, and turned down the avenue to Fiftieth Street. As the Cardinal reached the front entrance, he sprinkled it with holy water and performed the blessing ceremony. While the priests and choir chanted the "Miserere," the procession advanced

through Fiftieth Street, then through Madison Avenue and Fifty-first Street, until the main entrance was again reached. During this time the Cardinal sprinkled the walls with holy water. As the procession again entered the church, the choristers chanted the "Litany of the Saints," until all the clergy were within the sanctuary. The Cardinal and his attendants advanced to the bottom marble step of the grand altar and knelt until the litanies were finished. At the conclusion of this ceremony, all the acolytes, choristers, priests and prelates formed for another procession, and passed around the side aisles of the Cathedral, while the Cardinal sprinkled the walls with the holy water, when the procession returned to the sanctuary, and the dedicatory services ended.

As if they were part of the congregation, the musicians in the gallery had remained silent until the dedication was finished at 11:15 A.M. Then the hundred mixed voices, the solo quartet, the non–solo quartet, the Jardine organ with its treadle-pumping perspiring Irishmen, the full or-chestra—and at the musical helm, William F. Pecher—all of them launched into action, taking part in the first Mass ever held in St. Patrick's Cathedral.*

Vespers were scheduled for that evening at 7:30. To spell himself, Pecher had arranged for Cuban conductor Emilio Agramonte to lead the choir as he played. And after Vespers, he would have a great deal of work to do for the coming week.

---

* *Harper's Bazar*, covering the dedication, was staunchly Protestant to the end. While it was impressed by the "brilliant and effective music of the service," it also seemed to be amused by the use of holy water during the dedication (note the quotation marks): ". . . the cardinal performed the ceremony of 'blessing' the walls, and then returned for the 'blessing' of the interior. . . ."

St. Patrick's Cathedral, mid-1850s—only a few years after Archbishop Hughes had proposed a new edifice on "upper" Fifth Avenue.

A view from the gallery, taken during Pecher's time. The *Times* wrote, "A large and power-ful choir will be necessary at all times to properly sing the services; for without it, the voices would be lost in the great space of the building." The lighting system is visible in this view: multiple gas jets mounted atop each column's capital.

Photographed before the Archbishop's House, the Rectory, or the Lady Chapel was built, this view shows the rear wall of the not-yet-completed Cathedral. Note one of the two door-ways, visible at the left of the central bay. The wall would be removed to make way for the Lady Chapel nearly three decades later. (*Collection of The New-York Historical Society, negative no. 71261*)

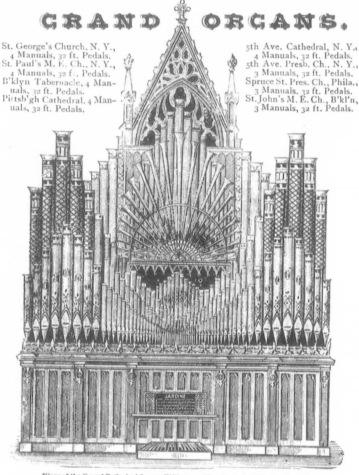

In the Jardine organ catalogue, the St. Patrick's instrument was touted as the pride of the shop. (*Courtesy of Jonathan Bowen/AGO*)

May 25, 1879. Dedication of the Cathedral (as shown in *Frank Leslie's Illustrated Newspaper*), with Fathers Young and Brown leading the procession while Pecher and the choir wait upstairs. Reports stated that even the outdoor crowd listened in rapt silence.

Chapter 2

MAMMON VS. CECILIANS (1879–1904)

Musical boys . . . are quite different from your sleepy, venal, stuckup, conceited, airish prime donne with their elaborate toilets, ribbons, feathers, fans, flowers, smirks and simpers. All of these but help to stop the ears by vulgarly attracting the eye.

Lyra Ecclesiastica

The late nineteenth century was a fascinating time to be a church musician. The job didn't carry the swank of centuries past, when choristers were lifelong retainers and routinely wore their robes in public as a declaration of pride, but it was possible for a musician to conduct an entire career in sacred music without losing face among his colleagues. This was definitely the case in cities, and in New York especially so; and at St. Patrick's Cathedral—the newest, the largest, the most exciting of churches—very much so indeed.

Several factors contributed to this climate, and they had absolutely nothing to do with religious sensibilities of any kind. The prime motivator was the city's big-time media culture in its first flush—newspapers and magazines were continually in need of material, and not a bit timid about hyping church-related events. Reporters used the same overenthusiastic accolades—or let fly with the same blasts of venom—to describe every performance they saw, no matter whether they were writing about sacred music, minstrel shows, grand opera, or the era's signature entertainment, the Broadway extravaganza. (Most church events were covered not by a newspaper's staff reporters but by college students, usually from Columbia University, who were paid a few cents a line for sitting in the congregation and scribbling the proceedings in shorthand as rapidly as they could.) Readers became conditioned to think about sacred music as just one more facet, albeit an "uplifting" one, of their week's entertainment package.* And for the first time since Mozart's day, the people making that music were promoted as celebrities. Multi-page newspaper spreads with photos, appearing at the beginning of The Season, gushed about them: "She comes from Canada, where she had already become famous . . .," "Among the foremost of our native tenors . . .," ". . . a quartet whose fame is widespread . . .," "Who of those fortunate enough to have heard Coker, the famous boy soprano at Trinity, will forget . . .". Such recognition was absolute catnip to those vocalists who were pining for the big time but feared the social exile of life as an opera singer. Divas like Adelina Patti were world renowned but unwelcome in good society; church soloists got their pictures in the paper but were still allowed to move among Nice People.

Furthermore, it was common knowledge that sacred music might offer fewer possibilities for the fabulous income that an opera star might pile up, but far greater potential for making a comfortable living. In that era a spot as a professional singer in a well-endowed church was an envied position, a springboard to lucrative concert and oratorio gigs, and a salary equal to that of many nonmusical professions. Or better: Witness the career path of the ultimate fast-tracker, Clementine De Vere. As the reigning diva of West Presbyterian Church, she had finagled a staggering $4,500 per year (in modern terms, something like $110,000), making her by most estimates the highest-paid church soloist in New York history. Clementine had been forced to suffer the indignity of reading all about her salary in the *Times*—indeed, many of New York's top-level soloists saw every detail of their incomes trumpeted in the popular press, a kind of gauche barometer indicating the degree to which their services were valued. But before the story was even published, she had soothed her feelings by moving on to the Met.

Such a career wasn't in any way a snap, because singers of that era had to be tougher creatures than their modern counterparts. Merely going through the motions of a chorister's routine was, by our standards, a chore. For instance, scheduling. The telephone was so intimidatingly new that it was regarded more as a scientific toy than a communications device. St. Patrick's itself didn't have one installed, let alone its music director or singers. Last-minute scheduling was done in a flurry of telegrams,

* A good example of this might be the ticket scalper who ran an ad in the *Tribune*, the morning of the Cathedral's dedication, offering "a few central seats."

or with notes delivered by messenger. This system was famously unreliable, and the please-fill-in-for-me-this-morning scenario usually ended with someone being embarrassed.

The standard joke was that singers "climbed to Heaven," because elevators to choir lofts were nonexistent. Anyone who wanted to visit the gallery at St. Patrick's had to do so by means of that four-story spiral staircase, unsure of footing and too narrow for more than one person to use at a time. Women would gather their cumbersome skirts about them, take as much of a deep breath as their corsets would allow, and hike. (Luckily the cage bustle, which had been a fashion rage and added a foot or more to a woman's rear projection, was going out of style just as the Cathedral opened.) Once ascended, both sexes (whatever the weather, men always appeared in jacket and tie, as well as a stiff collar) suffered. Forced-air ventilation was installed in the 1890s, but it never reached as high as the gallery, which had inefficient heating grates and no operable windows.* More so than the usual choir loft because of the extra height, the St. Patrick's gallery was dank in the winter and insupportable in the summer. People fanned themselves, dabbed themselves, and occasionally fainted.†

The gallery was illuminated by a number of multi-jet gas fixtures; they didn't help much. Gaslight consumed oxygen while giving off extra heat as well as gases such as ammonia. The only way to get brighter light was to use multiple jets, which used more oxygen while giving off yet more heat and fouling even more air—but gaslight was the only option available.

The music itself presented additional hurdles. Copies were made by lithography—sometimes sharp, sometimes not—or penned by copyists in a traditional, ornamental, nearly illegible copperplate script. Sight-reading

* The grates still are, and the windows still aren't.

† This problem was compounded by the Cathedral's physical plant, outmoded even by nineteenth-century standards. Many other churches in the city had well-planned parish houses with space dedicated to music preparation, but nothing like that had been allotted in St. Patrick's. Everyone working at the Cathedral simply had to get used to the idea of learning music, and making mistakes, in the gallery, in public. (On the other hand, the gallery would have its own restroom—the height of luxury in a time when plenty of New Yorkers didn't even have complete indoor plumbing.)

was an adventure for the sharpest vision. There was no technology of recordings for practice purposes, so every singer needed to be a pianist, or to know one. Musically unschooled singers were left in the dust. "Ear babblers," they were called.

What with the problematic climate control, dusty performance spaces, and other physical stresses, vocalists were notorious for raging hypochondria. The caution was justified. Most singers had to put out whether healthy or dog-sick, and they got little help from the medical community. Nowadays a singer afflicted with a throat problem can rely upon antibiotics, guaifenesin, hydriodic acid, acetylcystein, cortisone, prednisone, and more; the nineteenth-century singer's arsenal consisted of hot tea, honey-and-lemon, or gargles and "expectorants" that contained mostly alcohol. (Some thirty-five years ago, this author had the good fortune to know a gentleman who was then quite old. He had spent his childhood years in New York and had sung as a boy soprano during the 1890s. He said, "Our mothers always dosed us with all the patent throat medications, right before we left for church. They were convinced that it was good for us, and they used to compare notes on which preparation was supposed to be the best. The upshot was that some of us were always singing . . . well, a tad *drunk*.")

Singers in Catholic churches had also to contend with the rules of the Eucharistic fast, which in those years strictly insisted that the communicant must ingest *nothing*, not even water, starting at midnight before the morning's Communion service. The vocalist who intended to receive Communion but wanted a drink before singing had to choose between being hydrated and being honorable.

But in spite of newspaper nonsense, logistical problems, and the hazards of therapeutic booze, sacred musicians of that era had a gift that most of their modern counterparts lack—the knowledge that their efforts would be listened to with real, not manufactured, interest and appreciation. On this basis, if for no other, those long-ago singers can be envied.

Building a Music Department—Slowly

The Cathedral's dedicatory fuss was out of the way, and the day-to-day fuss was set to take its place. The morning after the dedication, the *Times* had weighed in with an enthusiastic piece, commenting on "the beautifully curved and painted pipes of the grand organ," and tossing a bouquet to the musicians themselves:

[A] burst of melody from the great organ and the brass and string instruments of the orchestra startled and delighted the ears of the throng, followed by the notes of the choir, above which, clear and pure, presently arose the voices of the soloists. The effect at the other end of the church was extremely beautiful, and dissipated at once any doubts as to the acoustic qualities of the building.

However, the same day's *Tribune* was readying a few swipes at St. Patrick's and the efforts made therein:

This brilliant and effective music of Haydn's is thoroughly well known. It is difficult (for it is very florid), and requires good singers to give it properly (this in all cases it did not have yesterday), but, while it is undoubtedly telling, it is not remarkably devotional in feeling. The solo singers were generally respectable, and one or two of them were very good, but the chorus was somewhat rough, and the noise from the combined orchestra and organ was sometimes too much for it.

The chancel organ wasn't mentioned (that end of the Cathedral would do with a temporary instrument until 1881, after which it was equipped with an Odell so insufficient for the space that most critics didn't find it entertaining to trash it in print), but the gallery organ seemed to be fair game:

An exhibition of this organ was given last Thursday evening, but at that time it was not possible to judge fairly of the instrument, for there were few people in the building, and though there was an unpleasant echo and the instrument seemed disagreeably noisy and altogether too loud for the cathedral—or for anything but the open air—it was thought that these defects would disappear when the building was full. But this did not happen. True, the echo had in great measure disappeared yesterday, but though the cathedral was as full as it well could be, this organ was still unpleasantly noisy, and other defects which had been noticed on Thursday had increased rather than diminished. . . . [T]here is neither richness nor dignity in the quality of the tone or the effect it produces. . . . [T]he pipes [are] decorated with much brilliancy, but not in the best taste.

This was as it would always be for music at St. Patrick's, a strange blend of slavish adoration juxtaposed with hostility of the who-do-they-think-they-are variety. (A case in point would be the society wedding that was delayed when the organist, mercifully unidentified, was twenty minutes late for the ceremony. The incident actually made the papers, complete with headline.)

William F. Pecher reacted by making no public sign acknowledging this fuss, or any subsequent one that would come his way. In action and bearing, he defined the position of music director (he always referred to himself as "organist") for the Cathedral simply by demonstrating each of the specific qualities that the job would ever require. He had technical skill combined with artistry, the patience to mold and teach volunteers, and the sophistication to inspire professionals while moving easily among star personalities. He had the self-discipline to maintain interest in his work, an invaluable trait in a musician who must perform the same repertoire year after year without succumbing to despair or cynicism. And not the least of his gifts was stamina. He may have been small and thin and already middle-aged, but to many he gave the impression of possessing great reserves of physical strength. This enabled him to deal gracefully with the demands of the work schedule, those repeated climbs to the gallery, the block-long walks to the chancel.

The only unusual aspect of his behavior was seen in his relationship with the press; while most New York musicians fought for attention, it seemed that Pecher did his utmost to avoid coverage. The *American Art Journal* slipped through the defenses when it interviewed him as part of an 1886 article, NEW YORK'S CHURCH ORGANS. The result sported passages that contained less information than insinuation:

> He was born in New York, but with maidenly reserve he objects to say
> when. He is, perhaps, forty years old, and lives a bachelor's life. . . .
> He is a composer of church music. He regards his facial appearance of
> no particular interest to mankind, and has sturdily evaded
> photographic temptations. Report says he is paid $2,000 per annum
> by the Cathedral. Here again Mr. Pecher thinks the public is
> inquisitive—unpardonably so. "It is not the public's business," he
> exclaims shortly.

Such blindsiding in print could make anyone publicity-shy, and the already shy Pecher only further strengthened his resistance to the media. (In his entire time at St. Patrick's he confined his own writings to occasional critiques of liturgical music. Otherwise, he was responsible for generating exactly *one* item for the popular press, a letter to the *Times*'s editor concerning the performance of music at a Cathedral funeral. Most of the letter's single paragraph was devoted to praising his soloist's work.) It would be years before he felt comfortable enough to allow *The Peterson Magazine* to interview him in any depth ("He is a man of large intellect, genial manners, aristocratic bearing, and for one so distinguished, possessed of an undue amount of modesty"). He even authorized the magazine to publish a photograph. That picture shows a man with a sharp nose, a lively, intelligent expression, and the moustache indispensable to the period.

However, newspaper reportage was to be among the least of Pecher's worries. An organization called The Society of St. Cecilia had been founded in Europe only a few years previously, dedicated to reforming the "inappropriateness" and "excesses" of sacred music that was then being performed in Catholic churches. Cecilians (as they called themselves) believed that the future of musical liturgy lay in ending those practices and replacing them with more "pure" forms—Gregorian chant, polyphony in the sixteenth-century mode of Palestrina (of all Cecilian-approved composers, Palestrina was the hero), and modern compositions with less of a "theatrical" bent. No "romanticism," no "sensuality," no "worldliness." No "complicated" harmonies. Nothing that smacked of "entertainment value." Obviously, no rewritten operatic ensembles ("operatic" was the ultimate insult for Cecilians; they hit a bull's-eye when the *Times* called for "a reform in the music now used in the Catholic Church on the ground that it is too operatic") or Haydn *Lord Nelson Masses*, no large orchestras, and especially no soloists emitting lovely noise for its own sake. This made for an admirable ethos, but it was wrenchingly different from business as usual.

Cecilians even had a standard of success to which they could point with pride: the Chorus of St. Cecilia, those well-trained men and boys over at the Church of St. Paul the Apostle who had so superbly anchored the St. Patrick's chancel choir and rendered the extensive chants during the Cathedral dedication ceremonies. Making their case in the brand-new "Marble Temple" was publicity too good for the Society to pass up, and their publication *Lyra Ecclesiastica* had a field day comparing the chancel choir ("the glorious music of Gregory") with the gallery choir (repeating the *Tribune*'s phrase, "not remarkably devotional in feeling"). But *Lyra Ecclesiastica* was completely out of the mainstream. THE GREGORIAN CHANT TO BE HEARD IN ALL ITS SOLEMN GRANDEUR may have made for an impressive headline, but most people, including a number of clergy, were ambivalent toward the prospect of having a steady diet of chant and chant alone. For that matter, Cardinal McCloskey himself was aware of and friendly toward the Cecilian movement but made no move to demand that Pecher implement its standards in his own cathedral.

His Eminence might just have been enjoying the singing too much to complain. After a period of fine-tuning, and plenty of resignations and replacements, Pecher wound up with a quartet of impressive soloists. At the very least, they were resounding soloists.

Each singer was, in the parlance of the day, a Sturdy Vocalist, or knew how to imitate one. Some came by their sturdiness naturally. Basso Charles Steinbuch was of the strongly constructed Liederkranz tradition (at one time singing *Götterdämmerung* excerpts with the Philharmonic), utterly unfazed by the size of the place or the amount or style of singing required on any particular day. Nor was tenor Christian Fritsch worried about a lack of voice; he had been New York's very first German-language Erik in *The Flying Dutchman*. Fritsch was hugely busy, and such a popular favorite that his engagement by St. Patrick's (his second engagement by Pecher; he had sung at St. Peter's some years before) was covered as a news item in the "Green Room" column of the *Police Gazette*, which provided readers with expert performing-arts criticism along with its famed images of minimally clad women: "If the other selections are as admirable we may expect to have in this city a choir equal to the most celebrated in Europe."

But Pecher had problems with his female contingent, problems that took more than a decade to settle. Possibly the ladies were daunted by the intensity of the Cathedral schedule, maybe overparted by the strength of their male colleagues. Or perhaps, as with Mme. Isadore Martinez, they had something better to do. She had skipped town instantly after the dedication (heading west for an opera job; she didn't even stay around for that evening's Vespers) and showed up only sporadically thereafter. The same was true for contralto Octavie Gomien, by all accounts second-rate but inexplicably active. That kind of on-and-off situation impeded Pecher's ability to build a solid music program, and both women disappeared from the Cathedral for good in 1885 after Cardinal McCloskey's funeral (in its coverage of the musical preparations for the requiem Mass, the *Times* wrote, "Mr. Pecher has already been compelled to refuse a number of applications, most of them made by vocalists of reputation").

St. Patrick's then experienced a dizzying parade of replacements, some who stayed one day and some who stayed longer, none of them to return. There came and went among others Armida M. Starritt (section leader promoted to soloist, and apparently a disaster), Mrs. Jones, Miss S. C. Hall, Emma Dexter, Miss McCullough, and Marie Groehl. Clementine De Vere clocked in a bit less than a full year, perhaps finding the position uncongenial to her theory of who, or what, was most important in the loft. Even greater frustration came in 1892 when Pecher hired a young contralto new to the city, Olive Fremstadt. Olive was already an astonishing singer, also a walking attendance problem; music critics were writing her up as the sensation of one concert after another, but she *never* seemed to make it to the Cathedral for major occasions, not even for that autumn's massively important Columbian Quatercentenary celebration. Worse, her AWOLs were apparently on short notice, because every news report of every service that took place during that season implied that no contralto soloist had been there to sing at all. Within months, Pecher had decided that he and Olive would go their separate ways, but she beat him to the punch. She left St. Patrick's and New York, wrapped up her training in Europe, declared that she would thereafter be a soprano, dropped the final *t* in her surname, and metamorphosed into "The Divine" Olive Fremstad, superstar diva at the Met and other places. She may not ever have actually opened her mouth to sing in the Cathedral, but she got a definite kick out of its name recognition; a 1914 magazine interview cooed, "One of her first engagements was as soloist with St. Patrick's Cathedral."*

* And then there was Effie Stewart, a self-promoting soprano who became a notorious figure in church music circles, if such a feat is possible. "Chosen from a host of applicants," as it went in a newspaper piece, she plied her shrill coloratura at St. Patrick's for three years before skipping off to Europe for further study and a shot (not entirely successful) at grand opera. When she returned and tried to plug herself back into the New York scene, the Cathedral's soprano position happened to be filled. Effie cleverly shopped herself around as a prodigal diva and wound up with a high-profile job, singing at "Dr. Parkhurst's" Madison Avenue Presbyterian . . . when a wealthy patroness sued Effie for nonpayment of the loans that the lady had made to support her during her Continental jaunt. The whole thing was played out in the press to a great deal of embarrassment on all sides, and during that time Pecher must have thanked his lucky stars every time he opened a newspaper.

At length, he chanced upon two singers who were exactly right for the situation. Soprano Katherine (also listed as Kathrine, Katharine, Kathrin, and Katheryn) Hilke didn't sing Wagner, but she did take a crack at the Beethoven *Ninth* for the Philharmonic. She was billed sometimes as a "dramatic soprano," but her actual repertoire implied that she was more probably lyric-but-loud; far more useful in a church context, that kind of vocalism enabled her to ride along effortlessly with her colleagues while still singing sentimentally enough to give listeners the impression of sugary sweetness that was essential for nineteenth-century sopranos. This particular trick was apparently one that she mastered too well, and it ultimately damaged her outside career—reviews tended to characterize her as dull. Nevertheless, in an era that preferred soloists of precisely that mode to sing at weddings and funerals, she was an invaluable asset to the Cathedral. And even though Hilke was an avid and indefatigable concertizer (during the six-week Lenten season of 1899, she chalked up seven performances of the Rossini *Stabat Mater* along with a Verdi *Requiem*), she had a high sense of responsibility and treated her St. Patrick's work as her primary musical outlet.

The final member of the quartet came to Pecher by happenstance. Christian Fritsch had found it necessary to leave, much too heavily booked to be available for the extra dates that the Cathedral so often required; he was happier with the more predictable schedule of Temple Emanu-El. Pecher filled the slot with Charles Kaiser, a tenor who was quite young but apparently didn't sound it. Kaiser was hired for *Samson and Delilah* with the Oratorio Society, and their Delilah was

> a Miss Mary Louise Clary, a young woman of Louisville, who has been studying in this country for two years, and made her first appearance on any stage at the public rehearsal Friday afternoon. Miss Clary achieved what may prove to be a disastrous success.
>
> This young woman has been gifted by nature with the most imposing contralto voice we have heard. . . . The power and quality of her voice are remarkable. . . . But—it is too bad that there must be

---

Litigations aside, Effie earned a genuine place in musical history when she allowed Thomas Edison to record her voice during her tenure at St. Patrick's. Her 1889 cylinder of "The Pattison Waltz" still exists—and many historians regard it as the first-ever recording of a "serious" singer.

a but—Miss Clary's knowledge of her art is still in its primary stage. . . . she sang fully two-thirds of her part just enough off the key to set a sensitive listener's teeth on edge . . . her phrasing at times was enough to make one gasp with astonishment. . . . Nevertheless the audience applauded her as if she had just come down from the heavenly choir, and Mr. Damrosch publicly shook hands with her.

Clary and Kaiser became friendly during rehearsals, he introduced her to Pecher, and the question was instantly settled. She accomplished her final work of vocal polishing while on the job, and the Cathedral was thereafter treated to an extraordinary instrument that could encompass everything from Bach and Handel to the Berlioz *Requiem*, with *Parsifal* thrown in for good measure. Clary became a bona fide hot property, in demand all over the United States for concert appearances, but like Katherine Hilke she showed admirable dedication to St. Patrick's by doing her utmost to limit out-of-town trips to the off season.*

It wasn't long before *Godey's Magazine* proclaimed to the nation, "One of the best tests of a singer's ability is connection with the choir of St. Patrick's Cathedral in New York." Pecher had at last put together a solo ensemble that could live up to the hyperbole, and its members would continue to do so for more than a decade. Steinbuch was the only member to leave—at that, because he retired, closing out his career in 1900. Pecher's other soloists stayed with him to the end of his life. Obviously he inspired loyalty and returned it.

Very Hardworking Singers

Making music at St. Patrick's, in the opinion of some, has been called "ready-made success." Possibly. But the truly gifted musician never rests

---

* In the spring of 1895, she even made her Broadway debut, sort of—unseen and unbilled, supplying the offstage "diva" voice for Virginia Harned in the original production of the Svengali tale *Trilby*. Her singing of "Ben Bolt" was so good that it became its own cult attraction for local theater buffs, and with no Sunday matinees to worry about in those days, she was easily able to fulfill her Cathedral schedule. But her stint in the play got her disinvited from a musicale at Chicago's Emmanuel Baptist Church: "[A]t a late moment the trustees decided, owing to the singer's theatrical connections, it would be better to dispense with her part of the program."

on laurels, and Pecher was more gifted—and more driven—than most. He seemed to know that unearned praise was worthless, and for every panegyric such as: "Among the Roman Catholic choirs that of the Cathedral, W. F. Pecher, organist, is not only the most famous, but has the most direct bearing on American music," there was a wholehearted slam (and this came after his first Christmas at the Cathedral, during what should have been a honeymoon period): "The choir had been reinforced to some extent. . . . A new soprano was one of the additions, from which the choir derived strength, perhaps, but certainly not sweetness."

The "hundred mixed voices" touted in 1879 had become a group whose total fluctuated wildly (this was the same problem that had plagued Gustavus Schmitz at the Old Cathedral) depending on the time of year, the weather, and the glamour of the service involved. In 1888, that *American Art Journal* interview estimated the gallery choir as numbering sixty members; in 1890, the *Metropolitan Church and Choir Directory* counted fifty. Impressive for a parish church, modest for a cathedral. However, Pecher knew that fifty productive members were preferable to a hundred dilettantes. Soloist and chorister alike absorbed one major lesson from their choirmaster: All members of the St. Patrick's choir were going to be very hardworking singers, otherwise they would no longer remain members of the St. Patrick's choir. Pecher drilled them relentlessly and in detail, striving to eliminate the "roughness" noticed by the *Tribune*. He was continually stretching their musicianship by exposing them to new works; the days of Mr. Harrison and the all-purpose *Lord Nelson Mass* were very much over, and a contemporary account credited the Cathedral choir with having a library of "over 200 masses." Many of them, even on ordinary Sundays, used orchestral accompaniment, a richness of sound that made Cathedral visitors gape in amazement. (They might have gaped for other reasons the Tuesday before Easter 1888, when a violinist—reported as having recently stopped drinking—smashed his instrument into pieces at the end of Pecher's orchestra rehearsal and promptly took off down Fifth Avenue, tearing off his coat and shoes as he ran. He was conveyed to Bellevue for observation.)

To expand upon the tradition begun by Schmitz, Pecher composed. With all those Mass settings already in the library, he had something different in mind: anthems, anthems that would showcase his choir's particular strength. That strength was already evident in his high-powered quartet and often considerable numbers. Sloppily executed, such a group's efforts would be heard as amateurish shrieking. Well disciplined, they held the potential for a thrilling sound. Most of Pecher's contemporaries would have refused even to accept such a sound in a house of worship. He reveled in it.

One need only compare two of his works to see the development in his style. There was the "O Salutaris" that he set for Mrs. Easton in his pre-Cathedral days, a droopy Victorian solo with periodic grinds-to-a-halt into which decorative cadenzas would be inserted. None of that for St. Patrick's; he wrote for the building, the power of the choir, the sheer exhilaration of producing sound in that space. By the time he set "Ecce Sacerdos" for Archbishop Michael Corrigan's silver jubilee celebration, the result was an astounding piece whose intensity still makes modern singers blink—shamelessly exultant, fiery even in its softest moments, a forward rush that models itself on the wilder moments of the Verdi *Requiem*. Other choirmasters may not have approved of such full-tilt choral writing, but then again few of their choirs would have had the mettle to execute it.*

Stretching a bit far in the opposite direction, Pecher often programmed the Allegri "Miserere" for Good Friday Tenebrae services during the 1880s. Considering that the piece is now considered an acid test of High Renaissance *a cappella* choral technique, and a vocal high-wire act to boot—plainchant passages alternate with two antiphonal ensembles, and the top soprano is required to hit (delicately) *five* high Cs—one wonders how his singers handled the piece with their slam-bang proclivities. No press reports evaluated the performance. (Then again, in those days the piece simply was heard with different ears. For a number of years it was also used as a centerpiece of the Cathedral's New Year's Eve "Watch" service, a choice that modern listeners would find stark indeed.)

Renaissance music was a very small problem, but the Cecilians, with their built-in disapproval, were a larger problem. The Society of St. Cecilia was able to inveigle St. Patrick's into hosting the opening of their "twelfth biennial convention" in 1890. It was quite a spread-out affair

---

* Just as in the days of Schmitz, Pecher obviously thought the piece was a one-off, never to be sung again. The choral score was discovered in the Library of Congress in time to be performed during the Cathedral's 125th anniversary year. Unfortunately the orchestra parts had long ago disappeared, and because Pecher had performed the organ part himself, he had never felt the need to jot it down.

with many participating clergy (none from the Cathedral) and a group assembled from a number of choirs to perform the works of Cecilian-approved composers. Pecher was nowhere to be found for the occasion, nor was any of his gallery choir. (Just as well: The sermon found fault with, among other things, "the fanciful performances of soloists, who were the servants of mammon six days and of righteousness but one day in the week, [and] had detracted from the dignity of church worship . . .".) The Cathedral's chancel choir was stuck playing host, however, and obligingly made itself part of the massive choral ensemble demonstrating the attractions of music by Cecilian compositional darlings Singenberger and Witt.

It had been obvious from the start that Pecher would have been far too busy to take on the creation and management of the chancel choir. Father Alfred Young having returned his Cecilians to 59th Street immediately after the dedication, singers were being recruited from the boys and young men attending the Cathedral's elementary school and Cathedral College (the Archdiocesan prep school for prospective seminarians). Their ranks were swelling, but strong leadership was necessary to turn mildly interested children and adolescents into listenable musicians. Father Anthony Lammel had been one of the eight principal cantors at the Cathedral's dedication. His musical and liturgical knowledge was impressive enough that he was asked to lead the chancel choir and train its members.

Over time, Father Lammel proved to be a talented conductor, an occasional composer (none of his music survives, either), and a very strong Cecilian who was not at all loath to express his views. An 1886 memo in regard to a proposed "Tantum ergo" by a composer identified only as Smith makes his position crystal clear:

> The music to the Tantum ergo belongs to the worldly style against which the church has repeatedly protested. Particularly objectionable are the following parts: Pages 4 & 5 contain Solos with Quartett [sic] accompaniment very much in the fashion of club quartetts [sic] and serenades; the organ and instrumental part adds to the evil effect. Out of taste is also the solo treatment of the Genitori on pages 13 & 14. . . . Though there may be more liberty for the composer in writing music for a Tantum ergo than in composing a mass, yet Smith's Tantum ergo is unquestionably better suited as a festival hymn for some joyful worldly affair than for churchmusic.

Such bluntness might make for friction with the man who had most probably submitted that music—Pecher. But Pecher's reputation was that of a man who respected opinions if they were informed ones. As it turned out, the point was moot: Lammel was more valuable to the Archdiocese as an ordained cleric than as a conductor, particularly in light of his administrative skills. By 1888 he had been yanked from the post to become pastor of St. Joseph's Church.

The Cathedral tried again with Father John A. Kellner. Quite young (he hadn't yet been ordained at the time of the Cathedral's dedication), even more artistically rounded than Father Lammel—he was known as "The Musical Priest," a rakish nickname for the time—Kellner was an ideal choice, and a solid success at St. Patrick's. "He stands very near to the Archbishop," confided the *Times*. So near did he stand that it was only a matter of time until the Archbishop promoted Kellner even more quickly than he had Lammel, sending him to New Rochelle to lead the newly consecrated St. Gabriel's.

Because the Cathedral had gone through two chancel choir directors in fourteen years, another approach was needed. Those previous directors had been priests; it was time to investigate the laity.

Part of Pecher's working style was his loose system of inviting young organists, conductors, or composers to "assist" at various times. Whether these men turned pages or played a bit, such a gesture benefited all parties involved, allowing them a taste of the Cathedral's milieu while helping Pecher to keep a finger on the city's musical pulse and giving him an informal file of musicians who might be useful for one purpose or another. P. A. Schnecker, William G. Dietrich, and Arthur Mees were only some of Pecher's occasional "assistants" who went on to later prominence in the choral music field as conductors or composers. (Another was George Fischer, who dropped his activities at the keyboard to concentrate on music publishing. As the head of J. Fischer & Bro., he would become a major force in Catholic church music.) Some of these introductions were made by other choirmasters; one who was particularly close to Pecher was Father John B. Young, choirmaster (he used the term "moderator") of the Church of St. Francis Xavier. French-born but a longtime American resident, he understood the necessity of such networking and fostered it whenever possible. Thus, in 1893 he brought a visiting fellow Frenchman to meet Pecher. Jacques-Marie-Pierre-André-Cécilien Ungerer—intermittently calling himself James—was newly arrived, working at St.

Mary's in Morristown, New Jersey, and thinking of relocating to New York. An organist who was an organist's son (his father played in the cathedral of Annecy), he had a European background and Belgian training that meshed perfectly with Pecher's Belgian background and German education. They got along so well that Pecher very soon asked him to join the staff as head of the chancel choir. Ungerer began work at the Cathedral that spring, aged twenty-one, and looking no older than the boys singing under his baton.

Perhaps from growing up in the business, Ungerer was immediately impressive. At the keyboard, he was an organist of serious ability. He was moving into composition, and his works would rapidly enter the Cathedral's repertoire. As a conductor, he was enough of the French taskmaster that he could get more and better work out of the boys than his predecessors had been able to get. And he and Pecher were so attuned to each other that they could perform the trick, germane to European cathedral choirs but very unusual in New York, of synchronizing the chancel choir with the gallery choir. For a number of years, an eagerly awaited Christmas highlight was "Adeste Fideles" in a Vincent Novello arrangement that caromed the music among Katherine Hilke, the chancel choir, the solo quartet, and the gallery choir, accompanied by both organs and a full orchestra. The effect was so spectacularly antiphonal that the *Times* commented with surprise on the "most impressive" music, "tossed, as it were, from one end of the vast building to the other."

There had existed during previous seasons, sporadically, a Cathedral-based community choir, and Father Lammel had been assigned to conduct it. The only record of its actually performing was during a single late-August Mass when the regular Cathedral choir was on its summer vacation; the usually loquacious *Times* refrained from discussing the results. Undaunted, Father Michael J. Lavelle (who took over as Rector in 1887) proposed in an 1896 memo to Archbishop Corrigan:

I propose to organize a Choral Society, which might be named St. Cecilia's Choral Society of St. Patrick's Cathedral, or something similar unto this. I would impress at least 100 members, everyone of whom will know something about music before they start, and of whom at least 20 will be men. If any person says that such an aggregation can not be formed out of our congregation, that man is simply laboring under a mistake.

As to the directorship of this proposed society, "Mr. Ungerer will be glad to help."

Subsequent events give the impression that Mr. Ungerer hadn't been consulted about helping. St. Cecelia's Choir, as Ungerer called it, was a thorn in his side for a number of years. There were nowhere near the 100 members projected; they didn't come to rehearsals; they couldn't execute the music; they lacked discipline. Soon enough, he would protest the whole setup, and St. Cecelia's Choir itself would fade into history.

In its permanent choirs, however, the infrastructure for quality music at St. Patrick's was in place and working so well that its reputation was spreading. The December 15, 1895, Sunday supplement to the *New York World* ran a full-page feature on the various attractions of St. Patrick's. (It wasn't a front-page article, however. That honor went to a "scientific" piece complete with illustration, entitled FRENCH SCIENTIST AND EXPLORER DISCOVERS A RACE OF SAVAGES WITH WELL-DEVELOPED TAILS.) The article expressed great admiration for the Cathedral's music and those who made it:

> The beauty and solemnity of the mass at St. Patrick's Cathedral is enhanced by the great choir, under the direction of William F. Pecher, who has been the leader since the dedication of the church in 1879. Properly speaking, there are two choirs—the grand, or "upstairs" choir, as the singers themselves call it, and the chancel choir.
>
> The grand choir is composed of seventy mixed voices, led by a double quartet. . . . The chancel choir is made up of sixty boys from the orphan asylum, ranging from five to twelve years of age, and is directed by Mr. James Ungerer, who presides at the chancel organ. . . .
>
> "The singers in the Cathedral choir have no sinecure," said Prof. Pecher to a Sunday World reporter the other day. "Early in September a year ago we began singing a different mass each Sunday, and during the year we had only about three repetitions. . . ."

If anyone needed more authoritative proof of the quality of music at St. Patrick's, it came only days later when the *World* proclaimed in a headline MELBA AT ST. PATRICK'S.

Nellie Melba, opera's diva of divas, was in New York and a few days away from her first Met performances of the season. Her secretary had recently married a well-connected young man, the ceremony taking place in Archbishop Corrigan's residence. Nellie had attended (finding the residence "austere"), and she and the Archbishop struck up an unlikely friendship. "The Archbishop was one of the most broad-minded men I have ever met," she wrote in her autobiography, *Melodies and Memories*, and continued, "As a slight return for the trouble he had taken about my secretary's wedding, I asked if I might sing the *Ave Maria* in the Cathedral, and I shall never forget the feeling, almost of awe, which I experienced as my voice floated out to the immense congregation."

The event was scheduled for Christmas morning, a holiday gift for public and press alike. Melba got star treatment, escorted up to the gallery by two volunteer ushers from the Young Men's Society (one reporter thought the ushers were "more useful and obliging than usual"). Carlos Hasselbrink, concertmaster of the Met orchestra, provided violin *obbligato* to Melba's solo. The *Times* was enchanted: "Her clear, belllike [*sic*] notes filled the cathedral. The efforts of Mme. Melba were a genuine triumph." The *World*'s reaction was less worshipful, tossing an inadvertent compliment to the Cathedral musicians: "Many hundreds of non-Catholics were present, and to most of them the singing of Melba was the great attraction; but, truth to tell, the rendering of the Adeste Fideles by the quartet, double choir, two organs and orchestra was far more thrilling and inspiring."

Also gratifying was Melba's response to Pecher as collaborator. She was famous for her slashing rudeness to those musicians she felt were beneath her, but he came through the experience unscathed.

Pecher Reinvents Pecher

Cathedral Bells was a souvenir book offered for sale at the Cathedral in 1898. Its pages were decorated with a number of illustrations purporting to show "important" areas of St. Patrick's that the casual visitor might not see. One of the more fanciful illustrations was entitled "Choir Gallery," supposedly a view of the choir in action with Pecher at the organ. Ladies are seated at the rail, singing, all of them decked out in the fashions of the day and demurely hatted. Rows of other ladies and gentlemen are arranged behind them. A man who looks like Charles Kaiser is standing next to the organ, delivering a solo, accompanied by a man who looks like William F. Pecher. (In a nod to the masculine ideals of the period, the artist has rendered Kaiser somewhat thinner and Pecher considerably beefier.) Imaginary scene or not, the artist has caught in Pecher's eyes an unmistakably sad and resigned look.

Pecher's life by this point had deteriorated into a treadmill. Aside from the Sunday Mass schedule, there were additional services, funerals, and weddings; at least one midweek choir rehearsal; soloist touchups; work with orchestra members; his own considerable organ practice; administrative work; coordinating meetings with clergy; trips to the College of Mount St. Vincent, where he headed the music faculty; and to supplement his income, he had opened his own studio, teaching piano and organ out of Steinway Hall. Being a celebrity musician as well as a celebrity teacher was very lucrative, but for a long time his routine had consisted of work and nothing else. He was in demand for interviews, but those few writeups to which he submitted made a point of referring to Pecher's "modesty," actually his own brand of personal reserve. It made sense in light of the sad events of his personal life. At the age of fifty-one he had taken a bride, twenty-three-year-old Gertrude Norwood, but only four years later she was dead. His parents were long gone. Ungerer was in many ways the person closest to him, protégé and best friend, the son he never had.

The coming of the twentieth century was an especially popular time for New Year's resolutions, and as 1899 gave way to 1900 (commemorated at St. Patrick's by the Cathedral's first-ever Midnight Mass, offered on New Year's Eve), Pecher apparently made a decision to transform his own life. He bought a vacation home in Stamford, a river town in upstate New York that boasted its own golf range. He plunged into the country club set, taking vacations to Lakeland and the White Mountains, his name appearing in society columns along with those of Rockefellers, Goulds, and Fieldings. He took part in whist parties and euchre tournaments, even winning a prize or two. Such activities now made him more visible, and more interesting to the public, than he had ever been in the past. But he hadn't pulled back from his Cathedral schedule; he was probably over sixty years old; and he was continuing to drive himself as mercilessly as he had for decades.

In the autumn of 1903 the *Tribune* was preparing to run a series of full-dress articles by Henry E. Krehbiel detailing the trends of sacred music in New York. The September 27 article, THE MODERN MUSICAL MASS, covered nearly an entire page and concentrated on the efforts of the city's larger-scale Catholic churches. It featured photographs of both Cathedral ensembles, posed with their directors before the Jardine. Ungerer, vested along with his chancel choir, looks tautly dignified. Pecher, seated at the console with the gallery choir standing by, looks gaunt, exhausted, and ill.

He was ill, more so than anyone imagined. In July, rushing out of town on business, he'd grabbed a quick lunch at a train station and was felled by ptomaine poisoning. NO HOPE OF RECOVERY, shrieked a headline (also in the *Tribune*, which would monitor the news of his health more closely than any other publication in the city). He was hospitalized for nearly two agonizing months—during which time he completely missed Pope Leo XIII's memorial *and* Archbishop John Farley's installation—before returning to Manhattan in mid-September. His homecoming occasioned W. F. PECHER RECOVERS. "He has just recovered from a serious illness, including an attack of pneumonia. . . ."

Pecher made it back to the Cathedral in time to pose for that *Tribune* photographer, but it was obvious that his constitution had been grievously undermined by the various illnesses. Only days later, he collapsed, this time from a heart attack. With an eye toward convalescing at his Stamford home, he was taken to a hospital in Yonkers, and ORGANIST'S ILLNESS NOT SERIOUS reassured readers, "It was learned that he is receiving treatment for heart trouble, but the doctors say that his case is not serious."

With spectacularly bad timing, Krehbiel's article hit the newsstands the following week.

Pecher's doctors changed their diagnosis and recommended treatment by specialists at All Souls' Hospital in Morristown. This would necessitate a month or two of absolute rest, possibly more, before he could think of returning. For the time being, St. Patrick's would have to manage without him. Neither Ungerer nor anyone else could possibly handle both choirs; Clemente de Macchi, a voice teacher and accompanist who was closely involved with music in the Archdiocese, had agreed at the time of Pecher's first illness to preside over the gallery choir. He would have to continue until Pecher was completely well again.

"These Parts Must Be Taken by Boys"

Giuseppe Cardinal Sarto, patriarch of Venice, had only that summer been elected to succeed Pope Leo XIII. As Pius X, he was determined to implement a number of reforms in the Church. One of those reforms was of particular interest to him, and it concerned music.

Eight years previously, the then-Cardinal had published a "pastoral" that took issue with the "light, trivial, scenic, and profane" music then being used in the churches of Venice.* The "pastoral" had no traction outside his own province, but within Italy—where sacred compositions by unabashedly operatic composers such as Donizetti, Rossini, and Puccini were highly appreciated, and polyphony was considered to be old-fashioned—it caused a sensation. The Madrid newspaper *Epoca* treated it as a harbinger of things to come. Not many Americans paid attention, except for those Cecilians who sensed a high-ranking champion of their cause.

As it turned out, their faith was well placed. One of the newly elected Pontiff's very first actions was to begin work on a *motu proprio* ("of his own accord") with the help of his old friend Don Lorenzo Perosi, a composer in the Cecilian style and *maestro di capella* of the Sistine Choir. The result, *Tra le sollecitudini* (loosely, "Among the concerns"), was promulgated on November 22, 1903—fittingly enough, the Feast of St. Cecilia, patroness of church musicians. It was then released in the Vatican's newspaper, the *Osservatore Romano*, on December 28. Within twenty-four hours it had been picked up by papers around the world. The *Times* headlined:

POPE ON CHURCH MUSIC
He Says Instructions of Former Pontiffs Must Be Observed.
Is in Favor of the Gregorian Chant, and Condemns the Use in Churches of Music Suitable for Concerts.
ROME, Dec. 28.—After long discussion with experts, principally with the famous composer the Abbé Perosi, Director of the Sistine Choir, the Pope has issued of his own accord a note on the subject of sacred music in churches.
In this note, which appears to-night in the Osservatore Romano, his Holiness formulates rules for church music, which recall the churches to a strict observance of the instructions issued by former Pontiffs.

* The Pontiff told of once celebrating a Mass and, as he began the Consecration, hearing two women launch into the operatic duet "Mira, O Norma." As the duet takes place between two Druid priestesses, he wondered if it was completely suitable for Catholic service.

The Pope, who is a passionate musical dilettante, condemns the transformation of liturgic [*sic*] music into compositions suitable for concerts.

The Pontiff is strongly in favor of the Gregorian Chant.

The Pontiff was indeed strongly in favor of Gregorian chant as the foundation of the musical Mass, to be sung by musicians and congregation alike. To go along with it, the rule stipulated, "Classic Polyphony agrees admirably with Gregorian Chant." Compositions in the "theatrical style," as it was called, were forbidden—including the works of master composers. Bands (and that definition included orchestras), pianos, and percussion instruments were forbidden. Organs were approved, but their more exhibitionistic applications were not. An organist could no longer take pride in the elaborate sound effects and decibel power that George Jardine had so proudly demonstrated to the press and public. The new rule expressly stated: "As the singing should always have the principal place, the organ or other instruments should merely sustain and never oppress it."

Then came the issue of women.

Singers in church have a real liturgical office, and that therefore women, being incapable of exercising such office, cannot be admitted to form part of the choir. Whenever, then, it is desired to employ the acute voices of sopranos and contraltos, these parts must be taken by boys, according to the most ancient usage of the Church.

This was a thunderbolt, and to many people the most controversial aspect of the *motu proprio*. Of course, the degree of controversy depended upon who was doing the talking at any given time. Some accounts used the barring of women as sensationalism—the *Tribune* ultimately ran a headline that included NON-CATHOLICS AND WOMEN CANNOT SING. Some, like *The Outlook*, ignored it completely. And others tapped into a vein of snickering misogyny—*The American Catholic* sneered that "not the least attention" would be paid to the rule, "else a warbling miss in the loft would not be permitted to make the Priest on the altar wait upon her concluding a four-and-a-half minute Amen."

Musicians knew the twofold realities of the situation better than this. First: Any Catholic church choir employing women would be effectively demolished, while its director scrambled to figure out a way in which it could be rebuilt. The second reality was sadder and more personal: As with other denominations, the music in most of New York's Catholic churches had for decades availed itself of talented women. Some of them (professionals) would be thrown out of work. Others (volunteers) would be barred from participating in an important aspect of their worship.

Tra le sollecitudini roared through the sacred music establishment like a firestorm. The opening days of 1904 were electric with more-or-less-scholarly articles in every publication, shrill discussions, and letters to the editor that grew steadily more heated. Some were signed with names, others with *noms de plume*, and they came in a torrent.

"Vox Urbis" was delighted with the *motu proprio* and detailed his reasons in an editorial for the Catholic magazine *The New York Freeman's Journal*. He had attended a Mass in an unnamed Italian city and found "the congregation, or better, perhaps, the 'audience,' had all carefully placed their chairs with their backs to the altar . . . gazing intently up into the choir . . . [as if] the place were a theatre instead of a church. And the choir was singing!"

Baltimore's James Cardinal Gibbons was quoted in the *Times* as saying, "In this country there has been little abuse, and we do not expect the Pope's letter to effect a change in the church music of America." (When later questioned on his views, his secretary would insist only that "he has been faultily and incorrectly quoted on church music.")

"Catholicus" wrote in, "The plain chant is not music. It is a barbaric jargon sung by priests and choirs who appear, from their performances, to know very little about it."

"Cantor" retaliated by suggesting that "Catholicus" educate himself by reading a list (supplied) of musical articles, "and I am sure he will be a little more careful when he speaks of or writes on that inspired music."

E. Francis Riggs insisted that plain chant alone was "the true church music . . .". Settings by Mozart and Haydn "were written at a period of debased ecclesiastical art. . . ."

A New Orleans priest, Father Scotti, wrote, "Bishops in the east have decided to remonstrate. We hope they will succeed, because the step would be the ruination of the choir here."

The *Los Angeles Times* reported the reaction of the Vicar-General of Kansas City, "This part of the encyclical will not be enforced in America. The abuses of church music have not appeared here, as they have in

Europe; and particularly in Rome. It would be impossible to get men and boys here to take the higher parts, and the churches could not afford it, anyway."

Conductor Frank Damrosch entered the fray when he was quoted in *The Church Economist*: "It is my opinion that the Pope hardly expects a literal observation of his instructions."

Rev. Nicholas M. Wagner sniffed that "wealthy churches . . . lack the sense of piety which demands the entire harmony of the music with the burden of the ritual." He also insisted, "[T]he chief obstacles in the way of reform are . . . the organists, many of whom would have to study over their course in music; the soloists, who are so easily dispensed with in true church music. . . ."

A rumor was circulating that Archbishop Farley would travel to Rome in order to ask the Pontiff for a reversal. The Marquise de Fontenoy, a columnist based in Europe, confided, "It is to be feared that he will fail in his mission, for Pius X is manifesting a firmness in the matter verging on obstinacy. . . ."

Finally the *Times* summed the whole thing up with its own editorial, rooted in common sense but utterly lost in the ensuing furor.

> The prelates of the Roman Catholic Church in this country either deny that they have advised the Pope that the carrying out of his recommendations with regard to church music is impracticable in this country or else they decline to discuss the subject. It is pretty evident, however, that in many, if not most, cases it is impracticable. A peremptory order to confine the singing in Roman Catholic churches in this country to male voices and to the Gregorian chants would be apt to result in at least a temporary cessation of church music altogether. . . .
>
> That women should keep silence in the churches is a precept as old as St. Paul. But it has been long and so extensively dishonored in the organ lofts that to banish from them the sex which is at once the more musical and the more devout would be to reduce many of those eyries to the condition of "bare ruined choirs." The conclusion which most Catholic pastors have probably reached for themselves, and which they would be pleased to have sanctioned from the Vatican, is that, in the actual condition of church music, the singing of women in church "tolerari potest."*

* *Tolerari potest* in this case translates to "can be tolerated."

The last time the press had asked Pecher for his opinion on this subject had been in 1899, when the Archbishop of Cincinnati had issued an edict forbidding the use of certain "operatic" Mass settings. Then, Pecher had straddled the fence, telling the *Times* that "from a religious point of view, there was no doubt that [the Archbishop's] attitude was justified." This time, reporters didn't bother to talk to anyone at St. Patrick's. In a way this was understandable: Many observers saw the Cathedral as the wealthiest of those "wealthy churches" and, musically, the most grievous offender. Those feelings were further justified when they could read (in Krehbiel's article of the previous September) a laundry list of *eighty-two* large-scale Mass settings then in use by the choir of St. Patrick's, most with the Cathedral's by-now-expected orchestral accompaniment, including the gargantuan Beethoven *Missa Solemnis*—a piece universally considered too enormous for church use, but one that had been performed at the Cathedral "on extraordinary occasions."

"There Was Never Any Hope"

During Ungerer's visits to the still-hospitalized Pecher, the two men had looked at the *motu proprio* from every angle, discussing whatever possibilities and options might be available to them. Uncomfortable as the situation might be, there was no option other than to wait. In the meantime, they had decided like most of the city's choirmasters to adopt a middle path, making no changes, until hearing more definite instructions from the Cardinal.

Doctors cleared Pecher for a return to work, and this cheered him greatly because he felt that he could assess the situation more effectively once he was back in the Cathedral. On January 20, 1904, he was officially released from All Souls' Hospital. But that morning, packing for his return, he suddenly crumpled to the floor. This time he had suffered a massive stroke, and his entire right side was paralyzed. Wrote the *Times*, "There was never any hope for his recovery after that."

He lingered for a month in semi-consciousness. On the afternoon of February 22, he died. The news reached papers as far-flung as San Jose and Duluth. The next evening, his body was brought to St. Patrick's and placed in the St. Anthony Chapel. Choir members, forming their own guard of honor, kept vigil until the funeral the next morning.

The music for the funeral mass was very hastily arranged, but singers from other choirs in the Archdiocese came to take part as their tribute to the man who had worked so single-mindedly for the Cathedral. Arch-bishop Farley had left for Rome on February 4; Monsignor Lavelle (he had been elevated in rank the year before) celebrated the funeral Mass and delivered the eulogy as well. Ungerer presided with stony composure in the chancel, as did de Macchi in the gallery.

The *Evening World* reported a congregation of more than 2,000.

William F. Pecher's death occasioned admiring tributes in print, even among those publications that had helped castigate the type of music he had fostered. "Vox Urbis" in *The New York Freeman's Journal*, so infuri-ated by the concert-type atmosphere promoted in churches, eulogized him as an organist "who had thrilled thousands." The *American Art Journal* ran an admiring obituary on February 27, stating that Pecher had been "respected and loved by all who were admitted to the inner circle of his musical and intellectual life. . . . Mr. Pecher wrote several vesper services and masses, which enjoyed considerable popularity, and one of them was performed at St. Peter's in Rome. He was one of the best posted men in America on the music of the Catholic Church."

After so many middling years, Pecher had been in the right place at the right time. His very individual vision, and his single-minded imple-mentation of that vision, made him the perfect choirmaster for St. Pat-rick's during the Gilded Age. Better than any of the city's other music directors, he had been able to balance the era's star-system tendencies with the requirements of the Catholic ritual. Some adherents of the Cecil-ian tradition would call the resulting music impious, disrespectful. Whether or not such had been the case, that music had admittedly existed as a source of pleasure for its listeners. The *motu proprio* signaled the end of this era, which coincided almost exactly with the end of Pecher's life.

He had left no heirs. Ungerer would display no outward signs of griev-ing for his mentor, and the ensuing months would be marked by a series of upheavals around St. Patrick's that would claim enough attention to obliterate the memory of William F. Pecher. With distressing speed, even his name vanished.

In 1928 there was a reference to him in the *Times*, the first in decades, contained within an article that celebrated Jacques C. Ungerer's thirty-fifth anniversary at St. Patrick's. It informed readers that Ungerer had begun as an associate to the Cathedral organist—"William F. Picher."

William F. Pecher, in one of his few published photographs.

A rare view of the Cathedral's original gallery, taken for the Jardine organ catalogue. Note that the photograph has been overdrawn to "show" the organ console. (*Courtesy of Stephen Pinel/Organ Historical Society American Organ Archives*)

Pecher leading his forces in the "Choir Gallery" drawing from *Cathedral Bells*.

Above: William F. Pecher and the gallery choir. *Below*: James C. Ungerer and the chancel choir. Pictures in the *Tribune* were an exciting honor, coming at a horrendous time. Pecher had been back at the Cathedral only two weeks after spending most of the summer in the hospital. In three months, the world of sacred music would be hit hard by the *motu proprio*; soon after that, the Cathedral's music department would be hit even harder by Pecher's death.

Chapter 3

ONLY THE RIGHT MEN, ONLY THE WHITE LIST
(1904–29)

> [O]nly men of known piety and probity of life are to be admitted to form part of the choir of a church, and these men should by their modest and devout bearing during the liturgical functions show that they are worthy of the holy office they exercise.
>
> *Motu proprio* of Pope Pius X

Because the process of grieving never fits into a business schedule, the early months of 1904 were a very black time for the musicians of St. Patrick's Cathedral. They were particularly so for Jacques C. Ungerer, who had just lost his mentor and closest friend, and whose job was about to become, for a while, impossible.

Not that it wasn't impossible for choirmasters in every Catholic church.* The impending changes hung over choir galleries like a sword of Damocles, bad because there was no timetable for their implementation, worse because they were taking place in a goldfish bowl atmosphere of publicity, worst of all for the musicians of St. Patrick's because the publicity became nationwide, and embarrassingly focused on every move they made. To top it off, the Cathedral was without a director of music. So, as it actually played out, the implementation of the *motu proprio* was an excruciatingly slow process marked by messy public relations, contradictory messages, and at the end an unavoidable amount of anguish.

The process began in mid-January, when the *Osservatore Romano* had issued a message that was intended to be helpful: "[T]he churches are

---

* Excepting organizations such as that of St. Paul the Apostle. That choir's devotion to strict Cecilian standards meant that they would have to change virtually nothing in their operation to conform to the *motu proprio*.

allowed to use their present music until it is possible to substitute it with the Fregorian [*sic*] chant." It provided scant comfort.

As the Marquise de Fontenoy had predicted, Archbishop Farley left for Rome at the beginning of February, not to return until Holy Week. Speculation began at once, in print.

> The Archbishop carries a letter from the American Archbishops to heads of the Church in Rome, one small portion of which, it was hinted yesterday, is in the shape of a mild protest from American Catholicism against the recent edict of the Vatican against the presence of female voices in church choirs. It is generally felt that the strict enforcement of the promulgation will work very great hardship here.

While the city—actually, the entire United States—awaited the outcome of Farley's visit, St. Patrick's was going through the ordeal of William F. Pecher's funeral. It was decided that Ungerer would act as interim music director until the Archbishop returned; his only option was to move forward, preparing for Lent, while doing his best to ignore the rumors and speculations, which were flying thick and fast.*

The confusion was merely exacerbated when Pecher and Ungerer's friend Father John B. Young of St. Francis Xavier gave a full-page interview to the *Times*. In it he attempted, clumsily, to define Gregorian chant.

> It is a free recitation of the text, with cadences, especially at the end of sentences. Its elements are either single notes or groups of two or three notes. Each syllable receives either a single note or one or more groups. In ancient notation the grouping was clearly indicated by what is called a neuma, resembling very much a shorthand character. . . .
>
> The general effect of Gregorian music is earnestness—gravity, if you please. The construction of the scales produces the effect of solemnity. Gregorian music expresses without exaggeration. It breathes sadness without despair, joy without extravagance. As compared with the music we know it is like the music of another nation. . . .
>
> It is because of the characteristics of Gregorian music that its introduction means the abolition of the mixed choir. With Gregorian

---

* One rumor was particularly tough to kill—the idea that women would be prohibited from singing *anywhere* on church premises, even as members of the congregation. However explained and denied, it would hang in the air for months.

music in use the proper place for the choir is in the sanctuary, to which women are not admitted. The choir must follow the movements of the chant as well as the music. The singers are supposed to be clerics, but in their absence boys and men can be employed. . . .

No doubt there are very few choirs at present which could render this music.

The strange aspect, where St. Patrick's was concerned, was that Gregorian chant had been regularly used as part of the musical service from the day of the Cathedral's dedication. But the rush of publicity had clouded the issue. The *motu proprio* was seen by the public only as a nebulous and badly-understood list of Don'ts, and Gregorian chant was regarded as something vaguely threatening and disconnected from the chants that so many worshipers had known for decades. It didn't help when Henry E. Krehbiel wrote a couple of articles in which he "detailed" the history of Gregorian chant and its terminology, complete with diagrams representing neumes in mnemonic verse, Romanic Letters, altius, levare, sersum, inferius, celeriter, and so forth. Most readers were stupefied.

As he had planned, Archbishop Farley returned on Holy Thursday. Before he had even disembarked from the *Favorite*, he was met by a clutch of reporters who questioned him in detail on his meeting with the Pope. He was enthusiastic about a number of subjects, but reluctant to comment on the *motu proprio* even when prodded.

"Do you mean that you will immediately dismiss all the women voices from your choirs?" was asked.

"I cannot say that. The question will have to be gone over very carefully by a committee competent to advise in such matters, but . certainly the wishes of the Holy Father will be carried out immediately."

Many people had been hoping that the Pontiff would reconsider his decision and were distressed that Archbishop Farley could offer them no concrete news. The unresolved situation made Easter a nerve-wracking experience for everyone involved with the Cathedral's music, particularly for any female who glanced at a *Herald* before heading off to church that Sunday morning. WOMEN SINGERS' LAST EASTER IN CATHOLIC CHOIRS was the banner headline to an article that "analyzed" the situation while inflaming it further (and uncomfortably spotlighting St. Patrick's personnel, as well as pointing out that Brooklyn and Newark had already switched to Gregorian chant and were in the process of dismissing all females from their choirs):

> As there are two women soloists in each church besides the members of the chorus, their disappearance will mean considerable personal loss, as well as a marked musical change. From Miss Hilke and Miss Clary, the stars whose voices, with the high priced salaries they commanded, made the singing at St. Patrick's Cathedral one of the special local attractions, down to the humblest church in the suburbs of Queens Borough the change will be enforced.

Members of the public spent Easter Sunday rubbernecking inside the Cathedral and out, cramming into every Mass to witness the musicians in action and perhaps to pick up some gossip. The *Tribune* commented dryly:

> Many in the large congregation were present because they had heard that the Easter mass would be the last one celebrated in the Cathedral for a long time with special musical features. The order of Pope Pius that women shall no longer sing in the choirs and that the music of the mass shall be confined to Gregorian and a few other approved selections, it is generally believed, will be carried out strictly in this diocese. . . .
>
> It was stated that the Cathedral choir had not yet received the notice that it would no longer be needed, but it is taken for granted by all connected with the Cathedral that it will soon be given.

A number of reporters spent their time in church carefully observing the women ("girls") of the choir as they tried, unsuccessfully, to maintain their composure. Along with the *Sun* and the *World*, the *Times* reported in detail:

> The music was on the same splendid scale for which the Easter services at St. Patrick's are noted, and the enormous congregation which crowded every available inch in the Cathedral to the doors was due no doubt partly to the fact that in all probability a musical programme of the elaborate quality rendered yesterday will not be heard in the Cathedral again. The Archbishop, on his return from his visit to Pope Pius X, announced that he would take steps to carry out

the Pope's wishes in regard to the restoration of the Gregorian chant, which has not been generally used for more than a century.

The Cathedral Choir, which includes Miss Katheryn Hilke, soprano, and Miss Clary, contralto, has not yet received any notice that it will be necessary to disband, but it is daily expected. Many of the members of the volunteer chorus of girls, who gave their services to the Cathedral, wept yesterday when they assembled before the mass, on the prospect of parting with one another. It is expected that the altar choir, trained under Prof. Ungerer, will be the nucleus of the new male choir.

If it wasn't entertaining enough for the public to see female choristers sobbing in the gallery, the Protestant publication *The Churchman* had its own laugh at the Cathedral's expense when it printed a blind item claiming that "ticket speculators obtained a practical corner on seats in the Cathedral and lustily hawked them in front of its doors." Then it took a jab at the music department:

> This was the last Sunday on which St. Patrick's Cathedral choir is to be suffered to render fugued music. Women singers are no longer to be employed. Occasion, therefore, was taken to announce a musical programme nearly every number of which will fall directly under the papal ban.

The rest of April passed with no real news. Some (but not all) of the country's archbishops met in Washington to discuss the question. Suddenly the *Times* was announcing POPE'S DECREE IMPRACTICABLE and reporting that Baltimore's James Cardinal Gibbons would be writing to the Pope in order to let him know that "it would be practically impossible to enforce the decree" and to "ask for advice and a modification." When asked about it the next day, the Cathedral clergy adamantly refused to climb aboard that particular bandwagon.

> Upon Archbishop Farley's return from Rome some weeks ago he announced that the Pope's wishes concerning the use of Gregorian music in church services would be carried out in New York as soon as possible.
>
> Father Lavelle of the Cathedral also declined to talk last night, declaring that the less said about church music as matters now stand the better it would be.

The Archbishop was involved in putting together an advisory group of clergy and musicians whose advice he felt he could trust, a "Diocesan Commission with a view of carrying out the instructions of the Pope on the reform of church music." The eleven members were announced on May 14; they included such Cathedral familiars as Fathers Young, Lammel, and Kellner—as well as Ungerer, who had finally been named the official "organist of the cathedral" on May 1. It would be a long process for the commission as well as for anyone watching its progress. The *World* published JURY PASSING ON THE CHURCH MUSIC, and related that the jury's work included not only dealing with questions of Gregorian chant and female singers but the tedium of combing through mountains of music to determine acceptability. "Each of the pieces approved is marked with a special seal, without which no composition is to be used in any of the Roman churches." While this went on, nothing would be publicly announced; things would proceed as they always had. This included Monsignor Lavelle's twenty-fifth-anniversary Mass in early June, which used soloists Hilke and Clary and the same mixed-voice choral setup that had always existed.*

Five weeks later the commission made its report to the Archbishop. The *Tribune* jumped on the story, although there wasn't yet a story on which to jump:

> The Rev. Father James H. McGean, pastor of St. Peter's Church, the chairman of the commission, told a Tribune reporter yesterday that he did not feel at liberty to say what the recommendations of the commission were as to carrying out the wishes of the Pope. He thought, however, that the Archbishop would give out the instructions to the pastors and the organists before September. As to the exclusion

* While the commission did its work, even Episcopalians got into the act. Bishop Henry Codman Potter of the Cathedral of St. John the Divine gave an extraordinary interview to the *Tribune* in which he expressed his distaste with "estimable young women" who sang operatically in churches, his "sympathy with the Pope," and his belief that young boys should be well trained both musically and otherwise. But the Bishop's alleged sympathy to Rome (among other things) might have been called into question when he continued, "In a community where thirty-five thousand Italian immigrants land in a year the time will come when an appeal must be made to the citizen soldier."

of women from the choirs, Father McGean said the commission had made no report. It was a delicate subject, he said, and depended on the meaning of the Pope, the interpretation of which was left to the Archbishop.

Pointedly, the article was headlined ARCHBISHOP FARLEY TO INTERPRET POPE'S WISHES AS TO WOMEN SINGERS.

At the same time that the *Tribune* was making do with inferences and innuendo, far more concrete news of the situation in New York was being printed in, of all places, Kansas City. A reporter from the *Kansas City Star* had somehow inveigled an interview from Ungerer—or Ungerer had assumed that there was no risk in airing his thoughts, as well as some music department business dealings, to a writer from the Midwest:

> [E]xcitement [anxiety] among the women choir singers of New York reached white heat, until May 1 witnessed the renewal of contracts with the soloists of St. Patrick's cathedral, St. Francis Xavier's and other leading metropolitan churches that support high salaried singers.
>
> "There is nothing in Gregorian music that women's voices cannot do most effectively," said Mr. Ungerer, the New York choirmaster of St. Patrick's cathedral. "The public seems to be laboring under erroneous ideas of the whole subject of Gregorian music and the purport of the Motu Proprio. It seems to think all figured music is to be abolished, and that church music of the future will in consequence partake of requiem—something mournful and monotonous. Unless there come from Rome explicit orders to abolish women they will certainly be retained at the cathedral.
>
> "The cathedral, in probability, will have no more Gregorian chant than it always has had. The Introit, Gradual, Hallelujah, Track, Offertory, Communion, which change with the feasts, have always been Gregorian at the cathedral. This has not been the case in other churches in this vicinity and elsewhere, and it is to effect this that the pope evidently wishes to make it compulsory. The Kyrie, Gloria, Credo, Sanctus, Agnus Dei will continue, as they always have been at the cathedral, to be figured music, but we trust of a higher order of composition. There is a lot of splendid modern music to displace Haydn, Mozart, etc.—music that sustains all the simplicity and solemnity of Palestrina. To bring the figured music to a higher standard

of excellence, it would seem, is one of the chief objects of the pope's decree, and it has not come too soon."

The summer went by with no further news except for one leak—an announcement (strangely enough, in the *Chicago Daily Tribune*) in July:

Archbishop Farley of New York has directed that hereafter no Jews or infidels or professed nonbelievers shall be employed in the choirs of churches in his diocese.

After which there was silence.

Until September 25, a Sunday. During that morning's Mass, the commission's report was read at every church in the Archdiocese and picked up by newspapers across the United States. BOY CHOIRS TO REPLACE SOPRANO AND CONTRALTO SINGERS/POPE'S WISHES CARRIED OUT, announced the *Times*. CHURCH MUSIC REGULATIONS/GREGORIAN CHANTS TO BE RESTORED—WOMEN BANISHED FROM CHOIRS came from the *Sun*. BARS WOMEN FROM CATHOLIC CHOIRS was the comparatively simple headline in the *Herald*.

The commission's report supported every aspect of the *motu proprio* without exception. It recommended also that Catholic schools teach a more formalized curriculum of music, that the Archdiocese establish a conservatory in order to train musicians in the approved repertoire, and that a catalogue be prepared in order to aid those musicians by offering a complete list of that repertoire. The report finished by quoting Archbishop Farley's words: "The quality of the music in our services will not suffer by the exclusion of certain compositions so long in favor with many to the detriment of devotion."

And that was that.

The situation was summarized by another *Times* editorial that appreciated the Pontiff's motives as well as the difficulties that were about to be created by the *motu proprio*'s implementation.

The authorities of the Catholic Church throughout Europe, and perhaps particularly throughout the United States, were undoubtedly thrown into consternation by the promulgation of the instructions of Pope Pius X concerning church music. The reforms which he laid down were so very sweeping that it seemed that their adoption would do away with what was commonly accepted as church music altogether.

Archbishop Farley's approval of the report of a commission appointed by him to consider the subject has been published. The report shows how radical a change from the present practice will be wrought by a sincere attempt to give effect to the Papal instructions. Every musician of taste will agree that the object of the instructions, which is to make church music more churchly, is a worthy object, from the point of view of art as well as of religion. But the means taken to assure this end will play havoc not only with the repertory but with the personnel of most organ lofts. The literal enforcement of the Pauline precept touching the silence of women in the churches threatens to reduce the singing to low mutterings until a race of boy choristers can be trained, while it is evident that a literal enforcement, by a priest not musically gifted, of the prohibition of music which does not "correspond to the words of the liturgical text without omissions, inversions or vain repetitions," would deprive the Church of some of the noblest music with which genius has stimulated devotion.

For the time, the influence of the Papal order upon the music of the Church, at least in this country, may be expected to be depressing. But since the purpose of the order is admitted to be commendable, it is to be hoped that, with a proper and not too literal adaptation of means to ends, it may ultimately result in a raising of the standard of Catholic church music, both in composition and execution.

There is no record of whether Katherine Hilke and Mary Louise Clary, or any of the female choristers, had been present in the gallery to hear the Archbishop's words. Very likely not. Only two days after the report, the Cathedral hosted the opening Mass of the third General Eucharistic Congress, the music of which "was sung by a picked choir of men and boys. . . ."

The process had been so long and draining that it had to an extent worn itself out. The official change was reported in the October 24 *Tribune*, but now it rated no more than a sidebar column.

Some of the new rules, chief of which is the elimination of women from the choirs, formulated for music in the Catholic churches of the city by the committee of laymen and clergymen appointed by Archbishop Farley to prepare measures in conformity with the Pope's desires, went into effect at the Cathedral yesterday.

At the 11 o'clock high mass a choir of sixty male voices replaced the mixed choir. The chancel choir of sixty boys took part in the services as usual, making an aggregate of 120 voices.

The Catholic historian John Talbot Smith would later write: "The reform in church music struck the diocese of New York with its fullest force, chiefly because the Pope indirectly urged Archbishop Farley to set an impressive example in so important a see." Smith's was an intriguing view that never crept into the popular press, but it makes complete sense in light of the Archbishop's unwavering insistence right from the start that he would abide by the *motu proprio*—as opposed to Cardinal Gibbons of Baltimore, who began 1904 by stating firmly that the regulations had nothing to do with *American* churches, then gradually edged back his position over a number of months until he was in complete accord with the Pope's wishes.

Oddly, after all the eavesdropping and snooping in which reporters had engaged during the previous months, no published account exists of a New York church's dismissing its female singers. The closest thing to an actual report was to come over a year later as part of an interview with, of all people, James Ungerer:

> There is always more or less difficulty in making a change in the singers in any church. . . . They made the change in a week's time, and Miss Hilke, the soprano, and Miss Louise Clary, the alto, stepped out one Sunday, and their places were supplied by male voices on the next.
>
> That there was some difficulty in trying to get a substitute for women's voices is shown in the increased number of singers. With the women's voices there was one regular quartet with two extra male voices to assist, while now there are three quartets of professional male singers with a volunteer chorus. The new order of things is as costly as the old, the present soloists being high-priced singers and receiving large salaries. And the result is not satisfactory after all. That is what J. C. Ungerer, the organist, says. . . .
>
> "Changing to male voices has changed the style of music entirely," says Mr. Ungerer. "It is impossible to get the same effects without women's voices, and then much church music is written for mixed voices, and I should be glad to see the order revoked."

(The *motu proprio* wasn't discussed much in literature, either. An extremely rare mention occurs in James Joyce's *The Dead*, as an ex-church soprano sings at a party and then makes her feelings plain to the guests: "... I think it's not at all honorable for the pope to turn out the women of the choirs that have slaved there all their lives and put little whipper-snappers of boys over their heads.")

Mary Louise Clary may have been personally hurt by her dismissal, but her career wasn't, because she was a well-established artist who suddenly had more open dates in her calendar. (Her husband happened to be a concert manager, which didn't hurt her situation, either.) Within months, she had departed for Europe and entered upon the German operatic scene with some success.

Katherine Hilke, however, was less fortunate. Her appeal had always been more locally based, and to a great extent tied to her association with St. Patrick's. She was instantly able to get another church job for the beginning of the 1904–05 season, that of soprano soloist at Calvary Methodist. But not much else came her way other than a few sympathy hires for concerts from old friends like Clemente de Macchi. (One of those concerts, a *Stabat Mater* for the Catholic Oratorio Society, was announced in the *Tribune*—in the same column that complained about the Easter music planned at the Cathedral: "[A] large portion of the old Easter glory is departed. . . . The Pope's rulings on the subject have banished the ornate music which used to heighten the gladsomeness of the Eastertide.") After a year or two of seeing herself described as "lately soloist of St. Patrick's Cathedral" and sensing the diminishing returns, she gave up on New York and headed to Europe. For "further study."

Aftermath of the motu proprio

Far more than careers or logistics had been changed by the musical upheaval of 1904. The *motu proprio* had affected the role of the choirmaster, underscoring his status as a lay minister while considerably reducing his authorial profile. The conductor with a strong and idiosyncratic vision was, quite simply, no longer a realistic choice for a Catholic church. During the next decade, Catholic music would be more suitable to the service but less interesting to the public—as would its musicians. And this change spread to non-Catholic music as well. The newspaper listings that had appeared at every holiday, carefully detailing the musical preparations of New York churches, began to dwindle. The impact of the change was summed up best, unintentionally, by the *American Art Journal*. The magazine's cover had always featured currently popular conductors or performers in midcareer such as Walter Damrosch, Theodore Thomas, or Met soprano Lillian Nordica. But the March 19 cover bore a portrait of Palestrina.

The singers' role would change as well, and drastically so. The full-page newspaper star treatments of church soloists, so prevalent just a decade previously, bypassed Catholic churches. And the vocally generous "distinguished soloists" of previous years were now being viewed as somehow inappropriate for the new repertoire.* The implication hung in the air that the less-engaged music now being performed would require less-engaging voices to perform it—and the possessors of those voices would have considerably less incentive for emotional investment (and longevity) in their jobs. Charles Steinbuch, the Wagnerian baritone who retired from St. Patrick's in 1900 after more than two decades, had been replaced by concert baritone Percy Hemus. But Hemus and his bantam-weight instrument stayed less than five years after the *motu proprio* went into effect.† *He* was then replaced by bass Gustave Holm, who sang only until it was discovered that he was a non-Catholic and, under the new regulations, ineligible to sing at the Cathedral. (This, along with his subsequent move to the Church of the Heavenly Rest, was deemed newsworthy by the *Times*.) There were other singers in this period—Graham Reed (once soloist with John Philip Sousa, then a baritone with the Brooklyn Opera Company, finally a voice teacher in Chicago), Stasso Berini, Nicholl Sebastian, Leo van Ljunghen, P. F. Notley, Frederick Percippe—to fill slots in the triple quartet mentioned by Ungerer. But it was a mark of

---

* Except in synagogues. An article in the *Washington Post*, written by the paper's New York correspondent, pointed out that music lovers could still find Big Liturgical Music at a number of the city's temples, along with choirs staffed by many of the same female soloists who had lost their Catholic church jobs. The article went so far as to inform readers of who was singing where, if they wanted to hear their favorites.

† Hemus wound up with some concert work, an unremarked solo recital, some touring operettas, and a few Broadway appearances. He finally found his niche as a radio actor for NBC—where he would die of a heart attack, moments before a broadcast, in 1943.

the period that their names didn't extend into other, flashier areas of musical history.*

For the occasional solo responsibilities required by the new music, Ungerer cobbled together an ensemble that would be known for years as the Cathedral Quartet. The name was a catchall, since its membership was actually quite fluid and depended upon the outside schedules of its singers. For instance, bass William F. Hooley was much favored outside of St. Patrick's—not for opera or concert dates, but as one of history's very first vocalists ever to work in the brand-new field of recorded music. The phonograph was a sensation across the United States, and companies such as Victor, Columbia, and Edison (engaged in manufacturing not only the machines but also the recordings that were played upon them) discovered that barbershop-styled male harmony groups were big sellers. They had also discovered that the sing-into-the-horn recording equipment of the time failed to record lower male voices unless those voices were particularly resonant. Hooley's sound was not only large but ringing with metal, which enabled him to "take" to disc easily. This put him in constant demand to anchor the lower end of the American Quartet, the Lyric Quartet, the Haydn Quartet, the Orpheus Quartet, the Edison Male Quartette, and the Heidelberg Quintet. It was grind work, indifferently paid, none of it glory-producing except for the occasional solo outing. (One of the first of those was spoken rather than sung, an 1899 rendition of Lincoln's Gettysburg Address. Many others were novelty pieces such as "Asleep in the Deep," which made a point of showcasing Hooley's evidently limitless bottom range.) After two decades of this routine as a pioneering studio singer, he died suddenly and inexplicably in 1918 at the age of fifty-six.

The Cathedral Quartet's top tenor was more lucky, and more durable, and he would become much better known. All of twenty-six years old, he

* One choir alumnus would achieve his fame considerably after the fact. Arthur Jarrett, a pupil at the Cathedral School, served as a soprano soloist at St. Patrick's until the inevitable voice change put an end to that. As an adult he developed a pop tenor voice and achieved big success as one of the first dance band "crooners." This led to movie roles with co-stars as diverse as Joan Crawford and Betty Boop, and radio superstardom in the 1930s as competition for the iconic Bing Crosby. Other Cathedral boy sopranos to become adult successes included film character actor J. Carrol Naish, as well as Jack Benny's radio stooge-and-tenor, Dennis Day.

had already sung at St. Patrick's . . . St. Patrick's Church, in Wilmington, Delaware. John A. Finnegan had been a machinist in a naval gun factory until he realized that he could sing; after that, he threw himself into the music profession, willing to do anything and everything to earn a living with his voice. He took any recital or concert work that was available. Like Hooley, he tried out the recording industry with some Irish songs as well as a few Dixieland rags. Unlike Hooley's, his output was issued on inexpensive local labels. As was the practice of the time, he made himself available as a hired entertainer at club events and political meetings. (He must have been good at it, too. His name was even listed on the sheet music of J. L. Feeney's labor song "Stick to the Union, Jack"— "Sung by the popular tenor vocalist *John A. Finnegan.*") He sang at a number of churches in Wilmington and then Washington, before deciding to attempt New York.

Choirmasters were realizing that the higher, lighter "Irish" tenor sound could also be viewed as an "Ecclesiastical" sound, a better fit for the new musical requirements than the more dramatic voices of years past. At the same time, Charles Kaiser was becoming more interested in voice teaching and decided that it was time to move on. This combination of events meant that John A. Finnegan would come to New York as the new tenor soloist of St. Patrick's Cathedral.

Finnegan blasted the stereotype of the badly trained, straining and shrill Irish "necktie" tenor by proving that he was very well schooled indeed, expert not only in church service but also in concert (conducted by Victor Herbert, no less) and oratorio—including Rossini's *Stabat Mater*, a part so high-flying that most tenors never attempt it, yet one of Finnegan's most frequent bookings. His sound was sweet but solid (an overwrought critic rhapsodized about "golden robustness that verges closely on the lyric"), and well focused enough to reach throughout the Cathedral's space. In years to come, he would be in demand for radio broadcasts and extensive recital tours, able to bring back some of the luster implicit in the phrase "Soloist of St. Patrick's Cathedral." He fulfilled the *motu proprio*'s requirements of piety and probity as an active member of both the Knights of Columbus and the Friendly Sons of St. Patrick. And he would achieve the greatest longevity of any soloist in the history of the Cathedral.*

---

* Cathedral connections meant that both Finnegan and Hooley would be on tap for various Catholic-sponsored events. Their names show up repeatedly in Carne-

But those days lay in the future. The ears of the public had been conditioned by decades of Mozart and Gounod—also Hilke, Clary, and their lush-voiced sisters—and they were disappointed by the comparative austerities of Mitterer, Lambilotte, and boy trebles. The extent to which the Cathedral's musical stock had fallen was demonstrated when Metropolitan Opera manager Heinrich Conried launched a legal attack against New York's "Sunday laws," which prohibited certain types of entertainments on the Sabbath. To provoke a test case, Conried scheduled a Verdi *Requiem* in defiance of the statute and took the stand himself at the resulting trial. The *Tribune* covered the trial and reported gleefully:

> One of the questions asked of him was:
> "Is the 'Requiem' sung in just the same manner as it is sung in the Cathedral?"
> "No," answered the director, quickly. "It is presented in much better form; better singing, better music, better everything."
> This caused a general laugh in court.

Lest anyone miss the thrust of the article, the headline read REQUIEM SUNG BETTER AT OPERA HOUSE THAN AT CATHEDRAL, HE SAYS.

Such public perception (especially because St. Patrick's had absolutely nothing to do with Conried's case) made it more than clear that "church" music in New York was now regarded as something considerably different from—and inferior to—"real" music.* But as far as the Cathedral was concerned, its music would for a while be less interesting than the image of its musicians.

This was the situation at the 1908 wedding of Gladys Vanderbilt to a Hungarian count. The wedding took place at the Vanderbilt residence, not at St. Patrick's. Nonetheless, the chancel choir was in attendance.

---

gie Hall performance lists for St. Patrick's Day as well as Columbus Day concerts—mishmash-type evenings that steered both men into dangerously unfamiliar waters, requiring them to sing hit tunes from works including *Rigoletto*, *Aïda*, *Ernani*, *The Creation*, and *Lucia di Lammermoor* (the "Sextet," including their choir colleague Nicholl Sebastian), and even confections like "Doan Ye Cry, Ma Honey." Perhaps fortunately, those performances weren't reviewed.

* About this time, a new insult gained currency among musicians. It referred to the recent crop of church music that supplied liturgical correctness but not much else: "Sacred Ragtime."

Because there was a quick ceremony instead of a nuptial Mass, the only choral music was a single piece from Gaul's oratorio *Ruth*. (A popular dance orchestra supplied the rest of the music for the ceremony.) *Town and Country* didn't concern itself to write about the choir's singing but approved of their role in the stage picture; they were the personification of angelic choirboys, their job to march before the bride in the wedding procession.

"I Fear No Labor as Far as Strength Allows"

To the extent that a musical organization takes on the personality of its leader, there was indeed a new era at St. Patrick's.

William F. Pecher had been a reserved man who gradually relaxed into the public aspects of his role at the Cathedral—truly charming reporters with his personality in some of those later interviews, allowing himself to accept the friendship and hospitality of people who admired his work. He even took part in the playtimes of the rich when he accompanied the occasional society soprano in a hotel musicale. And the choristers of St. Patrick's made no secret of the fact that they not only respected him but loved him deeply.

James Ungerer, though, would never be given to fun, play, or casual friendship. The old cliché "living for his music" applied far too strongly to him. Some years after his death, his friend Alastair Guinan wrote a memorial tribute that contained a key to his personality:

> Mr. Ungerer's essential character was marked by a certain austerity of demeanor which prevented many from discerning what was known, perhaps only to his most intimate friends & pupils—a fundamentally gentle, sympathetic, & understanding nature, humorous indeed, but profoundly wedded to rectitude. "High principled" would be the best word to describe him, if one were restricted to a single term. . . . [T]he modesty of his exterior & the quietness of his manner effectively concealed the richness of his gifts so that they were fully appreciated only by those who were privileged to share some degree of intimacy with him.

Those privileged ones were few and far between. Whether his "rectitude" came from paralyzing shyness, deep-seated personal conflicts, or a genuine anxiety disorder, Ungerer's response to the very public nature of his position was to retreat from it. He was pleasant but formal, capable of little backslapping or camaraderie. After his remark to the *Times* in 1905 that he would be glad to see the *motu proprio* revoked, almost none of his subsequent opinions made it into print. (Nor were they much sought by the press; the word apparently had spread.) He permitted himself scant recreation other than an occasional trip to Europe to visit family members. He indulged in no luxury and few comforts, not even in his domestic arrangements; for decades, his address was at the Capitol (formerly the Knights of Columbus Hotel), a modest residence hotel within walking distance of St. Patrick's, where he would live in a room-with-bath. Another old cliché put it more succinctly: His only true home was at the keyboard.

Ungerer may have been shy, but he could never be called a coward; the high-principled component of his personality made him absolutely capable of speaking out when he felt the need. As far back as 1898, he had written an indignant memo—three pages, single-spaced—to the Rector and trustees. In several sections, it detailed a number of problems existing in the music department (it's enlightening that none of those problems involved William F. Pecher or the gallery choir) as well as his ideas for solving those problems. The first section, entitled "The Chancel Choir," spared no one, including himself:

> Having directed the Chancel choir for the past five years, I find that its work apparently efficient is far inferior to that of a well equipped choir and its progress entirely barred and unsatisfactory.
>
> . . . I can not stop to teach rudiments where there is a constant demand for ready work at short notice. . .

The second section, "The Seminary," recommended—in verbiage that would still apply today:

> We need a good contingent of male singers. No doubt a ready element and active co-operation on everyone's part can be found at the Seminary. But while some may be musical and some not, all need instruction and training.
>
> A class compulsory to all should be given weekly—this would embrace "History and Method," "Interpretations of Gregorian chant" and "Congregational Singing." Again all voices should form a choir taught in two sections, embracing theory and singing and modern

music. Following this plan you would afford every clergyman a knowledge he should have. . . . It would take two years perhaps to organize a Choir as I would like to have. It is impossible to do it with any outside element and I fear you will never have a strong organization unless you fall back on the Seminarians.

The next section took in St. Cecelia's Choir, which had long been anathema to Ungerer. Musically, he could function as a professional or an educator but balked at the idea of serving as social director for a recreational group. He wanted to reorganize the choir from the ground up:

I would run St. Cecelia's choir on a different plan: Admit all worthy young men and form a practical singing Society. Would undertake to perform some of the big works in the Cathedral this winter: taking our Chancel Choir and Seminarians as a nucleus St. Cecelia's choir assisting we could give the "Messiah" around Christmas and the "Stabat Mater" and others in Lent.

Those improvements never occurred, and St. Cecelia's Choir would soon disappear from the scene completely. There was a halfhearted effort (not Ungerer's) to revive it in the early 1920s, but to no avail. The idea of a Cathedral-based community choir wouldn't be attempted again for another three-quarters of a century.

The final section of the memo, "Financial," is possibly the most telling in that it reflects not only Ungerer's sense of fairness but also the fact that it was intended to be an ultimatum. Also, that it was more or less ignored.

All the above to show a stationary state of affairs: The work hard and plentiful is very unsatisfactory to me for that very reason. When through Father Young's recommendation I was engaged for one year, I was given a salary of twelve-hundred dollars and promised a raise were I suitable. More than five years have elapsed now without a change. Should the desirable improvements not be made I see very little inducement to keep up my interest in the work.

Other Boys' Choirmasters in leading Churches of this City receive $3,500, yearly while the organists in the same churches only get $1,500. Their work is limited—mine is unlimited and perhaps thrice that of theirs. They may double their income from outside sources; I have positively no time or chance of doing so. I fear no labor as far as strength allows, but I would like recognition of same.

Ungerer would have some of these identical complaints ten and twenty years hence, finances among them. Whether it was a consequence of his B-type personality or the fact that he had begun as an assistant, he was by comparison one of the lowest-paid choirmasters ever employed at the Cathedral. That situation would improve, but not by very much, and it would ultimately come back to embarrass everyone involved.

However, St. Patrick's was extremely lucky in one respect—no matter how outraged his sensibilities, how overwhelmed he professed to be by any situation at any given moment, or how complicated his personal quirks made his dealings with colleagues, none of it would conceal the fact that James Ungerer was possessed of a great deal of talent. And he was able to implement his talent with a concentration that could produce exceptional results. That opening Mass of the Eucharistic Congress, whose congregation included more than a thousand prelates as well as the Vatican's Apostolic Delegate—and occurring a bare two days after the Cathedral had dropped its female singers—might easily have been a high-pressure musical disaster. Yet the *Times* was captivated by the choir's Gregorian chant: "The interpretation was German. That of to-day will be of the French and Belgian, and to-morrow the chant will be according to the Italian interpretation." With so many choirmasters still wrestling with the basic concept of chant, Ungerer's effortless command of the form's varying styles was something of a show turn, and a great assurance to Cathedral clergy.

The offertory for that service was Ungerer's own "O Salutaris." He had composed it in 1899, and it was so well received that it remained in the Cathedral's active repertoire for more than twenty-five years. A piece more tailor-made for the choirmen of St. Patrick's—or more indicative of the level of work that was expected of them at the time—can hardly be imagined. Written for *six-part* men's voices (when many New York churches had difficulty finding six male singers to begin with), it shows that Ungerer's musical vocabulary was unusually sophisticated for a church composer, with harmonies that have been described as Wagnerian Barbershop. The fact that it was performed repeatedly proves that the Cathedral's choristers, whether or not they were renowned soloists, were solid professional singers. (It proves as well that their vocalism was thoroughly understood by their choirmaster. The top tenor line alone contains ten high A-flats, four high B-flats, and one high C-flat. A composer doesn't write such a line unless he knows that he has voices able to execute it.) Even more fascinating in light of the piece's popularity is the fact that Ungerer never bothered to submit it for copyright.

Perhaps he forgot. He was easily as busy as Pecher had ever been, and with the implementation of the *motu proprio* possibly more so. Along with his Cathedral duties, he still taught, as he had since his arrival at St. Patrick's, at the Cathedral School. He continued to handle the musical training of seminarians. His particularly high visibility in the world of sacred music made it a foregone conclusion that he would be asked to serve on the organization committee of the American Congress of Catholic Organists and Choirmasters. This was a spinoff of the Society of St. Gregory, the main object of which was "to foster fraternal assistance and encouragement among its members, in the promotion of the cause of liturgical music according to the recommendations of His Holiness Pope Pius X. . . ." The Society was involved in the arduous process of compiling a brand-new hymnal. It was also in the process of compiling—using a number of sources, among them the New York Commission's efforts—a "White List" as well as a "Black List." Exactly what they sounded like, these lists (which were periodically modified and used well into the 1950s) were intended to provide a no-questions-asked guide for choirmasters who wanted to know what music was approved for church use. And what music was to be junked.

Such extra duties, added to the pressure of moving from chancel to gallery, made it incumbent upon Ungerer to look for assistance. So he turned to John J. O'Connor, an acquaintance from Morristown who had been organist at that town's Church of the Assumption. For his own training in Gregorian chant, the *Times* reported, O'Connor had "recently returned from the Isle of Wight, where for three months he was at the Benedictine Monastery. . . . There he was instructed in the method of singing and teaching the chant." O'Connor would take Ungerer's old post, presiding over the chancel choir and doing some occasional composing of his own. The arrangement functioned smoothly until the morning Mass of June 2, 1918, when Monsignor Lavelle requested prayers for John J. O'Connor, who had abruptly been taken ill. There was no clarification and no further news of O'Connor's status (nor even of the nature of his sudden illness) until the Mass of June 30, when Monsignor Lavelle announced to the congregation, "To-morrow at 9 o'clock there will be a solemn Mass of requiem for Mr. John J. O'Connor, during many years chancel organist of this Cathedral. He was a fine musician, faithful and devoted to his work. He deserves our prayers and constant grateful remembrance."

No records shed any definite light on the identity of O'Connor's successor over the next three years. Possibly Ungerer copied Pecher's old system of bringing in informal assistants for short stints to see how things would work out; perhaps he relied upon the help of such musically capable young men as were studying at Cathedral College or St. Joseph's Seminary. One assistant was Walter N. Waters, an organist-composer who had worked in a number of area churches, published an amount of choral music, and in his spare time served as secretary of the National Association of Organists. At his death, the *Times* would mention that he "served at St. Patrick's Cathedral for six years, including the period of the first World War. On the day of the armistice he played in St. Patrick's a special program marking the end of hostilities."

Ungerer finally struck pay dirt in 1922 with the newly ordained Reverend Robert E. Woods. As subdeacon, Father Woods maintained a full clerical schedule for more than a quarter-century, often celebrating Sunday's high Masses and giving sermons that were effective enough (and provocative enough) to be quoted frequently in the press. As a bonus, he was a wizard of time management. He was capable both at the organ and in conducting the chancel choir. He taught music at both Cathedral College and Cathedral Grammar School. He served as moderator of the Holy Name Society, the League of the Sacred Heart, and the Cathedral Club. For years, he sang the "Christus" in the Passion on Good Friday. (Starting in 1930, what leisure time he earned would be taken up with a project that had already been around for a while, the Catholic Theatre Movement, "trying to make every man and woman his or her own censor." Under his supervision another White List was issued, this one listing plays, and then films, that were judged suitable for Catholic audiences. Touted from the pulpit, in print and over radio, the idea failed to provoke much interest until it was reborn in other hands as the Legion of Decency.)

As had always been the case, major historical events would sometimes bypass the choir gallery completely, sometimes not. Of course the Cathedral musicians had taken part in the extensive celebrations that marked the 1908 week-long Centenary of the New York Archdiocese. Perhaps with a tip of the hat to Pecher's memory, Ungerer commemorated the gigantic ceremony of the opening Mass in the same manner as that of his mentor—by composing music for the occasion, a Kyrie and Gloria that were sung by the Cathedral Quartet along with an extravagantly augmented choir totaling 200 voices, the whole thing reinforced by the New York Symphony Society. Man and boy alike, Ungerer's singers maintained a punishing schedule, participating in six of the week's seven events.*

Even more overpowering were the celebrations that accompanied the Cathedral's consecration in 1910—a service of five hours, during which, reporters estimated, the Archbishop and his household (and the Cathedral choristers, as a necessary part of the procession) would walk four miles while making the required circuits of the Cathedral. For the Mass following the consecration, Ungerer composed his own *Mass, Op. 101*. When Archbishop Farley was made Cardinal in 1912, the new music came from sources other than Ungerer himself, but he coordinated an extensive program. (An example of the program's scope was the beginning of the procession, when the gallery orchestra launched into the "War March of the Priests," supplemented by trumpets—twenty trumpets.)

An indication of Ungerer's success was the fact that the Cathedral choir was viewed as not only good music, but good box office. In 1912, the *Titanic* disaster occasioned a rush of public support, culminating in a benefit held by the Women's Titanic Memorial Committee at the Century Theatre. Producer Daniel Frohman organized an extravagant lineup of performing luminaries, including George M. Cohan, Billie Burke, Ruth St. Denis—and, singing "Gounod's Sanctus" during the grand finale tableau, the full choir of St. Patrick's.

Ungerer and his musicians had additional visibility during the Christmas season of 1915, when Cardinal Farley granted permission for the churches of the Archdiocese, "for this year only," to hold Midnight Masses.

This is a return to a custom which was discontinued in this city twenty-five years ago, for at that time it was felt that at the midnight hour many persons attended the services merely from curiosity and as

---

* The exception would occur when Ungerer handed over the baton to his old colleague Father Young, who had coordinated the efforts of 5,000 New York schoolchildren, serving both as congregation and choir of their own special Mass. One observer said that the children sang "with remarkable unison."

a finale of a festive evening. The authorities of the diocese felt that the masses at dawn would possibly have more devout worshippers.

The Cathedral seems never to have held a Midnight Mass, hewing instead to the Old Cathedral's practice of 4:30 A.M. for its first Christmas service. But with Europe in the first throes of what would eventually become World War I, the Cardinal had felt that a Midnight Mass would be a suitable peace offering. A peace offering, but a splendid one, with opulent music: Everyone was instantly delighted with the Midnight Mass, and the response from congregations throughout the Archdiocese was so strong that the Cardinal was to repeat his "this year only" permission, over and over. "This year only" would show up as an annual notice in the New York press as late as 1924; after that, it was simply assumed that Midnight Mass at St. Patrick's was a certainty. From the Cardinal's one-time-only decision was born a tradition that turned into one of New York's, and ultimately the nation's, most emblematic holiday events.

That first Midnight Mass may have been a joyous occasion, but for Ungerer it had marked a difficult and awkward time, during which he'd left the United States, gone to France, and returned. The outbreak of the Great War in the late summer of 1914, involving as it did at the time only European nations, had seemed to have no effect upon music at the Cathedral. Or so people assumed. Ungerer's thoughts were never known publicly as he saw his country swept into the fighting. But by October, he had surprised everyone by arranging a replacement for himself and sailing to Europe to join the French Army. One can admire Ungerer's principles' being put into action, but it was an immoderately shortsighted gesture. He was forty-two years old, had lived as an American citizen since 1898, led a completely sedentary existence, and worked in a profession that had nothing to do with the skills needed in modern warfare.

Decades later, his obituary would report, "In January, 1915, he was declared physically unfit and discharged. He returned to this country on the last westward passage of the liner *Lusitania*, before her destruction by a German submarine."*

---

* Ungerer's replacement for those months was John Philip Foley, an organist who had already assisted at the Jardine on Easter Sunday 1905; he made himself available to take the gallery choir for the duration of the war. However, Ungerer's early return sent Foley back to his original post at St. Stephen's Church. (His pastor was a certain Bishop Patrick Hayes, whose own path would lead to St.

At the time, though, the only news of his military service came in a single terse paragraph in the October 1915 issue of *The Catholic Choirmaster*:

> Jacques Cecelien Ungerer, for twenty-two years organist of St. Patrick's Cathedral, New York, returned from France a few weeks ago, where he had served in the army in various capacities ever since the war began.

The episode would not be discussed elsewhere.

A New Friend from Italy

During these years, Ungerer would form an association that would prove to have immense repercussions in the history of the Cathedral's music, and in his own life as well.

Two Italian brothers, both organists, had been making waves in the music world. The elder of the two had lived in New York since 1894 and had made a reputation as a vocal coach. The younger brother had remained in Italy to pursue his studies and had made bigger waves; initial conservatory successes in organ, piano, and composition had led him to the Accademia di Santa Cecilia in Rome, to fistfuls of academic awards and official recognition (as well as a command performance before the king of Italy), and thence to the Vatican for a two-year stint as deputy organist.

In the spring of 1907, Father Young was in Rome on Vatican business. He knew that his organist Gaston Dethier was leaving St. Francis Xavier to pursue a concert career and that he would have to find a replacement. Perhaps S. Constantino Yon had recommended that Father Young watch his brother in action. Perhaps the young man needed no recommendation. Whichever way it happened, Father Young was sufficiently impressed to offer a three-year contract to Pietro Alessandro Yon. At the time of the offer, Yon was not quite twenty-one years old, the same age as James Ungerer when he had begun work at St. Patrick's.

Patrick's in a very different way.) Foley would spend another quarter-century in that job, becoming famous for the excellence of his boychoir. He also maintained a sideline in the 1920s and '30s, running Beaver Camp, a summer retreat for Catholic boys "from homes of refinement."

Only fourteen years separated the two men, but actually they were a generation apart. Ungerer had been a product of the nineteenth century, a model church musician who had survived the transition to the age of the *motu proprio* by knowing his job better, and executing it with more calm, self-effacing capability, than anyone else. In comparison, Yon was everything that Ungerer wasn't—totally informed as to the restrictions and requirements of modern liturgical music, but determined to prove that this music could be delivered with Italianate energy and the dash of a maestro. So soon after the upheavals of 1904, such positioning belonged only to a complete maverick.

Another factor would come to bear on the career paths of both men. The boisterous local press coverage of 1890s musicians was evolving into a more polished, national publicity network. Publications such as *Musical America* and *Musical Courier* were based in New York, but their influence stretched across the country. A high-profile New York musician (or one who wished to be) needed only to hire a press agent in order to whip up nationwide interest. Ungerer, being Ungerer, had no use for the process. Yon plunged in with gusto.

There were a few quiet years while Yon got his choral bearings and dispatched his first (mostly local) recital dates,* and then his name was suddenly a regular fixture in the music columns. That he was extraordinarily talented was without dispute; but part of his talent was an instinctive aptitude for effective networking, for compiling his own Rolodex of those in the business, and for the delicate process of distributing as well as calling in chits. Yon composed a song, "Qui te solo," and dedicated it to Met soprano Gina Ciaparelli. When she premiered it in a 1911 recital, he made sure that he would accompany her at the song's premiere. (This was good publicity for Yon—his first full-scale mention in the *Times*—and a composer's prerogative, even though it meant that her accompanist, the very distinguished Max Liebling, would be temporarily shoved from the bench.)

Within months, *Musical America* carried an extensive article describing a spaghetti party hosted by both Yon brothers at the Italian Club; the guest list included the well-known opera caricaturist Viafora. The article was framed not only as a personality piece but as a basic introduction to

* Yon later confided that he had been struck by a car during his first year in America. The accident fractured both wrists, putting him out of commission until he slowly and painfully recuperated.

the brothers (the editor of *Musical America* twirls pasta as he asks Pietro, "You are an organist?"), with a lengthy discussion of their musical views, some good-natured kidding of their Italian accents—and a Viafora caricature of the scene at table. Neither the Yons nor *Musical America* normally could have afforded his artwork to decorate a piece of journalism. But then again, Viafora was married to Gina Ciaparelli. . . .

Undoubtedly Father Young introduced Ungerer to his new organist. Despite their differences in personality, Yon soon became one of Ungerer's few close friends. Part of this stemmed from each man's admiration of the other's work. Yon would program Ungerer's "Terra Tremuit" no fewer than five times during Easter services at St. Francis Xavier. For his part, Ungerer arranged for public performances—"Jerusalem, Surge" was Yon's first composition heard at St. Patrick's, during the 1910 consecration Mass—and commissions. Yon produced a "Tantum ergo" for the Vesper service of Easter 1911 and, a greater compliment, an "Ecce Sacerdos" for Cardinal Farley's installation in January 1912. For Easter 1912, he went further and supplied a full Mass setting, the *Mass in G*, which took advantage of John Finnegan's solo capabilities (and of the Cathedral's largesse, scored as it was for a fifty-piece orchestra). All three compositions earned enthusiastic writeups in the *New York Times* and *Musical America*, along with photos of both Yon and Ungerer.

Those photos told more of Ungerer's stress level than it did of Yon's mounting fame. It had been only nine years since the *Tribune* had published its picture of Ungerer seated at the Jardine, thirty-one years old and still boyish. At forty, he had aged shockingly. Even so, the vacation shot with his friends is the only photograph in existence that depicts James C. Ungerer with a relaxed slouch, an unbuttoned jacket, and a smile.

Yon was able to reciprocate Ungerer's kindnesses when he and his brother opened the Yon Music Studios in 1914. While other musicians such as Pecher had taught privately, Yon's idea was to form a conservatory setting for aspiring liturgical musicians,* utilizing a small faculty of instructors whose work he respected. Constantino Yon had lived and

---

* Not only liturgical musicians. One composition student was a Yale graduate who had stumbled his way into the Broadway scene with a humiliating flop of a musical comedy. The young man studied with Yon for less than a year before realizing that he had to change his approach. But finally, Cole Porter found a musical voice of his own.

taught in the Carnegie Hall building since 1897, so it was logical for the brothers' joint venture to begin there. They were in cramped quarters; Carnegie historian Ethel Peyser would write of Pietro Yon, "At first he had a tiny studio, and for his little pipe organ had to use a small space under a staircase. He dreamed of having a spacious studio some day." His wish became reality as the Yon Music Studios expanded until their eighth-floor suite took in nearly the entire 57th Street frontage. Ungerer came on board in 1915 when he returned from his army stint in France, the teaching position (and supplemental income) he had ruefully mentioned in his 1898 memo finally becoming reality. He would give lessons in Gregorian chant and liturgy, in later seasons expanding his offerings to include organ, solfège, theory, and language.

Working so closely together meant that the Ungerer and Yon career paths would dovetail, run along the same track, cross—and occasionally veer apart. This was inevitable because their two personalities were so very different. At the root of it, Ungerer's ambition was not Yon's. It was evident that Pietro Yon was driven to bring something more to the experience of music at St. Francis Xavier, and his choir was becoming known for its quality.* But even though his name was gaining importance in the world of musicians, it was a name for connoisseurs; Yon was regarded as a talented church composer who happened to play recitals in the hinterlands. He wanted to prove his reputation at the organ, in New York City, before the general public. That chance came in 1914 when he was booked to inaugurate the newly installed organ at Aeolian Hall, an important musical bastion. The recital, including Bach, de la Tombelle, and two of Yon's own compositions, was a popular and critical success. The *Times* applauded, "He is an accomplished player, with an accurate and dextrous technique, with a sense of rhythm and the means of realizing it in his performance upon the organ." The recital set him apart as a particularly exciting musical presence, marking the beginning of Pietro Yon's personal legend.

* But it didn't do much for Yon's reputation when Joseph Young, a.k.a. Joseph Taylor, was arrested in 1913 as the mastermind of a gang that had committed a rash of well-planned armed robberies. On the stand, Young tried to defend himself by pointing out that, in the days before he Went Wrong, he had been part of the St. Francis choir—a piece of information that was quickly plastered all over the eastern seaboard.

Becoming a known quantity in New York gained him even more access to the city's talent pools. To provide variety on some of his programs, he founded the New York Gregorian Club, "consisting of twelve New York church soloists" (reported the *Musical Courier*). The club's personnel were drawn to a great extent from St. Francis Xavier ranks, but there were also men who sang at St. Patrick's, or would in the future.

Opera Magazine found the idea of a chant-oriented concert choir "intensely interesting." *Opera*'s critics and others liked the group's well-drilled expertise, but the comment of the *Times* on the Gregorian Club's first outing is significant: "Some might question whether there was not an excess of portamento and other emotional devices in music that is essentially impersonal in its expression." That remark gives a good indication of Yon's approach (also Ungerer's; by this time they were freely swapping singers) to the performance of Gregorian chant, and to choral blend in general. It had little to do with the taste of Ungerer's neighbor up the street, T. Tertius Noble, who had just arrived from England to assume the reins at the Episcopal stronghold of Saint Thomas Church. Noble had been determined to build his own men-and-boys ensemble along Anglican lines, but he was caustic when discussing the vocal material with which he was expected to work. He complained bitterly to *The Catholic Choirmaster*, "Most of the applicants possessed voices almost entirely ruined by that terrible disease—VIBRATO."

Neither Ungerer nor Yon bothered much with straight-tone singing; the Catholic tradition of the time preferred voices that were blended but not squeezed. (Choirmasters—and especially singers—who didn't buy into Noble's ideal might counter his "vibrato" epithet with something like the *New Music Review*'s dismissal of Anglican vocal style: "a hollow, wooden, flute-like whoop.") And in the decade after the shock of the *motu proprio* had died down, the pleasure of trained voices had begun to creep back into Catholic music. Plenty of those voices belonged to opera people or those who functioned within the opera world, and some liturgical music specialists were beginning to emerge. Yon employed baritone Leo de Hierapolis as well as two Canadians, tenor Léopold Christin and baritone Orphée Langevin.* Additionally,

---

* Christin made absolutely no headway in the New York operatic scene and became discouraged enough to return to Canada. He found success there, but only in his second profession, engineering.

as early as 1915 Yon had in his ensemble Serafino Bogatto, who sang no opera but would become a staple of Yon's musical ensemble throughout his life, moving into conducting as well as composition. Ungerer had among his own vocalists Finnegan and Hooley (who was lent to Constantino Yon for the opening of Saint Vincent Ferrer's new church building; the *Musical Courier* admired "his sonorous low notes"), as well as an arrival from Holland who had sung at the Royal Opera, lyric baritone Jan Van Bommel, who would figure strongly in the music of St. Patrick's in years to come.

One of the most well known of the voices belonged to Met superstar tenor Giovanni Martinelli. He had also become a close friend to Yon, close enough that they both bought summer houses in Monroe, New York. He was not only a renowned Canio and Otello, but—rare quality in superstars—a sport. He teamed with Hooley and young Met baritone Mario Laurenti to make what must have been an ear-filling trio at the Saint Vincent Ferrer opening. He showed up now and then for a solo outing at St. Francis Xavier. And the *Toledo Blade* reported on a benefit concert that had taken place in the late summer of 1917 for the Red Cross and Italian war relief. It was given in Monroe's unassuming Presbyterian church, borrowed for the occasion. The performers were Pietro Yon, Constantino Yon, and Giovanni Martinelli. "[Martinelli] seemed a little comically out of place, standing there on the ministerial platform, in his evening dress, and pouring out the passions and woes of Italian opera. But he did not seem to feel any incongruity (for which we rejoiced)," wrote the enchanted columnist. Along with snatches of *Pagliacci* and *Aïda*, "the enticing feature of his list was the first performance of Mr. Yon's The Infant Jesus, an exquisite Christmas pastorale . . . embodying, most ingeniously, the refrain of the Adeste Fideles."

Langevin recorded a number of operatic selections and art songs for Edison; the recordings reveal a very attractive French baritone. Nevertheless, his primary work was in coaching other vocalists (his ad in *Musical America* touted him as a "Specialist in French Diction/Particular Attention Given to Singers." Other than his church work and stints with the Gregorian Club, he made very few appearances. He did participate in two war benefits, the first in 1916 and the second, a monster affair at Carnegie Hall at which he sang the English national anthem, in January 1918. It was the Carnegie debut not only of Langevin but of the evening's organist—Pietro Yon.

The *Blade* got it almost right. Yon's own title for the song, properly in Italian, was "Gesù Bambino."

This most famous of Yon's compositions had been started, set aside, and picked up again; by the time of that September benefit, it was finally ready to be heard. The audience instantly fell in love with the song, so much so that Martinelli repeated it at St. Francis Xavier that Christmas. And the Victor Talking Machine Company had shown interest of its own. The *Blade* confided, "We have inside information that phonograph records . . . by Martinelli and a choir of boys are soon to appear."

The promise of a Victor Red Seal recording (which actually didn't happen until 1926) merely added to the song's soaring popularity and confirmed that Yon had written an actual hit, and not only for the sacred music market. In a period of rising Impressionist composers and the first stirrings of jazz, the sentiment contained in a pastorale was a genuine surprise—and, as has always been the case during wartime, a comfort sought after by many listeners. The melody was as recognizable as a lullaby; and like a lullaby, it had the quality of being remembered rather than composed. But it was sentimental without being mawkish, its simplicity complicated by major-minor shifts in the chord structure that added a strange dignity to the song. Best of all, it was performable by professionals and amateurs alike. While "O Holy Night" was (and still is) strictly a don't-try-this-at-home proposition, opera greats as well as children's choirs could give differing but completely valid performances of "Gesù Bambino." The song would achieve the near-impossible feat of surviving in the standard holiday repertoire, with important performances, innumerable recordings, and every kind of vocal and instrumental arrangement available from music publisher J. Fischer & Bro. Of all Pietro Yon's considerable output, it was the single piece for which he would be best remembered.*

In some ways "Gesù Bambino" was a convergence of some of Yon's most important relationships. At Yon's request, James Ungerer supplied a

---

* Yon obviously subscribed to Irving Berlin's dictum that one should never hate a song that becomes a hit. He always programmed it during holiday seasons, and he plugged it enthusiastically. So did James Ungerer; he featured it at St. Patrick's as early as Christmas 1918. And when the piano-roll manufacturer Ampico decided to offer "Gesù Bambino," it was able to list on the package "Played by the composer."

set of French lyrics. And the song's dedication read *A Francesca Pessagno, devotamente e con affetto* ("devotedly and with affection"). Francesca Pessagno, the object of the affection, was a young New Yorker, daughter of friends in the Italian community, who had come to the Yon Music Studios as a less-than-enthusiastic student. She would discover an enthusiasm greater than music when she dropped the studies to become Mrs. Pietro A. Yon.

The Pessagno–Yon wedding in May 1919 was another convergence of Yon's significant relationships, musical as well as familial. Father Young presided; Constantino Yon acted as best man; the St. Francis Xavier choirmen sang; James Ungerer conducted; and the organ was played by one of Yon's newest friends, Belgian organist Charles-Marie Courboin. This one-man dynamo had burst upon the music scene in Europe and then America, displaying both formidable musicianship and a swashbuckling lifestyle that was turning him into something of a matinee idol. (He had a well-publicized passion for sports cars as well as aviation, and he was a devoted connoisseur of wines and spirits. His daredevil *esprit* was apparently contagious. When Courboin and Yon both played under Leopold Stokowski's baton for the 1920 Wanamaker Musicians' Assembly, a photo shows them acknowledging the applause by standing at attention *atop the rail* of the orchestra balcony, a good thirty feet or so above the audience.)

Courboin had paid an extravagant compliment to Yon in his Aeolian Hall recital earlier that year, consisting as it did of nine works by Pietro A. Yon. Yon returned the compliment when he composed his twelve "Divertimenti," making a point of dedicating each of the pieces to an organist. Courboin was one of the dedicatees.

James Ungerer was not.

No one knows if Ungerer was asked to be a dedicatee. If so, he may well have refused. At this point in his life, he was strictly a liturgical musician who played virtually no concerts.* Considering the long, often

---

* The exceptions tended to be those events that had Yon as the obvious motive force, such as the 1921 Carnegie Hall concert for Fordham University. That one (interestingly, announced in the *Times* as "arranged by Jacques Ungerer") brought together the whole gang. The choirs of St. Patrick's, St. Francis Xavier, and Saint Vincent Ferrer's sang; both Yon brothers played; Ungerer conducted; and Martinelli soloed. Note that Ungerer didn't hit the keyboard at all during the concert.

anguished career path he had already traveled in nearly thirty years at St. Patrick's, he might be forgiven for behaving as if he had no interest in proving anything to anyone. However, given his juxtaposition with organists who were becoming media darlings—one of his closest friends (Yon) and one of his newest (Courboin)—comparison would be inevitable. Next to their achievements, his own career path seemed to be one of stasis.

Members of the press didn't bother with reasoning but preferred to make their own comparisons. When Yon played Ungerer's arrangement of "Frère Jacques" in a Chicago recital, the *Chicago Daily Tribune* reviewer praised Yon's "high powers . . . as musician and as interpreter" while referring to the piece itself as "quaint." The *Times* reviewed another Yon recital and mentioned Ungerer only as "a local colleague." And *Musical America* published a strange, unsatisfying interview with Ungerer:

> The great gray pile at Fiftieth Street, St. Patrick's Cathedral, is one of the city's noblest sights. And it is safe to predict, the music one hears at this church will seem as noble as that of any church service one has ever heard. Yet there is little that can be said about it, for of course it follows the prescribed lines of the Catholic service; its excellence is rather one of quality rather than of novelty, and excellence in music should be rather heard than talked of. . . .
>
> To Mr. Ungerer, the organist at the Cathedral, it seems probable that we are on the eve of profound changes in Catholic church music. . . . Mr. Ungerer feels a renaissance or at any rate a distinctly new development must be at hand. But he does not venture to predict what its nature will be.

In notable contrast to this piece, in which Ungerer seemed to be running away from the reporter and the reporter seemed to be thoroughly exasperated, elsewhere in the very same issue a headline trumpeted PIETRO YON'S RECITAL ROUSES ADMIRATION.

> [H]e played an interesting program and aroused the greatest enthusiasm with it. . . . [H]is Rhapsody, performed with enthusiasm and brilliancy, was rewarded with salvos of applause. . . . Mr. Yon convinced us that his superb musicianship, his technical skill both in manual and in pedal work and his fine sense of registration make him

a conspicuous representative of the contemporary Italian school of concert organ playing. . . .

As a patriotic prelude to the concert Mr. Yon played the "Star-Spangled Banner" and the "Marcia Reale" brilliantly, the audience standing.

The admiration that Yon was rousing, along with fistfuls of press coverage, was spreading to nonmusical as well as musical circles. In the spring of 1921, he was in Kansas City for a recital and masterclass when he saw a blind pencil seller in the street, discouraged by a lack of buyers. He engaged the old man in conversation and proceeded to empty his own pockets of change, surreptitiously dropping various coins into the man's cup. The pencil seller was gratified by the apparent new wave of customers. So was a reporter for the *Kansas City Star*, who caught the encounter.

Later that year, Enrico Caruso died in Naples. When New York commemorated his death with a requiem Mass (held not at St. Patrick's, where Caruso had been an occasional communicant, but at the more definitively Italian church of Our Lady of Mt. Carmel), the city's music community offered their services for the occasion. A selection of Met artists who had been particularly close to Caruso, including soprano Rosa Ponselle, sang. Serving as organist was another of the tenor's friends—Pietro Yon.

A high point came on New Year's Day of 1922, when it was announced that Yon had been elected "Titular Organist" of the Vatican by the Chapter of St. Peter. It was an astonishing, singular honor: The *Times* wrote that the appointment "has no precedent in the history of the Vatican." Congratulations flooded in from musicians the world over. Nonetheless, those who knew the inside workings of the New York music scene might be puzzled by the situation. Pietro Yon was, by popular acclaim—and now by Papal recognition—the most distinguished Catholic musician in the United States. He was a regular supplier of music to the nation's most distinguished church, St. Patrick's Cathedral. He was a close colleague of its choirmaster. But he was not a Cathedral employee.

The shadow of the future could be glimpsed when concert manager Ernest Briggs ran a full-page ad in the June 3 issue of *Musical Courier*. It announced that John Finnegan, star soloist of the St. Patrick's choir, was accepting dates for a two-month "Joint Concert Tour."

Accompanying him on the tour would be Pietro Yon.

The difference between Ungerer and Yon showed most glaringly in their approach to the new media that were gaining sway during the 1920s. Ungerer never recorded his work; nor did any other organist, because (wrote the infant magazine *Time* in 1923) "it has been impossible, it is said, to make successful gramophone records of organ music." A contraption was invented to make recording possible. It was demonstrated for the press—of course, by the most famous organist in the United States, Pietro Yon.

Then came the tidal wave of radio. Starting in the autumn of 1920, radio had been steadily evolving from the province of hobbyists to a genuine commercial enterprise. The technology of a "magic box," capable of grabbing talk and music out of thin air, had never been experienced before in history, and the public was largely uncomprehending (most newspaper articles found it necessary to refer to the thing as a "radio telephone") but enthralled. So were those first station operators, who were continually experimenting to make radio more interesting and more flexible. Someone at Pittsburgh's station KDKA had the idea of loading broadcast equipment onto a truck to transmit out-of-studio events at the same time that someone else at the station, a member of the Calvary Episcopal choir, talked his rector into offering the Sunday evening service as a test subject. The result was one of the earliest remote broadcasts, and the first-ever airing of a church service (the technicians wore choir robes to blend in with the surroundings). The response was hugely positive, indicating that liturgy would play a big part in radio's development. Thus, when New York's first commercial station opened—station WJZ, with facilities located in Newark, New Jersey—it made sure to offer its Radio Chapel on Sunday afternoons. This was a potpourri of whatever clerics and musicians could be induced to take to the air, and its program content changed weekly by religious denomination.

WJZ got around to Catholic fare on September 24, 1922, when Radio Chapel presented "music by the Cathedral Quartet, St. Patrick's Cathedral, New York." It was the first known broadcast in history to involve St. Patrick's. It was also probably a major pain in the neck. At that time, broadcasting at WJZ meant that performers needed to get themselves to Newark by train, where they were met by WJZ's car and driver. (WJZ employees acknowledged that the chauffeur was meant somehow to compensate for what was to come.) Once the participants had arrived at the radio station—located at the Westinghouse meter factory—the luxury treatment ended abruptly as performers were required to take the elevator to the top floor, exit to the roof, and then climb a ladder to reach the station's unventilated, windowless "penthouse studio." For this, the members of the Cathedral Quartet received carfare. The midafternoon broadcast time also guaranteed that they would miss that day's Vespers.

That would be it for a while. Protestant clerics had for the most part been enthusiastic about the idea of reaching into homes electronically; WJZ was soon able to replace Radio Chapel with regular Sunday broadcasts direct from Saint Thomas Church and West End Presbyterian. Catholic clergy, though, were ambivalent at best. Radio was in a way contrary to church practice. The *Times* interviewed a priest at the Cathedral, who thought that radio might be useful as a teaching tool for non-Catholics. But as far as regular parishioners were concerned:

> "The Catholic church requires of its parishioners actual physical attendance at mass every Sunday, and at masses on five or six feast days during the year," he explained. "Attendance over the radio would not answer."

St. Patrick's did allow WJZ to broadcast the Cathedral chimes on New Year's Eve of 1923, a half-hour program that was well enough received to be repeated on occasional Sundays. But no one on the staff, certainly not the Cathedral's music director, was fighting to have radio introduced into the Cathedral's sanctuary. St. Patrick's Cathedral would be one of the very last churches to embrace radio—and a major part of the push to do so, in years to come, would come not from James Ungerer but from Pietro Yon.

Yon Gets an Offer

Yon was rocketing to the kind of celebrity that would make him an American household name. *Time* found him interesting enough to dedicate an entire article to a review of his Town Hall recital, played to record attendance, which ended: "He showed how even the deepest-throated diapasons and most wooden bourdons can be made to sparkle under a rhythmic, bouncing, lively touch."

The *Times* critique of that same recital mentioned that "Mr. Yon has not appeared here in the past two years during which time he has been playing in over 100 cities in the United States and Europe." Part of that tour extended into France and especially Italy, and the response was ecstatic—so much so that the Italian Association of St. Cecilia requested that Pietro Yon, and Constantino Yon, be granted the Cross of St. Gregory the Great. The request came to the Archbishop of New York, the newly elevated Patrick Cardinal Hayes. Such a request was extraordinarily impressive. It could also not have helped but to make the Cardinal examine the Cathedral's relationship with its own organist.

In the extensive press coverage of Cardinal Hayes's elevation, most New York newspapers showed greater interest in the floral decorations the Cathedral was planning for the ceremony than in the musical preparations; the *Times* didn't so much as mention Ungerer's name. Then, when Catholic Charities had decided to broadcast the Cardinal's appeal in 1924—his as well as their first time on radio—the musical program was offered not by the Cathedral Choir and James Ungerer but by the boys of St. Stephen's, led by his old understudy John Philip Foley. "This is one of the best boys' choirs in the East," noted the *Times*, and the *Washington Post* took care to explain the situation: "The boy choristers of the church have achieved a position of high distinction among the chancel choirs of New York City, and it is peculiarly appropriate they should be selected for this program because His Eminence Cardinal Hayes as auxiliary bishop of New York was for some years the pastor of St. Stephen's Church." At Christmastime, when the *Times* printed its usual announcement of local churches' musical plans, St. Patrick's didn't even make it into the listing.

A microcosm of the situation could be seen in the January 1926 requiem Mass for Dowager Queen Margherita of Italy. A few days before, the *Times* reported, "Maestro Ungerer will be the organist. Beniamino Gigli and Giuseppe Danise of the Metropolitan Opera House have offered their services. . . . The chorus and entire musical program will be directed by the Italian organists, Constantino and Pietro Yon." But the day after the Mass, the coverage omitted Ungerer's name entirely, mentioning instead that Yon had played organ—and noting that the choir was that of St. Francis Xavier. The switch in personnel was never explained.

It's possible that Ungerer's work was deteriorating; it's also possible that the musical establishment simply felt him to be old news. Yon continued to support his friend, casting about for ways to involve him and keep his name before the public. A display ad in *The American Organist* had announced in October 1925, "Mr. Yon's recitals during the coming season will be directed as usual by Mr. J. C. Ungerer, manager of the Institute of Concert Virtuosi, and organist of St. Patrick's Cathedral, New York." The following summer, the ad read, "To our friends and patrons—A pleasant summer is the wish of Pietro Yon and J. C. Ungerer—Concert booking for next season is open—Write us somewhere in 'Europe.'"

But however it might be printed, the plain truth was that James Ungerer was associated with an extraordinarily high-powered talent, next to which his own accomplishments paled.

There is no way of knowing the Cardinal's thoughts during the months that he spent dealing with the back-and-forth correspondence that concerned the Yon brothers and the Cross of St. Gregory.* But it's a good guess that he began to focus on the fact that Pietro Yon was *not* working at St. Patrick's, and then to wonder why. From there, it would have been easy for him to conclude that Pietro Yon would be the perfect man to give a boost to the musical life of the Cathedral.

As the story is told in *The Heavens Heard Him,* a book subtitled "A novel based on the life of Pietro Yon" and co-written by his son, Mario, some years after his father's death, Yon plays a recital, after which he has a dressing-room visitor—Cardinal Hayes. Without beating about the bush, the Cardinal takes a seat and says, "I came to your concert with a double purpose: one, to hear good music; the other, to offer you the position of musical director at St. Patrick's Cathedral."

As it was revealed to the public, the story wouldn't be quite as tidily packaged, but any astute observer could see that changes were in the wind.

"An Organist Who Has Recently Come to the Cathedral"

The next two years at St. Patrick's were a very confusing time, when changes in the gallery seemed to be overlapping with changes in the personnel who would be responsible for the gallery.

For a number of years, complaints had been raised about the Cathedral's two organs. The Jardine, so highly touted for its power and complexity when it was first demonstrated, had in a single generation become

* That petition was unsuccessful; apparently Yon himself was never aware of it. But in early 1926 he was made, by order of the king, a knight: Cavaliere Ufficiale dell' Ordine della Corona d'Italia.

antiquated (those treadle-pumping Irishmen . . .) and frankly puny when compared to its more modern competition. The ridiculously undersized Odell in the chancel, at which everyone had sneered even when it was new, fared even worse. Changes had been considered as far back as 1905, when the *Times* reported that British organ builder Robert Hope-Jones "has been recently engaged in putting up in the cathedral loft a model of an instrument, and this is to be compared with the present one by the cathedral authorities. Additional interest will be lent to the Easter mass at the cathedral by the fact that Mr. Hope-Jones's model will then have its first public trial." The model was indeed tried—"He uses springs, valves, and cylinders and operates the organ by electricity"—but it generated no real interest from St. Patrick's. Nevertheless, musicians from other churches were touring the loft to check out the experiment. Within a year, the *Times* reported, "The result of this trial has been [an] order by the authorities of the Cathedral of St. John." (The instrument was budgeted at $50,000, not a bad outcome for a failed demonstration; it would be built by Hope-Jones's short-term associate Ernest M. Skinner. Not long after, Hope-Jones sold his patents and the firm morphed into the Wurlitzer Company. Skinner went off to do some organ building of his own.)

Over the next two decades there were sporadic whisperings about alleged "plans" for new instruments, even from highly respected sources such as British organ builder George Ashdown Audsley. Most of them amounted to wishful thinking, and none of them came to realization. Perhaps in frustration, the March 1924 *New Music Review* (which was, after all, the house publication of the American Guild of Organists) stated flatly of the St. Patrick's gallery, "[W]e have always maintained there is a wasted opportunity . . . where there could easily be placed an instrument that would rival anything in Europe."

Ungerer apparently agreed with this line of thinking; so did Monsignor Lavelle. The Cathedral's 1929 golden jubilee was in sight, and as part of the package of material improvements planned by St. Patrick's, it made complete sense to upgrade the central machinery of the music program. By late 1926, the *Times* announced a Cathedral fund drive under ST. PATRICK'S PLANS BIG IMPROVEMENTS (one of the requests was for "a first-class organ"). The response was strong enough that, by mid-1927, the headline was able to read NEW ORGANS AT CATHEDRAL:

The new organs jointly will cost $134,000, and will be made in St. Louis. One will be placed in the gallery, which is on the Fifth Avenue side, from where the present organ is played. Another will be in the chancel. A third will be an echo organ in the triforium. The instruments will have more than 10,000 pipes, 375 stops, two consoles and a string orchestra.

While the story had claimed that Monsignor Lavelle and Ungerer had been responsible for the "plan" of the organ, that wasn't precisely the case. Ungerer was a longtime friend of Ernest Skinner's and greatly admired Skinner organs. (It was easy for him to stop by and sample the wares, as the Skinner showroom was only three blocks away from the Cathedral.) But those in the know could glean from the "St. Louis" reference that the organs would be built by the firm of George Kilgen & Sons. Kilgen, renowned as much for its theatre organs as for its church instruments, was known to be a particular favorite of Pietro Yon; a Kilgen was being planned, with the help of Pietro Yon, to replace the outmoded instrument in Carnegie Hall; and a three-manual Kilgen would eventually be built for the Yon Music Studios. The scuttlebutt around town was that Yon, more than Ungerer, had been asked for his input regarding the organ design at St. Patrick's.*

Those who visited the Cathedral on Easter 1927 might not have noticed that Father Woods had relinquished the chancel organ. But if they had, they definitely would have been surprised by his replacement. The *Times* took the low-key approach:

> An orchestra accompanied the choir, led by Jacques Ungerer, organist of the cathedral. Pietro Yon was at the organ.

The *Herald Tribune* jumped the gun in its more gossipy *Music Notes* column:

> Pietro A. Yon, organist and composer, has been elected organist of St. Patrick's Cathedral, where he will take up his public duties on October 1.

---

* Yon's name was so thoroughly mixed up in the organ project that, in his book *The American Classic Organ*, Charles Callahan quotes a letter written in May 1927 by Skinner executive Henry Willis to another Skinner representative: "St. Patrick's looks like a cert for Balbiani unless you *go behind Yon* to the authorities, why not? Yon will never be any use to you so *down him*."

He will also continue to be in charge of the music at the Jesuit Church of St. Francis Xavier and give a limited number of recitals in America and Europe.

Whichever story was more accurate, Yon was now working at St. Patrick's with James Ungerer.

The years 1927 and 1928 moved very rapidly for the Cathedral music department, and if there were changes, they weren't being discussed with the public. More interest in the organ installation was shown by the *Times* than by the city's other papers, but on occasion the coverage seemed a bit stilted; it veered wildly back and forth from news of the nearly completed chancel organ to news of who was responsible for its design and installation, news of who would play it—and sometimes-convoluted attempts to attach a title to either man.

> The work of installing the first of the three new organs in St. Patrick's Cathedral is scheduled to commence next week. This will be done under the supervision of Jacques Ungerer, who has been the organist for many years.

That year's Christmas coverage included:

> A special feature of the service will be the rendering by Jacques Ungerer, choirmaster, of the "Missa Te Deum Laudamus," by Pietro Yon. . . . Another feature will be organ solos by Pietro Yon on the newly installed chancel organ, which will be played today for the first time.

By the beginning of 1928, the chancel organ was installed and "Pietro Yon, an organist who has recently come to the cathedral," was giving it an occasional public airing. And the *Times* clarified the arrangement.

> Beginning with the formal opening of the chancel organ in St. Patrick's Cathedral at a sacred concert and recital Jan. 30, Pietro A. Yon . . . will become associate organist with Professor Jacques Ungerer. . . . This is by appointment of Cardinal Hayes, Msgr. Michael J. Lavelle, the rector, and the lay trustees of the cathedral.

At the dedication, Auxiliary Bishop John Dunn would bless the instrument. (The console would be moved into the sanctuary, an unusual move that would allow the blessing as well as the music to take place in full view of the congregation.) The full choir would sing and Martinelli would be featured, along with Met baritone Mario Basiola. It was the kind of hot-ticket lineup that St. Patrick's hadn't seen in years, one that bore Yon's stamp.

Fair enough; because Yon was nominally the chancel organist, the event was going to be Yon's show. Ungerer, for his part, showed a great deal of modesty during this period. In describing the upcoming dedication, some members of the press were ignoring him outright, while others were trying to fit him into a scene in which he wasn't really a participant.* Two days before the event, the *Times* reported:

> [T]here will be a concert in which Pietro Yon, organist; Giovanni Martinelli and Mario Basiola of the Metropolitan Opera Company and the full choir of the Cathedral, under the auspices of Professor Jacques C. Ungerer, will take part.

The day after the dedication, the *Times* coverage wouldn't so much as list Ungerer's name.

Far more than had been the case at the Jardine demonstration fifty years before, the dedication was a major social as well as musical event in New York. Even though admission was by ticket only, a crowd estimated at 5,000 jammed into the Cathedral, and more people attempted to get in. T. Scott Buhrman, editor of *The American Organist*, was impressed not only with the event but with the near-riot that the event provoked:

> Before the hour of service began, the mobs broke through the police lines at the Fifth Avenue door and it was necessary to take unpleasant steps to restore order in the rear of this great Cathedral. All possible space was taken to the very limit of the Cathedral's capacity.

Those listeners who made it through the police cordon experienced a lush musical program quite different from George Jardine's slapdash "exhibition"; the tone was set by the program booklet, which announced at its very top APPLAUSE IS STRICTLY FORBIDDEN.† The music ranged from

---

* The program booklet for the dedication listed his name exactly once, on the frontispiece—"J. C. Ungerer, Director."

† The program also contained a photo of Yon sitting at the console. In his own copy of the program, Yon wrote at the top of the picture, "My Baby."

the Gregorian chant of Psalm 150 to Yon's own "Hymn of Glory," composed for the occasion. Martinelli and Basiola offered selections ranging from Verdi's "Ingemisco" to Perosi's "Pro peccatis," as well as Yon's "Ave Maria" and "Gesù Bambino." Yon himself played Bach, Gigout, Bossi, Renzi, and his own "Echo." Buhrman's article heaped lavish praise upon Yon while straining to keep Ungerer in the picture.

> Mr. Yon is the ideal organist for the Cathedral. . . . Mr. J. C. Ungerer remains as he has been for many years the choirmaster of the Cathedral. . . . This chancel organ is to be Mr. Ungerer's instrument. . . . [H]e has been so long identified with the Cathedral's music that he seems quite like a part of the Cathedral itself.

The evening was a huge success for Yon, and it apparently gave him a mandate to begin making changes. A week after the dedication, the organ was used in regular services and the *Times* mentioned in its coverage, "The proper of the Mass was sung by the new Gregorian quartet"—drawn from those men who had sung with Yon at St. Francis Xavier or in the Gregorian Club.

By Easter, it was obvious that the music at St. Patrick's was gaining in brilliancy, even if the *Times* could no longer remember Ungerer's name.

> Under the direction of Pietro Yon . . . the new associate organist of the cathedral, an elaborate program of Easter music was rendered by a quartet and special soloists who sang grouped about the new chancel organ, with Professor Yon at the instrument. Joseph [*sic*] Ungerer, who has been the organist of the cathedral for more than thirty years, played the gallery organ.

They did get it right three weeks later, announcing PROF. UNGERER TO MARK 35TH ANNIVERSARY AS ORGANIST AT ST. PATRICK'S. Celebrations aside, no one was taken into Ungerer's confidence, not even his friends, to discuss any aspect of the situation.

During the summer of 1928, Ungerer traveled to Europe for his usual visit. While in France, he received a letter from New York.

> My Dear Mr. Ungerer:
> Your card was duly received. I was delighted to learn you had such a pleasant trip. Hope you will thoroughly enjoy the stay among your relatives and friends. July was very hot and moist here. But I understand the temperature was just as high in Europe.

I have now to present a subject which calls for your best and most sensible consideration. Our people have decided to put the entire charge of the music in the hands of Mr. Yon. They are heartily appreciative of your good work for many years. But they have reached the conclusion that Mr. Yon will give the music they desire, and that he should be allowed to exploit his talents to the limit. This means that he is to be the Commander in Chief and that everybody must follow his lead with complete loyalty, docility and cooperation. Consequently, if you elect to continue, you must be willing to act happily, and with comfort to all, under his guidance; in a way that will give him complete satisfaction. Should you decide that this would be distasteful, I feel certain that our people would be willing to vote you a reasonable pension, and I would strive to have them make it equal to your salary to date. This proposition implies, of course, that you accept the situation gracefully, and that there be no incriminations [*sic*], or hard feelings. I had wished to speak with you upon this subject before your departure but things had not sufficiently matured. I can assure you of high respect from all, and of my own lasting good will and regard. Please let me hear from you as soon as possible.

Yours Very Sincerely,
Michael J. Lavelle

No records indicate a reason that "incriminations" or hard feelings would have been mentioned; nor does anything give a hint of what correspondence resulted or what negotiations ensued. The public knew almost nothing of what was going on behind the scenes. Coverage of that year's Midnight Mass listed Ungerer and Yon as "organists" (Martinelli sang), and on New Year's Day of 1929 the *Times* tried the gambit of referring to Ungerer and Yon as "co-organists."

On May 1, the thirty-sixth anniversary of his arrival at the Cathedral, Jacques-Marie-Pierre-André-Cécilien Ungerer formally retired from his position. And Pietro Alessandro Yon became the music director of St. Patrick's.

Working on His Memoir

Ungerer's personal history didn't end at all neatly. Some dramatic sensibilities might have preferred that he refuse ever to enter the doors of St. Patrick's again. But he was too much of a pragmatist for grand gestures;

also, he needed to attend to his cash flow. He spent some time on Yon's substitute list, playing at a high-profile Cathedral funeral in January 1930. In its coverage of the event, the *Times* referred to him matter-of-factly as the "organist of St. Patrick's Cathedral."

Of his post-Cathedral years, Alastair Guinan wrote:

> After his retirement from Saint Patrick's in 1929, Mr. Ungerer lived quietly in New York and, rejecting several attractive offers of posts of distinction, including that of Master of the Choir & Chief Organist at the Cathedral of St. Louis in Missouri, he pursued his studies & his musical compositions as well as a Memoir of the history of music at Saint Patrick's Cathedral, the manuscripts & supporting documents of which were bequeathed to his friends.

As opposed to William F. Pecher, who died while still at his Cathedral post, lionized by musicians, clergy, and public alike, Ungerer suffered that most ignominious of fates—to linger for decades, forgotten, still living at the Capitol Hotel. And still working on his memoir.

Along with its supporting documents, the memoir disappeared.

Jacques-Marie-Pierre-André-Cécilien (James C.)
Ungerer.

Viafora's Pencil Impressions of a Foregathering at Luncheon in the Italian Club, One Day Last Week. Left to right: Ludwig Wielich, Pietro Alessandro Yon, S. Constantino Yon, Viafora Himself, and John C. Freund, Editor of "Musical America"

Above: Pietro Yon makes his mark in *Musical America* with a Viafora caricature. *Right*: But the artist didn't stop there; soon after, he presented Yon with "The Organist," an unpublished caricature (sketched on the back of a menu). The body assembled from organ pipes, the multiple hands and feet— and the halo—effortlessly convey Pietro Yon's appeal. (*Courtesy of Loretta Yon Schoen*)

THE ORGANIST

The July 1912 *Musical America* published this shipboard photo of the Yon brothers
(and Ungerer, at right, traveling with them) heading back to Europe for the summer.
Heady stuff for a young and ambitious composer—but Pietro Yon would have been
yanked back to earth by the caption, which highlighted his then-more-famous brother:
Constantino Yon Spends Vacation in Native Italy.

Chapter 4

"PROFESSOR" (1929–43)

> If you have nothing to do, don't do it here.
>
> A plaque hanging in Pietro Yon's studio

In giving Pietro Yon authority over the music at St. Patrick's, the Cathedral was committing to a very grand experiment. He would receive a lavish budget and whatever personnel he deemed necessary to create the kind of music for which he was famed. To enhance the experience, there would be a tripartite organ, one of the largest in the world.

The idea was costly but absolutely logical. St. Patrick's was moving from national to international prominence, and its musical needs would be best served by a world-class musician who was also a world citizen. In this, Yon fit the bill perfectly. He was talented, extraordinarily intelligent, completely at home with important colleagues, well versed on a variety of subjects, gregarious as his predecessors had never been, easy with the press, delighted by the limelight, fitted out in Savile Row perfection,* and suavely good-looking to boot. Pietro Yon and his dark-eyed wife, Francesca, were a couple sought after by more than just the musical crowd.

In true Italian fashion, he had a sometimes-coltish sense of fun that showed itself in practical jokes. His son, Mario, would remember getting into their apartment-house elevator with his father, a neighbor, and her dog. Yon quietly slipped onto the elevator floor one of his joke-shop favorites, a plastic dog . . . dropping. He then casually called the lady's attention to her pet's "accident." Before she could recover from her embarrassment, he said, "No problem. I'll take care of it." Elaborately unfolding his handkerchief, he scooped up the offending item, wrapped it

---

* A magazine interviewer noted that, for Sundays, Yon preferred neckties in suitable liturgical colors—green for ordinary time, purple for penitential seasons.

in the handkerchief, and carefully inserted it into his trouser pocket as her eyes widened in horror. "There," he said, patting the pocket and smiling nicely. "All taken care of."

His greatest problem, during the spring and summer of 1929, would be that of organization. Not only was he responsible for filling out the gallery choir, finding a conductor for the chancel choir, and supervising the construction, installation, and impending dedication of the new gallery organ, but he was also supervising the construction, installation, and dedication of Carnegie Hall's new organ, which would occur the month before.

The wide-ranging music connections he had made over the years, combined with his determination, meant that those pieces fell into place very quickly. To lead the chancel choir: direct from Rome, the "Vice-Director of Music," Monsignor Joseph I. Rostagno. Formerly assistant director of the Vatican choir, he was a thorough musician whose ideas meshed very well with Yon's. He said in an interview, "The average choirmaster in America is a musician who turns his mind toward religious music once a week. Rarely is he an ecclesiastic musician who appreciates that the music of the mass is a definite part of the mass—an expression of worship rather than an embellishment." But Father Rostagno (he preferred not to use his title) wasn't a musical stick-in-the-mud. Twice, the "younger priests of St. Patrick's," as the *Times* called them, put together benefit performances of "classical and old favorite selections" for the Cathedral Club. At each, Father Francis Fadden, the Assistant Rector, accompanied a quartet comprising Fathers Robert E. Woods, John M. J. Quinn, C. Joseph Tytheridge, and Rostagno himself.

Yon was perfectly satisfied with the treble boys from the Cathedral School and the young men from Cathedral College. (They admired him greatly, although the Cathedral College students were typical adolescents, prone to giggles and spitballs. All of the boys invariably addressed him as "Professor.") As far as the professional vocalists were concerned, he knew the men already in place and had worked with some of them for years, so he wanted only to add to their numbers. John Finnegan would continue as he had for nearly a quarter-century, apparently with no decline; around that time, a critic was praising his "voice of uncommon range upward, with notable lyric quality." And Finnegan was joined by twenty-one other professional singers to make up what Yon called the

Male Soloist Ensemble, arguably the highest-powered choral unit St. Patrick's had ever known.

In the tenor section, Yon's old friend Serafino Bogatto would divide his time between singing at St. Patrick's and directing the music at St. Francis Xavier. He would be joined by De Los Becker, formerly of the Schola Cantorum (*Musical America* equivocated in 1907 that he had sung "with infinitely greater success than ever before"), one or two recordings, and not much else until his Cathedral days. Also new was Eugene (Eugenio, when it suited) Cibelli. He had been knocking around the music world as chaotically as anyone could, from his first appearance at the "Brucato-Rispoli Fencing Competition and Musical Concert" to a few discs of guitar- and mandolin-accompanied Italian songs for Victor. He did a season as a member of the New York–based San Carlo Opera, snickered at by critics ("an indubitably fine tenor voice, which he somewhat misuses through the nose. . . . [I]t is to be regretted that he quite funked his high B flat"), as well as a couple of stints at Chicago movie houses, strumming his Italian ballads in between features as part of the live stage show. The high, or low, point of that period came when he was required to share the bill with the then-current Miss America (who did not sing, dance, or entertain in any discernible way).*

The roster of lower voices would offer an uncommonly deep field, more so than any other choir in New York. Both Raimondo Scala and Imerio Ferrari dated back to Yon's days at St. Francis Xavier; possessed of seemingly indestructible basso profundo instruments, they would sing at St. Patrick's for decades. Likewise Hildreth Martin, who achieved some extra-Cathedral distinction as bass in the Ionian Male Quartet. A tintype of the then-voguish English Singers, the Ionians sang in a number of venues: madrigal concerts, holiday programs at ladies' clubs, scores of radio broadcasts, a couple of Town Hall recitals, guest appearances with the Dessoff Choirs. In 1929 they won a footnote in the annals of American musical history by premiering Virgil Thomson's "Capital Capitals"; in 1935, they accomplished the same in American governmental history by entertaining the Roosevelts at a White House state dinner.

---

* Cibelli's final career move was one of his best, and he could bring his guitar; it came in 1948, when he created the role of the Street Singer on Broadway in *The Madwoman of Chaillot.*

But Yon's baritones constituted a particular glory. Leo de Hierapolis (another St. Francis alumnus, and a man who claimed English, French, and Egyptian ancestry) had run the gamut from *Rigoletto* and *Lohengrin* in Philadelphia, an insane season of eleven operas in ten weeks in St. Louis, to a quick stop on Broadway for Pish-Tush in a revival of *The Mikado*. Once landed at St. Patrick's, he stayed put. Jan Van Bommel, however, varied his schedule with outside activity. He did the tour of New York concert halls in periodic recital programs (reviewers found his voice "of light, agreeable quality," "prov[ing] serviceable within its limits of tonal and emotional power") and threw in some radio work, such as a broadcast *Traviata* in 1925. He was also involved with New York's Dutch community, singing for Netherlands flood relief in 1926 and performing in New York celebrations for Holland's Princess Juliana a year later. (For that occasion the *Times* ran a photo of him in "native costume," complete with wooden shoes.) But the lion's share of his singing was done at—or through the auspices of—the Cathedral.

Then there was Carl Schlegel. He had shown promise even as a student, going through his early paces under the supervision of musical legends such as Cosima Wagner and Richard Strauss, and the Met signed him for his Wagnerian baritone in 1913. After that, little happened. Puccini used him in the world premiere of *Gianni Schicchi*, in a small role; but then again, nearly all of his Met roles were small. He took refuge in concert work and recitals—the critical response was always enthusiastic and, seemingly, always perplexed: "Carl Schlegel, who in stature and rich timbre stands higher among Metropolitan baritones than his name has in ten years' assignment of operatic roles. . . ." The Met remained unmoved and after thirteen years and nearly 400 performances dropped him from the roster.

However, he had done some of his earlier concertizing at Archdiocesan-sponsored events, which meant that his path had crossed Pietro Yon's. They had performed together in recital during his first Met season; also, Schlegel liked Yon's music and programmed it in some of his solo jaunts. Because both men knew the same people professionally, Yon would have been aware of Schlegel's employment situation. And as soon as he was in a position to do something about it, Yon brought him to St. Patrick's. The press coverage for Easter 1928 remarked almost with surprise, "Carl Schlegel, formerly of the Metropolitan Opera Company, sang during the recessional. . . ."

These men, with their individual strengths and ability to work together as a unit, became the core of the Male Soloist Ensemble. Yon responded not only with gratitude but also with an impresario's sensibility, setting them before the public in frequent solo assignments and tailoring his work for their particular voices. Another demonstration of his generosity would come as part of an interview in the *Herald Tribune*, his willingness to acknowledge their contributions: "Two singers . . . are with him as chanters, leading the Cathedral Choir into the sanctuary every Sunday at high mass. These men, Carl Schlegel, a barytone, and Leo de Hierapo [*sic*], a bass barytone, are priceless treasures, Mr. Yon said, for they know the mass as well as the priests."

Aside from their wildly varied career histories, an unusual feature of Yon's singers was their internationalism. Most of the Cathedral's singers had customarily been of German or Irish backgrounds. Yon employed men from a wide range of nationalities—including a good number of Italians. This went against the grain of many New York Catholics, who still felt that Italian congregants should worship in the lower church. Pietro Yon was going to raise eyebrows.

The Male Soloist Ensemble would have to sing from the chancel for its first months of existence, because the preparations for the gallery organ were as drastic as anything the Cathedral had seen for years. The *Times*—even more excited about the upcoming installation than it had been about the chancel organ—had interviewed Monsignor Lavelle the previous June, after the Jardine "gave out its final note," detailing the tasks required to make ready for the new Kilgen:

> "The fine new instrument made by the Messrs. Kilgan [*sic*] of St.
> Louis, is ready for installation at any time we may be able to receive
> it," continues the Monsignor. "But considerable time will be required
> to take down its predecessor. Then the choir loft must be rebuilt to
> make it fireproof. The Autumn will have arrived before we can hope
> to enjoy the new organ."

Once the corpse of the Jardine had been hauled over the edge of the gallery and lowered to oblivion, Kilgen's design would require that the gallery itself be greatly modified in order to accommodate the new organ's massive size and weight. That work waited until the beginning of 1929, when in the first week of January the *Times* was able to report that the gallery was "completely torn out." The article also quoted Monsignor Lavelle's opinion that the organ would be fully installed before Easter.

The Rector's view was over-optimistic because of the immense amount of labor needed to prepare the structure before anything could be installed. Over the next four months, the gallery itself was built forward six feet and reinforced with an iron beam that was said to be "capable of supporting 100 tons." Concrete flooring was poured to create a double-level loft, housing the organ console below (also creating space for orchestra musicians, when needed) and choir above. The old gallery had always been plagued by sightline problems, so a structure was designed of wraparound choir stalls that could supposedly accommodate one hundred singers in tiered formation. The stalls would be fabricated not of wood but of steel—simple of construction, fireproof as had been demanded, and remarkably uncomfortable. To blend in with the gallery's genuine wood, the stalls would be meticulously faux-painted in English quartered oak.*

Once the gallery was reinforced and enlarged, New York saw the first sections of the organ as they arrived from the Kilgen works in multiple railroad cars, each crate to be hauled to the Cathedral. Beginning in May, the four-manual console with its 166 stops, the 50-foot-high, 40-foot-wide organ case, and their interior workings were fitted together like a gigantic puzzle (and according to one report, the finished console spent several weeks being displayed in the narthex to stimulate interest). That job progressed rapidly, so much so that it was well on its way to completion when someone in New York realized that a vital part was still in St. Louis. The problem could be solved only by overnight delivery, something that is common nowadays but was so rare in 1929 that the story was told in the *Times*—not in the music columns, but in *Notes in Field of Aviation*:

> [I]t was found that if the instrument was to be finished on schedule airplanes alone could do the trick. The missing part, the electrical control operating the Repieno [*sic*], was loaded aboard the Universal Airways Chicago bound plane . . . the next morning it was delivered at St. Patrick's.

---

* The paintwork has survived its seven-plus decades of use with minimal wear—except for the spot where soloists are customarily placed. The railing at this area has worn down to the bare metal, in exactly the places where nervous hands might be prone to clutch.

Whether in the sky or on the ground, a very great deal was being made of the organ's Ripieno. What modern organists call a Mixture (and literally translated from the Italian word for "stuffing"), a Ripieno stop comprised several sets of high-pitched pipes whose bright (often *very* bright) sound lent vibrancy and brilliance to the instrument's tone. It was something that New York hadn't experienced much; when Constantino Yon commissioned a Balbiani organ with a Ripieno for Saint Vincent Ferrer, some listeners were excited; others complained that they had been nearly blown out of the church. Very soon, though, it was catching on. The Carnegie Hall organ would have a Ripieno, and so would the Cathedral's gallery organ. Columnists wrote of the Ripieno in almost mystic tones:

> It is very much the same as light, according to Signor Yon, which when looked at with the naked eye appears to be of one color, but when a prism is held up to the light immediately the several rays which constitute the basic color are analyzed and become apparent. The ripieno is the prism of the organ . . . blend[ing] these into a perfectly artistic sonorous ensemble.

By the end of the summer, the basic installation was nearly completed, save for the elaborate carved wood casework that would house the pipes. Very soon the organ would be ready for tuning and regulating. On September 7 came another missive from the *Times*, relaying Monsignor Lavelle's news that the organ had been "completely installed" and that the case (as well as that of the chancel organ, which had spent the last year unadorned) would be in place in another month. He concluded, "If this expectation can be realized, you can hope for a grand dedication and opening prior to Nov. 1 of our instrument."

It was good news—but it would be eclipsed by personal tragedy. On the same day that the *Times* article appeared, Francesca Yon died in Lenox Hill Hospital.

She had been born with a heart defect that had clouded her youth and caused her father initially to oppose her wedding to Pietro Yon; marriage, and particularly childbirth, were thought possibly to be dangerous. (Until their son, Mario, was born, she hadn't even told Yon of the problem.) The successful delivery of a healthy baby made them feel that the danger had passed, but intermittent episodes made it clear that her condition would only deteriorate. By that summer, Yon doggedly kept to his normal work schedule even though it was an open secret that his wife's health was steadily failing. When his sixteen-year-old pupil Robert Elmore made his concert debut, Yon insisted on attending; Elmore's mother, who knew the situation, was moved by Yon's gesture and thanked him for coming. Equally moved, he replied simply, "It's a wonderful thing to have a wife who will soon be with Jesus."

News of Mrs. Yon's death occasioned a large outpouring of condolences, stacks of notes, and an inch-thick sheaf of telegrams and cables from notables and friends in Europe and America: Martinelli, Gigli, the Met's manager Giulio Gatti-Casazza, Toscanini, singers from the Cathedral, students at the Yon Music Studios, Monsignor Lavelle, Cardinal Hayes, people who had heard him play in one city or another, people who had never met Pietro Yon but felt as if they knew him. From Ocean Grove, the New Jersey shore town to which he had retreated immediately after his wife's funeral, he replied to the Cardinal's note:

Please accept my sincerest thanks for Your most valuable prayers and consoling words of sympathy.

With the help of the Lord and through the prayers and sacrifice of my beloved Francesca I hope I will continue successfully my ideal and mission at St. Patrick's Cathedral.

Pray, do not forget my little family.

Your faithful and humble servant
Pietro A. Yon

Clergy, co-workers, and the public never knew it, but the next months would find him in the grip of a depression so severe that he contemplated suicide. His only antidote, as it had been during Mrs. Yon's illness, was to throw himself headlong into work and more work.

The dedication of the Carnegie Hall organ had originally been set for September 30. No one expected him to play that concert so soon after Mrs. Yon's death; it would have to be moved. Then there was Monsignor Lavelle's original plan of dedicating the Cathedral's gallery organ before November 1, equally impossible. Carnegie Hall quickly rescheduled its organ dedication for the night of November 4—but the Cathedral schedule was trickier. Five electricians were still working on the organ's "switchboard," and after that work was done thousands of pipes would have to be individually tuned. Further complicating things was the fact that Cardinal Hayes would leave for Rome at the beginning of October for at least a month, possibly more, of Vatican business. He had been in

Rome the previous year when the chancel organ had been dedicated; not unreasonably, he probably wanted to be there to dedicate the gallery organ. St. Patrick's decided to wait until the crunch was over.

The Carnegie Hall dedication was going to be broadcast on the major-market station WOR, itself the flagship station of a regional radio network. Yon had made his radio debut the year before with an hour-long recital, heard on two stations in New York and St. Louis; then in early 1929, his *Missa "Regina Pacis"* was performed on the CBS sacred music series "The Cathedral Hour." He had once conducted an open-air Mass before 750,000 people, but the CBS listening audience was easily twenty times that number. Radio had become big, big business, and an undreamed-of tool for reaching the public.

Yon felt that it was urgent to reevaluate the arm's-length relationship that St. Patrick's had maintained with broadcasting. On October 1, he wrote to Monsignor Lavelle:

I wish to report now on the question of the radio for the Cathedral.

I have been thinking and discussing with different people and with different radio stations the material, artistic and spiritual benefit of having the radio, as well as the objections.

Pro:

Financially—Although every Church of different denominations, including some Catholic, have to pay some radio stations to broadcast their services, the National Broadcasting Company has offered to give the service free of charge to the Cathedral. I gave the authority to my manager, Mr. Ienni, to try to get some money, and he has succeeded in having station WOR to agree (but not definitely) to pay $10,000 a year to broadcast our services.

Artistically—It will be a very strong boost for our musical organization and our new organs. We have at present everything to boost for, and the programs which I am preparing for the coming season are second to none. That is, artistically, we need not be afraid of any just criticism.

Spiritually—I believe that the Catholics all know that they cannot hear Mass through the air, and in case they do not, through the radio you could put them wise to that fact; but you would have, every Sunday, an audience of several millions instead of a few hundreds, and give an opportunity to the many Catholics living at a distance from New York to hear the services at the Cathedral. It would also be a means to attract a growing audience and importance for the Cathedral.

Con:

I am praying my dear Francesca every night to inspire me in all important decisions, and to keep me always doing things that will please the Lord and A.M.D.G. [*Ad maiorem Dei gloriam*, "to the greater glory of God"], and I kind of feel that when a highly sacred moment of the Mass is broadcast, which may enter an apartment of heretics, a dance hall or a store or place decidedly adverse and common, it would be sacriligeous [*sic*].

I spoke to several clergymen, and they answered that the people who would not be interested in such a program would tune out that station for another one to their taste; and some remarked that the radio in the Church would not be advisable.

My personal opinion is 80% for the radio, and 20% against it, and this is about the best report I can make.

In presenting these humble opinions to His Eminence the Cardinal, and after a decision, pro or con, has been reached, I will be perfectly satisfied with whatever that decision may be.

All the above is in reference to the Sunday High Mass and special occasions, but I do hope you will agree not only to have the radio for our dedication concert, but to make it pay, and to this effect I will report later.

This was a rather sticky situation for Monsignor Lavelle, because only the previous May there had been an interview stating that "Cardinal Hayes and the lay trustees of St. Patrick's Cathedral have determined to broadcast the sermons preached at the 11 o'clock high mass every Sunday morning. . . . The ritual of the mass itself, however, will not be broadcast. Whether some of the music by the choir is to be broadcast will be decided in a few days." Those broadcasts were to have taken place over WLWL (for We Listen, We Learn), a Catholic-programming station operated by the Paulist Fathers. But WLWL's government franchise allowed it to broadcast only two hours per day, and not the two hours during which Mass took place.

Yon's proposition, which would allow St. Patrick's to choose between a major New York station and a major American network, was intriguing (and possibly daunting to Cathedral authorities), but no decision was made. The idea of broadcasting any part of the Mass quietly fizzled, not to be revived for years.

Far more than this would collapse, exactly four weeks after Yon's memo, as the stock market imploded in the catastrophe of Black Tuesday. Many people were so heavily invested that they lost their entire savings in the wreckage. One of them was Pietro Yon.

Yon's First Steps

Pietro Yon's box office value, position at the Cathedral, and publishing contracts meant that he would have enough continuing personal income to weather the storm. Nonetheless, he was a widower with a nine-year-old son; his sister Lina was a dependent, living with them as the lady of the house; and a large number of people, both at St. Patrick's and at his studio, were relying upon him for their livelihood. He began to hustle as he had done in his younger days, filling the spaces in his calendar with extra bookings—and he involved his colleagues whenever possible, such as at a recital at St. Michael's Church in Paramus, New Jersey, to which he abruptly added a quartet of singers from the Cathedral ranks.

Stock market crash or not, the preparations for the Carnegie Hall program had to continue. They were hasty but logical, giving a nod to the original program performed at the hall's 1891 opening. Walter Damrosch would conduct the Oratorio Society, as he had thirty-eight years previously, in Mendelssohn's "Thanks Be to God" from *Elijah*. Yon supplied the backbone of the program, playing Ravanello, Bach, Skilton, Russolo, Guilmant—and Yon. Joining in for operatic arias from *Cavalleria Rusticana*, *Ernani*, and *Die Walküre* would be soprano Gina Pinnera and baritone Reinald Werrenrath. "The concert will be one of the brilliant social events of the season," wrote the *Times*, the day before the dedication. "Twenty-five debutantes of the Junior League will distribute the programs. The audience will include many musicians and artists, including the heads of the Metropolitan Opera Company and the Philharmonic Society. Admission will be by invitation only."

The evening was a smash, attended by a capacity crowd that included Mayor James Walker and then-Governor Franklin D. Roosevelt. But the day after, Yon had to return to the work of planning at St. Patrick's. It was November, Christmas was coming, and the dedication of the gallery organ had still not been set. The *World* reported that electricians were working on the organ's "10,000 magnets and about fifty miles of wire" during the Cathedral's open hours; after closing time, a staff of tuners took over, working through the night. This routine would continue throughout November, December, and January. It was extraordinarily costly work—the original estimate had nearly doubled, to $250,000—but the entire amount had come from the bequest of attorney John Whelan, part of a million-dollar–plus gift to the Cathedral.

In his earliest days at St. Francis Xavier, Yon had begun a practice of distributing small, nicely printed booklets which detailed the music that would be performed at various services. Starting with Advent 1929, he continued the practice at St. Patrick's with the handsome green-and-white *Advent and Christmastide Program*. The *World* wrote, "Announcement of the musical program, containing a forecast of Mr. Yon's selections for the coming month, is being distributed to pewholders at the Cathedral to-day. This is in keeping with the recently inaugurated policy of the church to develop a distinguished musical repertoire and to stimulate parishioners to take a more active interest in liturgical music."

Scheduled to preach at St. Patrick's at every Sunday High Mass during that Advent season would be a professor from Catholic University, Monsignor Fulton J. Sheen. He was announced in Yon's booklet, but so unknown in New York that the *Herald Tribune* identified him as "Fulton Sheehan." The two men worked well together, as each quickly recognized that the other was very good at what he did. And both of them felt that good performance values were admirable, even in a liturgical context. Sheen was able to call upon the Cathedral organist for musical-dramatic effects that another organist might not appreciate, or even comprehend. Before one Good Friday service, Yon received a hastily scrawled note in preparation for the Seven Last Words:

Dear Mr. Yon:

Will you kindly at the SEVENTH WORD supply an extremely SOFT organ background for the DIES IRAE which I will recite.

The cue will be:

Folding my arms across my breast—I will do that as I begin the poem.

Stop the background at the conclusion of the Dies Irae.

Thanks!

Dulcissimmmoooo!!

The softer the better—
God Love You.
Fulton J. Sheen

When they became friendly enough that Yon invited him to dinner, his practical joker's sense took over. Monsignor Sheen tucked into his meat course—impossible to cut, with the blunt-bladed knife that was at his place. At this point, Yon summoned his cook (taking part in the joke, and well rehearsed) into the dining room and administered a furious dressing-down, to Sheen's mortification. This went on until Yon dissolved into laughter.

(That time, Yon had been merciful. At another dinner party, a guest—also a cleric—dipped into his soup course and discovered, too late, that he had been served with a dribble spoon.)

Fulton J. Sheen and Pietro Yon may have clicked, but other clergy apparently weren't as taken with the idea of a choirmaster who had the temerity to advertise his activities on church premises. As the story (apocryphal, possibly) went, a priest (unidentified, naturally) confronted Yon about this.

The priest's complaint: "You *can't* think that people are coming to church merely to listen to *your* music!"

Yon's calm retort: "*You* can't think that people are coming to church merely to listen to *you* preach."

A New Organ, a First Broadcast

Yon had carefully tailored the Advent and Christmas programming for maximum impact, and to a great extent he was depending on his choristers. During the month of December alone, they would give an exhausting ninety-two performances of forty-eight different works: Gregorian chant, some warhorses, the Cathedral's first hearing of the Palestrina *Missa Sine Nomine*, a number of Yon's own compositions, and five performances of "Gesù Bambino." The programming gave full rein to his choir's musical and vocal assets; if it was designed to "stimulate parishioners to take a more active interest in liturgical music," it succeeded handsomely. And as a special bonus, the work on the gallery organ, and the gallery itself, had advanced to the point that both of them were ready for use. On Christmas morning, Yon played Handel and Widor, the Male Soloist Ensemble ranged around him.

That performance was more than a festive moment for Yon's men, as they would have to get used to a definite change in the gallery's acoustics. In the days of the Jardine, the organ's pipes had sat far back in the gallery and behind the choir, meaning that every singer's voice had a clear upward path to be naturally amplified by the Cathedral's central vault. Now, they would be dealing with an organ case so large that it sat literally above their heads, putting a "lid" on the sound. They also would be dealing with an organ that was four times the size of its predecessor. Members of the Male Soloist Ensemble, being for the most part opera-trained, weren't especially worried about projection; but from then on, Cathedral organists would have to exercise caution lest they swamp their singers.

January 1930 was an uneasy time for the United States as most people were worried about the state of the economy. But the Cathedral's music department was more directly concerned with the final push of effort needed to complete the tuning and voicing of the organ. It would have been a push to arrange the dedicatory program, as well—except that no one knew exactly when the dedication would take place. Cardinal Hayes was in Rome, where he had been since the previous October, having gone to make an *ad limina* visit to the Pope (a trip that was required to be made by high-ranking prelates, every five years). Once the Cardinal was at St. Peter's, the Pope had asked him to stay for Christmas—and the Cardinal wasn't about to refuse.

Cardinal Hayes didn't make it back to New York until January 21, arriving on the *Vulcania* and returning to St. Patrick's with a police escort. As he started walking up the Cathedral steps, he was able to hear the gallery organ for the first time; accompanied by five hundred children from the Cathedral School, Yon launched into "Home Sweet Home," followed by "Hail to the Chief," and finally "The Star Spangled Banner."

Now that the Cardinal was back in town, plans had to be immediately finalized. In four days the *Times* made the announcement that many people had been waiting to see, buried as it was in the fourth paragraph of its *Topics of Interest to the Churchgoer* column:

> On Tuesday evening, Feb. 11, Cardinal Hayes will dedicate the great new organ in St. Patrick's Cathedral. Msgr. Michael J. Lavelle, the rector, and Pietro Yon, organist of the cathedral and an honorary organist of the Vatican, are arranging the program.

—meaning that Lavelle and Yon would get a sum total of *seventeen days* in which to arrange the program, set the singers, set the orchestra, rehearse the whole thing, arrange for programs to be printed and tickets distributed—and there was still the question of radio coverage. . . .

The organist of the evening would have no problems. Yon's own repertoire was large enough that he had at hand, ready to go, a program completely different from any of the pieces he had played for the chancel organ dedication. Also, it would be an array of pieces that displayed the full range of the organ's capabilities: de la Tombelle, two pieces of Bach, Angelelli's *Theme and Variations*, and of course Yon. The centerpiece of the concert would be his own heroic *Concerto Gregoriano*, composed for organ and orchestra; Giuseppe Bamboschek agreed to conduct.

Martinelli, Yon's usual choice for star soloist, was in the middle of crunch time at the Met with a *Carmen* the night before the dedication and an *Aïda* the night after, meaning that there was no way he could take part. As a replacement, there was baritone Giuseppe Danise; he would be singing in the *Aïda* along with Martinelli, but he had some downtime before (and at the dedication, he would sing nothing more taxing than Dubois' "Deus Meus"). From the Cathedral end, de Hierapolis and Schlegel would begin the whole vocal works with the chant "Laudate Dominum." Both men had additional solo assignments during the evening, as did Van Bommel, Barchi, and Finnegan. The Male Soloist Ensemble, with extra ringers added to total a resounding thirty-four voices, would be shown to great advantage, along with the full choir.

Music may not have been a problem, but the short notice hurt the Cathedral badly when it came to the still-unresolved question of radio coverage. An event coming from St. Patrick's obviously couldn't be interrupted for now-a-word-from-our-sponsor; rather, it would have to be broadcast as a "sustaining" program, commercial-free, with the broadcaster itself paying for the time. NBC might have been interested in carrying the dedication back in October, but at this late date the network couldn't pre-empt its scheduled Tuesday-night lineup: the Eveready Program, the Wonder Bakers Orchestra, the Libby Orchestra, Johnson & Johnson . . . all major sponsors, all having purchased time on February 11. WOR would have had the same problem with its Nunn Bush Concert. Nor was WLWL an option—it went off the air at 8:00 P.M., exactly when the dedication would begin. Nevertheless, radio coverage was becoming more and more desirable not only because Pietro Yon wanted it* but

* This is especially intriguing in light of the 1930 census, which reported that Pietro Yon didn't have a radio in his home.

because the public response was so vociferous—5,000 tickets had been issued for the event, nowhere near enough to fill the demand. The extent of the demand was hinted at during High Mass on February 9, when Monsignor Lavelle mentioned the dedication but ended his announcement with the less-than-reassuring statement "As far as possible, it will be thrown open to the public."

No solution to the radio question was reached until the day before the dedication, when the *Times* announced that the dedication would indeed be broadcast by two stations of the BBC—that is, the Brooklyn Broadcasting Corporation. (Of course the news was also carried in the *Brooklyn Standard-Union*.) Stations WBBC and WCGU, operating jointly as "Brooklyn's Own Stations," had a strong bent for ethnic programming but were quite willing to take part in the event. Earlier in the day, they would offer the Friedopfer Entertainers, Jewish Science Talk, and songs from M. Platnick. In the evening, they would borrow network announcer Norman Brokenshire and make history by carrying the first-ever broadcast of a service taking place at St. Patrick's.

The obstacles were forgotten as the evening went off with its expected solemnity and musical polish; but in addition, there was the kind of crackling excitement that New York usually experienced at a Broadway opening night. More than an hour before the doors opened, a long line of ticket holders stretched down 50th Street, and Fifth Avenue itself was packed with a mass of people hoping to get in. T. Scott Buhrman of *The American Organist* was back (this time around, he was supplying program notes for Yon), and no happier with the crowd control than he had been in 1928: "The several dozen police rather mismanaged the crowds at the entrance, but the unpleasantness was soon forgotten inside the Cathedral. . . ." An astonishing crowd of 7,000 (reported the *Sun*) pushed inside to hear the event; another 5,000 people were turned away.

The *Herald Tribune* carefully listed the society members involved on the Dedication Committee. The *Evening World* was obsessed with the organ's mechanics ("There is only one organ in existence boasting more stops—that of the Cathedral of Breslau, Germany, which has 206. But the Breslau organ's motor is one of but 25 horse-power, whereas the Cathedral employs a 65 horse-power motor, which means that the total length and diameter of the pipes must be considerably larger than in the case of the Breslau instrument. . . ."). But, par for the course, the mainstream press didn't bother with the music itself. Only Buhrman mentioned the performances to any extent.

> An exceedingly handsome program presented many photos, a history of the Cathedral, a story about the organ, and the organ stoplist. . . .
> Mr. Yon's playing was at its best. The organ and choirs sounded gloriously in the great Cathedral. There is an echo, or reverberation, after a fashion; we're glad of it. It takes away the stiffness and glorifies the results of church music on a large scale. . . . Mr. Carl Schlegel's baritone solo parts were beautifully done, as also Mr. John Finnegan's tenor passages. Musicians should visit the Cathedral for the inspiration its services afford.

Buhrman was wowed by the entire experience, from the "exceedingly handsome" program to the choice of repertoire. Veering from that ultimate organ litmus test, the Bach *Fantasie and Fugue in G minor*, to Yon's own *Te Deum* ("magnificent, sometimes dramatic, always effective and appealing"), as well as such stylish curiosities as Giuseppe Danise's deliberately understated rendering of the Gregorian "Recordare," the evening was not only large-scale but musically sophisticated. Buhrman's article was headlined DEDICATION OF FOUR-MANUAL GALLERY ORGAN MARKS BEGINNING OF A NEW ERA IN CATHOLIC CHURCH MUSIC IN AMERICA.

Exceedingly handsome program, indeed; its Art Deco cover, sixteen pages, and twenty photos had obviously been printed at the very last moment because they featured a significant eleventh-hour change. Giuseppe Bamboschek wound up being stuck in Philadelphia for a week of extra performances and had to drop out of the dedication concert. Yon found an instant substitute in Paolo Giaquinto, a sometime conductor, vocal coach, pianist, and organist who had recently joined the Cathedral staff as Yon's "first assistant." Giaquinto manned the chancel organ as the choir entered to the "Hymn to St. Cecilia," then took the baton to conduct Yon's playing of the *Concerto Gregoriano*. The results were good enough that, soon after the concert, Yon promoted Giaquinto from "first assistant" to chancel organist.*

---

* Giaquinto was hired with a three-year contract, the Cathedral's usual way of doing things, and at the end of it he wasn't renewed; evidently he had argued with someone in authority when he shouldn't have. By the summer of 1933 he was back to vocal coaching, which would continue until the end of his career.

The general consensus was that everyone's work had been top-flight, including that of Giaquinto, Constantino Yon (he played for the *Te Deum*), Rostagno, the orchestra, and every vocalist. But the night had belonged to the new gallery organ. Also to Pietro Yon.

Depression vs. Oratorio

In the wake of the stock market crash, the first months of 1930 were surprisingly business-as-usual, although it didn't take an economist to see ominous signals in the air. Barely a month after the organ dedication, New Yorkers were heartened as they saw construction beginning on the colossal Empire State Building; but at the same time, an unemployment rally in Union Square escalated into a full-scale riot, the worst the city had seen in two decades.

St. Patrick's, in the midst of its preparations for Lent, was experiencing a strange sense of calm. Attendance was particularly heavy throughout the season, all the way into Holy Week (including the two-and-a-half-hour Palm Sunday Mass, an hour of which was taken up with the Passion, chanted by Fathers Woods, Quinn, and Tytheridge). Easter Sunday was jam-packed and no less lavish than it had been in the past, with the Male Soloist Ensemble at optimum power and a full orchestra assisting in the gallery. So far, collection totals seemed unaffected. The *Times* pointed out that the Cathedral's parish rolls might be shrinking, but the congregations weren't. This was attributed to a roster of distinguished guest preachers, as well as to "one of the most elaborate musical programs in any church in America. The addition to the musical staff as organist of Pietro Yon, honorary organist of the Vatican, and of Father Joseph H. Rostagne [*sic*] as choir director contributes much to this reputation."

That particular reputation would put Yon in a very uncomfortable position during the ensuing months as the depression became The Depression, making itself felt in a sudden and precipitous drop in collection amounts. The lingering sense of well-being evaporated. Churches across the United States were deciding that high-level music was an untenable luxury, slashing their budgets to the bone in order to save money. But at the same time, writeups such as the one in the *Times* were singling out the quality of the Cathedral's music department as a factor in the large crowds visiting St. Patrick's. There was also the sense that music at St. Patrick's *should* be of the highest quality, and that maintaining that quality was important, Depression or not. "There is no timidity about the future of congregations, the future support of the public, so far as St. Patrick's Cathedral is concerned," Buhrman wrote with absolute confidence.

The Cathedral was busy implementing programs to provide relief for parishioners in financial trouble. Yon was determined to do the same, as he had been doing since the Crash, providing his own brand of relief by giving employment, as regularly as possible, to as many musicians as possible. Although a number of years had seen no choral music at St. Patrick's during summer seasons, an abbreviated ensemble remained on duty through the summer of 1930, conducted by Paolo Giaquinto. At the beginning of Advent, Constantino Yon kept it in the family as he presented a Sunday-evening concert in Washington with singers from both Saint Vincent Ferrer and St. Patrick's. On Christmas Day, Yon brought in pupil Robert Elmore to take the console at the Cathedral. And when Yon played a recital date in Fargo, North Dakota, he took along John Finnegan.

But he wasn't concerned merely with doling out busywork to his employees. Plenty of vocalists had been thrown out of work by the Depression, and those men working at St. Patrick's knew that their comportment was as important to their jobs as their musicality. Yon made sure that they had ample opportunity to display their gratitude at events such as Cardinal Hayes's "At Home" reception, given every New Year's Day. It was a popular event with the city's Catholic society, and among the prelates, society members, and dignitaries would invariably come a group visit from the Cathedral choirmen, escorted by their conductor. No matter how strenuously they might have celebrated the night before (*after* they had finished singing the New Year's Eve "Watch" service, that is), they were expected to pay their respects to the Cardinal, hit formation, and sing nicely for the assemblage.

As the financial slump deepened in 1931, even the city's usually dispassionate news coverage was taking note of the unhappy mood. One article on local New Year's Eve plans mentioned that revelers would gather "with hope for a happy and prosperous 1932 and with little regret for 1931." For his part, Monsignor Lavelle became concerned about the cost of the music program. Musical organizations of all stripes were in trouble, large ones showing deficits and small ones folding outright. Most churches with anything more than a paid quartet were automatically slashing their paid music staffs. Giulio Gatti-Casazza made headlines when he "voluntarily renounced 10 percent of his salary" to keep the season afloat at the Met, which example supposedly prompted everyone else on staff to do the same. The Rector might have been inspired by the Met story; not long after it hit the press, he asked Yon to cut the choir budget by 20 percent. Yon, well aware that the Cathedral choirmen weren't paid on the same scale as Met singers, counter-offered to cut 10 percent and no more. The winner of that round has been lost to history,* but the Rector apparently conceded that a chorister was at least as useful as a diva, because the Male Soloist Ensemble retained its numbers throughout the leanest years of the Depression.

Hindsight has its ironies. Monsignor Lavelle regularly wrote lengthy memos to Cardinal Hayes, covering a number of unrelated topics. And as part of the very same memo in which he was objecting to music department costs ("My opinion is that the expense should be less, [even] if there never was any depression"), Lavelle himself provided the first mention of what would prove to be the largest and most important—and the most expensive—compositional project of Pietro Yon's career.

> Mr. Yon presented me with the libretto of an oratorio treating of the great apostle's conversion of Ireland. He proposes to write the music himself. I have gone through it and find it has some merit. If you deem it well, you could go through it in a couple of hours.

The libretto was inspired by the book *St. Patrick, His Life and Mission.* Yon thought it had possibilities as libretto material and called on his friend Armando Romano, who not only was cultural editor of the newspaper *Il Progresso* but known in Italy as a prolific author and playwright. Romano was intrigued by the story and fashioned a sprawling libretto that employed narration spoken and sung, choruses in every vocal formation, and a slew of soloists—all of it to be performed in both Latin and Italian. Apparently the Cardinal thought the libretto was worthwhile and gave his encouragement; when Yon returned from his summer vacation

* More than a decade later, a Cathedral soloist would note that "salaries had been higher and at the start of the depression everyone took a cut. At the time their salaries were cut they were told by Pietro Yon that salaries would be restored to their pre-depression levels when conditions improved"—which didn't happen for years.

in late September, both the *Times* and the *Herald Tribune* reported that he had already finished the music. "It will take me many months to orchestrate it, and then in the spring I wish to have it baptized here in the cathedral," he told the *Tribune* reporter, who continued, "Cardinal Hayes and Monsignor Lavelle, rector of the cathedral, are enthusiastic about the oratorio, he said, but there may still be obstacles of space and calendar to prevent the oratorio being played in the cathedral."

That statement was a euphemistic way of saying that there was a stumbling block to the idea of presenting Yon's, or anyone's, oratorio at St. Patrick's. In the wake of the *motu proprio*, musical events could not be presented in the church specifically as performances, but rather as services of music. That was why each organ dedication had contained a processional, a recessional, and a benediction, also why the 1928 program expressly forbade applause. Another factor was that, although those events could be ticketed, no money could be charged for the tickets; a discreet collection was the only way that attendees could be asked for cash. But *Il Trionfo di S. Patrizio* (in New York the title would translate to *The Triumph of St. Patrick*) would be a project much too large to be financed by passing a basket. Monetary patronage would be required before anything could be planned. Yon's hoped-for 1933 springtime performance date came and went with no further news of the oratorio's progress.

As it happened, Pope Pius XI had proclaimed 1933 to be a Holy Year, which in itself generated a number of additional large-scale events. Along with the usual Lent and Holy Week preparations, two weeks before Easter there was a gigantic Sunday-morning "Holy Hour" ceremony at Radio City Music Hall. Cardinal Hayes, along with Jewish and Protestant dignitaries, spoke to 6,000 people in the theatre, thousands more crowding 51st Street and listening through loudspeakers, and millions of international radio listeners. A massive combined choir provided the music for the occasion. And after the service, the St. Patrick's crew had to hurry back for Mass.

Only four days later, Yon took to the airwaves again with the Gregorian Club—revived, and this time comprising entirely St. Patrick's personnel—to sing his own arrangement of the Passion Story for an NBC broadcast. The work was initially untitled, but network publicity stated, "Yon's composition traces the familiar story of the Passion, Death and Resurrection of Christ," and the name stuck. (Not so the name of the Gregorian

Club. By chance, a local speakeasy had taken exactly the same name, and when Prohibition was repealed in 1933, *that* Gregorian Club understandably decided to go public. It might not have been a coincidence that, after the broadcast, Yon's Gregorian Club quietly reabsorbed itself into the Cathedral ranks and was heard from no more.)

Yon also had the task of finding an organist to replace the newly departed Paolo Giaquinto. Rather than go through the process of interviews and references, he took the path of least resistance by looking at his own organ pupils. In this case, the easiest path turned out to be the best: Edward Rivetti was a young New Jersey–based pianist and organist who had been working for the past year as musical director at St. Malachy's Church and fitting in musical odd jobs such as accompanying Paterson's Riverside Athletic and Singing Club, Inc. Rivetti was not only talented but also smart, likeable, calmly unflappable—and of Piemontese background, the same as Yon. He started at the chancel organ at the beginning of the 1933–34 season and quickly became not only a fixture at St. Patrick's (called in a single breath "Eddie-Rivetti" by just about everyone), but a second son to Yon.*

In the midst of it all, Yon was still casting about for possible oratorio backing. He had talked in detail with the president of the Friendly Sons of St. Patrick, Surrogate Judge James A. Foley. Foley thought initially that the Friendly Sons might be able to help with the finances. But as the project solidified, it became obvious that they couldn't possibly underwrite it in toto. *The Triumph* would require, besides its choral forces, eleven high-caliber soloists and a large orchestra; even with Depression economics, that added up to a very expensive proposition. In an attempt to keep interest alive, Yon arranged a private hearing of the score at his studio for Cardinal Hayes (to whom the score was dedicated), Monsignor Lavelle, and a few others. That prompted the *Times* to mention the project again:

---

* This relationship extended to matters beyond music. At dinner one evening they got onto the subject of regional dishes, Rivetti expressing his unfamiliarity with desserts of their region. Yon reared in disbelieving horror and instantly called in the cook: "From now on, whenever Eddie comes here, I want him to have *dolci piemontese!*" In accordance with that order, every time Rivetti came to dinner at the Yon home he was treated to new and increasingly exotic sweets, all of them made from traditional Piemontese recipes. It was a period he remembered fondly.

A few days ago an invited audience heard the first presentation of the oratorio. It will not be rendered publicly until Sunday, March 10, at which time the premiere will be the gala occasion of a celebration in the cathedral under the patronage of Cardinal Hayes.

Publicity didn't alleviate the Friendly Sons' worries, and sometime into the new year, Judge Foley wrote Yon informing him that they'd have to pull out of the project.

With the March 10 performance date hanging fire, Yon went to see Monsignor Lavelle, "all excited over bad news," as the Rector later wrote Cardinal Hayes with some displeasure.

> Now he wants to insist that we should underwrite it either by allowing it to take place in the Cathedral with charge for the tickets, or in some public hall, always with the implication that the Cathedral make up any deficit that may be incurred. There are two objections to his plan. First, I know you do not care to have an enterprise of this kind in the Cathedral, particularly where there is a charge for admission. Secondly, Oratorio is not a popular entertainment. . . . [M]y personal wish is that you write that in view of the general financial situation it is inopportune for us to take such a risk this year.
>
> I am sorry to bother you with this matter but if I do not, he will. He has a great reputation as a musician but he rarely gives us the sort of music that our people care for.

It undoubtedly didn't help Yon's case when, during the meeting, he had told Lavelle that the project would probably cost five to six thousand dollars—in modern terms, about $90,000. For a single performance.

Although the Rector's comments were born in the heat of dispute, his two objections were valid (and borne out by the Cardinal's reply: "Tell him that the *Trustees* of the Cathedral are not in a position to stand any expenses; nor can we use the Cathedral for any admission"). In order for Yon to proceed with *The Triumph of St. Patrick*, a wealthy backer would have to suddenly appear.

Enter Humbert Fugazy.

A fellow Italian, son of banker and travel agency magnate Louis Fugazy, and heir to a seemingly inexhaustible fortune,* he had embarked

---

* In years to come, Humbert's nephew William Fugazy would become even better known to New Yorkers as the head of Fugazy Transportation and its fleet of limousines.

upon entrepreneurial life with lawyer Bart Manfredi. Fugazy had spent the 1920s promoting boxing matches, some of which were wildly successful while others were such disasters that they earned him the nickname "Hard Luck Fugazy"; in the early 1930s he tried the idea of a steamship-turned–floating restaurant, which sank before it ever opened. By 1934 his interest had turned to music, and he entered negotiations to take over the Hippodrome National Opera Company ("to create a new opera public from the world of sports and other amusements," he said ingenuously). In comparison to the Hippodrome Opera scheme—which earned a single day of press coverage, then instantly collapsed—getting Yon's oratorio on its feet would be a snap.

By late March, the arrangements were finally in place. The performance date would be April 29. The venue would be not St. Patrick's but Carnegie Hall. It had been agreed that the oratorio could be announced as occurring "under the patronage of His Eminence, Patrick Cardinal Hayes." This in itself was attractive enough to draw more patronage from a wider circle, including musical notables (Arturo Toscanini and Gatti-Casazza), political figures (Mayor Fiorello La Guardia and former Governor Alfred E. Smith), society luminaries (Mrs. William Randolph Hearst, along with the previous president of the Friendly Sons, Justice Francis J. Martin), and distinguished clergymen (Monsignor Stephen Donahue of the Cathedral staff—and, for all his earlier annoyance, Monsignor Lavelle himself).

Yon had written the title role of St. Patrick for Martinelli's voice, but Martinelli wouldn't be available for the performance because of the pushed-back date; on the day of the premiere he'd be sailing for Italy and a contract with the Florence May Festival. Yon decided to use Met tenor Frederick Jagel, who sang a good chunk of Martinelli's repertoire when Martinelli wasn't around. Also from the Met would be baritone Millo Picco; soprano Santa Biondo was listed as "formerly of the Metropolitan," having left the roster after three seasons. The other two female soloists would be mezzo Frances Iovine and soprano Elizabeth Slattery; the other men would be Cathedral stalwarts—Finnegan, Cibelli, Schlegel, de Hierapolis, Scala, and Ferrari. Ruggero Vene, an Italian composer-editor who had been working in Rome as assistant to composer Ottorino Respighi, would switch gears to make his U.S. debut as conductor. With the rest of the Cathedral Choir as the core, filling in the choral sound would be a "chorus of sixty singers drafted from leading church choirs."

New York's publicity machine was working overtime to turn *The Triumph of St. Patrick* into a Major Event, and newspaper readers were deluged with articles that examined every aspect of its history and production. A week before the premiere, the *Times* carried four separate mentions of the work, including a display ad and a radio schedule. "WORLD PREMIERE/Notable chorus of 60 artists/other eminent soloists" . . . "Both in its organization and in the manner it was written the oratorio is described as one of the most unusual ever presented in New York" . . . "The proceeds are to go to charities which will be designated by Cardinal Hayes" . . . "Mr. Yon himself will be at the organ and the orchestra will include sixty men from the Metropolitan . . . ."

Such attention might have proved nerve-wracking for most composers. Yon's own method of relaxation was to perform with the Philharmonic. Twice during that final week of rehearsals, he played an all-Bach program under Toscanini's baton, also at Carnegie Hall.

At Mass on the morning of April 29, Monsignor Lavelle added a plug for *The Triumph* to his announcements, ending with "We would love to see every one of you in attendance." City newspapers reported that the first act would be broadcast on station WJZ. Olin Downes's Sunday music column in the *Times* carried a quarter-page portrait of Pietro Yon and mentioned that *The Triumph* would have its world premiere that evening.

From nearly all accounts the performance went off beautifully, marred by only one problem—many audience members weren't there at the start. Most papers didn't even mention this. The *Times* speculated, "The concert began before an almost empty hall downstairs, perhaps because of the change to daylight saving time yesterday. By the middle of the program, however, a fair-sized house had assembled." But Samuel Chotzinoff, in his "Words and Music" column for the *New York Post*, interpreted the absence of audience in a writeup that managed to be snide as well as bigoted, claiming that Cardinal Hayes's endorsement should have resulted in a crowd of Irish stampeding into Carnegie Hall; the turnout had "shattered another myth of racial solidarity." (As well, he pointed out that few were interested in oratorio because it was a "lazy form" of opera, minus costumes or scenery.) About the libretto, he wrote,

> We first behold the young Patrick as a Christian shepherd. . . . Even
> at that tender age the young slave shows all the symptoms of sainthood

and goes around blessing everything. . . . I could not help feeling a little sad at the plight of the Druids, for ever since I heard "Norma" at the opera I have valued these pagans for many excellent Christian qualities.

And Chotzinoff dispatched the music at a stroke by suggesting that the tunes would be good for musical comedy.

For its own part, the *Times* might have been exasperated by all that publicity it had been printing because it weighed in with a particularly crabby review. The performers were liked; but the reviewer wished that they had been given something else to sing:

> Unfortunately the musical material was almost entirely undistinguished; sentimental, derivative and banal. . . . [O]ne looked in vain for musical ideas of exaltation or nobility or dramatic power. . . . One would like to record this work as a significant addition to American music, ecclesiastical or otherwise, but unhappily this is not the fact.

Critics without a particular axe to grind were much more enthusiastic about the performance. The *Sun*'s critic thought of Bach-style narration and was impressed by Yon's use of three narrators. (Yon named them "Storici," a term used in Passion settings of the Renaissance; tenor, baritone, and bass, throughout the evening they often sang unaccompanied. That might have driven the average opera singer crazy, but the roles were sung by Cathedral men who were not in the least bothered by it. In fact, "Storicus" Raimondo Scala wound up as one of the critical hits of the evening.) The *Herald-Tribune* also liked what it heard:

> [A]s a rule, Mr. Yon is at his best as a creative musician in this work in his choruses, although the arias are always melodious and grateful for the voice. . . . The performance deserved praise, especially in its unity and dominating spirit, which reflected much credit on Mr. Vene's conductorship.

That review picked out a particular moment as one of the evening's high points, the chorus "Sia laudato il Signore" (listed in English as "Chorus of the Earth"). It was the single piece on which all critics agreed, even the unimpressed *Times*.

The most passionate review, over a page long, came from *Musical America*:

[L]et me make clear that this is not one of those contemporary pieces designed to arouse controversy. Mr. Yon is no experimenter in unpleasant sounds. . . . In its beauty and simplicity it would, indeed, be difficult to find a passage in contemporary music to rival it. It made a profound impression. . . .

At the organ the composer officiated in a distinguished manner. His Cathedral Choral Society of some sixty voices not only sang with superb tone, but with technical assurance. . . .

It had been a stimulating, also tiring, experience for the musicians of St. Patrick's. Even so, its glamour was put into perspective two days after the performance as the Cathedral's own Monsignor Donahue (who had sat with Monsignor Lavelle in Carnegie Hall) was consecrated Auxiliary Bishop. The ceremony was splendid, all three hours of it, and featured the Cathedral Choir.

And just in case anyone might forget what the choir had been up to lately, one of the musical selections was the chorus "Sia laudato il Signore."

Triumph in Chicago, Triumph at St. Patrick's

Some personalities might have worried about overexposure after the hype associated with *The Triumph of St. Patrick*, but Pietro Yon was too busy to give it much consideration. In early 1935, the *World-Telegram* ran across the top of a page ELOQUENT HANDS GUIDE CATHEDRAL CHOIR IN REHEARSAL, a photo series of Yon conducting a runthrough from the console. Its half-dozen shots show him with arms flailing in a variety of angles, his face blazing with concentration.

That period wasn't completely pleasant. In January, the sobering announcement came that Father Rostagno was resigning, calling a halt after his two-year assignment had somehow lengthened into six years. Before he left, he gave a press interview in which he said that he had been pleased by some, but not all, choirs in New York (St. Patrick's and Saint Vincent Ferrer made the cut); he also revealed, surprisingly, that his favorite "modern" liturgical composer was Joseph Ryelandt. "He will return to his native Italy on the *Rex* next Saturday," reported the *Times*, "where he will devote his time to research in the Vatican library for old manuscripts on church music, preparatory to publishing a book."

Still, Yon had lost none of his enthusiasm for St. Patrick's or its music and periodically checked the Cathedral School boys for signs of musical aptitude. It was a low-key procedure designed to put the children at ease; the entire class would be asked to sing a simple tune while "Professor" Yon walked up and down the aisles, his ear alert to vocal quality. One of those children, now a venerable man, remembered the day some seven decades past when Yon visited his classroom. As the boy sang along with his schoolmates, Yon stopped briefly next to him and listened for a moment, then patted his shoulder and murmured, "You will do other things with your music. . . ." And he continued on his way.

Yon himself was doing a wide variety of things with his music. In April he participated in the Industrial Arts Exposition—right across the street from the Cathedral, at Rockefeller Center. Midwestern engineer Laurens Hammond had perfected an electrically operated "pipeless" organ and was ready to unveil it to the public. Yon was asked to play the new instrument for a gathering of press representatives, and he showed off the virtues of the Hammond Organ to a very high-powered group of "invited guests" including Fritz Reiner, Lauritz Melchior, Helen Jepson, Gladys Swarthout, Rosa Ponselle, George Gershwin, Sigmund Romburg, and of course Martinelli. (The guests were impressed: Gershwin was the first to buy a Hammond for himself, and Laurens Hammond was nicely launched. When he became successful enough to open his own show-room "studio" in New York, Yon dropped by to play for the press opening.) From there, he plunged into five performances of two different programs with the Philharmonic—the world premiere of Sonzogno's *Tango* and the Beethoven *Missa Solemnis*. All of this activity took place in the days immediately before and after Easter, which required him to schedule those events around Holy Week services, along with his usual duties. One of those duties was hosting: Martinelli and Toscanini liked to meet with Yon at his Carnegie Hall apartment for ravioli dinners. A very convenient locale, either before or after a performance.

As 1935 gave way to 1936, the focus moved to Chicago, as a plan developed to have George Cardinal Mundelein's Cathedral Choristers make their first concert appearance in *The Triumph of St. Patrick* with local soloists. Yon was undoubtedly glad of the revival. He was probably glad of the distance as well, because the resulting publicity had little to say about the oratorio and much more to say about the matrons who were sponsoring the event: "Mrs. McLaughlin is chairman of the patroness committee and last Wednesday she gave a tea for the other women interested in the affair. . . ." While the work was being readied for its March 9 hearing, the Chicago press seemed to be evenly divided between the music and society columns. (And there were features such as coverage of the dress rehearsal, when Orchestra Hall was filled to capacity with an invited audience of Archdiocesan nuns; it made for an eye-popping news photo.) Yon attended the performance, accompanied by Monsignor Lavelle, and took the stage at the end for a bow amid the audience's cheers.

With the Chicago production came an additional benefit. Whether as a result of Cardinal Mundelein's interest or the success of both performances—or if it had all been planned in the first place thanks to Humbert Fugazy's backing—less than three weeks after the Chicago concert, St. Patrick's announced that it would host its own Cathedral-sponsored performance.

This time the scoop was provided by the *Brooklyn Times-Union*: ARIONS ARE HAILED BY MONS. LAVELLE/REHEARSE ORATORIO THEY WILL PRESENT AT ST. PATRICK'S CATHEDRAL APRIL 26. Yon regarded it as a prime opportunity, because he had written *The Triumph* specifically to be performed at St. Patrick's. But as he planned the event, he realized that some changes would have to be made in order to fit the music to the Cathedral's space. The sixty voices of the chorus, so impressive in Carnegie Hall's superb acoustics, would lose their punch coming from the gallery of St. Patrick's. A much larger group would be needed, and Yon found them in the Arion Singing Society of Brooklyn. The Arions were capable; they were also numerous. (The *Times* listed them as having 300 singers in the gallery for the performance. If that estimate was true, they would have had an extraordinarily claustrophobic evening. They also would have broken every fire law in existence.)

The Arion Singing Society, however, would present one problem that would require Cardinal Hayes's help. They were a mixed choir, and women hadn't sung in the Cathedral gallery since 1904. A dispensation would be required. (It was granted.) The *Times* overdramatized the episode, and inaccurately: "[T]he first time in the history of the cathedral that a mixed chorus has been admitted to the choir loft to give a special performance. . . ."

As both Yon and Rivetti would be busy at their respective consoles, Arion conductor Leopold Syre would handle the conducting.* The soloists would be basically the same, except for a few changes. At last, Martinelli would be in New York and available to sing the performance. (The only problem occurred when Yon decided to switch the Italian libretto to English for the Cathedral performance. Martinelli had learned his role in Italian, and he was firm in his determination to perform it that way.) Santa Biondo gave way to Lola Monti-Gorsey. Probably in a gesture of equality, Jan Van Bommel was given the role that had formerly been sung by Carl Schlegel. And John Finnegan's "Storicus" was assigned to a new member of the Male Soloist Ensemble, John Griffin. Griffin was a newspaperman-turned-tenor who had started singing in Chicago movie houses, moved to radio, and finally became a headliner of "Roxy's Gang." This was the pride of producer "Roxy" Rothafel, a company of vaude-ville-style performers who provided stage shows for movie palaces (and it appealed to the lowest common denominator; at one point Griffin was announced to sing "a fine composite of 'Laugh, Clown, Laugh' and 'Ridi Pagliacci'"). In 1934, newly based in New York and with his Roxy days behind him, Griffin performed for the Liederkranz Club—on the same program with Carl Schlegel. Schlegel undoubtedly introduced him to Yon, and by early 1936 he had been installed as a front-rank Cathedral soloist.

The original late-April performance date had to be moved to May 10. That didn't hurt attendance a bit because press reports estimated an astounding 7,000 listeners, including Cardinal Hayes himself and a large slice of New York's clergy. Keeping it within the framework of a service of music (and providing an opportunity to give some solo work to those men who had lost their roles), the performance would begin with a pro-cessional (assigned to John Finnegan) and end with a benediction (that went to Carl Schlegel). Yon and his musicians had an extremely good night; the consensus was that this performance equaled, or surpassed, the premiere. The *New York American* felt that nothing more was needed but to reprint the high points of its earlier Carnegie Hall review.

* Reviewers liked Syre's work, and Yon must have, too. A year later he collabo-rated with Syre as guest artist for the Arions' holiday concert at Carnegie Hall. And he joined them for a third Carnegie outing in 1940.

An even more enthusiastic review came from columnist John Festeneck, who was frankly bowled over by every aspect of the evening—even if he did get the title of the piece wrong, referring to it as *The Glory of St. Patrick*. Probably the most endearing part of his review came toward the end when he carefully noted, "I beg Mr. Edward Rivetti to accept my sincere assurance that at no time did the virtuosic mastery of Mr. Yon's organ performance leave the slightest disparaging reflection on his own competence and skill as an organist."

Festeneck, as it happened, wrote for the *Paterson Morning Call*, Eddie Rivetti's hometown newspaper. And whether it was because of a teacher's pride in his pupil, or because he was so amused by the columnist's title flub (blazoned across the page in a headline, at that), Festeneck's was the press clipping that received pride of place in Pietro Yon's own scrapbook.

Talk of the Town

Unfortunately, the success of *The Triumph of St. Patrick* was a unique event—there is no record of the oratorio's being performed ever again in New York. Over the next few years, Yon tried to repeat his achievement with other titles, none of which caught on with listeners. *Christ the King* received two performances in October 1936, both of them on the same day at the Brooklyn Academy of Music, and all that is known of the piece is the soloist lineup (the usual Cathedral men, assisted by Father Woods and Millo Picco). The *Road to Golgotha* was sung once only, at St. Patrick's. *The Quest* was referred to in a newspaper interview as "being neither cantata nor oratorio, but requiring soloists, a large choir and an orchestra." Such extensive requirements probably sank it. After its single reference in print, *The Quest* was never mentioned again.

However, the fortune of these projects had no bearing upon the fact that Pietro Yon was not only a master of his craft, but a particular treasure for New Yorkers. Monsignor Lavelle's onetime comment, that Yon rarely gave St. Patrick's the sort of music that the people cared for, was contradicted by the fact that both he and his choir continued to be a draw both inside the Cathedral and out. A look at music listings for various holidays in the late 1930s shows programming that changed little from year to year. This was the music that resonated most strongly with congregations and clergy at St. Patrick's; whether or not Yon found it repetitious, he was happy to offer it. And listeners responded in kind by according the Cathedral choir almost mythic stature. The St. Patrick's name had such appeal that, for several years, the Waldorf-Astoria ran display ads in New York papers to announce its Christmas Day "tea-concert." The featured entertainers were listed in large type: John Griffin and Jan Van Bommel.

Yon himself had traveled far from the image of a church organist. Exactly how far he had traveled was made plain when he received the ultimate seal of approval, Manhattan-style—a writeup in the "Talk of the Town" column of *The New Yorker*. The writer obviously had a great time with Yon, describing his flashy wardrobe ("not at all like our conception of a cathedral organist") and his interest in popular music (mentioning his days at St. Francis Xavier, when he would sneak over to the vaudeville houses of Union Square and listen to ragtime . . . and Yon went even further, admitting that he liked swing bands). The article even pointed out that Yon had adopted American manners: On a visit to Italy, one of his brothers greeted him with a click of the heels—Yon's reply was a clap on the back and a hearty "Harya, pal?" And he said that he wouldn't live anywhere but in New York.

However, the *New Yorker* article didn't point out that Pietro Yon was absolutely unable—and unwilling—to slacken his pace. He might not be traversing the country in the freewheeling way of his earlier years, but New York recitals were becoming more frequent for him. He was also accepting a sheaf of other assignments, serving on committees for the Choir Music Festival and the Child Welfare League, playing for events sponsored by the Municipal Opera Association, Columbia University's Casa Italiana, or as part of the entertainment at the Catholic charity event The Emerald Ball. An extreme example of Yon's workaholic tendencies came on Christmas Day of 1938: After he had played Midnight Mass of the evening before, and then the Mass of Christmas morning, he headed to Bethlehem, Pennsylvania, to conduct a mid-afternoon "Community Christmas" broadcast for WABC.

On top of all this work, he was deeply involved with his pupils' career progress. When Mabel Nichols wrote a Christmas carol he liked, "Christ-Child," he not only programmed it at St. Patrick's for the Christmas Eve carol service but made sure that the media heard about it. And when Robert Elmore made his Carnegie Hall debut, one of his program selections was Yon's *Concerto Gregoriano* in its organ-piano arrangement. Yon himself played the secondary piano part.

Another important pupil was Yon's own son, Mario. Even as a teenager he was a great help to Yon in his work, a talented organist . . . and a gifted mimic. This gift was very useful around the Cathedral; Yon could be occupied in the chancel moments before a Mass, and Mario was able to begin a prelude at the gallery console, playing in exactly his father's style. This enabled Yon to make his way upstairs without even having to break into a trot. Yon told one interviewer, "If he would put his mind to it he could probably beat me at my own game." But, perhaps from watching the effort his father would habitually exert in order to be a winner at that game, Mario wasn't wedded to the idea of music as a career.

Yon's work at St. Patrick's would prove to be one of the few constants in his life as accomplishments became intertwined with leave-takings. In late 1937, his father died in his hometown of Settimo. Yon arranged a memorial service at the Cathedral, for which he brought out a Mass setting that he had composed years earlier in memory of his mother. It had been heard only once before, at Francesca Yon's funeral.

Cardinal Hayes had been slowing his public pace since experiencing a serious heart attack in 1932, and then another cardiac episode in 1937. Even though he was seen less frequently in public, he was still active in Cathedral administration and still appreciated his employees, especially the head of his music department. During the spring of 1938, in a surprise move he appointed both Pietro and Constantino Yon as Knights of St. Sylvester—if not the Cross of St. Gregory, very nearly as impressive. Both Yon brothers were delighted with the honor, but it turned out to be a parting gesture. During the predawn hours of September 4, the Cardinal suffered a massive coronary and died in his sleep.

Yon received the news at his vacation home in Italy. He immediately headed for New York, but sadly there was no way he could arrive in time to coordinate, or even to attend, the Cardinal's final rites. (Rivetti filled in, playing the Dead March from Handel's *Saul*, which had been played for Cardinal Farley's funeral some twenty years before. The Cathedral choir was supplanted by the Incarnation Choristers, singing Palestrina and the Rheinberger *Requiem*; and a choir of seminarians from St. Joseph's contributed some of the extensive Gregorian chants.) On the day of the funeral, Yon was at sea on the Italian liner *Saturnia*. It offered its own memorial Mass as a gesture of respect.

He responded to the Cardinal's death as he always had, in music. The *Times* reported, "Pietro A. Yon, organist and musical director of St. Patrick's Cathedral, announced on his return from Europe yesterday that he had started work on a composition in the form of a eulogy to the late

Cardinal Hayes. It will be entitled 'Go, Happy Soul.'" Actually, Yon's work would consist of polishing a piece that had been written three years previously. A writer for *Musical Digest* had been one of the very first people to hear it:

> Circling my way round the eighth floor pandemonium of student musical effort in Carnegie Hall the other day, I came suddenly upon the sonorous peal of an organ responding to a master touch and the luscious tones of a baritone in a lovely but unfamiliar song.
>
> The last strain had been lost in the medley when I became aware of an open door, an inquiring voice, and my embarrassing position as an eavesdropper. Only the indulgent courtesy of Pietro Yon saved me from an unceremonious eviction. But, favored of the Gods, I had been an unbidden guest at the first exploitation of Mr. Yon's latest brain child, "Go, Happy Soul," by none other than the pride of St. Patrick's Cathedral, Leo De [*sic*] Hierapolis.

The piece gained a life of its own, and it was performed at a number of the Cathedral's final rites for people as diverse as brewer and New York Yankees owner Jacob Ruppert and Met conductor Gennaro Papi. But the serenity displayed in the song would be jarringly contrasted with events soon to come.

The year 1939 was a very complicated one for the Cathedral, and for the world itself. The death of Pius XI in February was commemorated in elaborate stateliness the world over, with an estimated 6,000 congregants taking part in the ceremonies at St. Patrick's (still without a titular head; Bishop Donahue had been elected Administrator after Cardinal Hayes's death, as a temporary arrangement). But a month later, the election of Eugenio Cardinal Pacelli as Pius XII gave birth to plans which would involve millions, plans that had never been attempted before and that pointed in the direction of the world's new instant media culture. The Cathedral remained open to the public throughout the night of March 11–12, carrying through its loudspeakers an international shortwave broadcast of the coronation ceremonies that would take place in Vatican City starting at 2:30 A.M. New York time. The hookup included local coverage; starting at midnight, Pietro Yon started the proceedings for the Cathedral congregation, as well as for the NBC radio audience, with an organ recital. And Yon's friend Monsignor Fulton J. Sheen followed up with an address. It may have been an exhausting night, but both Yon and

Sheen were on duty for the next morning's solemn pontifical Mass. Sheen was joined by Bishop Donahue; Yon was joined by his full choral forces, along with Martinelli and baritone John Charles Thomas as soloists for Yon's "Tu es Petrus."

Equally large celebrations were planned when Archbishop Francis Spellman was named to succeed Cardinal Hayes. He made a spectacular entrance into the New York Archdiocese, crossing the state line from Connecticut with an "entourage of twenty-five motor cars and a large police escort" (reported the *Times*), and his drive into Manhattan was witnessed by a quarter of a million people standing along the way. Five thousand people alone were waiting for him in front of the Cathedral's archepiscopal residence. Also waiting for him as he entered were Pietro Yon and the St. Patrick's choirmen, who promptly launched into "a hymn of greeting." The following morning, 7,000 people in the Cathedral, 50,000 in the streets outside, and unnumbered radio listeners witnessed as Spellman was formally installed as Archbishop of New York. At the height of the overpowering ceremony, the full Cathedral choir was joined by the St. Joseph's seminarians to sing "Ecce Sacerdos" as Spellman proceeded to the altar.

Even though the Archbishop theoretically had the right to replace Yon with any choirmaster he wished, that wasn't going to happen. Far less of a musical connoisseur than Cardinal Hayes had been, Archbishop Spellman was nonetheless happy with Pietro Yon's work. The music program of St. Patrick's would continue to operate exactly as it had for the past decade.

New York went through a strange dichotomy of emotions during that spring and summer. On one hand, there was the 1939 World's Fair, opened that April, with stupendous exhibits and its overall theme of a peaceful, utopian "World of Tomorrow." Fair organizers were particularly proud of the Temple of Religion, a large nondenominational structure underwritten entirely by private contributions. The Temple was designed to promote religious understanding to fairgoers by providing informational talks and music, the music to be "more embracing than any other festival music ever given." Organists and choirs from across the United States came to New York to perform at the Temple. Yon and the St. Patrick's choir had already been asked to appear in October 1940, as a special attraction during the Fair's closing days.

But the day before Spellman's installation, Nazi Germany and Italy had entered into the "Pact of Steel" alliance. Europe was moving toward the inevitable outcome of war.

With Rivetti left in charge of the music, Yon left for Italy at the beginning of July, ostensibly to visit relatives and play some recital dates. Soon after he arrived, he played for the Pope, after which they went behind closed doors for a few minutes. What they discussed wasn't revealed; the *Times* reported only that the Pontiff "sent his special blessing to St. Patrick's choir and all of Mr. Yon's pupils."

Barely a month later, it became obvious that the international situation was deteriorating rapidly. As had been the case with James Ungerer a generation before, Yon found himself on the wrong side of the Atlantic with war threatening. He booked passage on the *Conte di Savoia*, set to leave Genoa on August 24, only to find that the sailing had been canceled.

The next three weeks were a nightmare, as he tried Paris and the *Normandie*; another cancellation. From Paris to Trouville, Trouville to Le Havre, he met with canceled sailings at every port and was preparing to try Bourdeaux when he heard that the *Conte di Savoia* had rescheduled its sailing. Back to Genoa.

Most of his fellow passengers (a distinguished bunch, including European royalty, American millionaires, Met basso Ezio Pinza, and the Japanese ambassador to Italy) had been anxious to leave Europe as soon as possible; one woman took a 400-mile taxi ride in order to make the sailing. Fortunately the crossing was uneventful, and the *Conte di Savoia* arrived in New York on September 23. The *Times* was on the dock to interview a handful of the ship's passengers. One of those passengers was Yon, who said unequivocally, "Whatever happens, the best thing for the United States is to keep out. If we go in we will again be the goats."

His apprehensions proved to have been well founded; Germany had invaded Poland on September 1. War had begun.

Yon didn't know it at the time, but he would never return to Europe.

Even though the United States was still officially neutral, the emotional impact of the war was felt at St. Patrick's only three weeks later when the Cathedral hosted a Mass to honor Polish Day at the World's Fair. There had been a previous Polish Mass in May, given to mark the opening of the Fair's grand Polish Exhibit. Then, Yon had played, the full Cathedral choir had sung, and Monsignor Lavelle had offered a prayer that "war drums would be muffled." But in mid-October, with Nazi forces in occupation and mass murders of "Polish intelligentsia" having begun, this Mass turned into an electrifying display of national anguish. Yon played again, but now the Cathedral choir was supplanted by the Perth Amboy (New Jersey) Polish Choir, underlining the sense of ethnicity so well that some attendees wept. Archbishop Spellman declared that "Poland will never die." But neither he nor anyone else knew what the future would hold.

St. Patrick's itself received a particularly heavy blow only three days after that when Monsignor Lavelle, eighty-three years old and weakened by heart disease, died on the evening of October 17. The full choir sang the "Miserere" as his body was brought into the sanctuary for public viewing; for the funeral three days later, Yon conducted them in one of Lavelle's favorite hymns, "In Paradisum," as he was buried in the Cathedral crypt. Monsignor Lavelle had been a personification of the Cathedral's history, having come to St. Patrick's less than a month after its dedication and remaining there for sixty years (a record that has never been equaled by any Cathedral employee). He would be missed by many congregants, and also by Pietro Yon. Over the years, the two men had engaged in some heated sparring matches; but there were also moments of crisis, personal as well as professional, during which Lavelle had proven to be fiercely supportive.

Father Joseph Flannelly had been brought on to the Cathedral staff in late 1938 as Assistant Rector, and he was appointed Lavelle's successor with the title of Cathedral "Administrator." One of his first tasks was to oversee the preparations for the broadcasting of Midnight Mass 1939. Even though more and more Cathedral events had been offered on radio—the Pontiff's coronation, the dedication of the gallery organ, Archbishop Spellman's installation—they had been unique events and not regular Masses. Now the choir's 11:30 carol service would be carried locally on WMCA, and the Mass itself on WOR and the Mutual Network—a first for the Cathedral, and the beginning of a new tradition.*

---

* That first broadcast also put St. Patrick's on the clock, so to speak. In previous years, no Mass would begin until the celebrant gave the signal. Once radio became involved, that authority had been transferred to the control booth, and a radio Mass scheduled for a specific time would begin *on the dot*. That punctuality has continued into the present and the television age, most blatantly evident on Christmas Eve at the Midnight Mass. At 11:59 P.M., every single person in the Cathedral

Although Pietro Yon's creativity continued unabated, in 1940 and 1941 the escalating tensions of the world situation were of more consequence than any music. In March, Archbishop Spellman was invested with the *pallium* in a lavish ceremony. ("Worn only by the Pope and Archbishops, the Pallium, a circular band of white wool about two inches wide, signifies their duties as spiritual shepherds.") Frederick Jagel hadn't been heard in a Cathedral context since appearing in *The Triumph of St. Patrick*, and Yon brought him in as guest soloist. It was the sort of thing that used to generate headlines. But Archbishop Spellman gave an address in which he "praised the peace efforts of Pope Pius XII and President Roosevelt," and the *Times* account of the ceremony was headlined SPELLMAN DEFENDS U.S. PEACE MOVES.

The news coming from Benito Mussolini's Italy distressed many Italian-Americans, and Pietro Yon—member of the Sons of Italy and the Knights of Columbus, proud American citizen—was no exception. From the distance of New York City, he could act only in the capacity of goodwill ambassador. On Monday of Holy Week, Yon, Martinelli, and the Cathedral men performed for CBS over its shortwave frequency:

> International Station WCBX of the Columbia Broadcasting System presented a program of liturgical music . . . which was beamed to Italy and rebroadcast throughout that country by the Italian government's broadcasting system. The program, one of a series designed to strengthen the ties between the American and Italian people, consisted mainly of music from "Passion, Death and Resurrection." . . .

Ties weren't strengthened by this gesture or any other, and the situation would become ever more strained. When the commissioner general for Italy to the World's Fair, Vice Admiral Giuseppe Cantu, died of a heart attack, his funeral at St. Patrick's prompted an awkward moment when some in the congregation insisted on greeting his coffin with the Fascist salute, others raised a halfhearted hand, and American officers in uniform (reported the *Times*) pointedly gave "the usual military salute."

---

gives attention—not to the Cardinal's entrance or the trappings but to the broadcast floor manager stationed in the choir loft. A near-comical hush ensues. In absolute silence, clergy, congregation, and choir strain to hear as she counts down the final seconds to the five-four-three-two-one "hand-off." *Then* the Mass begins.

That Easter, Yon pulled out the stops with an extravagant lineup: The Male Soloist Ensemble, the Cathedral College choir, and the Cathedral Center Club choir were joined by soloists Cibelli, Van Bommel, boy soprano David Roberts—and for extra luster, Martinelli and John Charles Thomas. "This is one of the most elaborate music programs ever arranged for a solemn feast at the Cathedral," wrote one reporter. But the big news was Monsignor Fulton J. Sheen's headline-grabbing sermon in which he condemned the friendship between Adolf Hitler and Josef Stalin.

John Finnegan hadn't been slated for solo work at that Easter service or for the Italian broadcast. In fact, the last time his name appeared in print as a Cathedral soloist had been in 1936, at *The Triumph of St. Patrick* (and that night he wound up indisposed, with John Griffin having to take over his duties). But he was still respected as a cornerstone of the Cathedral music department, preparing to mark his thirty-fifth anniversary at St. Patrick's on May 1. Also, he had been for decades an active member of the Friendly Sons of St. Patrick, frequently appearing as soloist with their glee club. On the evening of April 12, Finnegan left his home in Queens to sing with the Friendly Sons at their annual concert. While waiting for a train in the Roosevelt Avenue station of the IND subway, he suddenly collapsed, victim of a heart attack. He died immediately.

His funeral took place at the Cathedral before a congregation of more than 1,000. The full Cathedral choir, as well as the glee club of the Friendly Sons, sang at the Mass. Yon told *Catholic News*, "He was one of the finest artists I ever knew, a hard and sincere worker and a perfect example of what a Catholic artist should be when serving his Church and his God."

Finnegan's death was a jolt—few of the Male Soloist Ensemble were young men, and no one could help but feel the usual reaction to a colleague's demise—but the Cathedral choir was strong enough to be musically unaffected. John Griffin, in fact, had in recent years been viewed as the *primo tenore* of St. Patrick's. He had become one of the most important soloists of the Friendly Sons, and as a bonus he was doing a surprising number of radio appearances. Most of these were fifteen-minute runthroughs of his Irish-tenor repertoire. Griffin wasn't a bit choosy about the venue. He would appear on virtually any station no matter how small, and at one point he was programmed to sing *during* a local newscast, in between stories. All this activity paid off handsomely in recognition value when he was asked to appear as a headliner at the final full day of the 1940 World's Fair, singing in open-air concert at the huge Court of Peace with Met soprano Ruby Mercer.

The Cathedral choir had shown up at the Fair a couple of weeks before Griffin's solo bout, along with Yon, Rivetti, and the WPA's New York Civic Orchestra, making their appearance at the Temple of Religion. This time around, the theme was American-Italian Week, with announcements that Yon and his men would appear in "a special program of religious music of Italian origin"—an all-Yon program, with his *Mass in E-flat* as the program's centerpiece. Apparently the performance went off with its usual polish, but the timing was not the best; many commentators felt that the original theme of the Fair in 1939, "Building the World of Tomorrow," had soured. In somber acknowledgment of the world situation, the 1940 edition of the Fair was renamed "For Peace and Freedom."

With the war spreading into other countries, many Americans seemed to feel that the upcoming holiday season would be the last truly peaceful one for a long time. And as "Gesù Bambino" had instantly struck a chord in the public consciousness during wartime 1917, so it did in 1940; when the *Times* listed the Christmas music being offered in New York churches, Yon's name showed up an extraordinary thirty-two times (most of them, offerings of "Gesù Bambino"). Midnight Mass at St. Patrick's featured Nicola Moscona and the usual Cathedral choristers; but the next day, the Cathedral Quartet had to be on call for a 9:00 A.M. broadcast of "Solemn Mass, from the Holy Name Mission for Homeless Men."

Not long after that, Yon was briefly hospitalized for what was probably hypertension, resulting in the inevitable advice to slow down. He incorporated a nap into his daily routine, but otherwise the advice was ignored. Yon was isolated from the Italian branch of his family and worried (as did all fathers of young men) about the possibility of America's entering the war, and his only coping mechanism was that of work. He threw himself into more recital activity. It wasn't enough to occupy him. He wrote a hymn for the liturgical procession of the Ninth National Eucharistic Congress in St. Paul: "Our Eucharistic Lord" was sung by the 80,000 participants. It still wasn't enough to occupy him. Finally, he decided to go into business—as a manufacturer of sporting goods.

While he had always been enthusiastic about golf, playing was nearly impossible in the terrain of his hometown of Settimo. Sometime during a vacation in the mid-1930s, he had dreamed up an alternative and named it Kangaroo Golf, utilizing wooden pegs dubbed "kangaroos" rather than golf balls, along with block-shaped wooden tees, wickets, markers, and, to carry the "kangaroos," what *Time* described as "a canvas pouch not unlike a carpenter's apron. . . ." Yon formed a company to manufacture Kangaroo Golf sets. They were available at several locations, among them the Fifth Avenue department store B. Altman ($12.50 plus shipping). Kangaroo Golf, Inc., produced a brochure describing the game and featuring testimonials from enthusiastic Kangaroo Golf players, among them such sporting figures as film actor Roland Hayes, soprano Gladys Swarthout, and the loyal Martinelli. Kangaroo Golf didn't catch on to replace regular golf, but it was a good try. In any event, Yon had no intention of giving up his day job.*

That June, Ignace Jan Paderewski—lionized pianist, also Poland's one-time president, living in New York exile at the Buckingham Hotel—died of pneumonia. Because of his dual position as musical legend and national leader, his funeral was not only musically distinguished but carried off with full military honors; his casket was loaded onto a horse-drawn caisson and brought to Pennsylvania Station, there to proceed to Washington and burial at Arlington National Cemetery. During his funeral, the full Cathedral choir performed

> some of Paderewski's favorite music, specially selected by Pietro Yon. . . . Paderewski's own Nocturne was played by Mr. Yon at the organ as a prelude. Don Lorenzo Perosi's mass, which Paderewski had admired, was sung by the choir of eighteen voices, and was broadcast by short wave to all countries. . . . [T]he organist played the Chopin Funeral March, prominent in Paderewski's own repertoire, and the coffin was carried out.

Yon played at St. Patrick's that summer; in October, the Cathedral men were involved in the Mission Sunday broadcast for NBC, same as the year before. The Christmas season was approaching, but most people were waiting for the world's powers to decide on their next move.

---

* It was around this time that a discouraged young man wrote to Yon, whom he had never met, asking if there was any point in pursuing a career in music. Yon replied with a sympathetic letter stating, in effect, that the act of making music was vital to a musician—but also pointing out that, in his mid-50s, he himself had just started a new, completely nonmusical business, and that giving free rein to all of one's interests was always something to be encouraged.

December 7, 1941, would be the second Sunday of Advent. The *Times* announced the day before that the sermon at the following day's 11:00 A.M. Mass would be delivered by the Reverend Leon Harvey on "Christ's Advent Through Mary." At 4:00 P.M., Father Woods was scheduled to speak on "Christ Our Saviour."

But well before the start of that day's Vespers, New Yorkers would be glued to any available radio, listening to reports of the air attack on Pearl Harbor.

World War and Homefront Loss

The headlines said it all: ENTIRE CITY PUT ON WAR FOOTING, also CITY CALM AND GRIM AS THE WAR WIDENS. Some of the initial coverage involved St. Patrick's. Two days after the United States declared war on Japan, New York held its first air raid drill and the *Times* reported its effect upon the city's churches. While Riverside Church had a minister assigned to a bullhorn for crowd control and First Presbyterian announced that the upcoming Sunday sermon would be entitled "How to Act in Air Raids," Monsignor Flannelly explained the St. Patrick's position: "Once the clergy start a mass in the Catholic Church it must be finished. . . . [Monsignor Flannelly] was in the middle of a mass at the cathedral Wednesday morning during the air raid alarm and it was not interrupted. . . . [I]t was said that Roman Catholic congregations were free to leave a mass at any time, though the clergy at the altar were not." Not that Cathedral security was lax: ID cards—ADMIT ONE TO CHOIRLOFT—were required for entrance to the gallery. Yon himself had a card. Across its width he had written PERMANENT.

As Archbishop Spellman (who was Military Vicar of the United States Armed Forces) and St. Patrick's plunged instantly into the war effort, so did Pietro Yon. When the Archbishop blessed the National Catholic Community Service Clubhouse in December, Yon brought along a quartet to make music for the occasion. Only days after that came the era's first wartime Christmas, with all of the city's churches determined to provide a familiar, comforting holiday—one headline read 'AS USUAL' PLACARD OUT FOR CHRISTMAS. The music was up to its usual standard, but there was a difference in the markedly increased number of uniforms conspicuous in the Cathedral during every service.

In early 1942, Mario Yon claimed one of those uniforms by enlisting in the army. Mario's father attempted to enlist as well. Pietro Yon had been a 1917 recruit at the time of the first World War but had been discharged when it was discovered that he had a "floating kidney." Now, at age fifty-five, he tried again. His offer of military service was appreciated but rejected, with thanks. He would be far more effective in serving the country from his Cathedral post.

Yon's worries over his son would be compounded, in a nonmilitary way, when Mario wanted him to meet Gloria San Venero. Not exactly to "meet" her: Gloria was the daughter of Francesca Yon's closest friend, and Pietro had known her since her birth. But Mario and Gloria had become seriously involved and were thinking of marriage. Yon responded in his usual ways. First, he invited Gloria to dinner; then, he sneaked a whoopee cushion onto her dining chair. They instantly became friends.*

Early 1942 was a punishing time for the United States because so much of the news was negative. From Italy, there was no news at all. Yon finally became worried enough to contact Archbishop Amleto Giovanni Cicognani, Apostolic Delegate to the United States in Washington. The Vatican was maintaining a neutral position in the war; perhaps the Archbishop could help in getting a cable through.

> I am extremely sorry to disturb Your Excellency, but I must beg you to please help me to get news to and from my beloved family in Italy. . . .
> I pray that my plea may be granted as the hardest thing in life is indeed to be cut off from the family.

Cicognani replied only five days later:

> I have received your letter of February 22nd, and have already sent a cable message through the Vatican, including the text as written by you.
> The cost of this cable amounts to $4.21.

Yon did what he could for the war effort by making himself and his singers available for myriad benefits and ceremonial appearances such as the "Make-Believe Peace Party" sponsored by the Catholic Writers Guild

---

* Gloria became considerably closer to Mario when she followed him to his army post near Kansas City, where they were married. When Yon heard the news, he wrote the newlyweds a letter: "Gloria, you may have come in through the window instead of the door. Nevertheless, you are family and I love you."

and the dedication of a new wing for St. Clare's Hospital. After a Holy Week made more strenuous in the heightened emotional climate, Yon and the Male Soloist Ensemble trekked over to WQXR's studio after the Easter Sunday Vespers to give an evening broadcast. And one Sunday evening involved, after Vespers, two special Masses—one at 5:00 and one at 7:30, each one broadcast on a different station.

As well, there was the Grand Gala Concert and Children's Summer Fund Benefit, held at Carnegie Hall for the Sons of Italy. Many Italian-Americans were mortified by Italy's position in the war; one news article noted that "pictures of Mussolini were taken from store windows or turned to the wall" in Italian neighborhoods. Yon joined Martinelli and a clutch of Met singers including Licia Albanese and Salvatore Baccaloni, with Giuseppe Bamboschek at the podium, to offer topflight music along with some cheerful fundraising. However, as concert time neared it was decided to use the occasion to honor fifteen Italian-American servicemen who were missing in action. What was originally a light evening became something very different as the names of the missing servicemen were announced and their relatives filed up to the stage. Nearly all of the women were dressed in black; nearly everyone on the stage was in tears.

Even a supposedly private event could become a lightning rod for public feeling. In early November, Broadway legend George M. Cohan died of cancer. Along with his prodigious output of more than fifty plays and musicals, he had written the song "Over There," so much the rallying cry of the First World War—and still being played in 1942—that Cohan had received a Congressional Gold Medal. His funeral at St. Patrick's caused a mob scene, with 4,000 people packed into the Cathedral and another 2,000 standing outside. Cohan had been an extroverted actor but an unusually private individual; although there were 100 honorary pallbearers, during the funeral no eulogy was read. Nevertheless, as the coffin passed, Pietro Yon gave Cohan his own tribute—a soft, haunting organ improvisation based upon "Over There."

The Cathedral College students who had always functioned as Yon's volunteers were moving either into accelerated ordination or various branches of the service; but the members of the Male Soloist Ensemble were for the most part far beyond military age. Leo de Hierapolis, who had sung with Yon since 1915, left St. Patrick's in 1940. Even though Carl Schlegel was still on the payroll as a Cathedral soloist, he was in his 60s, ailing, and had sharply curtailed his involvement. Two baritones came in as replacements: Gerard Gelinas, who had been an early semifinalist (but not a winner) on the "Metropolitan Opera Auditions of the Air"; and Rosario Tremblay, who showed up as a Cathedral soloist but did little singing elsewhere. Both men were gone within a couple of seasons.

That year's Midnight Mass, along with every other aspect of New York nightlife, was being conducted according to "dimout" regulations designed to avoid the glare that might turn a city into a target. The exterior of St. Patrick's was plunged into darkness as surrounding street lights were fitted with hoods to direct their light downward, turning the structure into a looming hulk against the night sky. Inside the Cathedral, the *Times* noted, almost nothing had changed except for "many more men and women in uniform in evidence." Yon even programmed the *Mass of the Shepherds* as he had the year before.

It might have been a measure of expediency—he had programmed it for Advent—because his schedule was as heavy as it ever had been. There were Cathedral duties, war-related duties, and compositional duties. His mass *Thy Kingdom Come* had been sung at the Cathedral the previous June, and another Mass setting, *Fortitudo Martyrum*, was ready by February 1943. Additionally, Yon had family duties. His new daughter-in-law had suffered a miscarriage, after which she had returned east to live with her parents for the duration. Gloria spent a great deal of time with Yon and his sister, visiting for regular lessons—not in music, but in chess. Father- and daughter-in-law became very close during this period.

Early 1943 would be a particularly crowded time, with "Navy Church Sunday" being followed by another Polish Mass (this one offered in commemoration of war dead). As for Lent and Holy Week, the Cathedral would make an effort to accommodate the vast numbers of wartime swing-shift workers by expanding its schedule—on Good Friday, worshipers would be able to choose from *two* three-hour "Agony" services, at noon and 7:00 P.M., each one complete with music and Monsignor Sheen's commentary. And on April 4, the Male Soloist Ensemble gave another Sunday evening broadcast on WQXR.

Five days after the broadcast, Yon lunched with his sister and then retired for his afternoon nap. She heard a thud and entered her brother's room to find him lying on the floor, unable to move or speak. Badly frightened, she instantly called the house physician; when the man came to the Yon apartment, he found not only Yon in distress, but Lina Yon in the throes of a massive heart attack. Within fifteen minutes she was dead.

Pietro Yon had suffered a stroke that paralyzed his entire right side. The city's press said nothing about it at the time. The *Times* printed an obituary for Lina Yon that carefully sidestepped her brother's illness, then waited until Easter Sunday to mention it in any detail:

> For the first time in more than fifteen years, Mr. Yon, musical director of the cathedral and honorary organist of the Vatican, was not at the great organ on Easter Sunday. He is seriously ill in Columbus Hospital. Edward Rivetti, his assistant, played and directed.

As time passed and it became apparent that Yon's recovery might take months, it was decided to move him from Columbus Hospital to the Long Island home of Gloria's parents for long-term care in a better atmosphere.

Rivetti was handling the end of the choir season, but it was unquestionably a two-man job and some provision would have to be made. Even so, with the news of Yon's illness an open secret, St. Patrick's began to receive unsolicited applications from organists who wanted to replace him—some of them coming as early as the week after he was hospitalized. One such application came from Yon's ex-assistant Paolo Giaquinto, an extraordinary letter:

> In the event that there be a vacancy for an organist and choir master owing to the sickness of Maestro Yon, for whose recovery I fervently pray, I beg to apply for consideration. The needs of the Cathedral choir are well known to me and I do not hesitate to submit my qualifications, conscious as I am of my abilities and experience. . . . [I]n your Cathedral I was Chancel organist for many years. . . . I would gladly dedicate my life to such a glorious task irrespective of time and sacrifice and feel in my humility that I could give you full satisfaction. Awaiting the honor of a personal interview and more detailed information of mutual interest, I beg to remain. . . .

Monsignor Flannelly answered each applicant with a short and coldly pointed note stating that, at the moment, there was no vacancy. Yon's doctor was cautiously optimistic, and those at the Cathedral were taking a wait-and-see attitude.

That summer, Yon made some gains that were reported not in the New York press but in the national music journals. The June *Catholic Choirmaster* described him as "slightly better from a critical illness," and that same month's *Diapason* reported "news from his bedside which indicates that he is making slow but sure gains. . . . He is still paralyzed on the right side and cannot speak, but the doctor feels that it won't be long until he will be talking." However, as September approached it became apparent that Yon's recovery wouldn't be that rapid or, unfortunately, that complete. The Cathedral would need to consider a replacement, at least until Yon might be able to resume his duties.

Charles Courboin and Yon had for decades maintained a friendship based not only on professional respect but on mutual understanding—the kind of friendship in which Courboin would always be sure to spend the day with Yon, after the death of Francesca, on the date of Yon's wedding anniversary. He had spent more than three decades crammed with recital activity and organ design consultations. Lately he had been shuttling between Baltimore, heading the organ department of the Peabody Conservatory, and New York, where he had for eight years been giving weekly broadcasts on WOR. He understood the situation. And he was currently without a church position.*

On October 2, most of the city's papers announced that Dr. Charles-Marie Courboin had been appointed to St. Patrick's "for the duration of the illness of Pietro Yon." Courboin played at the next day's Mass, beginning with a Bach fugue.

In its coverage of Courboin's appointment, *The Diapason* reported that "latest reports indicate a gradual improvement" in Yon's condition. But it wouldn't last. During that month and the next, Yon's condition worsened. Early on the morning of November 22—the Feast of St. Cecilia—he died.

His funeral took place on the 25th, attended by a congregation of more than 1,300. Toscanini was there; so were the many anonymous musicians, as well as nonmusicians, who felt touched by Yon's work. And there were clergy from the Cathedral and nearly every other church in the city. Courboin led the choir, which included not only the Male Soloist Ensemble but a number of former members, in Yon's own *Mass of Requiem*. A *Daily News* photo showed the recessional as the coffin passed: pallbearers including Mario Yon, Constantino Yon, and Martinelli; choirmen lined up on either side, faces contorted in an effort to maintain self-control.

---

* Courboin's son, Robert, related another factor: that Yon was able, during this period, to indicate his own preference of Courboin as a successor.

The *Times* wrote, "At the conclusion of the mass, the choir sang the lament from the Tenebrae of Good Friday, 'O all ye that pass by this way,' to music composed by Mr. Yon."

End of an Era

Pietro Yon's time at St. Patrick's had been bracketed by national catastrophes—the Depression at the beginning, World War II at the end. Still, he had prevailed handsomely.

His spectacular celebrity had occurred in a time when the organ was a popular instrument, choral music hadn't yet been labeled as "longhair," and the rise of jazz hadn't engulfed the world's musical perceptions. But the same media culture that had vaulted Yon and the St. Patrick's choir to fame had changed musical tastes in less than a generation. A popular organist had once been Pietro Yon, playing Bach and his own works; now a popular organist would be nightclub performer Ethel Smith, playing "Tico-Tico." And the Cathedral Choir would henceforth be pigeonholed as "church music," replaced in the public's affections by the semi-pop repertoire of Norman Luboff and Roger Wagner. Yon had engineered a glamour time, a golden period for music at St. Patrick's; but his achievement could never be duplicated.

The next years in the world of classical music were swamped by modernism, during which Yon's insistently melodic output would fade from esteem. The *Musical News and Herald* wrote that he was "known rather by trifling piffle than by his really meritorious Sonata Chromatica," and *Commonweal* suggested that his works fell "into the 'greasy' classification."

Pietro Yon had enjoyed the media machine and used it to great effect, but it had a tendency to instantly swallow the memory of those same people it had once vaunted. In 1947, writer Patty de Roulf penned *Sonata Romantica*, a scenario for a film biography based on Yon's life story. It didn't sell.

Pietro A. Yon, during his Cathedral years.

Shortly before Christmas 1929, the *Morning World* gathered Yon's brand-new Cathedral Choir (including the Male Soloist Ensemble, his boy choristers, and volunteers from the Cathedral Club Choir) for a photo—taken only weeks after the stock market crash that would plunge the nation into the Great Depression.

The Kilgen Organ Company snapped a publicity photo of the newly installed gallery organ in the rebuilt gallery—a view that gives a workout to amateur detectives. Note that the organ may be there, but the choir stalls aren't . . . proving that the picture must have been taken in the last weeks of December 1929. (Non-detectives simply can note the holiday wreaths hung on each column, which also provide a clue.)

Assistant Organist (and right hand) Edward Rivetti (*left*) in Yon's studio, watching his teacher in action. (*Courtesy of Dianne Rivetti*)

Yon and his men broadcast for NBC with radio hosts Monsignor Thomas McDonnell (*left*) and Archbishop Spellman (*right*) on Mission Sunday 1941. Less than two months later, Pearl Harbor would be attacked and the nation swept into World War II. (*Courtesy of Loretta Yon Schoen*)

Chapter 5

THE MORE THINGS CHANGE (1943-70)

> He is first and foremost musician, but he combines with that the roles
> of aviator, motorist, speed-boat pilot, mechanic and fond father. One's
> first impression of Mr. Courboin is of great virility. He is a tall man,
> broad-shouldered and slim-hipped. His face, vivid and animated in con-
> versation, in repose is that of the vision-seer, the dreamer, the idealist.
>
> Press kit for Charles-Marie Courboin

For the leadership of its music, St. Patrick's had traveled a cir-
cuitous path from the days of the modest William Pecher to the reclusive
James Ungerer to the ebullient Pietro Yon. Now it would encounter the
more complicated personality of Charles Courboin.

In a way, Courboin was a perfect successor to Pietro Yon because they
shared not only similar traits but similar histories. Like Yon, Courboin
had been a *wunderkind*, organist of Antwerp Cathedral at age sixteen and
an enthusiastically received virtuoso recitalist in various high-powered
European locales. After arriving in the United States, he worked at a
number of churches in New York and Pennsylvania, breaking up his duties with an extremely heavy schedule of concert activity and—very unusual for "serious" organists of that period, but something that Pietro
Yon had also tried—even a stint as a theater organist in Buffalo. Both men
had married their students (and Mabel Courboin had been a talented
enough organist to work at church positions of her own). His abilities
had garnered him his own mark of royal favor, Knight of the Order of
the Crown of Belgium. Yon was a prankster; Courboin was a walking
encyclopedia of jokes, rhymes, and limericks, blue or otherwise. As a
performer, Yon would do anything rather than disappoint an audience;
Courboin obviously agreed. At least once while he was driving to a recital, his love of speed (one of his cars had been rebuilt to accommodate

an airplane engine) had resulted in a pre-performance crackup. Bandages and all, he showed up and delivered the goods.

And while some other organists may have had Yon's talent, few of them had the same happily productive relationship with the media. Courboin was one of them. In 1937, he had been asked by Mrs. Eugene du Pont to play for the wedding of her daughter Ethel to President Roosevelt's son Franklin Jr. This produced a sheaf of press and radio coverage, all of which Courboin seemed to enjoy (assuring reporters that there would be "no swing music" at the ceremony, confirming that his pre-ceremony selections included not only Bach but the president's favorite, "Anchors Aweigh," chuckling over the fact that security protocol insisted he be driven to the church with a police escort), and it snowballed into his very own "Talk of the Town" interview for *The New Yorker*. The between-the-lines tone told almost more than the column itself, on one hand describing his musical talent and the hundred-plus organs that he had designed, but playfully contrasting the musician with the bon vivant as it told of his pilot's license, his slight Belgian accent, his physical appearance, and his invention of the Courboin cocktail: "Dubonnet, Amer Picon, and grenadine, in we forget what proportions."

This kind of publicity prompted a number of people, primarily those who didn't work at St. Patrick's, to think of Courboin as a duplicate Yon. Not quite. There were plenty of differences between the men, but some of them were subtle. For instance, Courboin didn't share the ultra-focused personality of his predecessor. Pietro Yon often spent leisure hours in composition or finicking practice, either at the Cathedral or his Carnegie Hall studio; but Charles Courboin, who lived far uptown in the Washington Heights section of Manhattan, preferred to spend his downtime on 69th Street at the arts-and-luxury Lotos Club. Yon's closest relationships were with his family members; Charles and Mabel Courboin maintained their tightest personal bond with lifelong friends Firmin Swinnen and his wife, Augusta.* And then there was the issue of authority: Yon had always

---

* Swinnen was a fellow Belgian who had also played at Antwerp Cathedral; in the United States, he had made his considerable fame as organist at the Rivoli Theatre, as well as at Longwood Gardens, the spectacular arboretum Pierre du Pont had developed near Philadelphia. The two couples were so close that they had bought a quadruple cemetery plot.

had some trouble maintaining discipline during rehearsals, while Courboin radiated an air of power which guaranteed that he had only to walk into the gallery to create order. The Cathedral College students might be in mid-spitball, but a single glance from Dr. Courboin could stun them into obedient silence.

Certainly Yon and Courboin handled the matter of publicity in very different ways once they were installed at St. Patrick's. Throughout his tenure, Yon had continued to maintain his publicist as well as his clipping service. But Courboin—the man whose press kit had once appeared to belong more to a silent-screen star than to an organist—seemed to turn his back on the image he had so carefully crafted. Once Courboin was functioning at the Cathedral, his name almost never appeared in the "celebrity" columns.

As part of his Cathedral equipage, he was inheriting the Kilgen organ, built as it had been to Yon's specifications; it wasn't much to his taste, but any changes would have to wait because of cost and wartime restrictions. He was also inheriting the Cathedral College forces, significantly reduced because of war; the Male Soloist Ensemble, which would remain virtually intact in its personnel although instantly and forever losing its title (henceforth it would be known, less imposingly, as the Men's Choir); and a nonexistent boychoir. The Cathedral School had closed in 1942, victim of its own neighborhood's change from residential to commercial. That had ended the next-door stream of boys available to sing at St. Patrick's. As a result, the boychoir had disbanded during Yon's last year.

Additionally, Courboin was inheriting the implacably loyal Serafino Bogatto, singing (no longer first tenor; he would move steadily down, all the way to the bass section), acting as emergency organist, and conducting—in the 1941–42 season, he had prepared the choristers for Erno Rapee's Radio City performance of the Mahler *Eighth Symphony*. (Some of those choristers had been Cathedral boys. A *Times* publicity photo showed Rapee conducting them while Bogatto stood by, his tight-lipped expression daring them to make the slightest mistake.)* And as chancel organist there was the equally loyal Eddie Rivetti, who had more than proven the full extent of his worth during the last months of Yon's life. But Rivetti had recently received his draft notice. While he was in the

---

* Bogatto even did some composing, writing a setting of "Haec Dies" that was used at nearly every Easter of Courboin's tenure.

process of being rated and re-rated for service, Courboin let it be known that he had a new permanent assistant ready and waiting should Rivetti go to war. (No names were named, but most likely this was organist Gérard Caron, a Canadian who had come to New York on a governmental grant to study with Courboin and had proven himself valuable enough that he was quickly slapped onto the Cathedral's substitute list.) Archbishop Spellman countered by himself making it plain that, no matter how long Rivetti might serve in the military, and whoever might function as his substitute during that time, his job at St. Patrick's would be waiting for him upon his return.

But those were issues to be addressed in the year to come. Courboin's first major Cathedral assignment, after conducting Pietro Yon's funeral, would be to pay tribute to his memory at the "Month's Mind" service scheduled for December 23. Midnight Mass would take place less than thirty-six hours later. Courboin acknowledged that he was replacing a prolific and beloved figure, as well as a close friend, by programming his own favorites but inserting "Gesù Bambino" at each and every Christmas service. The *Times* wrote on Christmas morning: "For the first time the music for the Christmas mass was under the direction of Dr. Charles M. Courboin, recently appointed organist and choir director at St. Patrick's, succeeding the late Pietro Yon, who died several weeks ago."

A single glance at the *Times* music listings for that season told of a definite change in house routine—and illustrated the single most important difference between Yon and Courboin. Pietro Yon had been the prodigious organist who was besotted with vocal beauty, both solo and choral, and had gone to extraordinary lengths to make the Cathedral a prime setting for its display. Charles Courboin, however, was more purely an organist. A prodigious one, without a doubt, tagged "last of the heroic organists" fairly early in his career. But his own musical language and strengths emanated from the console, not the choir stalls. Hence it was no surprise that, from the moment he began, the Cathedral's musical identity—the "signature sound"—changed. The choral repertoire list became shorter, more iterative, and considerably leaner in its vocal imperatives. The opera-stars-as-guest-soloists immediately vanished. Virtually all solo work would come from within the ranks of the choir, there would be less of it, and the singers who rendered those solos would be far less likely to see their names set before the public. Very quickly, the musical identity of St. Patrick's became that not of a choirmaster's but of an organist's church.

None of this was to say that Courboin was uninformed when it came to choral performance; rehearsals of the Men's Choir were as detailed as they always had been, if not quite as deferential to the choirmaster. At one session, a particular phrase hadn't been coming out to Courboin's satisfaction. Although he was no trained vocalist, he ventured to demonstrate what he wanted by singing it. "There," he said with a smile of pride, turning to the senior member of the bass section. "What do you think of *that*, Signor Scala?"

Raimondo Scala replied gallantly, "Maestro, you have a beautiful voice. Just not for *singing*."

Then there was the matter of composition. Whatever his predecessors had done, Courboin hadn't been playing coy with *The New Yorker* when he shrugged off the idea of writing his own music. (One of the few times that he did, confecting the theme for his own radio series, *The American Organist* wrote dishearteningly, "Here's a lovely piece of music, but what can you do with it?") As programming was announced for Easter 1944, Courboin matter-of-factly scheduled *five* pieces by Pietro Yon but penned nothing himself. Throughout his entire tenure at the Cathedral, his own name would rarely, if ever, show up in composer listings.

It might seem that St. Patrick's was renouncing its former commitment to a high-profile musical program, and in a way it was. After two years of round-the-clock effort and crushing war news, the conflict was at last turning toward Allied victory. Americans were more heavily involved than ever, including New Yorkers and everyone at the Cathedral: Archbishop Spellman himself would be absent for months at a time, making repeated and physically punishing trips around the world to minister to the fighting troops. Perhaps in reaction to the emotional strain, popular culture in 1944 craved escapism and sentiment—*Going My Way* was one of the hit movies of the year, and some bandleaders reported that GIs were requesting "White Christmas" instead of swing tunes. Many visitors came to St. Patrick's hoping for music that could comfort rather than challenge them; Courboin's programming might have seemed unusually chaste a decade earlier, but now it fit perfectly. When former Governor Alfred E. Smith's wife, Catherine, died in the spring of 1944, at her funeral the Cathedral Choir sang primarily Gregorian chant.

Much of the music department's time during that year and the next would be channeled into the task of supplying music for an extraordinary number of wartime weddings, a phenomenon that was repeated at nearly every church in New York. (While St. Patrick's didn't claim a record-breaking total of nuptials, the Church of the Transfiguration reported that it was their heaviest year ever.) Compared with the usual splashiness of a Cathedral wedding, many of these ceremonies were very small affairs; some were performed under a time crunch, while others had to show ingenuity in order to overcome wartime shortages. With gasoline rationed to three gallons per person per week, one bride got around the problem by driving herself to the Cathedral in a horse and buggy.

One wartime wedding would be more lavish than any other that year, at least musically. Rivetti had been deemed eligible for military service in early 1944 and joined the navy. One of his first leaves came the first week of May, when he headed straight back to St. Patrick's to play for that Sunday; a couple of months after, he returned for another leave, this time to be married in his local Paterson church. The entire Cathedral music department was there, with Courboin playing and the Men's Choir singing, and many of the guests were part of the New York sacred music scene. Rivetti's brother (also a serviceman) was best man, which prompted a snag in the ceremony when his military flight home encountered a two-hour delay. It was an extremely hot July day and the guests might quickly have become miserable, but they were happily distracted as the St. Patrick's forces, Courboin, and the other guests pitched in to give an impromptu concert until the best man finally could get to the wedding.

Some of the Cathedral singers were new employees, as the Men's Choir experienced its first major personnel changes in a long time. A surprise had come during the spring when Jan Van Bommel tendered his resignation from St. Patrick's after nearly thirty years of service, pulling up his New York stakes in order to head to California where he had an offer "coaching singers at Metro-Goldwyn-Mayer" (reported *Catholic News*).* There was also the loss of Carl Schlegel, whose health issues had

---

* Quite likely the MGM job didn't work out. As they did with performing talent, film studios frequently offered prospective coaches six-month contracts with no guaranteed renewal. By the late 1940s, Van Bommel was functioning on the West Coast exactly as he had functioned in New York, as baritone soloist for various

kept him from the Cathedral since well before Yon had suffered his stroke. Monsignor Flannelly had retained him on the payroll in the hope that he could return, but his illness only worsened, and he would spend his final months in an area nursing home before his death the following year. As Courboin would find, those particular vacancies would be extraordinarily hard to fill.

With Rivetti off to war, Courboin lost even more coverage when Gérard Caron left the Cathedral to take a full-time job at the French-speaking Church of St. Vincent de Paul. Bogatto could plug some of the resulting holes in the schedule but not all of them, and it became obvious that someone would have to be found to take the position of chancel organist for the duration. After some hectic months, it was finally agreed—halfway through Holy Week—to bring in temporary help. Albin McDermott (regularly organist at Bishop Donahue's Church of the Holy Name) and Patrick Daley had been two of the previous applicants for Yon's job; a memo handwritten on Lotos Club stationery states that they would play some scheduled Masses and Vespers. (An asterisk at the bottom of the memo carefully specifies "During Mr. Rivetti's absence.")

Nonetheless, a shuttle of temporary organists would help no one. Going back to the list of applicants, Courboin hit upon Brooklyn-based Charles Lauria. He was not only good, he was available—and he was amenable to the notion of working at St. Patrick's as a long-term employee who would then give up his place upon Rivetti's return. He agreed to start in the fall, at the beginning of the 1944–45 season. That settled, Courboin went off to vacation, leaving Bogatto to conduct, and McDermott to play, during that summer's record-shattering heat wave.

The major events of the period had little to do with music. Americans had been tensely awaiting news of the Allied invasion of Normandy, and the commencement of D-Day was jarringly confirmed for New Yorkers on June 6 as bells began to ring from St. Luke's Lutheran Church at 4:00 A.M. Even in the pre-dawn hours, worried crowds made their way to city houses of worship to pray for the safe return of their loved ones; hundreds poured into St. Patrick's even before the first scheduled Mass at 7:00 A.M., and before the end of that day 75,000 people had streamed through the Cathedral.

---

churches and choral societies. At his death in 1960, *Variety*'s obituary didn't even mention the studio.

For New Yorkers, the concentration on war news was interrupted in October when Al Smith died exactly five months after the death of his wife. "The Happy Warrior" had been not only a wildly popular figure among the city's residents but also a Papal Chamberlain and a devout communicant at St. Patrick's. Archbishop Spellman accorded him the honor of lying in repose in the Lady Chapel with instructions that the Cathedral would be kept open as long as visitors came to pay their respects. For the funeral Mass, the *Herald Tribune* reported, the men sang the Perosi *Missa di Requiem*; as Smith's coffin was carried out of the Cathedral, Courboin played the Guilmant "Marche Funèbre."

That holiday season was a high-strung time, as the end of the war was tantalizingly in sight, yet uncertain. Courboin and the Men's Choir had extra duty; the Archbishop, himself a poet, had written a piece for the occasion, "A Prayer for Children." WOR broadcast his reading of the poem at 10:00 P.M. on Christmas Eve, accompanied by the choir's singing. Courboin and the choir then proceeded directly to the tasks of 11:30 carols, broadcast on WMCA, then back to WOR for Midnight Mass itself. Then on to Christmas morning and, finally, the holiday's Vespers.

The year 1945 alternated between unbearable stress and exaltation. With the war in its final stage, rumors of imminent victory had been circulating for months; but they were suddenly forgotten when President Franklin D. Roosevelt, only recently inaugurated for an unprecedented fourth term, died in April of a massive cerebral hemorrhage. As did many of the nation's churches, the Cathedral responded with a votive Mass, sung to an overflow-capacity congregation. At the conclusion of the service Courboin played "Taps" followed by the national anthem, both pieces in muted renditions that were received by mourners who stood in silence with bowed heads.

New Yorkers were so anxious to look forward to a day of celebration that the city's houses of worship were making preparations far in advance. The *Times* wrote in April:

> Extensive arrangements have been made by the city's churches and synagogues to be on the alert for announcement of V-E Day and ready to throw open their doors for special services at hours as yet unannounced in many cases. . . .
>
> Te Deum, the universal prayer of thanksgiving of the Roman Catholic Church, will be sung after a mass of thanksgiving at 12:15 p.m. on V-E Day at St. Patrick's Cathedral.

(For that matter, since the previous October the Cathedral had displayed a schedule of V-E Day thanksgiving Masses, set to take place on a date that no one could predict.)

When they finally occurred, V-E Day and (later that summer) V-J Day resembled each other as every incoming report of victory drew immense crowds into Times Square, gathering around the fifty-five-foot-tall replica of the Statue of Liberty that had stood before the Times Building for the past year as a symbol of the War Bond program. On V-E Day, a *Times* reporter was struck by the contrast between the unrestrained party atmosphere in Times Square and—notwithstanding the scheduled thanksgiving services—the anxiety displayed inside St. Patrick's:

> Many were smiling, but others cried softly as they knelt in prayer. A few women were in mourning. There was joy in the realization that the war in Europe was over, but it was tempered with the sobering knowledge of its price in blood and of the enemy still to be defeated.
>
> One woman leaving the cathedral summed up the general feeling when she said to a companion: "This is no celebration for me. My kid is still in danger."

V-J Day rumors began several days in advance of any official news, and by Sunday, August 12, the tension was excruciating. The *Times* reported that Archbishop Spellman waited during that morning's Mass for some definite word, "ready to read his special peace prayer that had been read throughout the Roman Catholic Archdiocese on V-E Day"; at the other end of the Cathedral, Serafino Bogatto waited with the summer choir, ready to launch into the "Te Deum." No announcement came, no "Te Deum" was sung, and the Archbishop had to leave after Mass on a previously planned trip to the Pacific war theaters.

When President Harry S. Truman finally made his official announcement of the war's end, it was Tuesday evening. No organist and no singers were on the premises at the time.

Postwar Music for a New Cardinal

Those with long memories could recall Pietro Yon's first days at the Cathedral, his well-delineated plans for the music program. The general expectation was that the postwar calm would allow Courboin to implement his own plans. However, it didn't work that smoothly.

The neighborhood surrounding St. Patrick's was continuing its inexorable change from residential to commercial, evidenced by the plot just north of the Cathedral, which had held variously the Boys' Orphan Asylum, a private home, and the Union Club. Now it was being redeveloped by the retailer Best and Company for its new department store. While blasting for the foundation was taking place, a one-hundred-pound piece of the Cathedral's stone trim shook loose from the percussion and fell to the sidewalk. Worshipers were uninjured; but the Cathedral's organ, which had been repeatedly jolted along with the Cathedral, was less lucky. Courboin's first task upon returning from vacation was to contact the Kilgen Company in the late summer of 1945 for repairs both immediate and long-term.

The damaged organ may have contributed to the fact that the music of St. Patrick's seemed to go through a fallow period. That autumn saw the death of tenor John McCormack; his memorial at the Cathedral made little mention of the music. Press coverage of Christmas services had more to say of the scaffolding over the newly damaged Cathedral façade than it did of Courboin or the choir.

But two days before Christmas 1945, the musicians experienced a moment of out-and-out magnificence. For most of the year, rumors had been circulating that Archbishop Spellman might be named Papal Secretary. Before the morning Mass on December 23, Spellman heard other and far more thrilling news: he had been nominated Cardinal. Courboin's choirmen got to be the very first Cathedral representatives to announce this to the congregation, of course musically: As the Archbishop approached the altar at the beginning of Mass, the Men's Choir replaced the scheduled processional with "Ecce Sacerdos." Only a few worshipers caught on. It was a moment later that Monsignor Flannelly clarified the situation for the benefit of the nonmusical public—"Within the last two hours we have received from the Eternal City news of the nomination to the College of Cardinals of four Americans, one of whom is our own Archbishop."

After the Mass ended, Spellman returned to his residence to greet well-wishers and the press.

[H]e was again greeted with "Ecce Sacerdos Magnus" sung by the cathedral choir as a spontaneous gesture. After the serenade Cardinal-designate Spellman shook hands with Dr. Charles M. Courboin, director, and the members of the choir, expressing thanks for "all you have done" for the cathedral.

Archbishop Spellman headed to Rome the following February for his elevation. When he returned the first week of March, the new Cardinal was greeted not only in two full-dress services at St. Patrick's but in a ceremony at the Met—so crowded that seats had to be set up in the orchestra pit. (He began his address by wryly observing, "In my wildest flights of imagination, I have never pictured myself on the stage of the Metropolitan Opera House.") Courboin and the Men's Choir (and Rivetti, who had been discharged from the navy in December) were on hand to provide music. For added luster they were assisted by radio soprano Jessica Dragonette, not only a media megastar but a friend of both Spellman's and Courboin's who had been honored by Pope Pius XII with the Holy Cross *Pro Pontifice et Ecclesia*.

Among the clerics who had accompanied the Cardinal to Rome had been Father William T. Greene, a recent transfer from the Church of the Holy Cross. Since the previous year, he had become a fixture at St. Patrick's, known for his provocative and timely sermons. He had a musical bent, enough so that the Cardinal named him chairman of the Archdiocesan Committee on Church Music. He was astute in matters of publicity as well, arranging a concert of Met stars to benefit the Marianite Sisters of the Holy Cross. His speaking style was sufficiently attractive that, when WNEW broadcast the Cardinal's message "The Meaning of Christmas," he read it on the air himself. He was becoming not only a trusted confidante of the Cardinal's but a musical force at the Cathedral, named Moderator of the Choir. So it was no surprise that he began to put forth various ideas to extend the scope of music at St. Patrick's.

Whatever Courboin thought of Father Greene's ideas, he didn't immediately deal with them because his attention was being consumed by other problems. For one thing, he was about to become a first-time grandfather. (Because son Robert and daughter-in-law Rosemary lived in New Jersey, the Swinnens helped out by lending their house to the Courboins during the summer so they could be nearby.) He also had a recording contract with RCA Victor, which wanted to issue discs of him at the Kilgen—surprisingly, the first time that a St. Patrick's musician would be recorded at St. Patrick's. But the Kilgen was still undergoing repairs and wasn't ready for the microphone. Courboin's recording would have to wait until 1947.*

* Once the recording was finally issued, the *Chicago Daily Tribune*'s opera-besotted music critic Claudia Cassidy was unimpressed: "For the record, not for

Then there was the problem of replacement vocalists. For the past four decades, St. Patrick's singers had tended to fall loosely into either of two categories. One type was the man who had gained plenty of experience (and sometimes renown) from the concert or opera spheres; he might be slowing down his pace, but had plenty of mileage left. The second type was a man with a modicum of talent, no clear plans for the future, and a willingness to be molded. James Ungerer had employed both types of singer; Pietro Yon had opted for the former; but Courboin seemed to prefer the latter. During the first postwar years, he coped with the loss of Van Bommel and Schlegel by hiring singers such as Franklin FitzSimons, Herbert Nystrom, and Wilson Lang. FitzSimons was a Juilliard alumnus, a baritone who in two decades had made almost no imprint on the music scene. The other two were tenors: Nystrom was a recent arrival from Sweden and had sung a recital or two (one review mentioned "a pleasantly lyric quality, if without profound expression"). Lang's credentials were even more off-center. He had come to St. Patrick's from Chicago-based radio, with a New York stop in between at the Royal Palm Lounge of the Park Central Hotel (on the same bill with mentalist Lady Esther), and a stint as backup singer for a Broadway revival of *The Time, the Place and the Girl*. Lang would gradually take over the duties of John Griffin, who had begun working on the editorial staff of the decidedly nonmusical trade magazine *Crockery and Glass Journal*. In reverting to his journalist's roots, Griffin was slowly trimming his once-frenetic musical schedule.

It may have been a good time for Griffin to pull back, because Monsignor Flannelly was showing himself to be markedly different from Monsignor Lavelle in his sense of musical-liturgical propriety. In a note sent to Courboin, congratulating him on the choir's Easter performance, he included some guidance which proved that his preferences were light-years away from the style once practiced by Pietro Yon:

> [P]ermit me to remind you that solos are not exactly according to the mind of the Church. In non-liturgical functions, e.g. Novena devotions or weddings, solos do not offend any law. I noticed during Holy Week

---

me." Record buyers disagreed with her, making the album a financial success for Courboin. A half-century after the fact, *The American Organist* would write, "He referred to this set of discs as his 'Bing Crosby Album,' and he used part of the revenue to buy a black Cadillac sedan."

and again on Easter that several parts of the Liturgy were sung as solos. I will appreciate your not doing this again. Whenever a solo is called for by a composer, I suggest that two "cantores" sing that phrase, e.g. two tenors, two second tenors, two baritones or two basses.

More public, and far more humiliating for Courboin, were the problems caused by an attempt to upgrade the Cathedral's choral repertoire—an attempt that misfired badly. Oklahoma-born composer Roy Harris had for more than two decades been making a name for himself as an exponent of musical "nationalism," most of it in the form of symphonies and orchestral pieces. During the 1930s and '40s, his work had been enjoying a vogue in Philharmonic concerts and on radio broadcasts. Harris had written some amount of vocal music as well, and by 1947 he and Courboin were discussing the possibilities of his writing a full-length Mass setting to be premiered at the Cathedral by the Men's Choir.

Why this alliance was being cultivated was a mystery. Cathedral congregations, and Cathedral clergy, still preferred *motu proprio*-driven composers such as Ravanello, Witt, and Perosi (and those same listeners had demonstrated time and again that St. Patrick's was still very much a Yon house, too). A liturgical work in Harris's unabashedly dissonant Modernist style would be at best an interesting novelty for the Cathedral, but virtually without precedent. Nonetheless, as St. Patrick's went ahead with its season,* Harris went ahead with his composition. The Mass was projected to be ready for its first performance on Easter Sunday 1948.

But in February, Harris gave an interview to the *Times*. The article was headlined COMPOSING FOR CASH / HARRIS PROVES COMPOSER CAN GET PAID FOR WORK. Harris was quoted as saying:

It suddenly occurred to me that I was living in a twentieth century civilization where cops and janitors and everyone else got paid for being what they were. Everybody except "composers." It followed, therefore, that if I wasn't paid for my music I wasn't really a composer.

---

* One feature of the season was the first-ever Cathedral appearance of the Catholic Cadet Choir of West Point. On the Sunday after Easter 1947, eighty cadets served in the chancel, while another eighty sang in the gallery. The Men's Choir was wedged into the only remaining space—in the lower loft, next to Courboin at the console.

So I decided never to write again except for a fixed sum of money agreed upon in advance.

The concept was entirely reasonable, but—as was the habit of Roy Harris in much of his public pronouncements—the story was delivered with a dash of cockiness. Then, as part of a listing of his triumphs both musical and financial, later in the article there came a single sentence:

An Easter Mass will be performed this Easter at St. Patrick's Cathedral, New York.

Other composers had written on a commission basis (Pietro Yon, for one), but it had been more informal—and none of them had paraded that fact before the public, especially not in a victorious tone. Apparently, Father Greene was infuriated. The Mass was dropped from the Cathedral schedule so abruptly that the story made it into national as well as local periodicals. Father Greene told *Time* that the implication that the Mass was written for cash was "not only untrue, but distasteful."

Years later, music commentator Nicholas Slonimsky would write that Harris's "royalties" were to have come not from the Cathedral directly but from a planned recording of his Mass. Nevertheless, the *Times* article, and the subsequent brouhaha in *Time,* had given the project a mercenary tinge that Harris had a hard time living down.

The Mass for Men's Voices was performed later that spring—not at the Cathedral but at the Columbia University Festival of Contemporary American Music. Reviews were lukewarm-to-negative, with phrases like "We find Mr. Harris' poly—shall we make a vile pun?—phony," "Musically it is sterile," and "gauchery." Worse, someone writing program notes had the idiotic idea of trying to get mileage from what was left of Harris's Cathedral connection; concertgoers read that the Mass had been "written at the request of Dr. Charles M. Courboin, musical director of St. Patrick's Cathedral in New York." That particular line got plenty of attention, none of it flattering. The *Times* wrote that "A listener expressed amusement at the composer's statement." The *Washington Post* also quoted the program note, smirking, "It seems safe to prophesy that the work will never be heard in that edifice."

It never was.

"Fifty Boys Recently Organized as a Choir"

Money had become a major problem among Courboin's employees, as economic inflation had gripped the country during 1947 and was only intensifying during 1948. Nearly every worker in the United States was affected, including musicians, and among them the members of the Men's Choir. Choirmen were paid on a sliding scale, as they had been throughout Yon's time, according to their length of service and the amount of singing they did, but none of them earned what could be called full-time income. And the buying power of that income had diminished by nearly a third since the end of the war.

June saw a flurry of correspondence regarding money matters. Courboin first sent a note to Monsignor Flannelly, asking "permission to have a committee call on you to discuss the possibility of salary increases due to the high cost of living." Flannelly responded:

I have received your note suggesting an increase in salary for the members of the Choir. I have given it some consideration and will give it some more. I understand fully how difficult it is for people to try to meet the terrible current costs of living. However, I must also remember that the Church income is suffering because of these same high costs of living. The income of the Cathedral for 1948 has been down about $100.00 a day when compared with 1947. I, therefore, do not see how we can increase salaries.

On the other hand, I believe that we must curtail our expenses. I am thinking seriously of reducing the Choir to twelve members. Perhaps this would be the best season of the year to make this reduction so that those released might find employment for themselves in other choirs. . . .

If I determine upon this, I will appreciate suggestions from you and Father Greene as to just what singers will be retained.

The choirmen then asked John Griffin, as a respected senior member, to intercede on their behalf. He wrote Monsignor Flannelly (on *Crockery and Glass Journal* letterhead):

While the cost of living was increasing one and three-fourth times wages throughout the country increased a bit more than three times in the same period, but during the so called period of "easy" money and high salaries, the choir did not enjoy the benefits of increases.

I read in the paper only the other day that by agreement salaries paid to cleaning women were fixed at $1.00 per hour, unskilled laborers over $2.00 per hour, and bricklayers approximately $3.60 per hour. No special skill or preparation is necessary to handle jobs of that sort, whereas a singer must train and keep in training if he is to do his job properly. Yet the choir members of St. Patrick's Cathedral average approximately $2.00 an hour for their work, as compared to the above scales.

Monsignor Flannelly thanked Griffin for his "interesting" assessment, but by that fall he had decided on his course of action.

I have given much consideration to the appeals made by the Choir for increases in salary. Since the income of the Cathedral has been decreasing this year, I cannot see my way to raising the fixed salaries.

Furthermore, with the added expense of the coach for the Boys' Choir plus the salaries I will have to pay to the male altos, I must ask you to reduce the size of your present choir. This last I want to do as equitably as possible. To men who have given many years of service, I propose to give a pension. I must ask you to confer with me in this matter.

In a couple of paragraphs, Monsignor Flannelly was hinting at a series of changes that would remake the entire music department. During the course of the 1948–49 season, some of the oldest members of the Men's Choir were retired and given a monthly pension.* Their vacated spaces would be filled by a handful of male altos, absent from St. Patrick's since 1942. Finally, the musical focus—which had for decades concentrated upon the Men's Choir—would change radically.

For there would be, once again, a boys' choir.

Not exactly "once again." James Ungerer and Pietro Yon had used boy trebles, as a necessary substitute for female voices (and Ungerer had gone on the record as less than delighted with the results, in that 1905 *Times* interview). But those boys had almost never been featured as members of their own group with a particular musical identity. During the 1940s and '50s, however, boychoirs were a big thing in American popular culture, and Cardinal Spellman had decided that the time was right to establish the Cathedral's own group of singing boys. The Cardinal enlisted the

---

* This was initially $25.00. Flannelly sent a letter with the first check: "I have hesitated to retire the older members. However, voices do grow old and they must give way to youthful ones. This law applies to every walk in life."

help of Father Greene, as well as Courboin, to find a Catholic boys' school that would serve as a source of treble voices. They hit upon St. Ann's Academy, nearby on Lexington Avenue, and with the Brother Director's consent began to canvass the boys for interest and talent. Fifty boys were chosen. Beginning in the spring of 1948, they spent the first three days of each week in after-school sessions, working on music basics and voice building. On Thursdays they were bused to the Cathedral, along with a handful of the Academy's Marist Brothers riding along for crowd control, for further work with Father Greene and rehearsals with the Men's Choir.

Because the gallery offered less-than-optimum rehearsal space (and it had never provided any office space), the anticipated crowd of boys made Cathedral authorities realize at last that it was necessary to create a dedicated music area. The only solution that could be found was to break through the wall of the gallery into the north spire in order to build a "choir rehearsal room." The room—located a few steps above the gallery floor, and sharing the spire with the Cathedral bells hanging some twenty-five feet above it—was made ready for the boys' first rehearsals. To give it the greatest possible floor space it mimicked the spire's shape, which meant that it was octagonal, which played havoc with the choral sound during working sessions. Furthermore, because the room was fitted into the spire it was windowless, which (given the hygiene standards of most young boys) played havoc with tempers and respiratory systems. Still, it was the choir's own space, the first music room St. Patrick's had ever had constructed.

By the start of the season, not only were the various pieces falling into place, but there was an air of anticipation that hadn't been seen in the music department since the days before the war. The boys would make their first appearance on December 13, Gaudete Sunday, singing Müller's *St. Benedict Mass*. Assuming that went well, their next date would be for Midnight Mass. It went well enough; and the next time they sang they were not only heard—but seen. On *television*.

In contrast to the Cathedral's years-long resistance to radio, St. Patrick's was becoming involved with television at exactly the right time. Until then TV had been a locally based proposition, primarily centered on New York and one or two other East Coast cities. But 1948 was the industry's watershed year, with an explosion of activity. It was minuscule in comparison with radio; a nationwide total of only 350,000 TV sets (half of them clustered around the New York City area) were served by fewer than three dozen stations. Nevertheless, TV programming was viewed with wonder and fascination by most people. And, as in the early days of radio, it was interested in the church. Two years earlier, WABD, flagship station of the short-lived DuMont network, had televised the Christmas Eve Carol Service of Grace Church, a first for the industry.* This time Midnight Mass from St. Patrick's would be carried by three of the nation's four TV networks. (DuMont opted to return to Grace Church for its service, its 8:00 P.M. time allowing the network to be off the air well before midnight.) Those with long memories might have chuckled nostalgically, the day before the Cathedral telecast, when a "spokesman for the archdiocese" pointed out to the *Times* that "the obligation of Catholics to attend mass on Christmas could not be fulfilled via television. . . . [T]he physical presence of the worshiper" was required— virtually the identical comment that had been given about worship via radio in 1924.

Radio broadcasts from the Cathedral had required microphones, wires, technicians, and a remote truck. That first telecast relied on all those items, plus a number of massive cameras stationed in the aisles and the gallery; two-inch-thick cables running from those cameras, turning floors into obstacle courses and requiring ushers to continually warn congregants against tripping; and, to accommodate the low-resolution video of the time, a plethora of additional lights that were blazingly strong enough to raise the temperature inside the Cathedral—especially in the gallery. That Christmas Eve happened to be a particularly cold night with temperatures bottoming out in the mid-20s, which kept the congregation from sweltering. Choristers upstairs, however, were rather less comfortable.

Even with these drawbacks, home viewers were impressed, and so were the print media. On Christmas morning, the *Times* wrote:

> The midnight mass at St. Patrick's Cathedral . . . was televised for the first time with remarkable success. Close-ups of the Cardinal and his assistants . . . came through with unusual clarity . . . as viewed on a set receiving the WNBT telecast in the Times Square area. . . .

* That choice may have had something to do with the fact that the WABD studios were located only a block or so away from Grace Church.

In the singing was heard for the first time since the war fifty boys recently organized as a choir by the Rev. William T. Greene, archdiocesan music chairman.

(The reference to a set "in the Times Square area" is its own bit of television history: At the time, so few people owned sets that the reporter was likely catching Midnight Mass at either of the two places where a set could reliably be found—a TV dealership, or a bar.)

Not only was the television broadcast a success, but so was the performance of the Cathedral's newest singers—so successful that the musical focus shifted instantly from the Men's Choir, where it had been concentrated for nearly twenty years, to the boys' contingent of the Cathedral Choristers.

Video Stars, Singing Safe Music

Within months the Boy Choristers (their official title) were a much-appreciated presence, not only at St. Patrick's but in many homes throughout the country via increasingly frequent TV and radio broadcasts. But they enjoyed no entitlement. If anything, they were working as hard as the members of the Men's Choir, constantly drilled in deportment as well as musicianship. The discipline even extended to their attire, as Father Greene (elevated to Monsignor in 1950) designed a uniform for the boys, complete with its own insignia and a military-style cap, and they were expected to be properly turned out whenever they were on Cathedral premises. Father Greene's design eschewed the usual cassock and surplice that boy choristers had worn at the Cathedral since 1879; for services, the boys now covered their uniforms with capes of flamboyant green and gold, thus guaranteeing that they would be noticed at all times whether or not they were singing.

Even though the Cathedral choir had appeared on radio for years, television proved to have much more star-building power. This, combined with the idea of church choirboys becoming TV personalities, struck some observers as hysterically funny. In 1952 *The New Yorker* saw fit to run in its "Talk of the Town" column the following item: "Notice received by a ten-year-old St. Patrick's Cathedral chorister: 'Choir uniforms must be worn at all services and telecasts.'"

Choir life wasn't all drudgery for the boys, as Monsignor Greene made sure to build playtimes into the schedule. During Lent, the boys were part of St. Patrick's services on Wednesday and Friday evenings; Monsignor Greene arranged for them to decompress by playing stickball on the Cathedral's outdoor terrace when they weren't needed. And every New Year's Eve, they were on the schedule for the Cathedral's two "Holy Hours"; between those services, they were taken to Rockefeller Center in a group for some ice skating.

TV audiences got to see the boys again during Midnight Mass in 1949,* but not in 1950; that year's Midnight Mass telecast came from Boston's Cathedral of the Holy Cross. (Christmas Eve viewers who wanted to see the boys had to content themselves with watching them on the CBS variety show "The Arthur Murray Hour," which paid St. Patrick's a flat fee of $500.00 for their services. Their appearance was at 9:00 P.M., after which they had to hustle directly back to the Cathedral for the carol service and Midnight Mass.) It would be one of the last times that television audiences went without Midnight Mass from St. Patrick's; the following year it was restored to the NBC schedule, where it would stay for another two decades.

To an extent, the boys were getting more attention than the music program itself. In an October 1949 *Times* article on sacred music in New York, the Cathedral was mentioned exactly once, in the last paragraph: "Among Roman Catholic houses of worship, St. Patrick's Cathedral and the Church of St. Ignatius Loyola give prominence to the musical selections for the liturgy." The choral repertoire had thinned to a list of tried-and-true pieces. As the *Lord Nelson Mass* had been a staple of the Cathedral a century before, now Courboin leaned upon the Refice *Missa Choralis*. Throughout his tenure, it would invariably be programmed on Easter Sundays, the centerpiece of an unchanging trio of selections that included the Bogatto "Haec Dies" and the Yon "Christ Triumphant." The Pontifical Mass of Christmas Day employed the Refice as well (always paired with Handel's "Hallelujah Chorus"). The West Point cadets relied on it even more wholeheartedly, singing it during their visits in 1948, 1949, 1950, 1951, 1952, 1953. . . .

The more intriguing music at St. Patrick's was found at the organ. When the Kilgen company had been called in to repair the damage caused

* To keep the boys alert for Midnight Mass, the mothers of St. Patrick's boys tended to insist that their sons take a nap early in the afternoon of Christmas Eve—the last thing the boys wanted to do.

by Best and Company's dynamite, Cathedral authorities decided that it was a good time to work in the changes that Courboin had wanted from the start (and he knew exactly what he wanted, because decades earlier he had been a "tonal adviser" to the Kilgen Organ Company). This would be the first of a number of modifications, and it was heralded in a splashy Kilgen advertisement in the August 1950 *American Organist*:

> The Kilgen Organ in the grand Cathedral was installed in 1927. . . .
> [I]t is one of the largest cathedral organs in the world. It has been
> recently been redesigned tonally under the direction of Dr. Charles M.
> Courboin, famous organist who presides at the Cathedral. The result
> of this revision is greater clarity of speech, artistic brilliance and an
> ensemble that can only be called magnificent. Those who have heard
> the redesigned organ have acclaimed it a literal masterpiece.*

Along with the interest generated by the new sounds coming from the Cathedral's organ, there was something of a guess-what's-next atmosphere engendered by the Cathedral's organist. Only sporadically would Courboin inform the news media of his own choices of music for preludes and postludes—he preferred to leave his selections to the inspiration of the moment. Even so, a scheduled piece would sometimes be scrapped at the moment his fingers were descending to the keyboard; one visiting organist heard him say nonchalantly, "I'd rather play something else. . . ." Switching gears, he would do so, completely from memory. Making the experience even more involving for listeners was the anticipation of the moment when Courboin and assistant Rivetti might man their respective consoles to "trade" improvisations, back and forth. Both the gallery and chancel consoles had been fitted with lights on toe switches; one man would build a musical theme to its own climax and then flash the light, a signal for the other to pick up the thread in part of a back-and-forth game that fascinated many. Rivetti, who enjoyed these liturgical jam sessions as

* Kilgen wasn't the only company that tried to get press mileage out of the work being done at St. Patrick's. The following July's *American Organist* carried an ad that described, with pitched excitement, the organ's new *motors*: "[T]his magnificent 4-manual gallery organ has been in operation since 1928. . . . It is powered by a forty horse-power Spencer Orgoblo. A smaller Orgoblo is used on another 3-manual instrument near the sanctuary, also redesigned." Note that both advertisements were inexact about the date of the installation.

much as Courboin (he called them "duels"), wasn't the only musician to take part: One day Courboin traded improvisations with his old friend, titanic organist Marcel Dupré, in New York on a visit. That event was spontaneous, neither announced nor recorded . . . and unfortunately not repeated.

But this was music for connoisseurs. Most of the liturgical music of the 1950s could be labeled "safe," and that label applied to music being performed at some of the most prestigious venues. Even the coronation of Queen Elizabeth II in 1952—for that period, what might be called the most high-profile use of sacred music in the world—relied upon compositions of past masters (such as Handel) and elder statesmen (such as C. Hubert H. Parry and Ralph Vaughan Williams). Because music in Catholic churches was hewing to the dictates of both the White and Black Lists, it was even more "safe," and St. Patrick's offered no exceptions during this period. Courboin kept to his regular list of composers, except for the rare occasion when he tipped his hat to a compatriot (Pentecost 1954, which featured the *Missa Exultet Orbis* by fellow Belgian Camille Van Hulse) or a friend (that year's Midnight Mass, offering the *Missa Pontificalis* of his old pupil Joseph J. McGrath). Nor did he rock the boat with his own work: His "Ingrediente" (probably Courboin's only piece of choral writing for the Cathedral), composed for Palm Sunday 1955 and dedicated to Flannelly, was so stolidly workmanlike that it was ignored by the music community at large. For that matter, the 1957 funeral for Arturo Toscanini, attended by many of the world's foremost musical personalities, was enhanced by nothing flashier than the Perosi *Missa de Requiem*. (The *Times* called the music "simple" and "unpretentious.") The greatest excitements occurring in the Cathedral music department were nonchoral: the installation of an elevator to the north spire room and the electrification of the chimes, which had been mostly silent since 1946.*

The performers themselves were certainly not asked to be groundbreakers. Events such as the annual Catholic Charities telecasts tried to

---

* The chimes, which had in the past been rung by hand or by a mechanical clockwork arrangement, were now played from a small keyboard located in the choir loft. Courboin's grandson remembers visiting the gallery as a very small boy, his grandfather pointing to the various keys as he "helped" by pressing them. As far as the elevator was concerned, Courboin's son states that it came about simply because his sixty-something father was no longer fond of climbing stairs.

be subtle about the fact that the Boy Choristers were valued almost more for their emblematic appeal than they were for their singing. Outside the Cathedral, the boys were viewed, more pragmatically and as a unit, as a hot property. When CBS put together a TV version of *The Man Who Came to Dinner*, the producers pulled out the stops with an all-star cast including Monty Wooley, Joan Bennett, Merle Oberon, and Buster Keaton; and for the play's wacky Christmas Eve scene, which used a boys' choir, they went straight to Courboin to get a contingent of the Cathedral boys. (One of them shrugged, "All we had to sing was 'Deck the Halls.'") A year later, Warner Bros. began production on *Miracle in the Rain,* with its climactic scenes taking place at St. Patrick's; not only did the company come to New York for location filming at the Cathedral, but rumor had it that the boys' voices were being used on the soundtrack. For that matter, when *Cosmopolitan* wanted to do a photo shoot showing a fashionably dressed model entering St. Bartholomew's Church, the editors didn't even look at any other church's choirboys but booked Boy Choristers Joseph McQuade and his twin brother, Michael, to pose with her.

Sometimes the emphasis on the boys could become a bit nettling to their adult colleagues. When RCA recorded *Perry Como Sings His Favorite Songs of Worship* in 1950, the boys were included in the project (along with RCA's other contract artist, Courboin); not so the Men's Choir. Nevertheless, the men—who were producing the identical sound they had first achieved under Pietro Yon—were still respected as the musical motor of the group. At the week-long Catholic School Music Festival of 1951, the Cathedral Choir was scheduled to top off the entire works with a Town Hall concert. The men were regarded as an essential component of the evening, enough so that the Cathedral gave them the somewhat left-handed tribute of picking up the rental cost of their dress suits.

And the men's expertise was absolutely necessary in complicated liturgies, if only for purposes of stage management. The *Times* account of Palm Sunday 1951 offered a particularly good example, in which the Men's Choir, the Boy Choristers, and the Cathedral College choir participated. The ceremonies required singers to sing (audibly) from behind closed doors in the vestibule, for other cantors to respond from within the Cathedral, and for the procession to move with the deacon and other ministers. All of these tasks fell to members of the Men's Choir.

These were highly involved rituals being enacted by very disparate groups that came together only once or twice weekly, and it was logical that their leaders might experience friction. Especially given that, while Courboin was a decisive and outspoken individual, so was the Choir Moderator, Monsignor Greene—and he had a pulpit from which to speak. Nearly each week, his sermons were quoted in the *Times*. Some of them touched on musical matters; without fail, every article included the accompanying line "He is chairman of the commission on church music of the Roman Catholic Archdiocese of New York."

Courboin finally decided to write a memo to Bishop Flannelly (who had been elevated just before Christmas 1948). In it, he very thoroughly aired his feelings.

> The main point is the uncertainty about the precise duties and responsibilities of the Choir Moderator. You will recall that the office was instituted about four years ago, shortly after His Eminence had mistaken for tardiness the belated arrival in the choir loft of two of our singers, Messrs. Marcoux and Meli, who had been helping the College boys in the Sanctuary.—It seems to me that such things as the balance of the choir, interpretation of the music as well as its choice, even the organ stops selections, and the like should be my responsibility, and that the Moderator of the Choir should confine himself to the disciplining of the choir should the occasion arise.
>
> However, the unexpected announcement on occasion that His Eminence, the Cardinal, has ordered Msgr. Greene to have the choir do, or not do, a particular thing makes it very hard to preserve the proper discipline and unity, for of course the members of the choir never know where responsibility and authority reside, and are expecting new orders from His Eminence through Msgr. Greene that may countermand at once and without warning whatever I have said.
>
> [I] regret to say that I consider Msgr. Greene's knowledge of music to be both incomplete and inadequate, with a correspondent deficiency in musical taste. He would have plenty to do if he confined himself to the discipline, for as you may know, this leaves much to be desired. One does not expect young boys to be angels, but there is room for improvement in the matter of decorum during the sermon and other parts of the Mass.

There is no record of a reply. However, Bishop Flannelly must have been aware of the situation for some time. The previous summer, one of the Cathedral's newest staff priests, Father Francis X. Duffy, had been sent to the Pontifical Institute for a year's course of study in choral music and Gregorian chant. By the time Courboin wrote his memo, Father Duffy was back at the Cathedral, diploma in hand.

During all of this Monsignor Greene continued his practice of moderating, coaching, issuing those occasional orders to the choristers, and seeing his sermons quoted in the *Times*. LIVING OF EACH DAY TO FULL COUNSELED was the headline on September 24, 1956, describing his most recent sermon:

> "Each day is a new life, each sunrise a new birth for the individual, the beginning of a new existence, a new great chance to put to new and higher uses the results of past living."

The subject proved to be an appropriate farewell; almost immediately thereafter he was gone from the Cathedral, having been abruptly named pastor of the Church of Our Lady of Perpetual Help in the Westchester County village of Ardsley.

With Monsignor Greene's position thus opened, Father Duffy was asked to take over as Choir Moderator.

The Passing of Ungerer

At about the same time, the story of James Ungerer was playing out to its sad conclusion. His promised memoir unpublished, new compositions unwritten, he had dropped almost completely out of sight since his departure from St. Patrick's. A few choirmasters still programmed his music, primarily his "Terra Tremuit" at Easter, but his name had faded from most memories. Whatever royalties he earned weren't lavish; he still lived frugally, as he had for decades, at the Capitol Hotel. Some years before, it had been turned into a YWCA residence, but Ungerer had proven to be so attached to the place—or so obviously cowed by the prospect of finding new quarters—that he was allowed to remain there "under a special arrangement."

By 1953, when he reached his eightieth birthday, plagued with severe arthritis in his hands (which he had long attributed to the heavy touch required to play the Jardine in the Cathedral gallery), his vitality had started to falter. Soon it became apparent that he would have to move to a nursing home. The Mary Manning Walsh Home had opened the previous year, close to the Queensboro Bridge on Manhattan's East Side, and

Ungerer decided that it would be his best choice—provided, of course, that he could afford it. Considering his current pension of $166 per month, that wasn't going to be possible.

He then wrote a letter to Bishop Flannelly, laying out his financial situation simply but in bleak detail.

> I applied for admission to the Walsh Home last week because my health condition appears to be deteriorating more rapidly of late.
>
> Was told of the thousand or more applications already on file—also, the monthly terms for occupancy ($200.—for a room—$137 for a ward bed).
>
> While I realize that "beggars can't be choosers," I find the ward proposition distasteful—and incompatible with my temperament, as regards the minimum requirements of a fair measure of contentment.
>
> If & when my admission goes thru, I should desire the room accommodation for which my funds are not adequate.
>
> Would you be willing to raise my allowance to meet the $200.—monthly charge—the whole check thus going to the institution, while I would try to get along on a small annuity, $60.—to defray incidental expenses.
>
> I enclose a letter from Monsignor Lavelle, at the time of my resignation, to show that he intended my pension to be equal to my salary at the time ($2,400.)—the Board of Trustees, however, decided on the lower figure ($2,000.).
>
> Please do not think I am making any sort of claim;—indeed, whatever your decision, I shall remain grateful for your kind attitude and personal support in the past & with God's help hope to be spared any insurmountable difficulty in the future.
>
> > I remain, as ever,
> > Gratefully,
> > J. C. Ungerer

On the Cathedral's copy of the letter, Bishop Flannelly made a single note: a calculation of the difference between Ungerer's pension and the amount needed, accompanied by the firm phrase "We will pay this and supplementary every year."

Ungerer was thus able to move into a room in the Walsh Home. The additional funds allowed him to retreat even more completely from the world, until he died "after a short illness" (so read his death notice) on November 8, 1957. His death didn't even make it into the obituary notices of *The American Organist*.

In earlier decades, large congregations had filled the Cathedral to take part in the funerals of William F. Pecher and Pietro Yon; but Jacques-Marie-Pierre-André-Cécilien Ungerer had outlived nearly everyone who cared about him. Bishop Flannelly, assisted by Bishop Donahue, performed the Requiem Mass in the Lady Chapel.

There was little music. There also were few mourners in attendance. The *Times* had noted in Ungerer's obituary, "Funeral private."

Returning Ladies and Recording Stars

Pope Pius XII had been a fervent admirer of Pius X, and his actions proved this when he beatified him in 1951, then declared him to be a saint in 1954. Finally he decided to commemorate the fiftieth anniversary of the 1903 *motu proprio* by issuing an encyclical of his own on the subject of liturgical music. *Musicae sacrae disciplina* ("Discipline of sacred music") was promulgated on Christmas Day of 1955.

Music historians would refer to *Musicae sacrae disciplina* as a "Christmas present to choirmasters" because it maintained the spirit of *Tra le sollecitudini* but relaxed its stringent dictates. It reaffirmed the primacy of Gregorian chant as the absolute of liturgical music, as well as classic polyphony, while allowing that some works (of composers such as Mozart, Rossini, and Haydn) that had been banned for the past fifty years might have merits of their own to make them suitable for Catholic worship:

> In this journey, although sometimes slowly and laboriously, [sacred music] has gradually progressed from the simple and ingenuous Gregorian modes to great and magnificent works of art. To these works not only the human voice, but also the organ and other musical instruments, add dignity, majesty and a prodigious richness.

And there was a further relaxation of the rules:

> Where it is impossible to have schools of singers or where there are not enough choir boys, it is allowed that a group of men and women or girls, located in a place outside the sanctuary set apart for the exclusive use of this group, can sing the liturgical texts at Solemn

Mass, as long as the men are completely separated from the women and girls and everything unbecoming is avoided. The Ordinary is bound in conscience in this matter.

This was remarkable—if only because there was virtually no reaction to it. Compared with the *motu proprio* of 1903 and the months of white-hot press coverage it had unleashed, *Musicae sacrae disciplina* was almost ignored in the media. The *New York Times* didn't even bother with the story. *Time* tried somewhat halfheartedly to be entertaining in its coverage: "[V]oices raised in praise and gladness have always been part of the Christian faith. But the sound is sometimes unholy."

The *Washington Post and Times Herald* tried to keep to the story but ended by spinning off on a tangent, discussing the fact that the Archdiocese of Chicago had forbidden the use of certain compositions, among them the Wagner and Mendelssohn wedding marches and the Schubert "Ave Maria."

And no publication mentioned a thing about the return of women to the choir gallery.

Perhaps the idea was no longer a shock, because more than one parish had been using mixed choirs since the war years and before, their pastors turning a blind eye to the gender issue. For its own part, St. Patrick's during this time had one luxury that it didn't have in 1903—no reporters invaded the choir loft, and no one asked Cathedral representatives to comment upon the encyclical.

Musicae sacrae disciplina was clarified and further detailed by 1958's *De musica sacra et sacra liturgia*, but by then there was barely a ripple of public reaction. Both documents would be helpful to confused liturgical musicians; even so, they had little effect on the music that was being performed at St. Patrick's and absolutely no effect on the people who performed it. Women would sing in the St. Patrick's parish, but not at the Cathedral—rather, at its newly constructed satellite, the Chapel of Saints Faith, Hope and Charity on Park Avenue. When it opened in late 1958, it was dedicated with the help of the Cathedral Choristers, but after that its music was provided by an all-volunteer, all-female choir. Thus was born The Chapel Chorale. They would be praised, somewhat avuncularly:

The progress of the Choir in perfecting an ever increasing repertoire has been steady and gratifying. Unreservedly we hail the buoyant esprit de corps of this volunteer group. Our observation of them reveals that they really enjoy association with one another in their choir life. Their enthusiasm is boundless, whether it be for a birthday party, for a gathering around the coffee cups after High Mass, or for a new project to enhance the beauty of our Church services. When constructive criticism is given they are always humble and make every effort to improve. When they are given any encouragement they are very grateful.

As busy as the ladies of the Chapel Chorale may have seemed, their male colleagues at the Cathedral were busier. St. Ann's Academy moved out of the area before Monsignor Greene had departed, and one of his last Cathedral duties had been to arrange for All Hallows Academy, a Bronx-based school, to take over the supplying of boys for the Cathedral Choristers. Locally based choral director Fred Short had worked with the boys from their St. Ann days; he would continue to oversee their initial training, after which they would be phased into the choir.

And by this point all singers at St. Patrick's had to move quickly; along with their regular schedule of Masses and special services, the Cathedral Choristers always had to be ready to sing at outside events. There were Communion breakfasts, most of them at the Hotel Astor; Christmas tree lightings at New Jersey's Bergen Mall and midtown's Bryant Park; even the opening of the Four Seasons Restaurant in 1959. Located in the trend-setting Seagram Building, it was the city's newest, most modernistic dining environment, and the fact that its managers wanted to have Cathedral choirboys as entertainment was something of an incongruity. However, they did; and they were offering not only dinner to the singers, but also limousines to take them home. (After all, it was a school night.) Father Duffy remembered the evening: "I had told them that the boys would be perfectly fine with hamburgers, but they wanted them to choose whatever they wanted. So there they were with great big menus that they could hardly read . . . the waiter came and the first lad said—'I'll have a hamburger and a Coke.' So did each of the other boys. . . . When they went home, they were disappointed—disappointed that none of their friends were there to see them getting out of the limos."

Father Duffy's schedule meant that he was regularly busier than any Cathedral singer, carrying a full load of clerical responsibilities as Associate Master of Ceremonies (and within a few years as Master of Ceremonies, giving him even more to do), heading the St. Patrick's Information

Center, and fulfilling his duties as Music Moderator. His juggling capabilities would be tested even further in the summer of 1959, when Roulette Records approached Cardinal Spellman with the prospect of recording two albums of Christmas music. At the very least, it was an odd idea: Roulette was only in its second year of operation, concentrating on rock 'n' roll, some jazz, and a few Italian pop imports. Almost nothing in its catalogue pointed toward either sacred or choral music.

Nevertheless, the Cardinal liked the idea and asked the Music Moderator to make plans for upcoming recording sessions. Father Duffy was alarmed. It was already July, the boys were on vacation, and nothing had been selected or rehearsed, let alone recorded. But the Cardinal was firmly confident in his belief that those details could—and *would*—be managed in time to have an album on store shelves by the Christmas season.

The whole project presented difficulties, and not only because of the time crunch. The Cathedral itself would be a tough venue for recording sessions, available only during late-night hours, with midtown traffic clearly audible through its windows at all hours, and its reverberation providing an acoustic nightmare for engineers. (When Courboin recorded his organ album in 1947, technicians had to fiddle continually with microphone placement to counteract the problem. Even so, the *Wall Street Journal* had griped about the sound: "The recording does not do justice to the tonal colors of the different stops. . . .") Rather than deal with those issues, Roulette chose to record at Webster Hall, an East Village ballroom that had been converted into recording space. Additionally, not only the venue but the sheer amount of music would present problems. The boys' 1950 jaunt with Perry Como had been accomplished in a single day because they'd had to record only two selections for a 78 rpm album; now, the LP era was demanding that they come up with twenty-four finished tracks. Some of the music would be fairly new; more of it came straight out of the choir's usual repertoire. "Gesù Bambino" and "Carol of the Indians" were the off-the-rack published arrangements that the Cathedral had always used, as was "Carol of the Bells."

Starting in early September, boys and men embarked upon concentrated, exhausting rehearsals. Very soon after that, they (along with Eddie Rivetti to man the studio's undersized electronic organ; Courboin stayed out of the project) headed to Webster Hall for a series of recording sessions that ran anything but smoothly. Father Duffy recalled, "We spent ten days recording . . . my job was to ride herd on the kids while we went through this grueling experience. On the bus downtown. Then off you go. . . . Then we'd do it again. Then we'd do it again. Then we'd do it again. *Then* we'd do it again. By that time everyone was ready to tear me apart. . . . *Then we'd do it again.* . . ."

In spite of the chaotic schedule, the result—the first volume of it, any-way—made it into stores by early December, in both monaural and stereo versions. *Saint Patrick's Cathedral Choir Sings Christmas Carols* gener-ated polite interest on both coasts: The record reviewer for the *Los Angeles Times* was taken with the album's version of "Carol of the Bells" (also released as a single, perhaps with a view toward radio and jukebox play), while Roulette Records attempted its own buildup with a large ad in the Sunday *New York Times*. But in the late 1950s, each holiday season saw the market glutted with a wide variety of Christmas albums. Unless those discs caught on with the public, most of them were banished to half-price bins by January. The St. Patrick's album was one of these casu-alties; its sales had been no more than respectable.

The following year, *Saint Patrick's Cathedral Choir Sings Christmas Songs, Volume 2* was released without publicity. It sank like a stone.*

Changes at the Vatican, Changes at the Cathedral

The year 1958 would begin a period of high stress for the musicians of St. Patrick's; there were events of worldwide importance to the Church, but they were juxtaposed with intense personal tragedy. The tragedy was Courboin's, and it was particularly wrenching because it took place in his own household.

Mabel Courboin was an attractive woman with a slightly husky voice. She enjoyed and craved cigarettes. In the late 1940s, she began to suffer from arthritis and the family doctor prescribed the new treatment using cortisone. The dosage and understanding of the medication was [*sic*] not yet perfected, and the result was a woman who became a virtually speechless and crippled invalid. The smoking habit

---

* Even so, Morris Levy, Roulette's legendary president, would remember the two albums fondly in a 1986 interview with the *Los Angeles Times*. Still hanging prominently in his office was a photo of him shaking hands with Cardinal Spellman on the Cathedral steps.

continued, as it was her one "outlet," and it caused her death in 1958. Either a match or a cigarette ignited her clothing where she was seated while Courboin was in another room taking a phone call. By the time he realized she was in trouble and got to her, she was already badly burned and survived only a few days in the hospital. Her funeral was held in the Lady Chapel at St. Patrick's.

In the face of such a blow, it was probably fortunate that most of the Cathedral's other main events at the time didn't focus on the music department. Neither the 150th anniversary of the Archdiocese, celebrated on Easter Sunday 1958, nor the subsequent commemoration of the laying of the Cathedral's cornerstone some weeks later produced much coverage of the music accompanying either ceremony. Then, after four years of steadily declining health, Pope Pius XII died in October; St. Patrick's responded with a Solemn Pontifical Mass—sung not by the Cathedral Choristers but by the sanctuary choristers of Cathedral College. When Angelo Giuseppe Cardinal Roncalli was elected Pope John XXIII less than three weeks later, the Cathedral's response was perfectly suited to the moment, although it had nothing at all to do with the choir.

> The monsignori and priests filed across Madison Avenue [from the Villard Houses, where the Chancery offices were located] to St. Patrick's Cathedral. There they were joined by the cathedral staff. The group, numbering about fifty, sang the Te Deum. The Most Rev. Joseph F. Flannelly, Auxiliary Bishop and administrator of the Cathedral, led this hymn of thanksgiving.

In contrast to the nightlong music-filled ceremonies that had taken place in 1939 to usher in the reign of Pius XII, this time there was no announcement of planned musical tributes. Nor would there be any. As the rock 'n' roll–saturated 1950s were segueing into the 1960s, it was more than obvious that sacred music was losing its hold on the general public, whether it was being performed at St. Patrick's or anywhere else. That attitude was underlined by a piece in the *Times* (and pieces in the *Times* were becoming rare) entitled MUSIC SWITCHED AT ST. PATRICK'S TO COPE WITH A DEPLETED CHOIR. Its sole point being the fact that Rivetti had been forced to change the planned Mass setting to accommodate his short-staffed summer group, the article was a silly, much-ado-about-nothing item that would never have been written about any other church choir in the nation.

He lacked a complete choir for the selected music. . . . Two tenors had failed to report and a third arrived late. As Mr. Rivetti explained the situation: "We need a team before we can make a musical line-up."

Not the music, but the structure of the Mass itself, was being called into question by more and more Catholics. This had been going on quietly for decades, and a group called the Vernacular Society had gained a number of adherents (although some of their meetings took place in secret). Nevertheless, when the *Osservatore Romano* announced in January 1959 that the new Pope intended to convene the Second Ecumenical Council of the Vatican—the first such meeting since 1870—the news created gradual but steadily mounting shock waves throughout the world. During the nearly three years that it took to coordinate the first session of the Council, there were rumors of extravagant, possibly unwelcome, changes to be wrought upon Catholic rites.

But during that time the Mass remained unaffected. Catholic sacred music as well remained unaffected, especially so at St. Patrick's. The repertoire hadn't been modified. Courboin and Rivetti were playing what they always had played—evidently with success, as Courboin was honored once again by Belgium's king with the title Chevalier of the Order of Leopold. And while Courboin might have been willing to dispense with Eddie Rivetti in 1943, that attitude had undergone a complete reversal as Rivetti's dedication and professionalism had proven him an invaluable assistant.* Not only did the two men come to admire each other deeply, but in the wake of his wife's death, Courboin became a welcome presence in the life of the Rivetti family.

As for the vocal music, the choral repertoire and even the singers were much the same as they had been for a long time. (They not only enjoyed working together but were a particularly sociable group. Sundays had a set routine, as after High Mass the men and their families would adjourn in a group to West 46th Street for luncheon at the Italian restaurant

---

* Rivetti's dedication sometimes resulted in his being spread a bit thin. Every Holy Week, he was booked not only with all of his Cathedral duties but also with an early Easter Sunday service at the Holy Name Mission. While he played, his wife and daughter would wait outside the Mission, parked on the Bowery in the family car (with orders to keep the doors locked) until Rivetti was finished. Then they'd head back to St. Patrick's for the High Mass.

Barbetta, in those days an inexpensive neighborhood eatery. That party would usually last until it was time to return for Vespers.) A number of the members of the Men's Choir had clocked two decades or more at St. Patrick's; Raimondo Scala and Hildreth Martin had each put in a whopping thirty-plus years.* The general atmosphere in the music department was one of if-it-ain't-broke-don't-fix-it, and while some listeners snickered, just as often they had to admit that the results could be impressive. One such observer remembered watching the Men's Choir at Vespers: "They'd come out, they were older than God . . . but they *sang*."

The Cathedral's music was untouched even by the forces of the Early Music Revival. Groups of original-instrument performers and straight-tone choirs that specialized in unearthing "ancient" works were invading some churches, listened to by audiences that were small but slowly gaining in numbers, dubbed "baroqueniks" by *Time*. The results were encouraging listeners to think more carefully about the music made by those groups, and their own church choirs, in a way that Pietro Yon's Gregorian Club hadn't attempted. By the early 1960s, even neighborhood choirmasters were talking about Baroque pitch and learning how to refer to Josquin Des Prez by offhandedly using only his first name. (A strange barometer of the trend's effect could be seen in the holiday music listings of the *Times*—not even because of the listings themselves, in which Purcell and Pachelbel were showing up more and more frequently. For decades, those listings had been decorated with photos showing the city's church choirs in action. Around this time one photo featured the choristers of the Church of the Transfiguration, a group in the vanguard of the Revival; in the back row, one of the choirmen was proudly holding a lute. *That* had certainly not happened in those pages before.) But if the sound

---

* Those recordings that exist show that the lower voices wore their years surprisingly well. The Cathedral tenors didn't fare as happily, as some loud passages were marked by stridency and a tendency to wobble (although soft passages were as ethereal as they had ever been). Courboin may have tried to shore up the tenor section with one 1959 hire, Gino De Lilla, an Italian opera singer who had just moved to New York. He did large roles at small companies and small roles at large companies; a 1965 writeup in *The Albuquerque Tribune* told readers that he "has appeared at La Scala, Covent Garden, Lisbon, Germany, France, Switzerland and Portugal. . . . Before his move to this country, he spent three hectic years giving 500 concerts throughout Italy with the Festival of Mantova."

of the Cathedral Choristers might be labeled "male choir" (or, more deri-
sively, "glee club"), they didn't care; they had been producing that sound
for decades and no one had complained. Lute or no lute, the general
feeling was that the Early Music Revival didn't apply to them.

The various forces pulling at the Church's fabric began to make their
case in the media, some of them bringing up the subject of sacred music.
When Rome's Pontifical Institute of Sacred Music celebrated its fiftieth
anniversary, the Pontiff used the occasion to point out, "[I]t is a duty to
make sure that the Latin language maintains its regal scepter and its noble
dominion in all solemn liturgy." *Non-solemn* liturgies could avail themselves of popular hymns in the vernacular; but Latin "is permanently
connected with the sacred melodies of the Church of Rome, and is a clear
and splendid symbol of unity. . . . It must continue to maintain its sover-
eign position to which it has every right."

St. Patrick's stayed out of this discussion, getting no closer than an
article in the November 1962 *American Organist* that giddily celebrated
the Courboin-modified Kilgen—"Full organ is known to invoke diverse
reactions from listeners, from shivers of the spine to pronounced weak-
ness of the knees"—while mentioning absolutely nothing about the choir,
the form of the Cathedral's music, or any possible changes that might
ensue.

One of those changes stunned the world when the Pontiff died of
stomach cancer in June 1963, less than five years after his election. St.
Patrick's responded with a pontifical requiem Mass, and worshipers
packed into the Cathedral as Courboin led the Men's Choir in the Perosi
Missa di Requiem.

The voice of the choir's soloist, Gina [*sic*] de Lilla, carried softly and
reverently through the cathedral as heads bowed in silent prayer. The
6,000 mourners, more than 70 per cent of them women, filled the
pews, stood in great unmoving masses in the side aisles and crowded
the four side doorways.

Not even three weeks later came the election of his successor, Pope Paul
VI. News reports wrote not a word about any music. (However, the
Times was particularly enthusiastic about the homily, delivered by the
now-elevated Monsignor Duffy.) Some people wondered what would become of the Vatican Council, but the new Pontiff promptly announced
that the Council's work would continue, resuming that autumn.

Then the events of that November would make many Americans forget about the discussions of the Council.

As with Yon and Ungerer before him, Eddie Rivetti held a professorship at Cathedral College, where he taught Gregorian chant. Robert Ritchie, one of Rivetti's students (and a future Cathedral Rector), remembered the afternoon of Friday, the 22nd, and the moment when an ashen-faced Rivetti came into the classroom to break the news that President John F. Kennedy had been killed by an assassin's bullet.

Neither Rivetti nor Courboin was able to get to the Cathedral immediately, but the clergy did their utmost to comfort the 20,000 people who visited St. Patrick's that day when they first heard that the president had been shot. Bishop Flannelly broke the news to the congregation at 2:30: "We have just been informed that President Kennedy is dead. May God have mercy on his soul."

> For a moment, there was not a whisper in the huge cathedral. Then a muffled wail, subtle as smoke, crept over the crowd. Women bowed down sobbing and men cradled their heads in their arms. . . . Bishop [John J.] Maguire led the congregation at St. Patrick's in singing the national anthem, something that is rarely done in a Catholic church.

The next morning, the Cathedral held the first of what would be four requiem Masses for Kennedy. The *Times* was there, describing the overflow crowds, the seminarians and clergy chanting the "Dies Irae" (while pointing out that it had been heard the previous June at the requiem for Pope John XXIII), and the fact that congregants displayed "little outward emotion." At the end, Courboin, at the galley organ, played "Taps."

At which point, noted the *Times,* it began to rain.

Viva Papa!

By late 1964, the Vatican Council had instituted its first proposed changes in the Mass. They may have been historical ("the most sweeping changes in the liturgy since the Council of Trent," claimed the *Times*), but when they were introduced to the public their importance was swamped in a sea of confusion. The *Times* detailed all of this in a long article, seizing upon the new and unfamiliar aspects of the Mass—the English language (except that Latin was still intended to be used at places like St. Patrick's "where there are usually foreign visitors"); hymns, or rather the fact that the congregation was being specifically directed to sing them; and the new characters of the lector and the "commentator" (a type of M.C. for the Mass, and soon to be discontinued). As to any proposed changes in the music, there wasn't much news:

> The high mass presents a special problem because of the settings of the classical Latin by noted composers. A few musical versions have been written for the English text, notably one using American folksong themes, but their use is expected to be limited.

The Cardinal, who had participated in the Vatican Council, had gone on the record as considerably less than enthusiastic about the results. So did plenty of other people. Brooklyn churches held "demonstration Masses" to teach grumbling parishioners the new routine. As far as the "new" music was concerned, the reaction fell just short of open rebellion. One man said, "I feel like I'm a member of a children's chorus, having to sing this wretched little hymn out loud." Music directors were finding that Gregorian chant had an alien flavor when sung in English. The folksong-themed pieces written to English texts met with little favor from congregations or musicians. The French priest Joseph Gelineau had tried to fit psalmody into a system that was meant to be usable by anyone; he composed innumerable settings that were meant to be singable but that came across as mechanical.

While both *Time* and the *Times* had made a point of carrying unflattering comments about the music that might be used in the new Mass, Courboin simply worked around the problem. And so did most of the city's other Catholic choirmasters, according to the music listings for services such as those for Christmas 1964. Other than tossing in a few of the lumpy Latin-to-English translations that had become available ("Cry Out with Joy to the World"), nearly all of those choirmasters were stubbornly fitting into the holiday services the music with which they—along with their choirs and congregations—had always been familiar. To many liturgical musicians, it seemed to be a Chinese puzzle: Rivetti, for one, would spend years at the self-imposed task of translating the Cathedral's favorite Latin settings, then trying to fit those translations to their music in a way that would scan gracefully. Such effort was not only daunting, but depressing.

The Revised Mass wasn't the only subject of interest to the city's Catholics. The 1964–65 World's Fair had opened that spring—in the same location as the 1939–40 Fair, and using much of the same physical layout. One of the most popular exhibits was the Vatican Pavilion, which had made the astonishing gesture (thanks to Cardinal Spellman's request) of arranging for Michelangelo's *Pietà* to be displayed. Of the Pavilion's more than 27 million visitors, most of them boarded the exhibit's triple-level moving walkway to get a glimpse of the *Pietà*. But in contrast to 1939 and the vigorous musical programming that had been one of the attractions of the Temple of Religion (much of it featuring St. Patrick's musicians), tastes had definitely changed. This time there was no Temple of Religion. Music, to the extent there was any, was being provided by such sources as visiting high school bands at the General Cigar Pavilion and the 600-bell Coca-Cola Carillon—and for that matter, most people would leave the fairgrounds humming the theme song incessantly played at the Disney-designed UNICEF exhibit, "It's a Small World." Neither Courboin nor the Cathedral Choristers would be featured at the Fair.

The Cathedral music staff would, however, be involved in an event without precedent when the Pontiff visited New York in October 1965. Never before had a Pope visited the United States. And Pope Paul VI was coming to New York City in a whirlwind fourteen-hour trip—specifically to address the United Nations, but also to visit St. Patrick's, to celebrate a gigantic open-air Mass at Yankee Stadium, and then to the Fair to finish with a visit to the Vatican Pavilion. Nearly all of it would be televised, nationally and internationally.

Even though the Pope would be visiting St. Patrick's for less than twenty minutes, the Cathedral, along with the city, went through weeks of preparation. Some of it was the usual housekeeping (with a twist; girls from Catholic schools drew lots for the honor of polishing the Papal throne). Some of it was less usual, such as a number of intensive bomb sweeps, and the police check of clerical supply stores to keep tabs on suspicious characters who might be seeking priest's clothing. The *Herald Tribune* noted that, over the weekend, Cathedral workmen had installed a bronze plaque next to the main entrance:

HIS HOLINESS, POPE PAUL VI
ON HIS ARRIVAL
FOR THE FIRST PAPAL VISIT
TO AMERICA
CAME TO THIS CATHEDRAL

TO ADORE
THE BLESSED SACRAMENT
4 OCTOBER 1965

The evening before the Pontiff's visit, onlookers began to gather in the streets around the Cathedral, enduring temperatures in the low 40s in an all-night vigil to form a crowd that by the next morning would swell to almost 50,000.

The next morning, St. Patrick's was filled with its own crowd of 4,500 invited guests. Courboin and the Men's Choir were stationed in the gallery (along with rifle-toting Secret Service agents, as well as a photographer from *Life* magazine), ready with the music demanded by the occasion: the Papal March, Ravanello's "Tu es Petrus," and Ambrosini's "Oremus pro Pontifice" to be sung after the Papal blessing. Eddie Rivetti was ready at the chancel organ, his wife, Ann, and daughter, Dianne, seated on a bench near him. The Pope was expected to arrive at noon. Some observers had wondered about the "propriety" of over-enthusiastic crowd reactions both outside and inside the Cathedral (in 1965 the idea of applause in a Catholic church, or for that matter any other kind of demonstration, was nearly unheard of), and before the Papal arrival Monsignor Duffy addressed the issue by announcing to the congregation, in formidable understatement: "We are not making any announcement concerning your reaction to the Pope's arrival. We leave that to your own emotions or devotions."

Everyone took him at his word. The Pontiff's motorcade arrived in front of the Cathedral twenty minutes early, and those inside heard a sudden roar from the crowd in the streets. With Bishop Flannelly escorting, the Pope entered the central doorway—and as the organ launched into the Papal March, Dianne Rivetti remembered, "it was something like an explosion" as the congregation leapt to its feet, many people (even clerics) jumping up to stand on their pews, nearly all of them shouting at the top of their voices as the Pope walked down the aisle to screams of "Long live the Pope!" and its Italian equivalent, "Viva Papa!" Then, reaching the altar, he seated himself as Courboin and his men offered the Ravanello.

The Pontiff's blessing of the congregation, his address to them, and afterward, walking around St. Patrick's to greet the cheering crowds—the whole experience was a high point for New Yorkers. And it had been a unique moment for Courboin—who was presented with a Papal medal for his efforts—as well as for the Cathedral musicians.

However, that was the sum total of the music department's involvement with the Papal visit.

That evening's Mass at Yankee Stadium (held before a congregation that the *Times* estimated at 90,000) had its music provided by a chorus of 225 local seminarians, and beforehand the prelude music was given by the Princeton University Pro Musica Brass Ensemble, playing Palestrina and Schütz. When, as his last stop after the Mass, the Pope visited the Vatican Pavilion at the World's Fair, he was serenaded by the band from Cardinal Spellman High School.

Vatican II and a Very Public Funeral

The Papal visit may have been a high point, but it marked the beginning of the end for the Cathedral Choristers under Charles M. Courboin.

American culture had splintered into warring factions, all with provocative labels—the Establishment, the Anti-Establishment, the Drug Culture, the Counterculture, the Sexual Revolution, the Social Revolution, the TV Generation . . . and the Vietnam Generation, as the national involvement in the Vietnam War further divided the country into hawks and doves. And all of it was taking place during a time so openly hedonistic that it had been dubbed the Swinging Sixties. No wonder many people felt there had been a steep decline of interest in churchgoing.

For Catholics, some of the feeling might have come from confusion: The changes in the Mass wrought in 1964 by Vatican II were themselves being changed again and would be changed several times more until they would arrive at a final form in early 1970. While some people were exhilarated by the alterations, others were openly dismayed, and yet some others were stoic. The clergy, including Cardinal Spellman himself, were doing their level best to accommodate those changes. When he celebrated a thanksgiving Mass for the fiftieth anniversary of his ordination, the press account remarked upon a major difference in the sanctuary, a "simple altar" that had been added thirty feet in front of the main altar. The *Times* noted that the Cardinal had offered the Mass from the new altar (and that the altar had been his idea), and added:

> This was to encourage full participation of the congregation in the prayers and hymns, most of which were in English, in keeping with the recent liturgical reforms in the Catholic Church.

But that comment on English hymns was one of the last times that Courboin's musicians would be mentioned, even obliquely, outside of a major Cathedral event.

The lack of interest was probably inevitable. With so much public attention being focused upon the form of the Mass, there was little left over for the music. An alarming number of Catholic churches had responded to the changes by dismantling their music programs outright, while plenty of other choirmasters who were still striving to make music in the new Church felt that they needn't have bothered. Nearly all of the new repertoire consisted of hastily confected Mass settings, hymns, and other service pieces whose musical value was so dubious that they would disappear faster than any White List composition ever did. But at the time, such musical upheavals weren't limited to Catholic choir lofts. Many Protestant churches were subjecting their music to even more drastic changes, supposedly to "keep up with the tastes of the people," actually more often as a desperate ploy to keep a congregation's interest alive. The Reverend Bryant Kirkland, pastor of Fifth Avenue Presbyterian, the Cathedral's neighbor a few blocks to the north, gave an interview at Christmastime which demonstrated that his congregation had changed its approach to the holiday season more radically than any Catholic church would dare:

> We have to have certain pieces of music, grind out the same three or four messages, the Wise Men, Star of Bethlehem, and so forth, which are all so worked over—and use the same symbology. I care for a more creative approach.

Reverend Kirkland had addressed the problem by programming a concert at which Duke Ellington led a performance of his "In the Beginning God," complete with jazz combo and liturgical dance. Next to such extreme and attention-grabbing ideas, the *Missa Choralis* evoked nothing more than a shrug.

Writer Thomas Day would later comment on precisely this period, insisting that "[the] ideal of exuberant, splashy, Great Master music, with orchestra, was considered a scandalous aberration. St. Patrick's Cathedral on Fifth Avenue, under Cardinal Spellman and even earlier, would serve as the prestigious model and would shape the musical tastes of American Catholicism." That theory may or may not have been accurate. But the

Cathedral's musicians would have been surprised to hear it. Their impression was that most people just weren't paying attention.

There was another, darker problem. Courboin was over eighty years old and beginning to experience physical tremors, which instantly gave rise to the rumor that he was suffering from Parkinson's disease. (Robert Courboin has stated that this was never the case—that his father was actually suffering from a condition called Depuytren's contracture, in which tumor formations cause the fingers to bend immovably toward the palm. The condition can be triggered by work that chronically stresses the hands, as well as by injuries. Considering that Charles Courboin was an organist who had been involved in more than the usual share of auto crashes, it stands to reason.) Some observers said that the tremors would disappear whenever he began to play. Even so, Courboin was forced to start missing occasional Sundays at St. Patrick's. Rivetti loyally jumped in to pick up the slack.

The next milestones in the Cathedral's history underlined the fact that, in some minds, splendid music seemed no longer to be particularly required for Catholic worship. After more than twenty-eight years as Archbishop of New York that had turned him into an important figure on the world stage, Cardinal Spellman died of a stroke in December 1967. His death was a shock to the music department; his reputation was that of a tough boss, but he had enough of the personal touch that he would be regularly invited to, and would attend, the testimonial dinners that were held for retiring choirmen. His funeral was a major event, covered in exhaustive detail by every newspaper and every TV network. *Time* wrote of the pageantry and the high-powered guest list, which included everyone from President Lyndon Johnson to a delegation of senators from South Vietnam. But its only reference to the music was the post–Vatican II omission of some of it: "Notably absent from the service was the beautiful but chilling sequence Dies Irae."

In its numerous articles covering the Cardinal's funeral, the *Times* mentioned music one time: "During the service the congregation sang six hymns in English. The final one, 'For all the Saints,' is often sung at Protestant funeral services."

The following April, Cardinal Spellman's ex-secretary and Vicar General of the Archdiocese, Bishop Terence Cooke, was named Archbishop of New York (delighting Cathedral employees: a frequent comment in hallways was, "He's one of our own"). His investiture was a grand ceremony, also attended by President Johnson and a galaxy of notables. And the *Times* wrote of the music, in toto, "It is all in English now, Protestant hymns are sung, and the congregation sings and speaks responses to some of the prayers."

National tragedy occurred soon after midnight on June 5 when Senator Robert F. Kennedy of New York, forty-two years old and in the midst of his presidential campaign, was cut down by an assassin's bullet in California. The country reacted in shock and disbelief; Kennedy had long been considered the heir apparent to his late brother's mantle. His body was flown to New York, to lie in state at St. Patrick's (which would be open for the entire day and through the night, if necessary, to accommodate mourners) until the funeral on June 8. That Mass would be televised to the nation.

As the first of more than 150,000 people began filing past Kennedy's coffin, funeral arrangements were being discussed. Military advisors had initially conceived their own rudimentary plans (including some discussions of the possibility of having Kennedy's body lie in state in the Capitol rotunda), but those advisors promptly learned that the Kennedy family members had their own ideas of what would constitute a proper funeral and were very firm in their determination to have those plans carried out. Music would play an important part. And the artists performing that music would represent a cross-section of the American music scene, as well as people who were important to the Kennedys. For the offertory, Leonard Bernstein would lead a contingent from the Philharmonic in the "Adagietto" from Mahler's *Resurrection* Symphony. Saramae Endich, a soprano prominent in the concert world, had been soloist in the Mozart *Requiem* sung at John F. Kennedy's funeral; she would sing the "Requiem aeternam" from the final movement of the Verdi *Requiem*. And the chant "In Paradisum" would be provided by a choir of nuns from Manhattanville College of the Sacred Heart.

But a problem arose when the senator's widow, Ethel Kennedy, requested that close family friend Andy Williams sing "Panis Angelicus" during Communion. Williams was immensely popular and the star of his own TV variety series, but he had made his fame as a pop crooner, and no one knew if he had the vocal equipment to handle Franck's music—or for that matter, if he even knew it. He met with Monsignor Duffy and Rivetti for a hastily arranged runthrough at the piano. As they thought would be the case, Williams didn't have "Panis Angelicus" in his repertoire. After a number of different options were suggested and discarded, someone suggested "The Battle Hymn of the Republic." They settled on that. Then Williams asked about his microphone placement, which caused further alarm: Cathedral soloists customarily sang from the gallery, and the gallery used no amplification. However, they could take advantage of Vatican II reforms that permitted a lay person to sing from the sanctuary. Williams could use the microphone at the lector's podium. Met tenor Richard Tucker would fill the gap at Communion, singing "Panis Angelicus" from the gallery.

The Cathedral Choristers (specifically, the Men's Choir) would have to provide the continuity that would keep these disparate parts from seeming like a jumble as they followed each other. There were whispers that Bernstein was concerned. He needn't have been. No matter how much they might have seemed out of step in the current music scene, Courboin's men had the skill to be on their best musical behavior, along with a performance style secure enough that they could collaborate fully with the soloists—not as a backup group, but as equal partners in the service.

At 4:30 in the morning of June 8, the all-night vigil of mourners was brought to an end, the crowds choking Fifth Avenue were moved behind barricades, and the doors of St. Patrick's were closed to prepare for the funeral Mass. Because President Johnson and other high-level government officials would be among the guests, the Cathedral underwent another bomb sweep. When the Philharmonic musicians showed up, Secret Service agents checked their instrument cases before they were allowed to enter. "We were surprised, though, that they didn't search our pockets," said the concertmaster.

By 9:50 A.M., Courboin and the Men's Choir were ready in the gallery, Rivetti at the chancel organ (this time without his family; the occasion promised to be tense enough that he had asked them to stay home and watch the funeral on TV), and Bernstein with his Philharmonic group was stationed in the ambulatory. Five minutes later, when the Kennedy family was seated, Courboin struck up the processional "All Hail, Adored Trinity."

It was very much a solemn occasion; but from a strictly musical standpoint, Robert F. Kennedy's funeral was an astonishment to millions of people who had forgotten the concept of quality music in the Catholic service. With no accompaniment other than the Men's Choir singing *sotto voce*, Endich gave a seamless rendering of the Verdi while the congregation listened in absolute silence.* Bernstein, "his eyes almost closed and his face contorted in concentration" (wrote the *Chicago Tribune*), "rhythmically moved his baton during the music that was a prayer from the 30 members of the Philharmonic." Tucker's performance of "Panis Angelicus" was, no surprise, as beautiful as anyone would expect.

Finally, after the Commendation, Williams—who had earlier served as one of the vigil-keepers at the bier—came to the lector's podium to execute the arrangement that had been frantically pasted together in a single day. Completely *a cappella*, he launched into "The Battle Hymn of the Republic," the men in the gallery joining him only for the refrain. Each verse built in strength, giving the choral forces more and more involvement:

> A few voices could be heard singing or humming quietly, and with each verse the chorus grew louder and more assured. Finally, as the end of the procession passed the flag-draped coffin, the cathedral organ and the choir in the balcony at the rear joined in at fortissimo level.

As the coffin got to the doors of the Cathedral and continued out to Fifth Avenue, the Men's Choir and Courboin reached full power, and Saramae Endich contributed a high, keening descant. The *Times* remarked that this was "for many worshipers the most moving moment."

Valedictory

Whether or not anyone had meant for it to be so, the funeral of Robert F. Kennedy had proven that compelling music still had a place in the Catholic service. A number of people seemed to agree. Columbia Records (which had recorded the entire service) included the music in its two-disc set *Robert Francis Kennedy: A Memorial*. Music critic Donal Henahan of the *Times* got the message as well, pointing out that the music had been

---

* Saramae Endich's appearance went virtually unnoticed by the media (press accounts didn't even mention her name), but it contained its own strange historical significance—it marked the first time in more than six decades that a woman would sing at St. Patrick's as part of a Mass.

the result of the "liberalizing influence" of Vatican II (including the use of the "Hallelujah Chorus" at the end of the funeral as a symbol of hope), and devoting an entire column to it:

> Protestant and Roman Catholic music, the singing of a television performer and a cantor, rousing music from the Civil War and symphonic excerpts mingled yesterday . . . in a way that would have been impossible a few years ago.

Others failed to get the message, however, and for the musicians of St. Patrick's their appearance at Kennedy's funeral served as something of a valedictory.

Those decision-makers now at the Cathedral seemed to have a different view of music's importance in the revamped Church. Archbishop Cooke wasn't in the least anti-musical; he played the violin, and many people remarked on his fine singing voice. But his personal style of worship was intensely focused on the Eucharist rather than on any ceremonial aspects of the Mass.* Clergy and laity alike, many people of that era followed that lead, considering music almost as an afterthought. Even the *Times* seemed to agree—starting with Christmas 1969, its once carefully detailed holiday music listings were "streamlined" to such an extent that the music information nearly disappeared. Now they read more along the skimpy lines of "Christmas Day—10 A.M.—Processional and Pontifical Mass."

Whether or not it was coincidence, the music department of St. Patrick's began at that point to disintegrate. After two solid decades of activity, the Boy Choristers didn't seem to fit into the post–Vatican II world. Their membership almost immediately dissolved. Because Monsignor Duffy was no longer needed as Choir Moderator, he would leave the Cathedral in 1970 to become pastor of St. Rose of Lima.

Courboin had been honored by Belgium yet a third time in 1968, when King Badoin bestowed upon him the Order of the Crown. But otherwise his situation wasn't improving, and his health problems were pushing him into semi-retirement. There were rumors that he hadn't played at the

---

* Cooke's philosophy, and his modesty, extended even to his elevation to Cardinal. At that time, he refused the ceremony of a full-dress installation Mass, preferring instead to celebrate the occasion by greeting the public on the Cathedral steps.

Cathedral since the Kennedy funeral. It had been necessary for Eddie Rivetti to quietly take over the choir's management, even conducting the Midnight Masses of 1968 and 1969. The feeling was that the music of St. Patrick's was in a holding pattern, not a satisfactory state given the revisions mandated by Vatican II that were still being adjusted and readjusted. A change would have to be made.

Organist of the Met and Other Places

In 1964, a young organist named John Grady had been placed on the Cathedral's substitute list; that spring, he got the lucky break of playing Cardinal Spellman's jubilee Mass. He then became even luckier in snagging the position of organist and choirmaster of the brand-new Holy Family Church, which opened at the beginning of 1965. The aggressively modern structure had been built within sight of the United Nations and was designed to serve its community. Grady was instantly plugged into that community, as well as its power structure.

Grady's year may have started off slowly (the *Times'* listings of Easter music carried a picture of him conducting the Holy Family choir—ten women and one man), but it got considerably better in June when he was named organist of the Metropolitan Opera. It got better still in October with the visit of Pope Paul VI, when one of the Pontiff's stops was at Holy Family for an ecumenical meeting. Not only did Grady put together a musical program for the occasion, but he had been given the honor of conducting the choir of seminarians for that evening's Mass at Yankee Stadium.

Within a couple of years Grady was able to move over to the Church of St. Agnes, where he formed The Concert Chorale, "a group of professional and non-professional singers who work under Mr. Grady's direction and have given many concerts in the metropolitan area. They are currently singing monthly in the Church of Saint Agnes; and they may also be heard on an NBC Network radio broadcast, each Sunday evening, at 11.05 o'clock." (So stated *The Memorial Requiem Mass for Jacques-Cécilien Ungerer*, the program booklet for a memorial to Ungerer that took place in 1969. The service had been a strange occasion, taking place not at St. Patrick's but at the Church of St. John the Martyr. The event was stuffed with music—including a generous handful of Ungerer's works—and listed Grady as the organist, along with The Concert Chorale as the singers. The coincidence of Grady's playing Ungerer's memorial was ironic in itself, made even more so by an additional line in the program: "Grateful acknowledgement is further made to Mr. Edward Rivetti, Organist of St. Patrick's Cathedral.")

When playing at St. Patrick's, Grady undoubtedly would have met the new Rector, Monsignor James Rigney, who succeeded Bishop Flannelly in late 1969. Monsignor Rigney was an outgoing individual who vividly remembered his first impressions of the Cathedral: "My predominant thought was, it's uninspiring. . . . You have to clean it up and somehow warm it up. You have to assure people they're not being greeted by a glacier. . . . I thought St. Patrick's needed a family. . . . The volunteers bring about the only unity outside the liturgy." This community-based thinking was a direct outgrowth of Vatican II imperatives—the Mass as a shared experience—and it would be only logical that such an ideal would take in the Cathedral's music. Rather than the previous model, which relied on high-quality professionals for the serious music production and used volunteers for tuneful window dressing (the Cathedral Club, and various permutations of the chancel choir), perhaps it would be a welcome change to involve the volunteers more deeply in the musical enterprise.

Seen in this light, John Grady fit the bill admirably. He had as much experience as any other New York choirmaster in the game of coaxing music out of volunteers, while at the same time his Met connections guaranteed that he had access to topflight professionals as well as the gravitas to deal with them. And he himself was well regarded as an organist.

On August 31, 1970, the *Times* unbent with a four-column writeup headlined ST. PATRICK'S NAMES MET ORGANIST AS MUSICAL DIRECTOR. Complete with a photo of Grady at the Kilgen, it was the kind of expansive article that hadn't been written about St. Patrick's in years:

> A new musical era will begin in St. Patrick's Cathedral next Sunday when John Francis Grady, organist of the Metropolitan Opera, will also become organist and musical director at the cathedral.
>
> Some significant innovations and departures from custom will soon follow. . . .

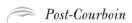 *Post-Courboin*

That same *Times* article had gone on to report, "The former cathedral music director, Charles Courboin, retired in 1968, and Mr. Rivetti has bridged the two-year gap to Mr. Grady." This had never become common knowledge. As far as the Cathedral's records were concerned, Courboin's retirement date would thenceforth be listed as 1970. He died on April 13, 1973, eighty-nine years old and spent. As with every other Cathedral music director before him, his funeral took place at St. Patrick's. Cardinal Cooke was one of the celebrants; Bishop Flannelly sat at the sidelines, several years retired and little more than a month away from his own death.

It was perhaps an indication of the era that there was absolutely no press coverage.

In the cemetery plot shared by the Courboins and the Swinnens, Charles-Marie Courboin was the last to be interred. A running joke through the years had centered on Courboin and Swinnen's mutual fondness for a favorite brand of cream ale, and their insistence that they were planning to be buried with several cases. It's not known if they were able to accomplish that project.

Charles-Marie Courboin, in a photo from the 1930s.

The entire St. Patrick's music department turns out for a Catholic Charities telecast. Boy Choristers are flanked by the Men's Choir, and headed by (*left to right, front row*) Charles Courboin, Monsignor William T. Greene, soprano Licia Albanese, and Cardinal Spellman. (*Courtesy of Joseph McQuade*)

Choirmen Serafino Bogatto and Hildreth Martin (*third and fourth from left*) had begun singing at St. Patrick's in the 1920s; they were still singing for Courboin in the 1950s. (*Courtesy of Robert Courboin Jr.*)

Chapter 6

BOYS AND GIRLS TOGETHER (1970–90)

> Whenever, for a liturgical service which is to be celebrated in sung form, one can make a choice between various people, it is desirable that those who are known to be more proficient in singing be given preference; this is especially the case in more solemn liturgical celebrations and in those which either require more difficult singing, or are transmitted by radio or television.
>
> *Instruction on Music in the Liturgy*

John Grady would tell friends that he had always dreamed of having one job—music director of St. Patrick's. Whether or not that was strictly true, most of his existence could be viewed as preparation for his work at the Cathedral, or at least a place like it.

Called "the first native New Yorker since William Pecher to hold the position" (incorrect but close; he was a Long Islander, born in Great Neck in 1934, and for that matter he himself would skip over Pecher's lineage with occasional claims that he was the first American *ever* to hold the post), Grady had jumped into the Manhattan sacred music scene early on as a boy soprano at venues such as the Church of the Blessed Sacrament and the Church of the Incarnation. At age thirteen he discovered the organ. This led him to Fordham University for undergraduate work, as well as to St. Ignatius Loyola for an assistant organist position. While he was at Fordham, his showman's instincts came to the fore when he joined the university's radio station, WFUV, became the station's director of music, and "initiated live broadcasts from areas of the city." Then came a brief interlude as a seminarian, sporadic private study with Virgil Fox (who at some lessons would become so angered with his student's casual level of preparation that he'd throw him out of the studio), more work at both Columbia University and the Juilliard School, and then John Grady was ready for the world.

Once his career began to move, he was able to add some alluring European credits with recital work at Notre Dame and Westminster

Cathedral. The press coverage of those excursions demonstrated that he knew the value of good publicity, and how to snag it, as well as Yon or Courboin had. In 1970, the *Washington Post and Times Herald* ran a large and hyperbolic article, four columns complete with portraits of both Grady and his organ console, headlined THE AMAZING MET'S ORGANIST. It was written by Paul Hume, who was not only the music critic for the *Post* but also a strident commentator on Catholic liturgical music. Coincidentally, he was also a professional friend of Grady's, as well as a now-and-then Met employee who contributed occasional intermission features during Saturday radio broadcasts.

As part of the article heralding his appointment, the *Times* had written, "At the Metropolitan, where he has been the organist since June, 1965, Mr. Grady must play the music that is set before him. At the cathedral, the range of his options will be restricted only by the limits of his imagination and his sense of what is fitting." Indeed, Grady was drawing up plans of the sort that had never been attempted before at St. Patrick's: concerts with full orchestra, chamber ensembles, and as a particular innovation, a Sunday afternoon series of organ recitals. This was a new and somewhat radical idea for any Catholic church, and a definite first for the Cathedral.

Such plans were typical of the extremely fragmented mood that characterized the "post-conciliar" period. The 1967 Vatican document *Musicam Sacram* had strongly promoted Gregorian chant as a touchstone in liturgical music but had encouraged "a period of experimentation" in new compositions and vernacular texts, and many music directors had interpreted that document as a signal not to promote Gregorian chant but to pursue Relevance by hauling out guitars and tambourines. (When jazz had revolutionized the world of music earlier in the century, the Catholic Church had remained impervious. Now, the inclusiveness of *Musicam Sacram* made it inevitable that Catholics would find themselves swamped by folk, even rock.) Grady would have none of it—"We don't have an indigenous folk tradition in the church. We have to borrow it from the Tennessee hills"—and was in fact moving in quite the opposite direction.

He was asked if he would hew to the line of serious, classical music. His one-word reply was "Yes." It leaped from his tongue with the finality of fiat.

Given the plans of other Catholic churches during the period, such an answer was bucking the trend. Considering the musical history of St.

Patrick's, no one was surprised. And considering Grady's own musical taste, those plans made complete sense. For a few years in the wake of Vatican II, a small group of the city's Catholic musicians who felt that they were losing a part of their musical heritage held weekly gatherings. Each meeting began with dinner, prepared by Paulist choirmaster and amateur chef Father Joseph Foley. "And after dinner," said John McManemin, one of the members (who himself had been a boy soprano in the days of Pietro Yon), "out would come everyone's *Liber Usualis*, and they'd sing chant." As a musical in-joke, the group members borrowed some Gregorian-chant terminology and nicknamed themselves The Quilismas. John Grady had been a Quilisma.

There was yet another change in store that was not at all heralded in the press, but one that would turn the Cathedral music program inside out: For the first time since October 1904, women would return as members of the St. Patrick's choir.

Such a decision would fit with the new sense of community that the Cathedral (and Cardinal Cooke and Monsignor Rigney) was fostering. It would show that St. Patrick's was solidly behind the spirit of the Revised Mass. And it would make it considerably easier to build a volunteer ensemble: Female singers have always been easier to find than men. For a professional core, Grady would get by with a mixed quartet. It would give him a solo ensemble while helping his departmental cash flow, shifting funds from the weekly choir budget to accommodate the extracurricular musical activities he was planning.

All well and good. However, there were a couple of problems in his path. First was a pre-existing situation, the fact that the Cathedral already had on its payroll the entire Men's Choir (the members of which he referred to privately as "sixteen leather-lunged Italians"), all of them having just finished the spring season, many of them preparing to slog through the hot months with Eddie Rivetti in the summer choir . . . and for Grady's purposes, each one of them superfluous. The exact way in which they were dealt with wasn't made public, but by the end of the summer, when Grady formally assumed leadership of the music department, every member of the Men's Choir had left the Cathedral staff.*

---

* Rumor had it that the men had been dismissed in a group, with the caveat that they "were invited to re-audition in the coming season." Whether or not any of them did so, not one would return to sing at St. Patrick's.

The second problem was more subtle and more pernicious. In the world of music, circa 1970, professional singers aimed to sing opera, period; concert singing was a step lower on the career ladder, and "church jobs" existed simply to pay the bills. This meant that the position which had been such a prestigious, door-opening credit for Katherine Hilke and Mary Louise Clary was no longer considered to be very important. To get any real dedication, Grady would have to be extremely lucky in his hiring.

The men were plucked directly from Grady's other environment, the Met—more correctly, the Metropolitan Opera Studio. At the time it was an informal training environment for promising young singers, financing lessons in everything from voice to stage combat, paying no fees and guaranteeing no Met performances to the participants but connecting them with musical jobs in lower-pressure venues. From this came bass-baritone Terrence Hawkins (fresh from the Bermuda Musical and Dramatic Society production of *The Barber of Seville*), as well as tenor David Griffith. Both had soloed at Manhattan churches, Griffith at Madison Avenue Baptist and Hawkins at Brick Church. And both would be gone from the Cathedral within a few years. Griffith would move to the New York City Opera, and soon after that to Frankfurt and Berlin, where he would settle permanently into the German system of opera-singer-as-civic-employee; Hawkins would go on to the Philharmonic, the Newport Music Festival, and the San Francisco Opera.

Both of Grady's women came from elsewhere than the Met. Mezzo Patricia Kelby wasn't part of the New York opera scene, but she was close to St. Patrick's—literally; she worked as advertising manager for *MUSIC/ The AGO Magazine*, whose Rockefeller Center headquarters were just across the street from the Cathedral. The office was a prime stop on the musical grapevine, and there Kelby had heard that John Grady had been auditioning a number of mezzo-sopranos without reaching a decision. She got herself introduced to Grady through an organist friend, demonstrated a particularly beautiful voice, and was promptly hired.

Grady had equally good luck with his soprano. Nadja Witkowska had logged time with a number of orchestras, some recordings, and a big fistful of the highest-flying coloratura roles with the New York City Opera. She wasn't bothered by live broadcasting, having sung twice with the NBC Opera (one of those times in color; the *Chicago Daily Tribune's* critic dubbed her "a beautiful cupcake"), and she'd more than proven her performance flexibility when she did a brief stint on Martha Raye's knockabout TV variety series "All Star Revue." On top of it, her path had already crossed Grady's in 1966 when he conducted her in the Poulenc *Gloria* for an NBC telecast. By 1970, when he was in the market for a Cathedral soprano, she came to mind again; he dropped by to hear her in a coaching session and liked what he heard. Perhaps because Witkowska had met Grady in midcareer, she showed the greatest stability of the quartet, staying at the Cathedral for Grady's entire tenure. Even so, with outside musical commitments she'd have to take off a day or two on occasion, such as happened six months into her first season when she made her own Met debut in *Lucia di Lammermoor*.

Along with his soloists, Grady would be responsible for hiring a brand-new character in the sanctuary—the cantor. The new *General Instruction of the Roman Missal* mandated:

> There should be a cantor or a choir director to lead and sustain the people in their singing. When in fact there is no choir, it is up to the cantor to lead the various songs, and the people take part in the way proper to them. . . . To fulfill their function correctly, these cantors should possess singing talent and an aptitude for correct pronunciation and diction.

With congregations proving themselves to be very, very ambivalent about being asked to participate in the music, some felt that an inviting personality was more important than vocal endowment. And a particularly inviting personality belonged to Stanley Carlson, a bass-baritone who had dabbled in nearly every branch of show business. He had put in more than ten years of character roles at the New York City Opera, starting on the second night of the company's existence in 1944. He had worked in radio and records and had parts in nine Broadway shows, all of them flops. And significantly, he had been one of the original Sing-Along Gang in the NBC series "Sing Along with Mitch," the granddaddy of karaoke, with its male chorus in pullover sweaters and its song lyrics running across the bottom of the screen for viewers. During each broadcast, the home audience was continually urged to "follow the bouncing ball" above the lyrics. If anything was good training for the job of coaxing a congregation to join in, that was.

Even more significantly, Carlson's good-natured folksiness was a departure in style from anything that had, musically speaking, ever happened before at the Cathedral. Without trying, Grady had presented a model of Vatican II style, vintage 1970. And Carlson had unwittingly created a prototype that St. Patrick's cantors would copy—or spurn—for years.*

While this lineup of musicians would constitute a radical change from those in the Cathedral's past, even more radical would be the music they were preparing to sing—a departure from the Cathedral's recent history of Refice and Perosi (which vanished from the repertoire completely; even Yon's music disappeared), and a bigger departure from the works chosen by most other churches, which in the post–Vatican II atmosphere were dull in the extreme. Grady restricted such pieces to service music, adding a heavy dose of oratorio excerpts served up as anthems, and some new compositions for variety. Such programming didn't please everyone, in particular some clerics. Grady, exhibiting a stubbornness for which he would become famous, ignored any complaints.

He also ignored the initial size of the choir. As with every New York choirmaster, Grady had a list of amateur singers who might be canvassed for interest (as the informal rule still went, the broadest hints were allowed, short of outright piracy). He might have been off-putting when he described what would be required of those people, because the hints produced a grand total of *nine* volunteers, giving him the smallest full-scale choir in Cathedral history. Undismayed, he merely spread the news that volunteer choristers would always be welcome to audition; moved the choir to the front of the gallery for better sound projection; and began his season with the bravado of a conductor who had unlimited vocal resources at his disposal.

Such bravado wasn't completely unwarranted, because he was John-Grady-of-the-Met, also John-Grady-of-St.-Patrick's. Those titles gave him access to a first-class talent pool, and he was ready to exploit it. Still, Grady got a prompt lesson in humility: The day after he started work at the Cathedral, St. Patrick's hosted the funeral for football coach Vince Lombardi. The congregation numbered 3,000 and included local, state,

---

* Grady had intended for Carlson to be the Cathedral's only cantor, but the frequency and number of services made that idea unworkable. Carlson was spelled by Grady's professional male singers when the choir could do without them. After a few years Carlson left and another Met Opera Studio alumnus, baritone Matthew Murray, was shuttled in.

and national dignitaries. There was a great deal of media coverage. Not a word of it mentioned music.

Moving resolutely forward, Grady himself inaugurated the Sunday-afternoon organ recital series on November 1, 1970, as the first recitalist. This was exciting for many of the city's organ fans—at the time, not a huge group—who were intrigued by the prospect of hearing the Kilgen played by other organists, in a more concert-oriented repertoire. (Because the concept of an organ recital series was a novelty for St. Patrick's, Grady didn't get much immediate response from organists. As a result, for the first eight weeks of the series' existence he was stuck playing four of the recitals.)

Just before the start of Advent, there was greater excitement when the *Times* ran a sizeable article, complete with headline, on the front page:

> Leopold Stokowski . . . conducted a tradition-shattering concert last night at St. Patrick's Cathedral before an audience of more than 2,500 that included Terence Cardinal Cooke.
>
> The throng that all but filled the spacious cathedral was invited before the concert to applaud "whenever you consider it appropriate."

For its very first concert ever (this was a matter of semantics—there had been those Yon spectaculars existing under the guise of "services of music"; but this occasion was offered to the public at $3 a ticket, the proceeds going to benefit the Cardinal Spellman Program for Retarded Children), St. Patrick's hadn't started small. The orchestra was top-flight, drawn from Grady's colleagues from the Met, and it was led by the lion-maned "Stoki," eighty-eight years old, still a magnetic presence on the podium and still enough of an international superstar to draw a capacity crowd. His participation made complete sense because he loved novel musical experiences as well as publicity, and a concert at the Cathedral offered both. The programming had something for everyone. Grady would play the Poulenc *Concerto for Organ, Strings and Tympani*. Stokowski, champion of modern works, had in May led the premiere of his friend Andrezej Panufnik's *Universal Prayer* in the Cathedral of St. John the Divine's gargantuan space; this occasion would provide him with a second, more easily controlled performance. And Grady and Stokowski collaborated on some Bach.

To form a choir that could stand up to the orchestra, Grady augmented the Cathedral forces by rounding up every additional chorister he could find—regardless of denomination, a specific request of Stokowski's (and a surprise to those who remembered the old "no Jews or infidels" rule: one bemused cleric told a reporter that the group was "'ecumenical' in its makeup"). The choir's job was the Panufnik, and a difficult job it was, because the twenty-eight-minute piece was referred to as "a solemn but sometimes unchurchly work, in which a frightening choral babble arose in the cathedral's rear now and then. . . ." The confusion was intensified by the addition of three harps, as well as some passages in which the harmonic structure left the singers on their own. Patricia Kelby remembered the conductor's matter-of-fact solution: "Stoki sent his assistant out to get us all pitch pipes."

The concert made news across the country, although the *Los Angeles Times* did mangle Grady's name: "organist John Brady." Even so, as the *Times* doted on the five standing ovations received by Stokowski, as well as his style, his attire, and his famous hands, it nevertheless commented bluntly:

> As an artistic event, this first program worked against large odds. Any orchestral program with organ in so large a space as this cathedral presents enormous problems of balance. . . . Mr. Stokowski and the organist, Mr. Grady, partly surmounted the difficulties, but only partly. . . . [R]esults were nonetheless muddy in sonority and rhythmically flabby.

No question that the concert was a milestone, but it was viewed far more as a news story than a musical event—an attitude that would continue for decades. Still, if Grady had wanted to remake the Cathedral as a concert venue, his wish had come true.

The next change, a very major one, came on the Sunday afternoon before Christmas. In the past, the Cathedral had maintained a strict Advent mood, saving its festal music until Christmas Eve. Now there was a difference: Grady collaborated with Alec Wyton, music director at St. John the Divine, to present—at St. Patrick's—The Festival of Nine Lessons and Carols. To some, this was a shock: The Festival was a beautiful service but unmistakably Anglican, and it hadn't quite made its way over to Catholic churches as a received custom. Also, it presented Christmas music before Christmas Eve.

Grady and Wyton went to great lengths to make the event a memorable experience, placing the Cathedral Choir in the gallery and the St. John's choir in the chancel for musical interest. To read the lessons between the choral selections, they had the services of Archbishop John Maguire (of St. Patrick's) and Bishop Horace Donegan (of St. John's). Grady read; Wyton read as well. And to read the fifth lesson, the visit to Mary of the angel Gabriel, they scored a coup by getting the services of Sir John Gielgud, who was then starring in the Broadway play *Home* and had a free Sunday afternoon. The day before the Festival, the *Times* ran a small and discreet notice as part of its music listings. That, combined with word of mouth—and the city's holiday ban on Fifth Avenue traffic, which created a pedestrian mall right in front of the Cathedral and encouraged crowds of walk-in listeners—was enough to draw a congregation estimated at more than 3,000 people. Again, the local press seemed mildly happy with the results but preferred to dwell on the historic nature of the service rather than on the music, though Paul Hume, Grady's *Washington Post and Times Herald* champion, offered three columns of unreserved praise for Grady that included a swipe at the then-still-living Charles Courboin: "Grady, who is also the organist of the Metropolitan Opera, has been hard at work. . . . [T]he improvements in the music that he has brought to that church are as welcome as they are long overdue."*

Four days later came Midnight Mass, the first one at St. Patrick's whose music would be modeled on Vatican II forms (Courboin hadn't changed any Christmas music during his final years), and an event when all of the refashioning would be displayed to the nation via NBC. Grady made a startling break from tradition that night by starting the Mass with a tympani roll (which was misinterpreted as hot-dogging, but he understood that remote broadcasts often didn't begin when they should and preferred that the opening hymn be heard in its entirety). Musically, he broke with tradition by programming the Cathedral's first performance of the Poulenc *Motets for Christmas*, then went a step further by commissioning a new anthem from composer/diarist/raconteur Ned Rorem. "Praises for the Nativity," scored for choir, solo quartet, and organ,

---

* Immediately after the Lessons and Carols ended and the congregation dispersed, Grady had to man the Kilgen to play that afternoon's organ recital. And the Sunday after that—two days after Christmas—he would have to play still another recital. Days like those might account for the moment, only months later, when he considered his schedule and sighed to a colleague, "I've created a monster."

would have its premiere that evening. Finally, perhaps remembering the glamour days of Pietro Yon and his guest soloists for special occasions, Grady decided to engage some star power of his own: Rising young tenor Placido Domingo was scheduled for *Andrea Chénier* at the Met on December 23, but he would nevertheless be happy to appear at St. Patrick's the following night.

That evening presented a few hard truths regarding Midnight Mass at St. Patrick's, as far as the music was concerned. The past decades had trained Cathedral listeners to expect their musical adventure at the organ rather than in the choir gallery, so the Poulenc *Motets* were received with more politeness than enthusiasm (although they would return again and again). But "Praises for the Nativity" proved to be a tough chew for the congregation, not to be repeated. Rorem remembered his work as "hard and lively" (he also complimented the Cathedral Choir as "clear and accurate"), and the piece seemed to have been tailored to the strengths of its singers, highlighting Nadja Witkowska's upper-range ease and Patricia Kelby's plush lower notes. But its musical idiom was uncomfortable to listeners who were looking forward to music more along the lines of "Adeste Fideles."*

Or "O Holy Night." The one unqualified triumph of that evening was Domingo's singing of "Cantique de Noel," so much of a triumph that it immediately created a tradition—from that Christmas Eve on, opera stars would gladly contribute their services to the Cathedral in order to sing that particular carol. Grady would write his own arrangement of the piece, properly highlighting the soloist. And congregations, along with the nation's TV audience, would assume that "O Holy Night" had always been a featured part of the Midnight Mass music at St. Patrick's.

A New Assistant and Some New Problems

Grady had made a successful start on his planned turnaround of the music department, but Eddie Rivetti hadn't been much involved in it.

Rivetti was a consummate gentleman and the most professional of professionals, a tireless practicer (his legacy from Pietro Yon) whose own skills as an organist were unimpaired, able to maintain responsibility to

* And in his 1993 book *Lies,* Rorem referred to the piece as "thorny." Whatever that means.

his work as well as a continually fresh interest in it. (During every wedding he played, he made sure always to strike what he called a "blue note." As he explained, it showed that wedded life wasn't all sweetness and light.) Each service was recorded in an "Ordo Book," in which he would list the singers, the music, and sometimes whether or not he had shaved for the occasion. And . . . he wasn't to Grady's taste.

Possibly it was that Rivetti had a pre–Vatican II mindset and mourned "all that gorgeous music" no longer being used at the Cathedral.* Probably it was that Rivetti had been mentored first by Yon and then by Courboin—daunting comparisons for a new supervisor. Very likely a major reason was that Rivetti had been working at St. Patrick's for thirty-seven years, longer than John Grady had been alive. While Grady and his choir had been perpetrating musical experiments in the name of the Cathedral, Rivetti had been stationed at the chancel organ on Sundays and filling in wherever else he was needed. That was the full extent of his schedule.

Around that time Grady heard an organ recital at St. Paul the Apostle, played by a young organist who had been working at First United Methodist Church in Westfield, New Jersey. He was very impressed, enough so to have a talk with the organist's agent, Richard Torrence.

Two days after Christmas, Torrence called his client: "How'd you like to be an organist at St. Patrick's Cathedral?"

Donald Dumler initially thought that the whole thing was a practical joke.

"He's waiting for you to call him, *right now.*"

Mystified, Dumler phoned Grady and they made an appointment for lunch the next day. Before the soup arrived, Grady cut through the preliminaries:

"When can you start?"

"First off, I'm not Catholic—"

"When can you start?"

---

* Rivetti's feelings were so evident that some of his supervising clerics became irritated. He later remembered an incident (without naming the church) when a priest strode into his office, with Rivetti sitting at his desk, and began to sweep armfuls of the "gorgeous" music from the shelves, dumping it into a wastebasket. After that kind of pointed demonstration, Rivetti had no option but to bring the discarded music home. Even then he couldn't bear to toss it out; not long before he died, he gave it to choir director Claudia Nardi.

"You haven't even auditioned me—"

"When can you start?"

There never was an audition. Dumler played a trial service or two during the last week of 1970, which clinched it; within weeks, *The Diapason* ran his glossiest publicity shot, along with an accompanying article.

> Donald Dumler has been appointed associate organist of St. Patrick's Cathedral, New York City, effective as of January 1, 1971. John Grady, organist and director of music of the world-renowned church, appointed Mr. Dumler to the post because of the heavy schedule of services, recitals and television broadcasts from the Cathedral. . . . [H]is duties at the Cathedral will be arranged so that both he and John Grady are available for concerts throughout the season.

Dumler's personal and musical roots were wildly different from those of every Cathedral organist before him. Born in 1938, he was the first non-Catholic in the Cathedral's history to be hired as a staff organist, and he'd spent his childhood not on the Eastern Seaboard or in Europe, but in Okeene, Oklahoma. As a boy, he listened to Midnight Mass on radio, idly wondering what it might be like to make music at such a place as St. Patrick's. When it turned out that he had an aptitude for the keyboard, he was taught piano from an early age; the most important outlets for his talent were supplying music (unpaid) for the dinner capping Okeene's annual Rattlesnake Roundup, playing (unpaid) for a telethon hosted by Ted Mack, as well as playing Christmas carols in a department store and making appearances (unpaid) on KGEO-TV's after-school music program "Malt Shop." After training with Mildred Andrews at the University of Oklahoma, he moved to New York for further study at Juilliard, all the while harboring vague hopes of a career playing for TV soap operas (which in those days didn't use orchestral accompaniment, relying on organists for their mood music). His New York résumé included a few odd jobs, such as manning the keyboard for a limited-run production of *The Stingiest Man in Town*; then he gradually found himself on the local recital circuit, which led to more-important recitals, which led to St. Patrick's. As for the soap opera dream, it would remain unfulfilled.

Without explanation, Grady assigned Rivetti to train his new organist in the Cathedral's way of doing things. Rivetti must have realized that Donald Dumler was being groomed to replace him; but he was careful not to let on, and Dumler found him to be unfailingly gracious and generous with his time. Still, it was no secret that Dumler was being asked to play a number of assignments that had previously been Rivetti's—as well as the organ recital series, an honor to which Rivetti had not been invited. Cut back to playing Sunday-afternoon services and not much more, Rivetti held out until mid-1972, then considered his options. He had played at St. Patrick's for thirty-nine years, the longest stretch ever for an employee of the music department. Most of that time had been a splendid experience. Rather than see the memory tainted, he decided to offer his resignation. Grady accepted it.

Cardinal Cooke sent him a note: "I pray that God will grant you great happiness in your retirement. . . ."

But retirement wasn't in the cards for Eddie Rivetti, as he was immediately approached by *two* churches whose pastors wanted his services— Guardian Angel Church on 10th Avenue, and Old St. Patrick's Cathedral. Both pastors were so insistent to have him on staff that they decided to work together, adjusting their schedules in order to allow him to take both jobs. This new career phase was flattering, but it took a lot of energy; Dianne Rivetti remembered her father driving (rapidly) between churches, charging up the stairs of one organ loft to play a service that he had just completed at the other. And the memory of St. Patrick's could still hurt. At times he would say ruefully, "When I was new, I played at the new Cathedral. Now that I'm old, I play at the Old Cathedral." But people at both the Old Cathedral and Guardian Angel made it plain that they were nothing but delighted to have him.

This was his pattern for the next eighteen years. By 1990, he was forced to retire because of increasingly severe arthritis, which had made playing impossible. A year later, he died. His funeral was at St. Patrick's. Donald Dumler served as organist.

If Grady had thought that by trading Eddie Rivetti for Donald Dumler he was getting a kindred spirit, he was mistaken. Grady loved being a center-of-attention performer, but he usually rebelled at the nuts-and-bolts processes of technical work and practice. Dumler, though, invariably sat down to a daily round of what he called "torture exercises" at the piano, followed each evening by practice at the organ. The routine was so inflexible that he would frequently answer his home phone with something along the lines of "I have eighteen minutes to talk." Grady was not only extroverted but possessed of a rapier wit that hovered on the edge of cruelty. Dumler was shy, courteous, empathetic, and gentlemanly to his bones. Grady could and would talk at length about theories of musicality. Dumler achieved his considerable effects completely by instinct; if pressed, he quoted Mildred Andrews' maxim "Make it boil." Grady was known as a stereotypical hard-drinking musician, although he was known equally well for his reliability at the Cathedral. Dumler, raised in the Baptist tradition, had grown up away from alcohol. (His own liquid indulgence was reserved for Sunday mornings: a Dr Pepper before Mass, followed by a second one after.) Those personal asceticisms became something of an affectionate joke around St. Patrick's, but the musical results couldn't be denied. Once he had gained a regular and visible platform from which to display his abilities, Dumler began to work with top-drawer musicians such as trumpeter Martin Berinbaum for a WQXR broadcast, and as a guest soloist at Carnegie Hall with the Collegiate Chorale as well as Stokowski's American Symphony Orchestra.

As for the choir, it had begun so tentatively that Grady hadn't ventured to buy robes for the singers; they were wearing the black cassocks, minus surplices, left over from Courboin's regime. But the group was starting to expand, slowly but steadily, as the events of the first season were demonstrating that making music in the Cathedral promised to be an interesting experience. To accomplish this growth, St. Patrick's was borrowing some of the membership-building devices used by the city's larger choral societies. In late August and early September, small ads would run in the *Times* inviting volunteer singers to audition for the likes of the New York Choral Society and the St. Cecilia Chorus; Grady began running his own ads, hoping to siphon off some of that talent. (At first the ads were considered rather *outré* for a church, but within a year some other New York choirmasters were copycatting Grady's idea.) The process was made ridiculously easy for would-be choristers, who could drop in on Sunday afternoons, "NO APPOINTMENTS NECESSARY." That open-door policy became its own small tradition in musical New York.

Once a singer did drop in, the casual atmosphere continued. Applicants were almost always handed a score of *Messiah*. Grady would mutter, "Please tell me honestly if you've seen this before" (without waiting for a reply), and he would launch into one of the easier choruses, not only playing but singing along with the more nervous auditioners. Singers who made the cut were often treated to Grady's own version of a St. Patrick's tour, which had little to do with everyday sightseeing as it took them into

No Trespassing territory, high into the south spire, even onto the catwalk suspended above the Cathedral ceiling. Then they were put on three months' probation. Once that period had been completed to Grady's satisfaction, they would ceremonially receive the ultimate recognition—a key to the choir loft.

The probationary period wasn't difficult, as most new choristers discovered that Grady (the first Cathedral choirmaster whose singers were invited to address him by his first name) had a rehearsal technique that was casual, too. He conducted work sessions from the piano, standing at the keyboard rather than sitting, often talking about the music he was playing, usually with a cigarette dangling from his lips (or set down on the piano's edge, burning yet another mark into the wood). Should the choir lag behind his tempo, he would bawl out, "I'm busy *dragging my grandmother's trunk!*" If things went completely awry, he would grind to a halt and comment dryly, "Close, but no refrigerator." And when a piece went well, he murmured his gratitude: "Leave it to you. You're loves, you really are. . . ." Singers adored it.

As 1970 gave way to 1971 (Grady had to play yet another Sunday-afternoon recital, in late January) and the season continued to unfold, a different issue was arising. But it was an issue that only an astute observer would notice. The recitals and their accompanying deluge of concert activity spoke firmly of hewing to the line of serious classical music. Nevertheless, at the same time, one of the Cathedral singers remembered, "The powers that be were a lot more interested in folk music." And *that* view was often shared by outside groups who held services at St. Patrick's, whose musical taste was absolutely not Grady's, but who were determined to have their way.*

This meant that the Cathedral had in effect two music programs, wildly differing, each jostling for attention. On the one hand, concerts at St. Patrick's were offering such heady experiences as the Verdi *Te Deum*, led by Zubin Mehta and featuring Met soprano Jeannette Pilou; a return engagement for Stokowski, conducting a swanky Christmas program with

---

* Considering the offerings of other churches at the time—St. Joseph's gave a concert entitled "From Renaissance to Rock," and Trinity Church programmed for Christmas Eve (in their own words) " 'For Unto Us a Child Is Born' by Handel with pre-recorded synthesized accompaniment"—maybe the Cathedral's presentations weren't all that far out of line.

guest soloist Benita Valente; Richard Yardumian's *Veni, Sancte Spiritus*, with Lili Chookasian;* even the premiere of *The Royal Mass of Mogho*, accompanied by four drummers imported from Upper Volta and a Harlem choir trained for the occasion in the More language, and applauded by Donal Henahan in the *Times* for "the sophisticated skill with which the composer interwove a bewildering array of stylistic threads into an affecting whole." On the other hand, there were occurrences such as the Mass held at St. Patrick's to celebrate Girl Scout Sunday; for a recessional, the organizers chose "I'd Like to Teach the World to Sing (in Perfect Harmony)." The congregation wouldn't have found the song in any hymnal. They knew it well, all the same, as it had begun life as a singing commercial for Coca-Cola.

With all that was going on in the music department, it could be most severely affected by events that had nothing to do with music. A study in the 1960s had cited the increased street noise of Fifth Avenue, which interfered with services when doors were left open for ventilation, as a good reason to install air cooling in the Cathedral. The work was begun in 1970, and the system was ready for the summer of 1971. (As with Courboin and Yon, Grady's choir was slated to sing through the hot months, whoever showed up.) But when the choir tried to sing in the newly cooled air, it was obvious that something was wrong. No one had thought to check on the acoustic consequences of the white noise generated by the system's blowers. And while those sitting in the congregation barely noticed the whoosh of air through ducts running along the triforium, it was enough to blot out a frightening amount of the choral sound. There was no way around it; the only solution was electronic. Microphones had been used on the altar and in the pulpit for decades, so now they appeared in the gallery. And very soon after, the *Times* would bark: "[I]t is certain that the amplification system was disadvantageous to the singers. It was impossible to gain any clear notion as to what the essential ensemble tone might be." In a period when classical music meant Opera and Opera was never amplified, quite possibly the inclusion of microphones devalued the music at St. Patrick's.

---

* That concert merited a multi-page cover article in *MUSIC*, complete with photos of both Grady and Dumler in action. The writer liked the performance but bewailed the Cathedral's acoustics, and the photos showed a sparse audience, nearly outnumbered by the performers.

But musical considerations meant nothing when compared with the disorder that was engulfing New York during those years and giving it the nickname "Sick Man of Cities." Unbelievably, the city itself was sliding toward bankruptcy: Finances were so rough that, when a Christmas-tree lighting was being planned at City Hall and the subject of music came up, officials tried to find a high school choir whose members could walk to the ceremony in order to save the cost of renting a bus. And whether it was true or not, conventional wisdom had it that Manhattan was dangerous after dark, the streets were unsafe, crime was rampant. This affected New York night life to the extent that Broadway theaters briefly pushed curtain times from 8:00 P.M. to 7:30, in order to expose theatergoers to less of the late-evening mean streets. A handful of New York churches even went so far as to cancel their Midnight Masses because so many parishioners were loath to be out late, even on Christmas Eve. Some of this atmosphere traveled to the midtown Fifth Avenue area; the Cathedral's rectory had been burglarized more than its share of times. Grady himself would remember an incident that occurred when he was practicing one late evening. It was close to midnight and the Cathedral was supposed to have been closed for hours, but he began to feel that he wasn't alone in the building; sure enough, he looked over the gallery rail and saw a disheveled man planted in the middle of the central aisle, staring up rapturously at the source of the music. The man called up in greeting, "You can come down now, little brother." (Grady didn't.)

Even during services, there was occasional trouble. Cardinal Cooke was Military Vicar for the United States, and his association with the Vietnam War—he frequently visited Southeast Asia, ministering to troops and invariably celebrating Christmas services—meant that groups protesting the war would target St. Patrick's, interrupting Masses with demonstrations against the conflict. (A group of the Sisters of Charity were the most visible, protesting each Sunday in front of St. Patrick's, and once arrested for staging a "lie-down" protest in the Cathedral aisles. Their activities became so notorious that a caller to the Chancery office, asking where to find the Sisters of Charity, was told in exasperation, "Have you looked on the floor of St. Patrick's?") War protests were unnerving in themselves, but sometimes the Cathedral seemed to be a target for anyone with a loud voice and a particular beef, as happened on the Sunday when a hood-wearing woman clambered into the pulpit during Mass to deliver a statement on homelessness. By then that kind of routine had become familiar, if annoying; Grady calmly laid into the full organ, drowning her out, until the police arrived.

St. Patrick's employee protocol stipulated that services were to be disrupted as little as possible, so for this occasion as well as less contentious ones the Cathedral musicians forged ahead with music-making. And it was a lot of music. The week leading up to Christmas 1971 was a good example of the pace the personnel of the music department were expected to keep: On December 19, St. Patrick's again hosted the Festival of Nine Lessons and Carols, this time with Cardinal Cooke himself leading the service. Christmas Eve brought Midnight Mass (and another stab at the Poulenc *Motets*). The day after Christmas was Sunday, with a choral High Mass, and the musical offering for the 4:45 P.M. recital was—the Cathedral Choir. Finally, Stokowski was there on December 29 to lead the choir in *Music for the Christmas Season.*

For volunteer singers without a passionate musical interest, these performances, and the rehearsals necessary to prepare them, could add up to an overwhelming time commitment. For professional singers with other career demands, the responsibility of working at St. Patrick's under John Grady could be more than they had bargained for. Understandably, some of those singers would decide to go elsewhere. Others stayed, excited by the high-profile events or the music-making or the sense of service to the Cathedral; they may have been cross-eyed with fatigue, but they developed their own coping mechanisms. Seasoned pro Nadja Witkowska had it down to a routine: "While John was playing, I was always hanging out in the *back* of the loft, learning the music, studying like crazy."

While those years might have seemed like chaos, the Cathedral's more-optimistic label for the period was "ecumenism." The Pontiff's decree *Unitatis Redintegratio* had asked for unity among diverse groups; and as both Cardinal Cooke and Monsignor Rigney were strongly enthusiastic about the trend, St. Patrick's participated in a range of activities that would have been unthinkable a decade before. The concert series received additional choral support from such diverse (and not necessarily Catholic) sources as the American Symphony Chorale, the Fordham University Chorus, and the choirs of Fifth Avenue Presbyterian, St. Bartholomew's, and Plymouth Church. The Cathedral Choir joined the choir of St. John the Divine, on their premises, for a Lenten concert—as well as their own Lessons and Carols services. The choir of Saint Thomas

Church came to St. Patrick's to participate in a "Prayer for Unity Service." Monsignor Rigney preached at Fifth Avenue Presbyterian, and even at Temple Emanu-El; Rabbi Ronald Sobel returned the favor, "the first rabbi in history to speak from the high pulpit." The Cathedral would make more headlines by hosting a joint Catholic–Lutheran prayer service, marked by the use of "Protestant" hymns such as "A Mighty Fortress Is Our God" (marked also by the congregation of 5,000 people, and the fact that they sat in ninety-degree heat because of a glitch in the cooling system; a news photo shows them during the processional, profusely sweating but singing lustily). While guitars hadn't made it into St. Patrick's, circus performers had—Los Muchachos, a Spanish troupe of 90 orphaned boys founded by a priest. Appearing at the Cathedral for a "circus mass," they juggled before the sanctuary railing, performed acrobatics as part of the Offertory, and received Communion in their tights. Archbishop Fulton Sheen was assisted during one Good Friday service by theatrical legend Cyril Ritchard, who "read some of his own meditations and selected passages of prose and poetry." (Ritchard, a devout Catholic as well as a stage-savvy one, appeared for the occasion in "a long black robe.") The whole idea was summed up in 1974 when the *Times* ran a display ad in commemoration: MASS FOR TENTH ANNIVERSARY/VATICAN COUNCIL II DECREE ON ECUMENISM.*

Ecumenism pervaded the Cathedral's musical life as well, as St. Patrick's became involved with a number of diverse projects. Some of them were new twists on old themes, such as the St. Patrick's Day Mass the year before, which had premiered a new Mass setting by Philip Green, film composer (responsible for over eighty scores, including those for *Masquerade*, *Victim*, and *All Night Long*) turned liturgical composer:

Bishop [Patrick V.] Ahern was principal celebrant at a concelebrated mass at St. Patrick's Cathedral. His fine tenor voice rang out in the

---

* Much of this activity took place in a construction-site atmosphere, as another alarm about the Cathedral's physical state had resulted in renovations that literally filled the space for nearly a year with a gigantic framework of scaffolding. The scaffolding blocked sightlines, played even more havoc with acoustics, and required portable closed-circuit TV screens to enable Midnight Mass attendees to actually see the Midnight Mass being celebrated. Fortunately the scaffolding had been removed by the time Los Muchachos arrived and needed flying room.

unfamiliar new "St. Patrick's Mass" by Philip Green, the composer. Mr. Green is a convert, noted Bishop Ahern.

"I don't think there'll be any conversions today," the Bishop said. "I just hope we don't lose any."

The concert series made a big splash in late 1974 with the Vaughan Williams *Dona Nobis Pacem*, featuring a number of the area's choirs as well as Benita Valente and Donald Gramm as soloists. But only months after, bigger news was made by legendary jazz pianist and composer Mary Lou Williams.

A number of the city's churches welcomed jazz as an alternative music form, and St. Peter's Lutheran had for some time been noted for its high-quality Jazz Vespers, but jazz had *never* been performed at St. Patrick's. In fact, concert proposals by Duke Ellington and the Newport Jazz Festival had been turned down. Undaunted, Williams—a Catholic convert—hunted down Cardinal Cooke to tell him that she'd written a Mass, "kind of noisy and loud." He replied, "That's what we need." And even though the work had already had previous life as the score for an Alvin Ailey ballet, she was hoping for it to be presented not as a concert but as service music. Once the Cathedral had decided to present *Mass No. 3* (which Ailey had renamed *Mary Lou's Mass*) and agreed to offer it as the music for an actual Mass, she re-scored it to be sung by a double chorus of children's voices. Thus it was performed in the Cathedral by students from four of the area's Catholic schools. The Mass was quite an occasion—cabaret queen Mabel Mercer served as a lector. And, wrote the *Times*:

> Despite the overflow attendance, churchly decorum was maintained throughout the service. When Miss Williams concluded her Mass with a driving, joyous performance of her setting for the 150th Psalm, "Praise the Lord," however, her listeners burst into spontaneous and extended applause.

But the Cathedral's music department hadn't been directly involved with *Mary Lou's Mass* at all. They were working on another project that bowed only five evenings later, rivaling *The Triumph of St. Patrick* in scope and size.

Laszlo Halasz had been a Broadway musical director, the first conductor of the New York City Opera, and by the 1970s leader of the Concert

Orchestra of Long Island. With the backing of the Nassau County Office of Cultural Development, he decided to commission a "folk mass" and to find a folk-based composer to write it. Alan Hovhaness, American-born but musically a world citizen, had been taken with the recent phenomenon of the folk mass as well as its popularity; he rapidly turned out both libretto and music for *The Way of Jesus*, a "folk oratorio." The score was eclectic, without a doubt. Hovhaness felt that much of his music was Handelian, but there were other sections that he referred to as "controlled chaos," and he pointed out, "I have three guitars accompanying a unison chorus several times." As the score was being readied, it turned out there wasn't a suitable performance venue available on Long Island. They contacted Monsignor Rigney, who thought *The Way of Jesus* was a fine idea for St. Patrick's. Hovhaness later said, "We were booked in before we knew it." So was Grady, along with the Cathedral Choir, like it or not.*

It was a large-scale performance, lavishly budgeted at $20,000—which was contributed jointly by the State Council on the Arts and Nassau County. The Cathedral Choir was supplanted by the All City Concert Choir; instrumental support came from the American Symphony Orchestra. Soloists were American tenor Brian Donahue; bass-baritone Ara Berberian ("long a champion of Mr. Hovhaness' music"); and, making an American debut that would soon lead to Met stardom and a major international career, Hungarian dramatic soprano Eva Marton.

With so many heavy hitters taking part, music critics were predisposed to enjoy the evening. It wasn't entirely free of hitches; Robert Sherman noted in the *Times*, "Maestro Halasz had to give a few cues twice, suggesting that a little more rehearsal time would not have been unwelcome," and mentioned that Hovhaness' guitar-accompanied sections had to be dropped from the performance, "apparently because of amplification difficulties." Nevertheless, the piece, the choir, and the soloists were all enthusiastically received. And the composer himself seemed to be satisfied, later telling the *Choral Journal* that *The Way of Jesus* was one of his most important choral compositions.

Jazz, folk oratorio, African tribal rhythms, controlled chaos: If Grady had ambitions of a "signature sound" to be heard at St. Patrick's, ecumenism was providing him with a real challenge. Flexibility was the order

---

* The music was quirky enough that choir members soon decided that they *didn't* like it, developing their own nickname for the piece that rhymed vaguely, and unflatteringly, with "Hovhaness."

of the day for the music department. Complicating matters was the high-profile nature of many Cathedral events, which made it especially important for Grady, and his musicians, to be able to roll with the punches. When St. Patrick's held "the first memorial Mass for a Jew" for Met tenor Richard Tucker, the Cathedral Choir deferred to soprano Martina Arroyo and the Metropolitan Opera Chorus. Bing Crosby's memorial Mass offered sections of the Fauré *Requiem*, but they had to be juxtaposed with an organ rendition of "The Bells of St. Mary's." And baseball great Casey Stengel's memorial was complicated when his good friend, Met baritone Robert Merrill, showed up—at the beginning of the service, completely unannounced—ready to sing "The Lord's Prayer." During the service, as the choir attempted to concentrate on "How Lovely Is Thy Dwelling Place," Merrill paced back and forth nervously in front of them, clearing his throat audibly and repeatedly, and at the moment before he sang he paused to ask Grady to turn off the microphones in the loft. Once "The Lord's Prayer" began, Merrill's anxiety evaporated as his voice rolled out in secure, Cathedral-filling splendor. Greatly relieved at the end of the song, he immediately left the gallery. And forgot his overcoat.

But there were times when rolling with the punches just didn't help. Walter Hook, another Met Opera Studio alumnus who had joined the Cathedral Choir, learned this the hard way when he was asked on short notice to sing both the American and Italian national anthems at the memorial Mass for slain Italian prime minister Aldo Moro. Hook had never even heard the "Inno d'Italia"; Grady gave him a hastily copied music sheet to study during the Mass. Unfortunately, the music staves had been copied out of order. And this problem was discovered only after the piece began, as it fell apart—in front of twenty concelebrating priests, most of them Italian; a congregation crammed with dignitaries both American and Italian; and the Italian radio/television network RAI, which was recording the whole thing for broadcast in Italy.

Complications to the Cathedral's plans could come from the most surprising quarters. The Vatican's Midnight Mass had customarily been held at the Sistine Chapel, a fairly small affair that was restricted to Vatican diplomats. But in 1973, the Pope decided to change the venue to St. Peter's. This move was greeted with such enthusiasm that it instantly became the norm, and the following year NBC jumped at the chance to televise the event. Still, the network had been regularly broadcasting Midnight Mass from St. Patrick's for nearly a quarter-century, with only that single break in 1950. If the network hesitated at dumping St. Patrick's, the hesitation didn't last long, and there came a major broadcasting hiccup for two Christmases during which NBC viewers saw the Vatican's Midnight Mass, and broadcasts from the Cathedral were limited to radio. Finally, local station WPIX decided to carry Midnight Mass from St. Patrick's. (At first it seemed to be an afterthought, as TV newspaper listings ignominiously shoved it in alongside the blurb for its traditional Christmas Eve treat of carols-with-video-of-crackling-fireplace, "The Yule Log": "Three hours of Christmas music, followed by Midnight Mass from New York's St. Patrick's Cathedral.")*

It was understandable that Grady was torn between very public events, with their prestige and their pitfalls, and the regular schedule of services and holidays, when he could maintain better control over the Cathedral's music-making. Holy Week of 1975 provided churchgoers with a perfect example of his tastes; during the week's services, Grady programmed selections from the Berlioz *Requiem*, Brahms *Requiem*, Bach *Mass in B Minor* and *St. Matthew Passion*, Stainer *Crucifixion*, and five movements from the Poulenc *Stabat Mater*. Lush programming, but not without its contentions. Before that year's Midnight Mass, the *Times* interviewed various Cathedral department heads. In response to Grady's musical plans, Monsignor Rigney told the reporter that he was " 'doing battle,' as he put it, to ensure that the Bach is balanced by 'enough carols for the common man'. . . ."

The Bicentennial at St. Patrick's

The United States Bicentennial was the most elephantine of national celebrations. In New York, the event had begun the year before with the

---

* In one way, staff and clergy may have welcomed the switch. During the NBC years, each Midnight Mass had been the subject of a critique in a post-holiday meeting—mandatory—with "Doris Ann," a representative of the network's Standards and Practices (meaning censors) Department. (One Cathedral staffer said, "She always wore a pillbox hat. She must have been born in it.") For these meetings, everyone had to troop over to the Rockefeller Center offices to hear her mild but pithy suggestions for on-camera deportment that represented the ideals of NBC religious programming: "Sit up straighter. Don't cross your legs like that. Don't pick up your toes when you're sitting. Or standing. Don't walk that way." Genteel as she was, Doris Ann assumed a terrible significance to a number of people around

ringing of church bells and special festivities across the city, including the Cardinal Hayes High School Band on the Cathedral steps. As July 1976 approached, most of the city's energies were taken up with Operation Sail, the approaching visit of tall ships—along with a plethora of ethnic celebrations, parades, fireworks, and other patriotism-themed events. New York churches were handling the celebration in their own ways, from the Brick Church "colonial service of worship" to Vespers at Trinity and Dutch Reformed services for buried soldiers.

Cardinal Cooke's schedule made him one of the busiest clerics in the city; he would begin July 4 at the southernmost tip of Manhattan with an 8:00 A.M. ecumenical thanksgiving service at Colonial-era stronghold Castle Clinton followed by a 10:00 A.M. Mass at St. Peter's on Barclay Street, then back uptown. He was busy the evening before, too, when St. Patrick's held its own Mass of the Bicentennial. It was a big occasion, with the Cardinal celebrating and Archbishop Sheen delivering the homily— and the lectors were television newsman Rolland Smith, along with "First Lady of the American Theatre" Helen Hayes.

The Fourth itself, as far as Cathedral personnel were concerned, was to be treated more as a regular Sunday. In practice, that wasn't quite the case; there were a surprising number of couples who particularly wanted to be married on the day of the Bicentennial and had booked their ceremonies at St. Patrick's far in advance. Those weddings had greatly inflated the regular Sunday schedule, and both Grady and Dumler were dividing the workload between them.

Dumler was sitting in his Parish House office in the early afternoon, able to hear Grady at the chancel organ playing prelude music for a wedding that would take place in the Lady Chapel at 2:00 P.M. The receptionist announced a visitor, a reporter from WPIX: "Are you ready for the bells to ring at 2 o'clock?"

Dumler was completely mystified. "Er . . . what?"

"We heard this would happen all over New York."

Dumler headed up to the reception desk, and for the next few minutes he, the receptionist, the reporter, and a priest hunted for a newspaper. They found a two-day-old *New York Post* and, sure enough, its schedule of Bicentennial events contained:

St. Patrick's, and the threat of her post-Christmas etiquette lesson cast a pall over their holidays.

2 p.m.—All bells in Manhattan ring for 15 minutes in honor of the moment the Declaration of Independence was signed.

But no one at St. Patrick's had done anything to arrange a bell-ringing session.

By this time it was 1:54 P.M. With no time to consult Grady and with the reporter in tow, Dumler sprinted the entire length of the Cathedral and up the gallery stairs, all the while trying to decide upon the appropriate music to play. Gasping for breath and with just a few seconds to spare, he switched on the power to the Cathedral chimes, leaped into position at the keyboard, and began "God Bless America" (which could be heard only on the street, because Grady's rendition of the Clarke "Trumpet Voluntary" was still blaring from the other end of the Cathedral). Suddenly he was enveloped in bright light: A WPIX cameraman had followed the reporter, and a microphone was shoved under Dumler's nose as he played: "How does it feel to be a part of this wonderful, historic occasion?"

Dumler's response, spoken in more-or-less rhythm, was, "I'm sorry . . . but it's very . . . difficult to talk . . . and play . . . at the same . . . time . . . especially when you . . . can't hear . . . what you're . . . playing. . . ."

The reporter had obviously expected something more profound. "Well . . . uh, we'll get out of your way." And he skulked off.

That clip made it onto the evening news, giving all of New York a taste of the Cathedral's observance of the Bicentennial.

Centenary and a Papal Visit

It was no secret that the reputation of the Cathedral Choir had suffered in its last days before John Grady took charge. But by the later 1970s, its prestige had come roaring back, and the leftover black cassocks had been exchanged for new choir robes of impossible-to-miss blue. Once again the musicians of St. Patrick's were considered Famous. It wasn't the kind of fame, based on musical superiority, that Pietro Yon's choir had enjoyed. It wasn't even the kind of fame that registered in that era's pop culture. But it was the kind of fame that swamped them with invitations to perform at outside events—events that had nothing to do with Cathedral services and little to do with the goal of high-caliber singing.

Such rapid-fire appearances, interleaved with the regular St. Patrick's calendar, tended to turn a chorister's schedule into a nightmare. The last month of 1977 offered a good example. December 4 was not only the second Sunday of Advent, but that evening Grady and the Cathedral Choir performed the Fauré *Requiem* and Handel's *Nisi Dominus* in "a memorial concert honoring Arturo Toscanini and Leopold Stokowski." The night after the concert, they were slated to sing at the Rockefeller Center Christmas-tree lighting. At the time the event was more Christmas-like and less bloated than it would later become, consisting of some traditional Yuletide music, a couple of well-known flash acts, and a half-hour local telecast on WNBC. While choir members were excited to be asked, most of the attention that night went to Andrea McArdle, barely fourteen years old but a sensation in the Broadway musical *Annie*.

Then came a smattering of more informal appearances. As they had done occasionally and would keep doing for some years, the Cathedral Choir presented Part I of *Messiah* in the public atrium of the Cathedral's newest next-door neighbor, the sumptuous Olympic Tower. And choristers took to the streets around the Cathedral for some neighborhood Christmas caroling. (One evening they had arranged themselves on the steps of Saint Thomas Church to sing when a musical passerby heard them—pop star John Denver. He was so taken with their music that he joined them for an impromptu version of "Silent Night.")

The final two choral events came the Sunday before Christmas—both of them on the same day. At 2:30, the Cathedral Choir teamed with the choir of St. John the Divine to offer the eagerly anticipated Nine Lessons and Carols. But as soon as the service was done, Grady, Dumler, and the choir had to head down to 34th Street to appear at the Macy's Christmas Carol Sing-Along. The Cathedral Choir was to be the primary musical underpinning of the evening, assisted by the Boys Choir of Harlem and the New Amsterdam Singers, and with starpower provided by Robert Merrill as well as cabaret songstress Elly Stone. The event was touted that morning in a relentlessly upbeat full-page *Times* ad:

> You'll be there, red-cheeked and merry, part of an immense New York family, lifting your voice in the joy of the season. . . . You'll be caught by the sweeping spotlights that will turn the night bright as noon in Herald Square. . . . On three giant stages that will turn Herald Square into a pine tree-forested arena. . . .

Merry or not, no one had allowed for the weather, and by the time they arrived at the location the city was in the grip of a sleet storm. As the "three giant stages" were open platforms, Macy's addressed the situation by passing out folding umbrellas to its entertainers. Two of the Cathedral's choristers stationed themselves on either side of Dumler, holding their umbrellas over him as he sat at a Hammond organ, trying to play while wearing gloves ("I kept thinking, I hope he doesn't get electrocuted," said one woman). Luckily, there were no major problems, and the event went off without casualties. Upon their release from Herald Square, Grady and his now-soggy crew wanted nothing so much as warmth and a drink; in a group, they escaped uptown to Rockefeller Center and the Rainbow Room.

After that, the Cathedral Choir could breathe a sigh of relief until Christmas Eve, but Grady didn't have that luxury. The evening of December 22, he was one of the twenty conductors featured at the "*Messiah* Sing-In" taking place at Avery Fisher Hall at Lincoln Center.

Nineteen-seventy-eight was to mark the start of the Cathedral's centenary year, which would begin late that summer, showcase a number of events, and end in May 1979 with a grand "Mass of Thanksgiving." Obviously, the music department was going to be closely involved, and a lot of Grady's time was taken up in planning sessions. But the centenary plans were suspended when Pope Paul VI suffered a fatal heart attack in early August. St. Patrick's offered a memorial Mass the next day to a packed Cathedral; because of the midsummer timing, it had to be done without choral support. Nor did the music department have much involvement in the rapid-fire succession of events that followed: the late-August election of Albino Cardinal Luciani as Pope John Paul I (the choir offered the "Hallelujah Chorus" at that Sunday's High Mass); the shock of his death only thirty-three days later; and the October election of Karol Cardinal Wojtyła as Pope John Paul II. (A few years before, Cardinal Wojtyła had visited St. Patrick's, where his picture was taken with some Cathedral personnel. Those photos wound up in a "discard" file, but Monsignor Rigney remembered them in time and fished them out before they were tossed.)

Once the new Pontiff had been duly elected and installed, the Cathedral returned to its celebrating. Cardinal Cooke kicked things off on November 1, presiding on the Cathedral steps over an opening ceremony attended by a crowd estimated by one reporter at 100,000 people, a ceremony that featured choirs, bands, and ethnic dancers. *Catholic News* reported that the celebration continued indoors:

> A highlight of the daylong program was the special "A City Singing" event. Outstanding musical organizations such as the Abyssinian Baptist Church choir, the Temple Emanu-El choir, the United Nations Chorus, and the choir from the Church of Sts. Peter and Paul in the South Bronx joined the Cathedral Choir and the audience in a unique performance of religious and patriotic music.

Some Cathedral music personnel were taken aback by the pile-on aspect of the evening, as well as their lack of input. The extent to which John Grady had any control over the programming of *A City Singing* (i.e., not much) was reflected in one of its final choral selections—the pop tune "What the World Needs Now (Is Love, Sweet Love)."

In the midst of all the hoopla, there was a line in the *Catholic News* article which proved that someone had done his homework: "Music for the noon program included many selections played during the ceremonies a hundred years ago." A nice tip of the historical hat, but it hadn't been Grady's contribution. In fact, the next offerings of the Cathedral's music department didn't musically address the centenary at all—Grady played a November 19 recital, and two weeks later the Cathedral Choir joined with the choir of Philadelphia's Cathedral of Sts. Peter and Paul to present Britten's *St. Nicholas*. Both events were exuberantly billed "In Celebration of Its Centenary"; neither of them consisted of centenary music.

That theme took a back seat during the Christmas season, but it resurfaced in the new year, and a week after Easter the New York press announced that Mary Lou Williams would give a repeat performance of her jazz Mass, sung by the Fordham University Preparatory School choir, on April 22. Wrote the *Times*, "The performance will commemorate the cathedral's 100th anniversary."*

* That "centenary" banner would be waved nearly until the end of 1979, when the Vienna State Opera Chorus appeared at St. Patrick's in early November. As the press release went, "The 100th anniversary of St. Patrick's Cathedral will be celebrated with a performance. . . ." People crowded in for the concert, but the attendance had little to do with an anniversary that, by that time, was six months in the past.

In the meantime, the Cathedral's choirmaster was preparing a centenary surprise of his own. As his predecessors had composed music for great occasions, Grady (who hadn't been known as a composer but as an editor and arranger) set himself to fashioning a "Gloria" setting for use at the Centenary Mass. Dumler remembered that the composition was adjusted and readjusted until the last minute: The "Mass of Thanksgiving for One Hundred Years of Worship and Blessing" was set for May 12, and Grady signed the final version of the "Gloria" manuscript, "New York 5/9/1979." Like Pecher's "Ecce Sacerdos," the work was built of unusually energetic choral writing, with Shostakovich-like orchestral interludes between verses and an introductory snare drum roll—as choristers crammed for the piece in last-minute rehearsals, they promptly nicknamed it the "War Gloria."

The Mass of Thanksgiving was the culmination of all the ceremonies. ("Of course it will go smoothly tomorrow" was the obligatory *Daily News* comment the day before. "After all, they've been getting ready for 100 years.") As a prelude there was an outdoor concert on the Cathedral steps, featuring "a group of young people dressed in bright Croatian folk costumes" and groups such as the Cardinal Spellman High School Concert Band—which saluted the occasion by offering the theme from *Star Wars*.

The Mass itself started with an elaborate procession that began on Madison Avenue, continued down 50th Street, and entered the Cathedral through its center portal as "clusters of colorful balloons were released." Matthew Murray was stationed at the cantor's desk; Grady, the Cathedral Choir, and a clutch of instrumentalists were ready in the gallery to launch into the entrance hymn, "O God, Our Help in Ages Past." Grady's programming made no reference to the music that William F. Pecher had chosen in 1879, but it cut a wide swath nonetheless. The selections ranged from the Gregorian "Credo" to the first performance of Grady's own "Gloria," anthems by Schubert and Brahms, and service music by Norman Dello Joio, as well as solo turns by Murray and classical guitarist Anton del Forno. And for the necessary all-inclusive spirit,

> Choirs from four parishes in the Archdiocese—Holy Name of Jesus, Kingston; St. Catherine Laboure, Lake Katrine; St. Charles Borromeo, Manhattan; Sts. Peter and Paul, [the] Bronx—sang in various languages during the distribution of communion. Each drew its music from a different ethnic source.

For most people it had been an impressive, sometimes gimmicky, ear-filling afternoon. But those close to Grady knew that he was hurt. He had discovered—during the Mass—that he had been the only composer that day to receive, inexplicably, no program credit. And the media didn't mention his contribution or even seem to notice it.

The season ended very soon after the centenary, after which the Cathedral's musicians headed for their usual summer pursuits. Grady almost always traveled to France during holidays, leaving Dumler to play during the off-season until the full choir reassembled. But this summer was alive with news, as rumors had flashed across the Atlantic that Pope John Paul II was considering a visit to the United States. By July, those rumors were verified (*Catholic News* confirmed the event with the clunky headline WILL VISIT HERE OCT. 2), and Grady had to rush back for some quick planning sessions.

An initial proposition was for the Pontiff to celebrate Mass at St. Patrick's, but that changed; he would instead pay "a formal visit" to the Cathedral on the afternoon of his arrival, follow that with an evening Mass at Yankee Stadium, and the next day return to St. Patrick's for morning prayers with an invited congregation of clergy and other religious. It was going to be an unprecedented occasion. The Pope's visit was going to last far longer than the twenty minutes Pope Paul VI had spent in the Cathedral during his 1965 trip. And it was going to be an ironic contrast for John Grady. The last time around, he had been the dark-horse musician who charged in to supplant the work of Charles Courboin. This time Grady would be the one under supervision—Cardinal Cooke had asked the Archdiocesan Music Commission to oversee, and its chairman, Father Dermot Brennan, to organize the whole thing.

Asking the two men to work together wouldn't be an issue. Father Brennan was a forthright admirer of Grady's work, so much so that he had invited him to sit on the Commission. "John served the Cathedral in an extraordinary way," he said. "He was invaluable to me. We sat down and planned the whole thing together."

It was a good thing that Father Brennan and Grady enjoyed working together, because the scope of this Papal visit (which included six American cities on its itinerary) meant that every plan was scrutinized by every official from every angle until it was approved—or changed. The Pontiff's initial stop at St. Patrick's was no problem; by general agreement, the music would be handled by the Cathedral Choir. The Papal Mass at

Yankee Stadium, however, was a vastly different story. Father Brennan had initially felt that the music could be performed by Grady's choristers, beefed up by a group of singers from area churches. "I thought that the choir could sit in the lower grandstand, so the structure could act as a sounding board. But," he sighed, "we heard that Connecticut and New Jersey had to be included. We ended up with a 1,400-voice choir . . . and there wasn't room for them where we'd wanted them in the first place." As to the prayer service that would take place the next morning back at the Cathedral, it was decided that the Cathedral Choir should be supplemented by a twelve-voice sanctuary choir of priests, nuns, and other religious, coming from the dioceses of Brooklyn and Rockville Centre on Long Island.

Even the music itself was to be scrutinized by a committee of American and Vatican representatives, meaning that Grady and Brennan had to travel to Washington to present their selections. Once there, they learned that their plan for Yankee Stadium—to have the choir accompanied strictly by an organ, as it had been in 1965—was actually smaller in scale than the plans of other cities. As far as the New York Archdiocese was concerned, that wouldn't do. "*Philadelphia* was having an orchestra, so *we* had to have an orchestra," said Father Brennan. When Grady and Brennan returned to New York, Grady sighed and phoned his contacts at the Metropolitan Opera to hire fifty instrumentalists. Father Brennan went to Carroll Music to buy a conductor's baton.

There was more traveling in store for the two music directors when it became plain that so many singers, coming from so many locations, would be impossible to collect in one spot for rehearsals. Grady and Brennan decided to have a handful of rehearsal locations scattered around the Archdiocese at area churches. Well and good, but it meant that part of their four weeks of preparation time would be spent behind the wheel, driving to those locations to coach choristers, many of whom had never even met them.

In the midst of all this preparation, St. Patrick's had to change gears for an extraordinary event—an interfaith service featuring an address by the Dalai Lama. The contrast between the two religious styles was remarkable (and somewhat comic) to the media. It also was apparently irresistible to many worshipers: There had been little advance publicity for the Wednesday-evening service, but the Cathedral was mobbed by a congregation of 5,000. And side-by-side with the musical exoticism presented by other guests at the service, the St. Patrick's musicians took part. Juxtaposed with "two lamas blowing on the Tibetan ceremonial horns, called 'gyalings,'" and "spirited choral singing and dancing by Buddhists" was the Cathedral Choir, offering all-American composer Randall Thompson's "The Last Words of David." At least one listener raised an eyebrow and claimed that the choir was "in comparison, tame," but the event had deeper significance than its music.

As the date for the Pontiff's visit approached, the city's preparations assumed a fever pitch, moving with unfamiliar efficiency. (For a planned Papal trip to Harlem, an empty lot was cleaned and covered with manicured grass, and a nearby abandoned building was completely removed, within two days.) Television reporting would be a little less intense; the *Times* commented, "The networks will be long on specials when Pope John Paul II comes to the United States next week, but short on coverage when his activities clash with football or baseball."

Grady and the Cathedral Choir were involved in one of those specials three days before the Papal visit, when NBC Radio presented "perhaps the most unusual entry in 'The Jeweler's Shop,' a three-act play written by the Pope when he was a priest in Poland 20 years ago. . . . The choir of St. Patrick's Cathedral supplies the music." This batch of choristers was unused to the art of radio broadcasting and the work was rather fussy, but the trip to the NBC studios was going to be one of their less-stressful jobs for the next few days. Security would be tighter than it had been in 1965; every Cathedral musician had to provide Social Security numbers, be vetted and cleared, and issued ID cards. (And the *Los Angeles Times* reported that New York detectives were once again "checking stores selling clerical garb to see if there have been any unusual purchases recently.") Street closings were going to prove a headache, and the tension level was rising around the city in anticipation of the event. Some New Yorkers were complaining, in the media and in print, about the inconvenience that accompanied a Papal visit.

But the personality of Pope John Paul II, and the effect that he could have on the public, made up for it. The afternoon of October 2 was gray and wet, with 10,000 people herded into the block around St. Patrick's. The Cathedral Choir was stationed in the gallery, offering movements from the Bach *B-Minor Mass* (and as a particular tribute a few Polish-language selections sung by Nadja Witkowska). When the Pontiff's open-topped limousine pulled up to the Cathedral doors, the gathering in the street erupted in cheers. Wearing a raincoat (and with Cardinal Cooke holding an umbrella for him), the Pope stepped cheerfully to the front door where a microphone had been set up. He chanted a benediction as the standees joined in, after which he said approvingly, "Very nice."

Inside, the orchestra launched into the Richard Strauss "Festival Entry," followed by a choral rendition of "O God, Our Help in Ages Past." None of Grady's choristers had been at St. Patrick's for the 1965 Papal visit, and it was a tough job to keep them singing rather than rubbernecking or pulling out cameras to snap photographs; but most of the music was drowned out in cheers as the central doors swung open and the Pope entered the Cathedral. One singer remembered the Pontiff's procession up the center aisle: "People were screaming, 'Long live the Pope!' And when he finally got up to the front, the first words we heard him say were—'That's right!'"

Many in the congregation howled with laughter, and New York began its love affair with Pope John Paul II.

The ceremony, and the Pontiff's address to the jam-packed Cathedral congregation, went by in a rapid blur: A TV reporter said that evening, "The ceremony was pared down . . . but the majesty of St. Patrick's lent to it that hard-to-describe excitement." Those responsible for part of that excitement, the Cathedral musicians, raced out of the building as soon as the Pope had left. Choristers piled into a bus, Grady and Dumler into a waiting car, and all of them were chauffeured, complete with police escort, to the Bronx and Yankee Stadium. From inside the vehicles, it was a memorable sight. "All the way up, the streets were packed solid with people, cheek to jowl," said Dumler. "Every block. It was amazing."

Once they had made it to Yankee Stadium, Cathedral Choir members met up with the other thousand-plus singers for a very hasty rehearsal. The size of the choir had forced it to be placed on the playing field, arranged in folding chairs. Some sort of choral seating formation had been attempted by assigning each singer a ticket, but Father Brennan noted that "there were more choristers than tickets. Some people sat two to a chair."

As an actual part of the Papal Mass, the music performed that evening was noted by few people, primarily by those who seemed surprised at its blend of traditional and more modern forms. In that sense, the musical choices ran precisely along the lines of Vatican II–inspired options: Grady's choice for the Papal entrance, the Brahms "Academic Festival Overture" (if he had to book a fifty-piece orchestra of Met musicians, he was determined to use them); the guitar-accompanied psalm setting, sung in "a folk idiom"; even a Gregorian chant "Credo," sung in Latin, which the next day's *Times* seemed to find upsetting. But most listeners were too happy to bother with details. Brennan and Grady traded conducting stints during the service, which was a good thing: By this time they were running on adrenaline. The Mass, which had started an hour late because of enthusiastic demonstrations in the streets of the Bronx, was made even longer by enthusiastic demonstrations by the 80,000 attendees—it didn't end until 11:00 P.M. And there was still the morning prayer service to come at 8:00 A.M.

Even before it had ended, the Papal visit was considered a spectacular success; *Time* called John Paul II "a beguilingly modest superstar of the church." The musicians of St. Patrick's had helped to make it a success, although the single musical "event" that had been noted by the media had nothing to do with the Cathedral: At the morning prayer service, the young priest conducting the sanctuary choir had begun perspiring with his exertions, and the Pontiff had strolled over to mop his brow for him. That particular moment made it into newspapers around the world.

After it was all over, Grady insisted on taking Father Brennan to the theater to thank him for his support. It took months to arrange a date, but they saw the latest Broadway hit play, which was a perfect choice in that it concerned two men whose lives intersect over the subject of music. Grady snagged tickets to *Amadeus*.

A City Singing and a Choral Family

And then it was back to business—which meant, in usual Cathedral fashion, that Grady would have to address a number of completely unrelated issues as they were tossed his way. Matthew Murray, who had spent less than five years at the cantor's desk but had sung for occasions including the Centenary Mass of Thanksgiving and the Papal Mass at Yankee Stadium, resigned from the Cathedral the week after the Pope left New York. Grady brought in another operatic up-and-comer who had been singing as a substitute in the loft for the past couple of years, baritone James Javore. It was no secret by this time that some excellent singers had proven to be less than excellent as cantors, but Javore showed himself to be a natural, offering the same type of bright lyric baritone that Murray had displayed along with a relaxed ease in front of the congregation.

One of Javore's earliest assignments would prove to be a test for all of the Cathedral musicians when Archbishop Sheen died of heart disease in December 1979. The Archbishop had become an instantly recognizable figure to Catholics across the United States, and a great favorite at St. Patrick's for more than fifty years. His funeral was guaranteed to be an emotionally charged event. Still, it went off smoothly, with the choir offering movements from the Mozart *Requiem*; as the coffin was being carried into the crypt, they sang the Fauré "In Paradisum." The funeral was broadcast, and one singer was surprised when a TV technician stopped her after the service, tears in his eyes, to compliment the choir.

In the meantime, John Motley, conductor of the All City High School Choir and the United Nations Singers, and one of the prime organizers behind the centenary *A City Singing*, thought his original idea could successfully be remodeled as a Christmastime performance—of course, to be presented at St. Patrick's. In a way, it was perfect. It was ecumenical. It would involve New Yorkers of all stripes, offering a kaleidoscope of holiday music, and the audience would be invited to sing along at intervals. Cathedral authorities loved the idea. It had only one drawback: It would be yet another Cathedral music event that wasn't generated by Cathedral musicians. As the centerpiece of the holiday offerings, Grady had been planning the C. P. E. Bach *Magnificat* along with the usual Lessons and Carols service for December 23, to be sung in tandem with the St. John the Divine choir. It was rather late in the game when he was informed that St. Patrick's would be hosting *A City Singing at Christmas* three days before his scheduled service . . . and, by the way, that the Cathedral Choir was invited to participate.

If Grady felt railroaded by this arrangement, he didn't let on to his superiors; and on December 20, the second of the ten acts offered during *A City Singing at Christmas* (which included a flutist, a Russian male chorus, a soprano, an Armenian boys' choir, and both of John Motley's groups) was the Cathedral Choir, singing two selections. In between acts, Motley energetically led the audience in Christmas carols. ("Oh," said Donald Dumler when he saw the evening in action. "A hootenanny.") The crowd was enormous, and *A City Singing at Christmas*—promptly shortened by music department members into the nickname *CitySings*—became one of New York's holiday traditions.

People may have been singing at St. Patrick's for a century, but now it seemed to be radiating extra glamour, and Grady was swamped with auditioners. It might have been the popularity of events like *CitySings*, or the high-profile visibility of the Papal visit. Grady, for his own part, was happy with the interest: Thomas G. Young wrote that Grady had told him of his determination "to increase the size of the choir to produce fuller sounds which would carry better through the cavernous interior."

And the city's musical press helped. Or maybe it didn't. Not only had the *Times* been carrying Grady's audition ads, but it supplemented those with comments such as:

> For something nice and civilized to do tomorrow, try auditioning for the choir at St. Patrick's Cathedral. No appointment is necessary. Just present yourself at 14 East 51st Street between 1 P.M. and 3. The choir's repertory is made up not just of sacred music. . . .

The implication that singing for the Cathedral Choir was simply a novel type of amusement for the singer—along with the fact that the notice appeared not in the music section but in the paper's *Going Out Guide*, next to suggestions for neighborhood walking tours and open-air entertainment—would probably have given fits to any other New York choirmaster, let alone a professional musician. But that was the way singing at St. Patrick's was viewed by many, many people. No surprise that the Cathedral Choir's numbers exploded—an ensemble of 60 choristers nearly doubled in size in only a few years. (A 1981 concert program listed 111 singers on the roster. Fifty-nine of them were sopranos.) The group's increased size even forced them out of the choir rehearsal room; from then on, rehearsals would have to take place, a bit inconveniently, in the parish house's largest meeting room. And still the choir continued to grow. Even though Grady auditioned every singer, some of them proved themselves to be dabblers who cared about the fun factor instead of the music.

And some were simply clueless, with no comprehension of Grady's, or any musician's, job. One chorister asked during a break, "So, John—when you're not at the Cathedral, where do you *work*?"

A few of the other singers blinked in surprise. Grady suppressed a smile and said patiently, "I'm the organist at the Metropolitan Opera."

The woman was puzzled for a moment, then suddenly brightened. "Oh! . . . So you play at intermissions?"

Grady, like Pecher and Ungerer and Yon, had arrived at a kind of tipping point as he reached his middle years. His mother had died in

1974, leaving him without family. There were no close personal relationships. In an effort to reorder his life, he had stopped drinking three years
after he'd begun work at the Cathedral, but his problems went deeper
than that. As one friend put it, "He was a guy who couldn't exist without
multiple crises blowing around him to certify that he was a Tormented
Musician." So he lived in an atmosphere of chaos, some of it self-gener-
ated, leaning heavily on his friends—his "Cathedral Family"—for support.
Some of those friends, like Dumler, would receive periodic 2:00 A.M.
phone calls during which Grady voiced his worries. (After a few years of
disrupted sleep, Dumler concluded that it was time to screen his calls; he
became one of the very first Americans to buy an example of that brand-
new technology, an answering machine.) Other music department members became de facto assistants. Every choir in history has probably had
those individuals who were willing to perform extra tasks, nonmusical
ones; St. Patrick's was no exception. Their helpfulness was invaluable to
Grady, who was piling even more work onto his Cathedral and Met
schedules, taking the baton for a series of orchestral concerts with the
Bronx Arts Ensemble, and tapped by RCA to record a Christmas album
with the Canadian Brass. The demands could have been overwhelming.
But because he had a gift for drawing people around him and deputizing
them to do what needed to be done, both his career and his life ran far
more smoothly than they might have. A prime example of this occurred
when he found that his East 70th Street apartment building was going to
be sold to make room for a new structure. The developers had found the
tenants new homes, but Grady hadn't done a thing about getting ready
to move. At the same time he learned that he would need surgery to
repair a hernia. This was not only a health issue but a logistical problem,
given that lifting and packing would be out of the question during the
recovery period. Most people would get the move out of the way before
visiting the hospital; Grady scheduled the surgery anyhow, pressing his
Cathedral Family into action. "There we were in his apartment," said
soprano Catherine O'Connor with a wry smile. "Some of us packing
boxes . . . some of us washing dishes. . . ."

At other times, the volunteer work involved plain old gofering. In early
1981, RCA approached Grady again, this time to discuss the possibility
of making a Christmas album of the Cathedral Choir with soprano Renata
Scotto. As opposed to the haphazard nature of the 1959 recording, here
was a major label offering collaboration with a top-rank opera star who

had spent much of the past decade as a major attraction at the Met. The repertoire was typical of the period's diva-makes-holiday-recording choices, with a load of carols, both the Schubert and Bach–Gounod versions of "Ave Maria," a single jarringly modern piece to exhibit musical integrity (John Corigliano's "Christmas at the Cloisters"), and, as the projected hit single, "O Holy Night." Eight of the album's fourteen tracks would involve the choir; Grady provided the choral settings. While he was giving the arrangements their final polish, Scotto decided that she'd like to include the Italian "pastorale" carol "Tu scendi dalle stelle." Grady didn't know it. This meant that alto Linda Catalo was sent downtown to Little Italy for sheet music at E. Rossi and Co., while Grady called around for a bagpiper to provide the "pastorale" element.

The choir was scheduled to meet the diva for two recording sessions during the second week of June; Grady would conduct, and Dumler would man the organ. Three days before recording commenced, Grady called Dumler into his office. "There's a problem. . . . She has a husband, and he's a conductor . . . she says if her husband can't conduct, she won't sing. And . . . um, they want me to play the organ for the record."

"Oh."

Both of them knew that Grady had signed a contract for the recording, but Dumler hadn't; the change in conductor meant that he'd have no chance of getting payment for any work he did. As a favor, he turned pages for Grady the first night of recording. After that, he stayed home.

With the choir in their usual places, Scotto in the lower loft, instrumentalists placed here and there, engineers continually adjusting microphones in an attempt to blend the choral sound, and recording equipment strewn everywhere—the mixing board was set up in the rehearsal room—choir members had to pitch in, directing people through hallways and relaying messages. When one session ran late and Scotto wanted a cup of tea, Catherine O'Connor was deputized to search for one. At 1:30 A.M., the only place in the immediate area still open was the Helmsley Palace Hotel, across Madison Avenue from the Cardinal's residence. She remembered that the late-night staff at the hotel got a kick out of it. "Here I was, running around in the middle of the night to get tea for an opera star."

Other than the switch in conductor, there weren't prima donna antics coming from either Scotto or her husband, (new) maestro Lorenzo Anselmi. Cathedral tenor Chris Cummings said, "We were told what a difficult person her husband was, and we'd better brace ourselves—he turned out to be a sweetheart." Anselmi even took the time to teach the choristers the Italian break-a-leg phrase, "In bocca al lupo." As for the diva herself, she had developed the reputation of being a sometimes spiky colleague, but she'd already worked with Matthew Murray in one of her operas at the Met (he'd been assigned to help her on and off a horse). Because of that connection, she had decided that members of the Cathedral Choir were closer to her than mere strangers.

It was a rare occasion for the volunteer choristers, because all participating singers were paid by RCA for their services. "We even got fourteen dollars extra, a penalty for 'noncompliance,'" said one. "Whatever that meant." Still, the recording sessions had their problems. The street noises, quirks of the organ, and other acoustical issues that had plagued Cathedral recording sessions in past years hadn't been addressed (the *Los Angeles Times* critic had complained about the apparently rackety sound quality of Grady's album with the Canadian Brass, dubbing it "overwhelming"). Added to that was the difficulty of getting the hundred-plus choristers on tape in a way that was both subtle and flattering. Microphones were pulled back, placed on long booms, dialed down by the technicians. All of this helped to some extent, but not entirely.

But the central issue lay with the soloist herself. Renata Scotto was then at the stage of her career when her vocal approach relied upon guts rather than finesse, and finesse was more in demand for Christmas music. In fact, at about the same time of the recording she had been starting rehearsals for a concert version of Verdi's *Macbeth* with the Ravinia Festival. When *Christmas with Renata Scotto at St. Patrick's Cathedral* was released in September, the critical verdict implied that she might have confused the two projects.

> Beware of veristically minded prima donnas bearing Yuletide gifts.
> The even line and sweet serenity demanded . . . never set easily on
> Scotto's equipment or temperament. Instead, she wrests every last
> conceivable ounce of meaning from these airs, with the results often
> squally and indecipherable.

The only mention of the Cathedral Choir, which came off sounding as if it had been recorded at a great distance, was dismissive: "reverent, if fuzzy, orchestral and choral contributions."

Part of Scotto's arrangement with Grady, and an oblique advertisement for the recording, was her appearance at Midnight Mass, singing the "O

Holy Night" arrangement that he had fashioned for her. She appeared again with the Cathedral Choir at another Rockefeller Center Christmas-tree lighting. It wasn't an auspicious night. A photo taken in performance shows the choir members—but one has to look carefully to see them, as they seem to be trying to back out of the way of a long line of Rockettes stretched in front of them, vivaciously performing the "March of the Wooden Soldiers." As for Scotto, the cover of the Christmas album had featured a photo of the diva in a lynx coat and hat (an image that became better known than the album). Perhaps to identify herself with her product, she appeared in those furs at the Rockefeller Center performance.

"There was a freak warm spell," said one of the singers. "It wound up being something like sixty-five degrees that night. And there she was, *really warm.*"

Thriving on the Pressure

With so very many singers, the Cathedral Choir was becoming a bit unwieldy, not only logistically but musically. Occasionally this manifested itself in small glitches. Sometimes it showed in more public ways.

Although *CitySings* was only a couple of years old, Grady gave the 1981 edition a shot of extra interest when Met tenor José Carreras agreed to participate. He opened the evening with the warhorse "Bless This House," then returned later to sing "Ave Maria" in the arrangement that Grady had written for Scotto's recording. The Cathedral Choir was sitting in the chancel choir stalls, ready for the choral backup. Carreras walked on; the choir rose. He began to sing. Some singers took a breath, some didn't . . . and because of that split-second of uncertainty, no one in the choir uttered a sound. Carreras finished "Ave Maria," absolutely solo. After which the choir sat down again.

At least Grady was having good luck with his professional voices (who often weren't required to participate in events like *CitySings*). These singers were no longer coming exclusively from the Met Studio; still, the Cathedral was getting the services of some solid musicians. Programs of the period boasted concerts, as well as services, that were being sung by the likes of up-and-coming Wagnerian mezzo Kimball Wheeler, soprano Dauri Podenski, tenor Gene West, mezzo Ellen Alexander, and bass-baritone Michael Riley. That same year, tenor Harry Danner, who had been doing the American opera circuit and had spent a few years on Grady's substitute list, joined the permanent ranks. He soon made himself valuable to the Cathedral, not only as a soloist but as a cantor as well. And basso John Calvin West, a mainstay of a number of regional opera companies, had first shown up at St. Patrick's in 1980 for a single concert. He'd return in 1984 as a permanent soloist.

Singers like those were glad to have the performance opportunity. It was becoming ever more rare for them. The Early Music movement that had begun some two decades earlier was gaining momentum, and New York's sacred music scene—as it was represented in the music journals, anyhow—was falling in with its stringent dictates. A commentator had written of "an increased interest in early music, including plainsong." That was an understatement: Many of the city's choirs had been ruthlessly transformed into vibrato-free zones. It was a welcoming atmosphere for light-toned singers, while the juicier voices preferred by John Grady were finding fewer and fewer sacred venues in which to work. At the summit of this mountain, organist Gerre Hancock had been spectacularly successful in capitalizing on the trend; starting the year after Grady began work at the Cathedral, Hancock had built the men-and-boys choir of Saint Thomas Church into a national phenomenon. Coolly precise in execution, straight-toned enough to cause a nosebleed, and devoted to works ancient as well as cutting-edge British, his choir members were the darlings of the musical cognoscenti. And apparently choosy: They hadn't collaborated with the Cathedral Choir since their joint ecumenical service in 1973.

But while so many New York choirmasters were relentlessly becoming (so went the local catchphrase) Earlier-Than-Thou, there was at the same time a stream of others who ignored the vogue. Their musical programs ran the gamut of taste, from singular occurrences such as the "Christmas pageant" performed by the children of the Church of the Heavenly Rest each December 24, "with traditional carols, live donkey and sheep,"* all the way to the extravagant load of music superintended by Jack Ossewaarde at St. Bartholomew's Church—whose choir complicated its duties

---

* That pageant was played on a gigantic platform erected over the church's altar; it stretched between the chancel stalls, oddly elevating the stage to the eye level of the adult choir members (who had no option but to sit through the whole thing). During one performance, an onstage lamb became bored with the action, trotted over to this author's music folder, and began to nibble.

by performing a full oratorio, every Sunday afternoon. (The solo requirements alone demanded endless relays of singers, and they came from all sources. Ellen Alexander, who had regularly spelled Patricia Kelby at St. Patrick's—and ultimately replaced her when Kelby left New York—spent a number of seasons singing at both the Cathedral and at St. Bartholomew's, having to monitor her schedule carefully to avoid double-booking.) And somewhere between these extremes fell the music program of St. Patrick's Cathedral . . . a group whose programming was lavish but conservative; whose sound, on a good day, could be lovely; and whose members sometimes tripped over their music. One chorister summed it up: "We often went in feeling very unprepared, then adrenaline took over. Grady managed to get performances that he had no right to get from us." That might have been the case. But if the old saw applies that it isn't about getting invited but about getting re-invited, then they must have been doing something right.

Pope Paul VI had first declared January 1 as a "World Day of Peace" in 1968, then Pope John Paul II had continued the custom; and the United Nations, in late 1981, declared an annual "International Day of Peace." St. Patrick's, collaborating with the Permanent Observer Mission of the Holy See to the United Nations, split the difference in its commemoration, as for a few years the Cathedral hosted a grand ecumenical service in the early spring. These services were high-profile occasions, made more so by musical programs that invariably included some very major operatic talent. The 1981 service featured star-of-stars tenor Luciano Pavarotti, singing between selections by the Cathedral Choir, offering the very suitable Verdi "Ingemisco" along with the very unsuitable Tosti "Non t'amo piu." Placido Domingo followed the year after; it was his reunion with the St. Patrick's music department, and he not only kept to sacred repertoire but involved the choir by choosing music in which they could participate. And in 1983, mezzo Marilyn Horne would join them.

The World Day of Peace services petered out after a while, but a more durable annual event was begun during the celebrations surrounding St. Patrick's Day in 1980 when the Irish choir Our Lady's Choral Society appeared not only at the St. Patrick's Day Mass but at a concert the evening before. The very enthusiastic response made it clear that an Irish-themed concert would be more than welcome around St. Patrick's Day; and the following year, the *Times* announced a concert featuring violinist

Geraldine O'Grady, tenor Tom Dillon, and the Friendly Sons of St. Patrick Glee Club (a reunion—the Friendly Sons had always been staunch Cathedral supporters, but they hadn't been involved with many Cathedral functions since the days of John Finnegan). By 1982 the concert had added readings by poet Galway Kinnell (who would win the Pulitzer Prize for his work the year after), as well as a title: *Celebration of Irish Heritage*. As to vocalists, it would attract identifiably Irish artists such as soprano Kate Hurney, who had sung opera and concert in Houston, Dallas, Tanglewood, and Zurich; and Frank Patterson, who had attracted international attention as "Ireland's Golden Tenor." With the cavalcade of acts already being displayed, there was little need for the Cathedral Choir to participate in the concert during its first years. But Grady lent to the enterprise Donald Dumler, to accompany whatever needed accompanying, along with someone from the vocal staff to open the evening with "Bless This House." And Harry Danner was once featured as the evening's tenor soloist, because he had the pedigree as well as the repertoire.

Those events were annual occurrences, but at this time the music department calendar went through a lineup of additional commitments that fell against one another like dominoes. Grady had joined the ranks of Cathedral musicians who had been given governmental honors when the French Ministry of Culture made him a knight in late 1981: Chevalier d'Ordre des Arts et des Lettres. The presentation meant an extremely quick trip to France, which wasn't in itself a problem; but at the same time, Grady was in the lengthy process of trying to put together a sanctuary choir, supposedly to sing at the 4:00 P.M. Sunday Mass. Monsignor Rigney and Cardinal Cooke had initially wanted an all-boy choir, which proved impossible to find. They decided upon boys' and girls' voices. Grady was in the process of hiring Keith Griggs, an organist who had been teaching music at the Anglo-American School and had experience working with youngsters, when it became apparent that there simply weren't enough children to make a respectable showing. The group would have to be composed of adults. Griggs gamely went forward with the altered plan, while he and Grady tried to figure out exactly how this choir would fit into the musical life of the Cathedral.

The following summer, Grady was invited to give a recital at Moscow's Glinka Museum. This was a political honor as well as a musical one, but it came at a particularly difficult time. Just before he was to leave for the

Soviet Union, St. Patrick's was slated to host a huge June 6 concert to commemorate nuclear disarmament talks at the UN. The "Symphony of United Nations" would feature two orchestras and 400 singers from 5 choral societies, and would climax with the *Ode to Joy*. And the singers of St. Patrick's were involved, as one of the five choirs. (They might have wanted to decline the honor; space in the chancel was so tight that choristers had to stand throughout the concert.) Although the *Times* had implied a relaxed musical atmosphere by listing the evening as "A Beethoven Sing-along," the choir still had to devote some amount of rehearsal time to getting familiar with Beethoven's music—and that time would have to be stolen, because the Cathedral Choir had earlier been scheduled to give its own concert.

The concerts finally dispatched, Grady left for his Moscow recital date—at which moment WOR-TV approached the Cathedral with its request to tape "a day in the life of St. Patrick's" for its religious-programming series "That's the Spirit!" to be broadcast in September. Dumler, left in charge, had the tasks not only of playing for the camera but of getting the choir to produce music for use on the soundtrack. He resorted to Grady's recycling trick, which meant that the Cathedral Choir filled most of the half-hour with those selections from the *B-Minor Mass* that they could rattle out automatically.

If there were choristers who resigned because of these extra commitments, their places were immediately filled by other applicants. For that matter, there were the people, like Grady, who seemed to thrive on the pressure. Others, like Donald Dumler, bore up and accepted it as part of the workload. And James Javore—who was trying to build an operatic career, but whose normal workload regularly included five weekend Masses, along with weddings and funerals—coped with the schedule by asking his agent not to schedule auditions at the beginning of the week: "On Mondays, my voice felt like hamburger."

Then there were the commitments that everyone found heartbreakingly difficult, but necessary. "Cardinal Cooke was wonderful," said Nadja Witkowska, remembering the days when the choir had been a small group that needed encouragement, and received it, from the Archbishop of New York. "He'd stand there in the garden and talk with you after a Mass. And he knew what he was talking about. He knew music." But the Cardinal's health was a serious issue, one that was discussed only in whispers.

Nearly two decades earlier he had been diagnosed with cancer, prompting a years-long battle that he had kept secret from most people. "At one point he had to have his salivary glands removed," said Father Brennan. "He couldn't really sing after that. If he was going to celebrate an outside Mass, he'd bring me along to do the sung portions." In the late summer of 1983, he learned that the cancer had returned; his diagnosis was terminal.

The next weeks became a vigil as the Cardinal's health declined, and the various departments of St. Patrick's set themselves to perform the tasks that must accompany death. Grady began to coordinate his forces for the various Cathedral functions that would take place. On October 5, the *Times* reported that the Cardinal was "close to death," that he had been listening to recordings of Gregorian chant and choral music, and that his staff had gathered at his bedside to sing his favorite, "Salve Regina." Early the next morning, he died.

Thanks to the Cardinal, the music department was well prepared in advance of his death. As the *Times* wrote, "He had requested the basic, unadorned Mass of Christian Burial. He chose the liturgical music, which ranged from baroque to modern." His funeral took place on October 10; that morning, a procession of more than 1,000 clerics, forming a line that stretched along East 50th Street and took more than 45 minutes to enter the Cathedral, participated in the Mass. In the words of the *Daily News*, Grady and his musicians offered "triumphant liturgical music": Purcell's *Solemn Funeral Music for Queen Mary*, along with movements from the *Requiems* of Mozart, Fauré, and Brahms. As the coffin was being carried to the crypt, Javore led the congregation in a final rendering of "Salve Regina."

As was the case with any large organization, some of the music department members had become close to the Cardinal while some newer members had barely met him. But the Cardinal had been more than just a fan of the music program. Over the past years, the Cathedral's accent on ecumenism had required Grady and his musicians to perform some unusual tasks, occasionally *very* unusual ones, for the sake of St. Patrick's; they had pitched in without complaint, and with an attitude of flexibility. Cardinal Cooke had always realized this, and had been grateful for it.

The Birth (Almost) of Choros Aristos

Whether it had been by design or accident, the Cathedral's music department had achieved not only a "signature sound" but a house style under each of its directors. So it did under Grady, settling into the form by which it would be viewed for the rest of his life. Grady himself contributed to the effect by cultivating his own image, that of the semi-bohemian conductor who shuttled between New York and Paris, who used extravagant gestures and worked in an office cluttered with music scores and cigarette ash,* the man who alternated between a notably brazen attitude in rehearsal ("You sopranos are a *disease!*") and a *grand seigneur* attitude at events such as Midnight Mass, which he would conduct in white tie and tails, sporting his French governmental decoration and maintaining tempo with an idiosyncratic, up-and-down bandmaster's beat that even his greatest admirers had dubbed "The Grady Conduct-O-Matic."

But when it came to his career path, he had far more in mind than mere publicity. Perhaps remembering his Concert Chorale of the 1960s, John Grady wanted to form a choral group, with the Cathedral Choir as its nucleus, that would sing at venues more concert-oriented than St. Patrick's. His Lincoln Center connections meant that this idea could be seriously explored. So for a year or so, the Cathedral Choir went through a period of collaborations—or perhaps a better term would be run-ins—with some famous music personalities.

Grady's warmup act in this venture came when NBC approached the Cathedral about participating in Perry Como's upcoming Christmas TV special, a tradition dating back to the 1950s. Each one had been very successful, and built around a theme; this year's special would feature a New York Christmas, showing "Mr. C" at such New York institutions as toy store FAO Schwarz and Balducci's Market. And the producers wanted to close the special with a scene of their star performing "Ave Maria" with the St. Patrick's Cathedral Choir. It would make a handsome tableau.

By November, the music had been rehearsed and everyone was ready for the scene to be taped. The Cathedral was closed early on the day of

---

* When the choir had abandoned the choir rehearsal room, to Grady's delight it became the official Music Office as well as the unofficial smoking lounge. This made for trouble when soprano Jessye Norman was the guest soloist for Midnight Mass. Asking where she might wait for her cue, she was pointed toward the Music Office—and upon opening the door, she was hit with a visible cloud of cigarette smoke. Grady, along with his orchestra members, had been puffing away during rehearsal breaks. Norman was understandably less than pleased.

shooting to accommodate the load-in of equipment and lighting, and the choir had a 6:00 P.M. call time, which everyone assumed would prove ample for recording the soundtrack and filming the scene. "It was only the one number, after all," said a chorister. Hundreds of votive candles were placed on the steps leading up to the chancel for extra atmosphere during long shots, and the choir was arranged on the steps to the high altar to make a living backdrop to Perry Como, who would stand front and center to deliver "Ave Maria."

But with the inevitable delays and retakes that always occur in video production, the evening stretched out longer and longer. Choir members stood in formation for one take after another as candles burned out and were replaced, dutifully lip-synching to their pre-recorded voices, without a provision made for a dinner break (and with no refreshments provided at all), until it was nearly midnight. By that time, Grady was so annoyed that he threatened to send the choir home; the producers made their own counter-threat, to sue if he did. Fortunately, not long after that exchange the session was able to wrap without the need to call any lawyers. "Perry Como's Christmas in New York" hit the airwaves in mid-December, to friendly notices ("The program is, as always with Mr. Como, in the realm of easy listening and viewing," wrote the *Times*) and good ratings. The Cathedral scene—which wasn't even mentioned by most newspapers— made a very attractive finale to the show . . . tuneful, serene, and without the slightest hint of litigiousness.

The Cathedral had its usual Christmas duties ahead, but this year they were complicated by the fact that Grady's wish had abruptly been granted. Leonard Bernstein had been preparing a benefit concert of the Mahler *"Resurrection" Symphony*, to be performed at the National Cathedral in Washington; those plans expanded to include a couple of mid-January performances with the Philharmonic. It seemed a good opportunity to give Grady's concert-chorale idea a try, and the Cathedral Choir was asked to participate. This meant that Mahler rehearsals would have to be scheduled along with Midnight Mass rehearsals (the Poulenc *Motets*, again, along with the usual ration of Bach and Handel), *CitySings* rehearsals, and everything else that was normally required on the Cathedral schedule . . . a lot of material to cover at a notoriously difficult time.

In early January, Bernstein sent a deputy to one of Grady's rehearsals to check on how the piece was progressing. Apparently, not well enough.

A chorister remembered, "We went through it, over and over. An assistant conductor from the Philharmonic came in to see how things were going, and . . . it was tense." No one knew Bernstein's exact reaction when the report reached his ears, but almost immediately, the musically expert New Amsterdam Singers were added to the lineup; rumor had it that they were drafted as reinforcements. The St. Patrick's crew was pressed into a number of last-minute rehearsals; rumor had it that Bernstein had taken Grady aside to issue a shape-up ultimatum. As a result, when the time came for the Cathedral Choir to meet their conductor, they were extremely nervous. But Bernstein's musicality and concentration swept them into the project.*

Before the opening performance, Grady gathered his singers together to warn them that he would be hiding in the audience for each performance and watching them, very carefully, for the slightest lapse in attention. The warning turned out not to be needed, as the piece came together with gratifying success. The *Times* was unqualified in its admiration for not only its conductor—"This was easily the most thrilling 'Resurrection' I have heard since—well, since the last one I heard Mr. Bernstein lead"— but its chorus, too: "[A] stageful of marvelously alert and responsive choristers: the Choir of St. Patrick's Cathedral and the New Amsterdam Singers."

The Cathedral Choir members were very, very relieved, but most of them were still inclined to give the maestro a wide berth. Not so alto Peggy Breslin, a native of Ireland (via Liverpool) who was afraid of nothing and nobody. After the first performance, she approached Bernstein to ask for an autograph.

"Who are you with?" he growled, glowering down at her.

"St. Patrick's."

"Oh." He snorted. "I never thought you'd make it."

Breslin drew herself up proudly. "Well, we *fooled* you, didn't we?"

She got the autograph.

Now that Grady had seen his concert-chorale idea in practice, he understood that it would have to be retooled to make it more attractive to

* One singer told of the Cathedral Choir's finally relaxing enough that, when Bernstein turned sixty-six on a rehearsal day, they serenaded him with "Happy Birthday." Considering that Bernstein's actual birthday wasn't until August, the story is likely muddled. But if it wasn't true, perhaps it should have been.

the city's orchestras. Still, he set to work with lawyer and Cathedral Choir tenor David Skoblow to incorporate the group. Before long, he came up with a name for it: Choros Aristos. But upcoming changes at St. Patrick's meant that the group's development would have to lie fallow for a while.

The Cardinal from Scranton

It was natural that New Yorkers (and not only the Catholic ones) would spend time and energy trying to guess who would be chosen the next Archbishop of New York. In the past, the choice had usually been a surprise to its citizens. This time it was a surprise as well to the man who had been chosen: Bishop John J. O'Connor, a former Naval chaplain with the rank of rear admiral who had been installed as the Bishop of Scranton all of eight months before. He told the *Times* that he had received a casual phone call from his friend Archbishop Pio Laghi, the Apostolic Delegate to the United States. Before hanging up, the Archbishop told Bishop O'Connor that he had been appointed Archbishop of New York—"I thought it was a joke," the Bishop explained.

He had been close to Cardinal Cooke, assisting him in the Military Vicariate; but preliminary reports showed Bishop O'Connor to be as extroverted as Cooke had been modest, a man who told a good joke, valued a good punch line, and made no secret of his likes and dislikes. His early public comments weren't precisely music-based, but anyone could read between the lines: Liturgically speaking, he said, "Don't call me conservative. I'm really *orthodox*." When he was asked his opinion of folk Masses, he replied that they were all right, provided the people who attended them didn't look as if they were going to an outdoor barbecue.

More direct still was the Bishop's comment at a preliminary meeting with Cathedral department heads, when without warning he turned to his new music director and said, "You should know, Mr. Grady, that I'm not very fond of the music of _____." (He had named a composer who was very much alive and active, a composer who had received many commissions—including one from Cardinal Cooke. There were reporters in the room, listening attentively. Grady broke into a sweat.)

If anyone, such as the music director of St. Patrick's, might be wondering about O'Connor's musical tastes, that person would need only to refer to the program from his installation as Bishop of Scranton the previous June. Those ceremonies had given choral works a decided back seat, focusing instead on Vatican II–styled congregational hymns such as "Be Not Afraid" and "Let There Be Peace on Earth." Finally, there was the broadest hint of all: When discussing his upcoming installation with media representatives, the Archbishop-designate said that he wanted to "keep it simple."

But keeping it simple was not a hallmark of John Grady. The installation of the Archbishop of New York featured the Cathedral Choir, a sizeable orchestral contingent, and Grady's usual big-occasion lineup of Brahms, Mozart, Byrd, C. P. E. Bach—and Grady; when the snare drum announced the beginning of the Grady "Gloria," the WNBC cameras happened to be focusing on Archbishop O'Connor and inadvertently caught him starting in surprise. For an offertory anthem, the forces combined to present the Bruckner "Ecce Sacerdos," a piece large-scale enough (and loud enough) that it might have been what prompted the *Times* to write, "From the rear choir loft the organ thundered, brass instruments pierced the air and the cathedral choir, robed in blue and gold, raised their voices. . . ."*

There was actually a good deal of thundering going on all over town. The well-funded 1980s were a flush time for classical music, Early Music for choirs or instrumental ensembles was enjoying a particular vogue, and the era seemed to be exemplified by the runaway success of the Pachelbel *Canon in D*. Sacred music, as well, was benefiting from the trend; many of the city's choirmasters were rooting through libraries and archives in an effort to unearth potentially fascinating material. In music listings, the accustomed Bach, Handel, Britten, and Vaughan Williams were interspersed with intriguing and less-familiar names such as Weelkes, Monteverdi, Wilbye, and Gibbons. For those who wanted to hear more recent works, Hoiby, Rutter, Warlock, and Robinson were on tap as well.

John Grady's response, at this point, was to do nothing that he hadn't already been doing. An exception came for Holy Week of 1984, when the *Times* listed Grady's own setting of "My God, My God, Why Hast Thou Forsaken Me" (but the piece apparently was so lightweight that it left no

* Six years later, when Bishop Thomas Daily was installed as Bishop of Brooklyn in 1990, a different *Times* reporter had the following take on the music: "From the rear choir loft, the organ thundered, brass instruments pierced the air, hand bells rang out and the combined choruses of the diocesan Schola Cantorum and the Choir of St. James Cathedral raised their voices. . . ." Coincidence, undoubtedly.

mark on the repertoire; years later, no member of the Cathedral music department could remember a thing about it). Otherwise, his season was devoted to the same works as always. That Christmas featured the Poulenc *Motets*, the usual Lessons and Carols with the St. John the Divine Choir . . . and to round things out, once again he slated the C. P. E. Bach *Magnificat*.

This seeming indifference to new or rediscovered works extended even to composers who were important to his own choir's history. Pietro Yon, for instance, had gone completely out of fashion in New York. Grady programmed not a bit of his music, and for that matter, during the entire decade of the 1970s the *Times* holiday music listings carried Yon's name precisely one time. Even though Luciano Pavarotti recorded "Gesù Bambino" as part of his very successful album *O Holy Night*, the song was viewed primarily as an interesting artifact. Then "Gesù Bambino" appeared for the 1983 *CitySings*—programmed not by the Cathedral Choir but by a Lithuanian vocal quartet. The response was extraordinarily positive, so much so that the piece immediately leaped back into the *CitySings* repertoire to be performed every year thereafter, by someone, in some arrangement. And within a year or so, Pietro Yon's name was showing up once again on New York choral repertoire lists. It's possible that this indirect plugging contributed to the rekindling of interest: If so, it was one of the few times during Grady's Cathedral career that he had actually influenced the city's musical taste. In any case, he didn't seem to notice.

None of these considerations bothered the general public, who still regarded the Cathedral as a Place to Be. In late 1984 Anna Quindlen wrote a long and affectionate article for the *New York Times Magazine*, detailing the preparations for the upcoming Christmas Vigil and its huge popularity: "In the last days of December . . . there is perhaps no hotter ticket in town than the one to Pew One, Center Aisle, for midnight mass at the great granite cathedral called St. Patrick's." She went on:

> There have even been scalpers at St. Patrick's. Five years ago, Monsignor Rigney ordered the notation on each ticket warning, "This ticket is never for sale," after he heard of a man who, after mass, said loudly that he thought it was scandalous that the church had taken up a collection when he had paid so dearly to get in.

But it was clear that the feeling about Midnight Mass wasn't dependent on its music. Speaking of the choir, its preparations, and its role in the

Mass, Quindlen dealt in generalities: the number of singers, the rehearsals for "the measured bars of the 'Magnificat' " and various hymns and carols, the choral "Adeste Fideles" at the beginning of the Mass on the stroke of midnight, the "Hallelujah Chorus" for the finish. All of the holiday music that Quindlen had admired in the article was music that had been done at the Cathedral before, that would be done there again, and yet again . . . a pattern that had been standard at St. Patrick's since the beginning of the century, and one that congregations seemed actually to enjoy. As to the man responsible for the music, he had received more direct press attention barely a month after Quindlen's article, when *New York* magazine published "John Grady's Organ Grind," a tongue-in-cheek detailing of Grady's hectic routine describing him as a "slender and precise man who has a look of permanent exhaustion" and listing his December 19 schedule: a choir rehearsal (which he would have to conduct in formal dress in order to be ready to run out at rehearsal's end); a taxi to Lincoln Center and his "*Messiah* Sing-In" guest-conductor stint; and at some point during the evening, a quick conference with the Met orchestra manager about the instrumentalists needed for Midnight Mass. Such articles made for fun reading, as far as the general public was concerned.

But, crammed schedule or not, a number of people in the outside music community felt simply that John Grady had stopped trying.

It might have had something to do with his new Archbishop, a man who cared passionately about the Mass and less so about the music that adorned it. As Grady was quickly learning, not only did Archbishop O'Connor have very definite ideas about what should and shouldn't be heard, but the Archbishop's office issued the music department a set of directives to implement those ideas. During a Mass, musical selections were not to be of a length to keep clergy waiting; offertory anthems were not to run longer than three minutes and twenty seconds. And congregational singing, more than anything else that happened musically at the Cathedral, was paramount in importance. (The new musical directives were enforced even during important events. When the Archbishop was elevated to Cardinal in May 1985, his "Welcome Ceremony" at St. Patrick's was an interreligious prayer service at which every bit of choral music was restricted to either the prelude or postlude. During the service itself, the musical program consisted of exactly two hymns, sung by the congregation—and the sanctuary choir, in one of their last major appearances.) Moments such as these might have given an observer the idea that extended choral works were no longer central to the music of St. Patrick's. And fair or unfair, the scuttlebutt around town was that the situation was Grady's own doing.

While no one talked about it, there was more to the situation. Grady was a man who liked to be the center of attention, personally as well as musically; this wasn't a problem when he had dealt with Cardinal Cooke, someone who had no need of the limelight. But now Grady had more than met his match in the powerhouse personality of John Cardinal O'Connor. (During his tenure in Scranton, his auxiliary bishop had referred to him as "a whirlwind, a big leaguer.") The Cardinal was aware of his own forcefulness and tended to underplay it with jokes; at the time of his elevation, a reporter asked him if he thought anything might change because of the honor.

"I doubt I'm going to become invisible," he quipped.

The O'Connor personality would require an adjustment on Grady's part that, perhaps, Grady wasn't able to make. Over the years, most of his transactions had been with Monsignor Rigney. The two men respected each other's talents, though they clashed on occasion. (Dumler witnessed the tail end of one of these encounters and tried to be philosophical: "Well, Monsignor. Perhaps John Grady is an angel sent from Heaven to test us." Rigney walked off a few steps and turned back. "Some of us," he said darkly, "don't *want* to be tested.") Now Monsignor Rigney was approaching retirement, to be replaced by Father Anthony Dalla Villa. Father Dalla Villa had served at the Cathedral for a number of years, most recently as Assistant Master of Ceremonies, becoming familiar with Grady's quirks as well as his outside employments. And he was very protective of St. Patrick's as Priority One, not to be displaced by the Met, Notre Dame, the Bronx Arts Ensemble, Choros Aristos, Grady's recital schedule, his vacation trips to France—and especially not with the amount of time that all of these extracurricular activities required. At a staff meeting, Father Dalla Villa made his feelings clear when he established his point by rising out of his chair to stand with legs in a wide stance. "You have one foot *here*, and the other"—he pointed—"at Lincoln Center. *And another in Paris.*"

Obviously, Grady's relationship with his supervisors was becoming strained. It didn't help when some of them, annoyed with his Francophilia, would phone the music office asking for "Pierre." And while he was personally as close as ever to his Cathedral Family, in musical terms his relationship with the Cathedral itself was beginning to fray.

One singer who had joined the choir at that time said, "It seemed that things were in a holding pattern."

This was inadvertently demonstrated on Good Friday 1985. That morning, media interest was generated not by any music being made at St. Patrick's but by the premiere of "We Are the World," a pop song that was being heard both recorded and live simultaneously at locations all around the world, as a promotion for African famine relief. One of those locations, which drew a lot of attention, was right on the Cathedral steps.

"This is the way to spend Good Friday," a man exclaimed to the *Times*.

Reservations and Hard Feelings

At a stroke, it seemed as if the plug had been pulled on most of the musical activity at St. Patrick's. The intense concert schedule, the recitals that cascaded one on top of another, abruptly ground to a halt. Recitals were sparse; full-scale concerts stopped outright. Even Cathedral-based events changed. Rehearsals ended early; the musical preparation for Masses became perfunctory. Grady's participation in *CitySings* (which hadn't been wildly enthusiastic even in its formative years) became even more casual—he would conduct the Cathedral Choir in their set and then send them home in mid-concert. A few times, Grady didn't even allow them to take part.

He offered no public explanation for this change in behavior, and he began to absent himself from the Cathedral more and more for outside bookings. Possibly because Father Dalla Villa had explicitly informed Grady that he couldn't accept outside engagements without permission, Grady tended to "get permission" by neglecting to mention any engagements until after he'd completed them. This was sheer stubbornness on Grady's part; some of his jaunts would have met with full clerical approval. Only a few weeks after Anna Quindlen's article had appeared in print, Grady traveled to Philadelphia to participate in the very first meeting of the Conference of Roman Catholic Cathedral Musicians. But the atmosphere had become charged with hard feelings on both sides, and by the late 1980s Grady was engaging in an open contest of wills with some of his supervisors.

Cardinal O'Connor was an exacting but fair boss, unfailingly gracious toward the choir and its director both in public and in print. He wrote about 1987's Midnight Mass, "Under the direction of John Grady, the Cathedral choir . . . [was] dazzling." In private, however, he had reservations. Father Dalla Villa wrote Grady, "The Cardinal feels, and I agree, that you have not yet accommodated the musical program so that it can be sung by the people at the 10:15 Mass." But Grady was absenting himself from the Cathedral to such an extent that, when the Cardinal wanted to discuss possible changes in the music, he sat down for some informal meetings with—cantor James Javore.

As for Father Dalla Villa, he wanted St. Patrick's to operate in a well-ordered, businesslike way, and to him the music department should be no exception. To that end, he implemented a number of organizational changes. Some changes were comparatively minor but made complete sense—such as the advance booking of a soloist for Midnight Mass. Grady's system had been simply to troll the dressing rooms at the Met a few days before Christmas, knocking on doors and casually asking, "Want to sing at St. Pat's?" It was utterly dependent on chance, sometimes produced last-minute switches, and meant that a soloist's name could never be printed in the Midnight Mass program. As of Christmas 1985, that had changed for good.

Other changes were born of the idea that a music department could be run like any other office department; these were less successful. It was during this time that Donald Dumler showed up one day to play his usual Masses, only to be told that from that time on (a nonmusical accountant's idea) he would have to punch in at the Cathedral time clock . . . and that he would be required to rack up forty hours per week, whether on or off the organ bench. Dumler suggested that his extensive home practice sessions might be applied to the weekly total—to no avail. "What you do on your own time is your own business," he was told. So for years he would spend countless hours practicing on a downstairs piano, sitting at his desk in make-work boredom, or haunting office corridors at the parish house.

There were moments during which the old excitement bubbled up. After undergoing two years of renovations, the Statue of Liberty was re-dedicated on July 3, 1986, and St. Patrick's held a commemorative Mass complete with a lengthy prelude concert featuring Grady, Dumler, the usual orchestral contingent from the Met, the Cathedral Choir, Anna

Moffo, Frank Patterson, Robert Merrill, and Simon Estes. It was a very capable lineup; a chorister recalled that one of the soloists was in the middle of an aria but still able to make two chattering sopranos shut up by shaking a fist at them, without missing a beat. Even so, such occasions were now rarities. In early December 1987, the Cathedral Choir presented *A Concert in Celebration of the Marian Year*, but the evening's centerpiece was, yet again, the C. P. E. Bach *Magnificat*. A year later, the *Times* listings for Christmas music conveyed an unmistakable message when it didn't list the Cathedral's offerings at all.

The music department was reinforced with the addition of a third organist to the roster. Alan Davis was a graduate of the North Carolina School of the Arts, studying in Paris with Mme. Marie-Claire Alain when Grady heard him play at the (Anglican) American Cathedral. He was impressed enough that he offered Davis a job at St. Patrick's. "I was very young, and far less than worldly," said Davis—and he had never set foot in a Catholic church, or even heard of St. Patrick's. Nonetheless, he came to New York to see the Cathedral and take in a Mass. That first Mass was a confusing experience, because members of a protest group were also in attendance and in the throes of a mid-Mass demonstration when Davis arrived: "Someone had told me it was a really strange service going on in a foreign language . . . and there were 150 people standing there all around the congregation, with their backs to the altar. I was thinking, 'This is *different* from the Episcopal service.'" Grady couldn't offer Davis a title, but he gave him solid employment, playing "everything" from weddings to 10:15 Masses, plugging the holes that Grady's and Dumler's schedules had left vacant.

There were numerous holes, because Grady was occupied with other plans. He had hit on the idea of resurrecting Choros Aristos as the next central project of his life, something that wouldn't supplant St. Patrick's but replace it. And while he didn't discuss it with his superiors, he talked about it at length with his Cathedral Family. Tenor James Poma remembers being asked to meet Grady at Holy Family Church, a meeting that was actually part of an audition day. "He wanted to spirit off some St. Patrick's choir members for Choros Aristos. . . . [A]s he put it, would we be interested in raising our own games?" The group's projected first season would consist of three large-scale pieces, flashy but familiar to St. Patrick's choristers (as well as their conductor): the Poulenc *Stabat*

Mater, Vaughan Williams *Dona Nobis Pacem*, and Puccini *Missa di Gloria*.

As for the Cathedral Family members, their concern was for Grady's employment situation. Few of them could absorb the fact that he might actually resign from the Cathedral. "How will you feel about leaving?" asked baritone Brendan Corrigan.

"Any benefit that I've gained from this job has already accrued," he replied stonily. "It'll follow me."

Still, he didn't make a concrete decision to leave. "It was as if he was waiting for some final thing," remembered Corrigan. "You know, the straw that broke the camel's back."

Hollywood Fame, New York Tragedy

Grady had always had a history of announcing major projects to the Cathedral Choir members with his version of a tease campaign, slipping out hints—"Very soon," he would say with raised eyebrows, "something important will be coming up." Along those lines, James Poma remembered walking into a regular Wednesday-night rehearsal and seeing, among the stacks of music intended for the choir, a completely new piece: Carmine Coppola's "Marcia Religioso."

"Sometime soon," Grady told his charges, "we're going to be doing . . . a film."

It was true. Grady had been approached by representatives from Paramount Pictures, who were in the process of filming *The Godfather: Part III* and wanted a sixty-voice choir to appear in the film's opening sequence, a grand cathedral scene in which mobster Michael Corleone is made a knight of the fictional "Order of St. Sebastian." The first two *Godfather* films had been whopping critical and financial successes; the third installment was virtually guaranteed to be a gold mine for anyone involved. As one singer exclaimed, "It was the *Godfather* series! The biggest thing in movies! You'd have to be crazy to pass up an offer like that." Grady apparently agreed; he signed a contract without consulting anyone from the Cathedral.

And with that stroke of the pen, he committed the most grievous error of his professional life.

For some years, Father Dalla Villa (recently named Rector, very soon to be elevated to Monsignor) had been nettled enough by Grady's outside activities. But it was far more serious and more public to have Grady working in a "gangster movie," and to have the choir appearing in that movie as well. Worse, scuttlebutt had it that the shooting script would be treating Vatican hierarchy as corrupt and ultimately murderous. Worst of all was the fact that Grady had enmeshed the Cathedral in this project without even attempting to secure permission in advance.

Grady's superiors were furious at his recklessness, and the situation was only exacerbated when Paramount asked for permission to film the scene at St. Patrick's. They were promptly turned down. Production scouts looked at a few other locations and finally hit upon Old St. Patrick's, whose pastor, unaware of any conflicts, agreed. That didn't help the situation, either. It was recommended to Grady—strongly—that he back out of his contract. The producers replied to that recommendation by threatening a lawsuit if he did. Whether or not Grady had wanted to cancel, he was stuck; so was the Cathedral Choir. St. Patrick's officials began to consider the ways in which they could minimize any negative publicity, or any publicity at all. In the meantime, the choristers began to rehearse Coppola's music.

The film's producers had initially offered each singer a flat fee of $50, with no residuals, for the two-day shooting schedule. However, one of the choristers was a member of the Screen Actors Guild. She reported the offer to her local union deputy, who sprang into action and forced the producers to offer standard SAG contracts (which guaranteed full royalties) to each chorister. Choir members were delighted with this turn of events, but most of them were unaware of any other legal back-and-forth—until they reported to the shooting location in early May. As they were being fitted for costumes, they discovered exactly how their publicity would be minimized: Each of them was being asked to sign, along with the contract, a declaration that they were acting individually and not as representatives of St. Patrick's. Additionally, neither they nor Grady would receive any screen credit for the film.*

* If Cathedral authorities worried about St. Patrick's being implicated, they would have been absolutely horrified at the director's original rough cut of the opening scene, which featured an unmistakable establishing shot of the Cathedral's exterior. As it was, a studio publicity photo of the scene was captioned MICHAEL RECEIVES THE ORDER OF ST. SEBASTIAN AT ST. PATRICK'S CATHEDRAL. Still, Grady's name appears nowhere—not in the screen credits, nor in any production listings. Same for the choir members.

On top of it, the final permission for Grady to go ahead was withheld nearly until it was time for filming to begin. "It was a hot spring evening," said James Poma. "I was sitting on the church steps with John—he was chain-smoking furiously, waiting for a call from the Archdiocese, telling him that he could proceed." When the call finally came, it had resulted in a delay for the crew, and an embarrassing cliffhanger moment for Grady. In comparison, the two days of rehearsal and filming went almost without incident (except for one chorister—not a professional actress— who was unhappy with the subdued lighting in the choir loft and kept calling down to the director between takes, "We can't see you!").

Donald Dumler hadn't been involved in the film; he had been told point-blank that participation might imperil his job. And while he was distressed at the loss of income, he was more worried by Grady's situation. "John had been told the same thing. He ignored it and went ahead anyway. They weren't happy about it." Things became less happy, and still more tense, as the summer progressed and it became plain that the film had been neither forgotten nor forgiven. (Grady told a friend that a number of memos he had received, on unrelated subjects, came to his desk with an accompanying stick-on note: REMEMBER THE GODFATHER.) Grady didn't respond directly, but by early September, *Times* readers could see his name listed prominently on two audition ads running on the same page—the familiar one for the Cathedral Choir, and a second ad, considerably larger, for Choros Aristos auditions.

The afternoon of September 26, Dumler was practicing in the rehearsal room when Grady walked in and pulled up a chair abruptly.

"Look, we have got to talk. Anywhere, but not here. *But we have got to talk.*"

"This sounds grave."

"Yes." And he left the room.

There was a rehearsal that evening, during which Grady seemed notably distracted and upset. When a group of choristers headed for dinner after the rehearsal, he declined to join them.

The next day, Dumler received a call; Grady hadn't reported to the Cathedral, and his phone was going unanswered. Peggy Breslin rushed to his apartment but couldn't get anyone to come to the door. They located a friend with keys, who entered the apartment.

The friend found Grady, half-dressed, lying on his bed. He had died of a heart attack.

In the days that followed, there were several versions of Grady's last actions. He had decided to resign . . . He had been asked to resign . . . He had written his resignation and delivered it to Monsignor Dalla Villa . . . He had written his resignation but hadn't delivered it . . . Heartbroken, he had gone home after the rehearsal, determined to write his resignation. . . .

Personal Demons

John Grady had been an energetic man who came to the Cathedral with a sheaf of extravagant plans for refashioning its music. But St. Patrick's turned out to be more interested in trying to absorb the demands of Vatican II. And Grady's plans were rooted in the opera house, the concert hall, and his own considerable personal demons, more than they were tied to the needs of the Cathedral. This meant that some of those plans would succeed, while others would be destroyed. As that occurred, Grady himself was destroyed in the process.

His death was so unexpected that his name would still show up in strange places as late as December, when he was listed as one of the conductors for the Avery Fisher Hall "*Messiah* Sing-In." Choros Aristos was stopped in its tracks; it (or at least its name) briefly resurfaced a couple of years later, directed by Met chorus master Gregory Buchalter, then disappeared for good.

As for *The Godfather: Part III*, the film that had caused so much trouble for the Cathedral and had prompted John Grady's final destruction, it was released around Christmastime. Choir members were shocked to find that, while their voices were heard on the soundtrack, their faces had been left on the cutting-room floor.*

---

* That was resolved when the trilogy of *Godfather* films was re-released on DVD in 2008. The set included two discs of extra features, one of which was the aforementioned rough cut of the opening sequence of *Part III*—and it contains a shot of Grady and the choir in full cry.

John Grady, in one of his favorite photographs.

St. Patrick's Cathedral entered the concert field in a big way with Leopold Stokowski leading the forces. (*Chris Sheridan*)

Principal Organist Donald Dumler, in a photo used at the time of his appointment as Associate Organist.

A mid-performance shot of Yardumian's *Veni, Sancte Spiritus*, 1972.

A Cathedral Choir member sneaked into the triforium to snap this dizzying view of Pope John Paul II, Cardinal Cooke, and cantor Matthew Murray during the Pontiff's 1979 visit. (*Courtesy of Catherine O'Connor*)

A behind-the-altar view of cantor, congregation—and choir—at the Cathedral's Centenary Mass of Thanksgiving. (*Chris Sheridan*)

Chapter 7

THE TRASH TWIN OF FIFTH AVENUE (1990-97)

> By far, the great treasury of church music . . . falls into the music for
> sung Mass. Every age has left us its contribution to that treasure. Much
> of this is able to be performed only by choirs that practice.
>
> *Sacred Music*

Almost as quickly as the news of John Grady's death was spreading through the ranks of choir members by phone, Monsignor Dalla Villa was sitting down to an emergency meeting with Donald Dumler to make the necessary arrangements—not only for Grady's funeral, but for some sort of stopgap measures to continue the work of the music department. Because of this, the Archdiocesan Music Commissioner, John-Michael Caprio, had been asked to take part.

The first order of business would be the funeral, during which the choir would have a major role. "You'll conduct it, of course," said Monsignor Dalla Villa to Dumler.

"Monsignor, I'm not a conductor!" said Dumler vehemently. As opposed to the legions of organists who prided themselves on nonexistent conducting skills, he believed without question that he was effective only when he left the baton to others. And Grady's funeral promised to have in the congregation a large contingent of Met and Philharmonic personnel, listeners to whom any slip-ups would be embarrassingly obvious. Rather than burden the choir with nervous and insecure direction, someone else would have to take the podium.

Before Monsignor Dalla Villa could even respond, Dumler turned to Caprio. "Why don't you do it?"

Caprio's schedule was as a rule insanely crowded, with activities spanning two states, and the upcoming week promised to be worse. Still, he shrugged in agreement.

"Of course."

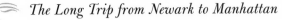

As opposed to the high-powered organists who had always headed the music at St. Patrick's, John-Michael Caprio had discovered early in the game that his own talents lay elsewhere.

Born in Newark in 1947, he had been educated in the Catholic school system. After that had come a great deal of study in various college settings: Depending on the biography, his name was connected with the New York University College of the Arts, Manhattan School of Music, Rutgers University, the Juilliard School, and the University of Notre Dame. Following the standard path of undecided musicians, he headed back to his home turf, playing at a few local churches and then becoming a music teacher at Paul VI Regional High School in the New Jersey town of Clifton. But his ambitions quickly clarified. "It was there," the *Times* later wrote, "that he undertook to train a touring chorus that alternately performed at such places as Trinity Church in New York City and the National Shrine in Washington." The touring chorus worked out so well that he "was asked to form a pontifical choir to perform for the Bishop of Paterson [New Jersey] at his liturgical functions." In 1973, he became director of music for the Diocese of Paterson; he also plunged into more intensive conducting study with Emanuel Balaban.

The result of that work came three years later, when the Ars Nova Chorale and Orchestra gave its first performance under Caprio's baton. Working out of his home base of St. Philip the Apostle Church in Clifton, the group began with the Vaughan Williams *Hodie*, a sizeable work requiring a mixed choir, a boys' choir, a solo trio, and a full orchestra. It was a big undertaking (Caprio later said that his friends "thought I had gone mad"), but even as a first effort it illustrated some major truths about John-Michael Caprio. He had a Barnumesque taste for large projects, richly produced. As well, he possessed a talent that would influence his career more than any musical gifts—an ability to mobilize large groups, even unwieldy ones, and to organize them toward his ends. In the sometimes haphazard Catholic-music world of the 1970s, such showmanship was excitingly unusual.

It was also expensive. So as he learned the art of running a concert choir, Caprio learned as well the various arts of cajolery, networking, and image-building. He wheedled free performances from well-known professionals. He built relationships with the local Chamber of Commerce, the New Jersey Arts Council, and something called Musical Arts of New Jersey; he even extracted donations from the local Musicians' Union. He honed a personality that combined the aplomb of a Toscanini with an unmistakable New Jersey scrappiness. And he made sure to look the part, sporting a stylish wardrobe, a height-of-fashion Afro (which in time would be supplanted by a hairpiece), and a full beard. Caprio's efforts paid off handsomely: Ars Nova performances were able to boast full orchestra, guest artists from the Met and City Opera—and on at least one occasion, a display ad in the *Times* larger than anything else on the page. All of this won him more serious attention, proven in 1978 when the opening of Ars Nova's third season was heralded by a full-length interview in the *Times*. Along with a photo of "the red-headed, red-bearded maestro," the article detailed his efforts to expand Ars Nova's reach, and the cause of professional classical music, in New Jersey: "'[W]e're worthy of their support. I have a dream that some day we'll build a concert hall in Passaic County.'"

It soon became clear that those New Jersey musicians would have to build the hall with someone else's help, as within months there occurred two events that would radically change Caprio's career path. In 1979, he was offered the post of music director at the Church of the Resurrection, located in the very upscale Westchester County (New York) town of Rye. For more than thirty-five years the congregation had enjoyed the services of organist-composer Dominic Tranzillo, but after his retirement there had been trouble finding a successor. Caprio made an immediate fit with the congregation. Even more significant, he struck up an instant friendship with the church's cantor. Tranzillo's daughter Jessica was a Juilliard-trained soprano, married to organist-harpsichordist Joseph Smith, and possessed of the triple gifts of an effortlessly beautiful lyric voice; superb diction; and a true liturgical musician's mindset, with no operatic ambitions whatsoever. She would become not only Caprio's assistant but a trusted confidante, and one of his favorite soloists.

At almost the same time, Cardinal Cooke made his own offer, asking Caprio to found, and to head, the New York School of Liturgical Music. The school would be based at the New York University Catholic Center and was intended to refine the skills as well as the tastes of organists, conductors, and even guitarists ("a means of sharing and perfecting our talents and improving the quality of our liturgical music in every Parish," wrote the Cardinal in a letter that was distributed throughout the Archdiocese). Caprio installed Jessica Tranzillo as his secretary, then set about fashioning a curriculum, staffing the school with every liturgical music specialist he could find.

These developments made Caprio more important in the New York area than he had been. But they also made his schedule a nightmare, because he was shuttling between his New Jersey home in Montclair, his school activities in Manhattan, and his choir in Rye. Something would have to give in this battle for priorities, and it was Ars Nova; the group's performance schedule began to dwindle, until by 1981 they would give some of their last concerts.

Still, Caprio wanted a venue for high-powered choral work, and his new church could be used as a base of operations. For additional vocal strength, he hit upon the idea of combining the forces of Rye's three major churches—Resurrection, the Anglican outlet Christ's Church, and Rye Presbyterian—to give joint holiday concerts. The newly installed organist/choirmaster at Christ's Church remembered his introduction to Caprio when he received an offhanded phone call in October 1982: "Okay, this is short notice, but my choir's doing this concert, and I thought it might be nice if. . . ." The *if* was a proposal for the three churches to collaborate on an early-December performance of Part I of *Messiah*—to be conducted, of course, by John-Michael Caprio. It was indeed short notice for a concert to be sung by three mostly volunteer choirs. But Caprio had the enviable gift of being able to tell singers on a Monday evening, "We'll rehearse Tuesday, Wednesday, and Thursday" in a way that they accepted without a qualm. The multi-choir concert was a success, enough so that the format was repeated annually, in one form or another, for the rest of his time in Rye.

As it turned out, that time wouldn't be long. Some musicians felt that Resurrection might prove a direct conduit to more visible work in New York churches, so it was no surprise when Cardinal Cooke asked Caprio to assume directorship of the Archdiocesan Music Commission in 1983. It was a distinctive honor—Caprio would be the first layman tapped to head the commission—but it made the issue of commuting more important than ever. It was then he learned of a house for sale in his hometown, the estate of recently deceased Met diva Maria Jeritza. The property, with its two houses and two carriage houses, was immense. Still, Newark at the time was a bad bet with its high crime rate, depressed property values, and crumbling infrastructure. These facts enabled him to bargain the asking price down by half. Then he told the story to the *Times* real estate section, posing at his front gate for a photo (which showed him in a linen suit, the Afro shortened, and the beard edited to what would become a trademark moustache). He was now that rarest of creatures in the New York City area, a substantial landowner. Less happily, he was still a long-distance commuter, shuttling between Newark, Rye, and Manhattan.

Both of those situations would change within a few years when he discovered the Delaware River town of Lambertville in southern New Jersey, directly across the water from posh New Hope, Pennsylvania. He found a small house in the area, named it Bridgegate (but he would invariably call it, drawlingly, "The Faaahm"), sold the Newark property, and rented a small apartment near the Archdiocesan offices for a pied-à-terre. Before long he was able to move his conductorial operations to Lambertville's St. John the Evangelist.

The last half of the 1980s were a settled period, with Caprio's public persona focused almost exclusively on his Archdiocesan role. That position, combined with his talent for schmoozing the media, meant that his opinions on liturgical music regularly made it into print. His quotes were worded to be not only informative but ever-so-slightly audacious: "I don't like to think of it that way, but making music is a business." "[T]he Romans have taken a bad rap, musically, for years." "I think guitar music is on the wane now." "The church should never be a salon or a concert hall for a composer to show off his skills." "We are not ready for a national hymnal because we have not aligned our taste levels."

But interviews didn't take the place of performance, and Caprio felt the need for more-concentrated musical activity than his church position was providing. Once again copying his Ars Nova model, he began to put together a group of instrumentalists and singers from the Lambertville area, the Riverside Symphonia, to perform at St. John's. He felt that popular, accessible music was vital to a new orchestra, so Riverside Symphonia's inaugural performance would feature such orchestral hits as *Eine Kleine Nachtmusik*, Barber's *Adagio for Strings*, and Jessica Tranzillo singing Mozart's *Exsultate, Jubilate*. The opening concert was set for October 6, 1990.

Which, as fate had it, would be exactly three days after John Grady's funeral.

Caprio and Grady had never been buddies; neither had they been at loggerheads, a fact that spoke well for both of them, considering that they had been thrown together in some professional near-collisions. Grady had spent a little time teaching music history and organ at the School of Liturgical Music, but maintaining that schedule had proven to be an off-and-on situation. After Cardinal Cooke's death, Caprio had filled in as conductor at a pre-funeral Youth Mass when Grady had been committed elsewhere. More blatantly, Monsignor Dalla Villa had been taken with Caprio's musical commentary—so much so that he had ordered Grady to meet with Caprio for "training" in the finer points of Cathedral musical programming. Grady didn't openly refuse, but that training session never took place.

Caprio was sensitive to all of that history and wanted to ensure that the funeral music would reflect Grady's own taste. So the programming featured repertoire that Grady loved and that Cathedral musicians had often performed: the Brahms "How Lovely Is Thy Dwelling Place," the Mozart "Lacrymosa" and "Ave Verum," and the Fauré "In Paradisum." The choir was called for a run-through—for most of them, their first meeting with Caprio. One chorister remembered the rehearsal, which began with Caprio well-dressed and cool-headed and ended with him seeming rattled, his clothing soaked in perspiration. (The rattled demeanor was unusual, but the perspiration was Caprio's reaction to any performance situation, stressful or not.) The service itself was a moving experience, particularly because of Cardinal O'Connor's sermon, during which he said, "The Cathedral Choir is an orphan without John Grady."

But Caprio was not moved as much as displeased. As far as he was concerned, much of the singing that day had been slipshod, and he blamed it on what he perceived as a casual attitude that had developed toward preparation and rehearsal. By the time the choir had arrived at "In Paradisum," a singer remembered, "we were awful. Weak. People were coming in and out as if we didn't know the music." To exacerbate the situation, almost immediately afterward Monsignor Dalla Villa had asked Caprio to serve as interim music director—a one-year commitment, during which a search committee would be formed to select a permanent replacement.

Caprio muttered to Dumler, "I've got a lot of work to do."

Then he went off to do some last-minute work for the Riverside Symphonia debut.

The Interim Guy

It was inevitable that, within days of John Grady's death, Monsignor Dalla Villa received the usual deluge of applications from organists who wanted to succeed him. One of them came with an accompanying packet of testimonials, topped by a grandiloquent letter attesting to the man's suitability—"[B]esides his ability as organist and choirmaster and gracious manner, we were particularly impressed with his family life, . . . his wife, and their two sons and daughter."

But Caprio—who was in the awkward position of serving as the interim music director while simultaneously sitting on the search committee to replace the interim music director—wasn't paying attention. During those weeks, he was trying to decide exactly which steps to take with regard to the choir. Jessica Tranzillo recalled, "He was saying, 'This is *St. Patrick's Cathedral*. This is the center of the diocesan universe.' He wanted the choir to be as good as, if not better than, the others." Still, he realized that he was filling a temporary assignment, one that used a large number of volunteers, and his usual sledgehammer style would have to be tempered.

So the choir was submitted to a gradual retraining process while the interim music director made heroic efforts to hold his tongue. Rehearsals became more intensive and more detailed; even the rehearsal breaks, which had become lengthy in recent years, were shortened. Attendance at those rehearsals, which in the past had been a fairly casual matter, was now required. He alternated between curt warnings such as *"Learn—the—notes!"* and comedy, adopting a fake Italian accent to remind the sopranos in wobbly moments, "No shake-a the voice, eh?" And the Brahms *Requiem*, the Bach *B-Minor Mass*, and all the other oratorio selections—what Grady had customarily referred to as "the Great Works"—were retired, as the choir's repertoire was pared back to simpler music. So much simpler was the music that, coincidentally or not, it vanished for a while from the broader public gaze. The *Times* music listings for Christmas 1990 and Easter 1991 carried not a single word of the Cathedral's programming.

Many people understood the motives behind the change. Some didn't, and at this point Caprio finally lost patience. One woman was upset enough that she confronted him: "Why aren't we doing the Great Works anymore?"

He snapped, "Because you can't sing them."

All in all it was a tough period for the members of the music department. Caprio was juggling the schedules of the Cathedral, the Archdiocesan Music Commission, the School of Liturgical Music, and the search committee as well; the Riverside Philharmonia was readying its holiday concert, complete with the Saint-Saëns *Christmas Oratorio*; and he was still, nominally, the music director at St. John the Evangelist—even though his efforts were primarily directed toward finding substitutes while the Cathedral situation decided itself.

In the meantime, plenty of hangers-on at St. Patrick's were waiting for the upcoming holiday season to provide the first real evidence of Caprio's abilities. A few eyebrows were raised when Caprio pulled the choir from the upcoming *CitySings*. But Midnight Mass itself provided no real surprises. Caprio offered music that was completely in the Grady mode, even to Grady's own arrangement of "O Holy Night" (rendered by Diana Soviero, who had sung a *Faust* at the Met earlier that evening but still had enough moxie to throw in a high C at the end of her solo). And for better or worse, there seemed to be no real change in the choir: In the final moments of the "Hallelujah Chorus" postlude, a soprano delivered an unintentional solo when she sang one too many "Hallelujahs."

While most listeners were reassured by Caprio's efforts, some singers weren't. Throughout this period a number of them would resign, publicly or privately. One of them later declared, "When you've worked with the people *I* have, it was a too-far-down experience."

This was a double-pronged comment, as John-Michael Caprio's detractors had two complaints. One of the complaints was personality-based: Caprio brought a different tone to the Cathedral's music department, and even his strongest supporters acknowledged it. "I can see where some people had a problem," said one singer who became a close friend. "Kind of brash. Mouthy. Some people couldn't deal with it."

The other complaint was based on Caprio's résumé. It was the résumé of a conductor rather than that of an organist, and this ran contrary to Cathedral tradition. Moreover, Caprio's curriculum vitae was the most modest St. Patrick's had seen in more than a century, lacking the international glamour and distinguished awards of a Yon, a Courboin, a Grady.

But as the search stretched from 1990 into 1991, it became apparent that no decision-maker at the Cathedral was particularly worried about the interim director's credentials. Instead, Cardinal O'Connor's sticking point was his insistence that the new music director be able to coax the congregation to sing. And this was a tall order. While the past two decades had accustomed many local congregations to the idea of singing during Masses, the vast majority of the people jamming St. Patrick's were occasional visitors or tourists—overwhelmed by the building, unfamiliar with one another, and completely disinclined to raise their voices. They hadn't sung under Grady; they weren't singing under Caprio. And this bothered the Cardinal.

It also bothered Caprio, though not exactly for the same reason. Although he would later admit (privately), "I *hated* it in the beginning," he had now come to realize that he wanted the Cathedral job, in fact wanted it rather badly. Now he became worried enough by the Cardinal's reaction to confide in David Skoblow.

> I remember that he called me, saying, "I don't how he expects me to do it!" We sat down and drafted a memo to try and explain that the congregation wasn't a local parish congregation, that they weren't used to the music . . . that they came to St. Patrick's to be entertained . . . that they were gawking . . . that they were there because they wanted to hear the choir. I don't know if it helped.

Although the search committee had combed through a goodly number of applications, not one applicant had been called in for an interview. When the members gathered in June 1991 for one final meeting prior to breaking for the summer, Monsignor Dalla Villa canvassed the room for opinions. It was then that Dumler, who had been close-mouthed during the search process, spoke: "Monsignor, you know the old saying—if it isn't broken, don't fix it. . . . I like the way things are now."

"You mean John-Michael as director of music?" asked Monsignor Dalla Villa. "The Cardinal will have a fit." He was particularly worried that Caprio's holding the Archdiocesan position at the same time as the Cathedral job might be viewed as a conflict of interest.

Still, there was no denying that the season had gone more smoothly than it might have in other hands. Monsignor Dalla Villa asked Cardinal O'Connor for his opinion on the subject of Caprio's working at St. Patrick's. "People are going to talk regardless of whatever you do," he said. "Do what you want."

The decision was revealed in an interoffice memo signed by Monsignor Dalla Villa, uncharacteristically brief, dated June 27, 1991:

Donald Dumler is now the official organist of the Cathedral.

John-Michael Caprio has been selected as Director of Music of St. Patrick's Cathedral.

Alan Davis is now associate organist of St. Patrick's Cathedral.

Not surprisingly for the period, none of the city's newspapers carried any word of Caprio's appointment—but then again, neither did *Catholic New York*. Even so, if that lack of coverage implied that the Cathedral's new music director wasn't capable of stirring up interest, those periodicals were wrong. As one chorister put it, "Coming into the room, you'd think there's five of him." It wasn't merely a case of personality: Caprio had obviously given a lot of thought to the changes that were needed in the Cathedral music program and was ready to implement his ideas, ruthlessly if need be.

That August, it seemed to be business as usual when the *New York Times* carried its audition ad for St. Patrick's, exactly the same one as had appeared for the past twenty years. But when the season began, Caprio announced that he had decided to get an honest assessment of his raw material by asking every chorister, professional or volunteer, to sing for him in private audition. For many, it would be their first audition since they had sung for John Grady. A number of them panicked. Soprano Dolores Nolan had joined the choir only months before, and she laid it on the line as soon as she walked into the room: "You will have blood on your hands if you don't accept me, because I will likely slit my wrists if you don't!" (Not only did Caprio accept her without a qualm, but she would ultimately show up in occasional solo assignments.)

Still, part of his audition process was to "cut out the deadwood," and other singers received less-diplomatic treatment. One hapless woman failed a sight-reading test miserably enough that she left the room in tears after Caprio announced, "If you can't sing this, you really don't need to be here." Another was scolded, "Your singing is not only flat, it's Merman-esque." There were more resignations, as well as terminations (which took place so quietly that most people had no clue of anyone's being axed). By year's end, the 120-plus singers of the choir had been trimmed to a group that numbered 76.

Caprio then fixed his sights on the department's finances. With few exceptions, both liturgical and extra-liturgical music had historically been funded by the Cathedral. But Caprio's concert plans were elaborate enough to warrant a budget of their own—something that he didn't want to leave to chance, especially because the United States in the early 1990s was in the midst of a financial downturn that might prove uncongenial to concert life. On top of it, the Vatican's Congregation for Divine Worship had in 1987 issued its declaration *Concerts in Churches*, a set of guidelines for nonliturgical music performances. One rule was, "Entrance to the church must be without payment and open to all." Concert-giving churches, St. Patrick's among them, compromised by charging admission only to a "preferred" area, which freed up the rest of the church for free seating but seriously reduced the possible income that any concert could generate.

An organized system of funding was obviously needed. To this end, Caprio met with David Skoblow to lay the legal groundwork for the choir's first-ever fundraising arm. In September, the newly named organization, Friends of Music, sent out its first appeal "to support the cause of presenting quality choral music accompanied by professional orchestra here in America's most famous Cathedral." The appeal went out only to choir members, their friends and families, and Caprio's personal mailing list. Authorities had refused to allow the Cathedral's own mailing lists to be used for this venture. That may have blunted some of the impact, but Friends of Music was nevertheless able to make a contribution to the $25,000 cost of Caprio's first concert on December 15, a Vivaldi *Gloria* that gave the St. Patrick's audience a closeup view of its new music director in action.

Four nights later came that year's *CitySings*, business as usual in its makeup and very obviously a sore point as far as Caprio was concerned. The choir hadn't participated at all in the previous year's edition; now they were programmed to sing three selections. But the Cathedral's music director objected to the tone of the event—the same tone to which John Grady had objected, in which the music had been carelessly chosen and the program "decorated" with mawkish clip-art drawings . . . and especially the fact that the Cathedral Choir seemed to be appearing as minor guests of the evening's organizers. James Poma remembered Caprio, standing in the ambulatory during the concert, his face set, muttering several times, "This is *our* house." Such fulminations had to do with more than pride of place. Caprio had definite ideas on music, but the showman in him had an even stronger sense of rightness in the performance of that music and was frustrated when a performance fell short.

But no matter what music was being performed, Cardinal O'Connor was still displeased with the fact that the congregation wasn't singing during Masses. Caprio tried peppering the congregation with choir members. It didn't help: The Cardinal was reputed to have said, "This is John Grady all over again." And after two weeks in a row when the offertory anthem had run longer than the prescribed 3:20, His Eminence had sharp words for his music director. That day, Caprio skulked into Dumler's office and sank into a chair. "Donny, I'm so depressed I could break down and cry right now." The issue wasn't resolved until Caprio (whose Archdiocesan office was close enough to O'Connor's that it would be easy to get face time) sat down with the Cardinal to convince him of his utter willingness to cooperate. Dumler remembered, "He told the Cardinal, 'Just tell me what you want.' He made it clear that he wanted only to please him. Finally, after that, the honeymoon began. And it lasted until John-Michael died."

While 1991 had been a rollercoaster, the general assumption was that 1992 would be smoother going. That wasn't the case.

On the positive side, Caprio's own musical taste was finding opportunities to declare itself. More than any of his predecessors, he understood the value not only of the classics but of more current composers such as John Rutter, as well as the ubiquitous Catholic pop that was showing up at so many parishes. This mindset created programming with the "liturgical correctness" that was a buzzword for the period; but as well, with a sense of lightness, of what's-next. On Easter Sunday 1992, he juxtaposed selections from *Messiah* with Haugen's *Mass of Creation*, the whole preceded by a brass ensemble offering Copland's *Fanfare for the Common Man*. (In times to come, an interviewer would ask him about this duality of taste. He framed it in quotable-quote language: "We have to present music that reflects the liturgy, but we also have to offer a variety of musical languages to speak to the diversity of people who come here." In private, he simply referred to himself and Donald Dumler, who unquestioningly supported his programming decisions, as The Trash Twins of Fifth Avenue.)

That year's *CitySings* finally bore the stamp of John-Michael Caprio, and it was evident from the appearance of the program (the clip art disappeared), the bumping-up of the quality of the musical selections, even the engagement of Temple Emanu-El's cantor Howard Nevison to open the proceedings with "Bless This House." But the showman's hand made itself apparent at evening's end. The concert had always ended with musicians and congregation joining in on "Silent Night," and Caprio decided that it would be a handsome touch to turn the carol into a candlelight processional, sung against a backdrop of the Cathedral's Fifth Avenue doors slowly opening to bring the city itself into the celebration (as he told his friends, "the Hallmark side of Christmas"). He was right; concertgoers adored it. And the moment would be repeated at the close of the program, every year thereafter.*

This may have felt like triumph, but Cathedral Choir members went through *CitySings* with the humbling memory of the previous Sunday evening's concert. Caprio had planned a swanky program, very much in his style: the Corelli *Christmas Concerto*; choral pieces that touchingly acknowledged the Cathedral's musical history ("Gesù Bambino," with the program note "Pietro Yon served as Organist-Director of Music at this Cathedral from 1926–1943," and Reger's "The Virgin's Slumber Song," annotated "This classic song was arranged for string orchestra by John Grady, who served this Cathedral as Organist-Director of Music from 1970–1990"); and, as the main event, the Bach *Magnificat*. Rehearsals were difficult (made more so by the coincidence of both Caprio's and accompanist Dumler's wrenching their backs), and after only a few sessions, one singer remembered the result as "a hash . . . we weren't getting it." Finally Caprio stopped short during a rehearsal and exploded, "I'm *not* going to put something in front of the public that you can't perform properly!" Although the *Magnificat* had been publicly announced, even in the *Times*, it was canceled forthwith; in its place was substituted the Vivaldi *Gloria* that the choir had sung the year before. Some people were embarrassed. Others realized that Caprio was playing for keeps.

As one of them sighed philosophically, "That taught us something."

The size of the choir might be shrinking, but the size of the paid staff was moving in the opposite direction, and Caprio's intent—that the music department be a reflection of his own taste—was evident nowhere as much as in his choice of professional vocalists. He felt that a large choir needed to be anchored by more than four voices; so, one at a time, other singers began to show up until the Cathedral had a resident paid octet and was heading for a triple quartet. As to the singers themselves, Caprio's preference seemed to be for well-trained musicians who could deliver the goods but weren't poised to run off to the Met. Cantor Charlene

* Almost every year. In 2007, this author was asked to write a short piece about Caprio for that year's *CitySings* program. It featured the story of the candlelight processional and the doors opening, and ended: "Watch for it tonight." Naturally, that was the first time the ushers forgot to open the doors.

Verkowitz was one of the first hires, along with tenor Arn Prince, a Manhattan School of Music graduate who had sung with the Santa Fe Opera and won first place in the Richard Tauber International Competition for Tenors. They were soon joined by sopranos Johanna Wiseman (who had sung a variety of orchestra dates, starred in a national tour of *Brigadoon*, and spent a few months on Broadway doing a small role in *The Phantom of the Opera*) and Patricia Thompson (familiar to Caprio from her work in churches throughout the diocese). Beth Clayton showed up with a knockout mezzo-soprano, good enough that Cathedral listeners would get to enjoy her vocalism for only a few years before she left to launch a career that would take her to the New York City Opera and other major venues around the world.

These were singers of the "emerging professional" class. This meant that, with a few exceptions, their sound would be youthful; younger than that of Grady's solo quartet, younger by far than the sound of Yon's very expert Male Soloist Ensemble. That youthfulness brought its own problems, working well for polyphony, sometimes less so when out-and-out vocal lusciousness was required. Also, "emerging professionals" were forever skipping off to take outside work. Yon and Courboin had strenuously objected to such jaunts if they conflicted with the Cathedral schedule; Grady gritted his teeth; but Caprio shrugged and willingly accepted the situation as a fact of modern musical life. Thus, he compiled the longest list of pinch-hitters that the Cathedral had seen in more than a century: Daniel Belcher, Barron Coleman, Steven Condy, Jennifer Diamond, Jeff Gardner, Mark Heimbigner, Jonathan Keeley, Richard Lissemore, Leslie Middlebrook, Jeanne Moniz, Lori Nassif, Pamela Olsen, Judith Parker, Michael Polscer, Nicole Rose, Andrew Schultze, Laura Tucker, Laura Van Teeple, Joseph Wiggett—they were only some of the vocalists who would show up, whether for a single Mass, a concert, or an entire season, and then might disappear again. Or perhaps they might sign on permanently. No one knew in advance, least of all the singers themselves.

Whether or not it was a cause-and-effect situation, from a public standpoint the choir's collective personality began to change as well. Every church choir bears an imprint of its members as well as that of its choirmaster: The Cathedral Choir had been mannerly and dignified under Pecher, an extremely close-knit family under Yon and Courboin, and a gregarious party under Grady. The fact that choir members might show up and not be certain of the people with whom they'd be singing couldn't be ignored, and it might have contributed to the fact that, under Caprio, the members of the Cathedral Choir developed a reputation for being imperturbable . . . and at times, less than the warmest of colleagues. All of these changes represented a major transformation in the role that professional singers would play at St. Patrick's, and it was enough of a shift that Grady-era soloists Ellen Alexander and Nadja Witkowska decided it was time to move on.

So did James Javore, and his departure left a difficult gap to fill. Jessica Tranzillo had frequently been available, helping out in the soprano section or manning the cantor's desk, but most days she was already spoken for at the Church of St. Francis of Assisi. And while Caprio had hired other singers with an eye to their cantorial possibilities—Arn Prince and Patricia Thompson would spend as much time cantoring Masses as they would singing in the choir—they were highly valued as choristers. The Cathedral schedule required a singer who could function purely as a cantor, and for this Caprio did some looking around at singers at area churches.

A young mezzo-soprano, Cori Ellison, was "an absolute freelance" who juggled a plethora of jobs around town: teaching an opera survey course at New York University, writing occasional pieces for the *Times*, singing extra chorus at both of New York's major opera houses (and writing English surtitles for City Opera) . . . and for several years, singing as a staff cantor at St. Paul the Apostle. She had been one of the many Cathedral Choir substitutes and knew Caprio, but she still found it puzzling when he called her during the summertime and asked, "Hey—would you be able to cantor Labor Day weekend?"

"Which Masses?"

"All of them."

Puzzled but willing, she sang five Masses over two days. Apparently someone was watching, and pleased with the results. Caprio phoned her again within a week. "Would you be interested in coming aboard?" She was.

Ellison turned out to be a find. In an atmosphere in which Cardinal O'Connor's outspokenness had turned the Cathedral into a major news center—so much so that his sermons often were quoted on evening newscasts, and several rows of pews had been removed to allow for a media platform—she was utterly poised in front of the congregation. Her gifts included not only a sympathetic voice, but an extra quality of communication. (One listener, Hollywood-style, described the quality as "It." Or as another put it, "She has this way of smiling while she sings.") Ellison would cantor not only that year's Midnight Mass but nearly everything else of importance that went on at the Cathedral for close to a decade.*

The preparation had taken longer than anyone had imagined, but John-Michael Caprio was ready to begin 1993 with both clerical support and financial backing, as well as a musical organization that he felt was ready to carry out his plans. Those plans were more ambitious than anything done at St. Patrick's in a long time. While they might seem interesting, no one knew how well they would be executed. And while those plans would have generated instant enthusiasm in other decades, things had changed enough that musical success at St. Patrick's was no longer something to be taken for granted.

Building a Music Machine

As John Grady had developed his Cathedral Family, Caprio had evolved not only a choir but an inner circle. Baritone Paul Zorovich said, "I got into the In Crowd when he found that I knew computers. I started installing software, I tagged along to go to breakfast after Mass, and the rest was history." Those individuals provided nonmusical talents, or financial contributions, or wisecracks (emphasis on the "brash" aspect, the more eyebrow-raising the better). In return, Caprio pulled strings when he could, providing theater tickets, invitations to participate in musical events that might be closed to other choir members, photo ops with the rich and famous—or the Cathedral Choir itself, provided gratis as accompaniment for important occasions. (Zorovich remembered the moment when he told Caprio of his plans to be married in Whitestone, and Caprio's immediate shift into flowery high dudgeon: "You . . . will . . . *not* . . . be married in *Queens!* You will be married *here*, with full choir and

---

* She also acquired that more ominous badge of New York celebrity, her own stalker. Until it ended with an order of protection, a man repeatedly wrote letters, waited for her at the Parish House door, proposed marriage or an alternative, and in the middle of one Mass that fell around St. Valentine's Day strode up to the altar rail while she was singing in order to ceremonially deposit before her a large heart-shaped box of chocolates.

organ!" James Poma had much the same experience when he got married; but when Caprio was rehearsing the choir for the occasion and noticed the groom-to-be singing along, he stopped the music dead. "*You're* not going to be singing. *Why* are you disrupting the balance?") Those people were extremely valuable to Caprio, and in the coming years, with the music department's calendar becoming continually more crowded, they would prove to be even more so.

Now that Vatican II was a distant memory to some people, there was a corresponding revival of interest in some of the older liturgical practices (such as the Mass According to the 1962 Missal, called by everyone the Tridentine Rite—officially proscribed for years but frequently celebrated by small groups of adherents in out-of-the-way churches, even in private homes). Caprio keyed in to this curiosity when he took his first musical shot over the bow only three days after the beginning of the year, as St. Patrick's presented its Vespers of Epiphany.

It was the first of what would be four Vesper services that year; the first Vesper service heard at the Cathedral in over two decades; and as it was a service that contained a very high proportion of singing, Caprio— who was hoping to move gradually into weekly Vespers—had been the motivating force behind it. As well, it was a marked departure from the Cathedral's usual brand of music. There was a new group of singers to execute it—the St. Patrick's Cathedral Chancel Choir (whose name would be changed within months, to the Cathedral Schola), a sixteen-voice ensemble comprising Caprio's soloists, bolstered by whatever volunteer singers he decided were up to the task. And those singers were performing works by William Crotch, Gerre Hancock, William H. Harris, John Hilton, Healey Willan, Charles Wood: composers whose output was basically Anglican in style, almost unknown at the Cathedral.

More Anglican-styled music was in store when St. Patrick's added to its Holy Week schedule a sung Tenebrae on Good Friday, a somber and impressive service that had vanished from the schedule during the 1970s. Its main drawback, from the perspective of Cathedral Schola members, was that the schedule required it be held at 9:00 in the morning; and while Caprio's first effort concentrated on the chanted Lamentations of Jeremiah, every following Tenebrae would feature the Allegri "Miserere," famous for its five high Cs and very much in vogue at a number of New York churches. The programming made the service a solemn delight for listeners. The hour made it unpopular with most of the Cathedral sopra-nos. (Especially when it began to be televised. On one occasion, the camera caught the soprano at the moment that her high C cracked, linger-ing on her look of consternation.)

Still another change involved the look of Cathedral programs, an area with which no music director had bothered to concern himself since the days of Pietro Yon. Caprio felt that programs should be uniform, identi-fiable, and attractive, qualities that they had rarely achieved during the previous forty years. To lend a hand, he consulted Father Timothy Shree-nan, a staff priest at St. Francis of Assisi, not only an organist himself but computer-literate (in those days, an unusual talent) and well versed in graphic production. The two men—who were close enough that Caprio invariably called him "Timmy"—would literally remake the look of printed materials at St. Patrick's.

On top of it all, the subject of fashion intervened when Caprio decided that the choir should be equipped with new robes (finding the choir's blue robes "too Protestant"). The new design was a compromise between his own ideas and those of Monsignor Dalla Villa—and the resulting robes were magenta, with a large design embroidered on the front in gold, the "P" of the Chi-Rho transformed into "SPC" for a Cathedral monogram. This made the robes nothing if not unique. And after one appearance at Midnight Mass (so went the legend), it caused WPIX-TV producers to ask Caprio for an alternative for the choir to wear on camera; apparently the robes photographed very badly in the gallery. From then on, Midnight Mass would be performed in concert dress.*

Caprio was forced to deal with not only vocal and sartorial but also mechanical upheavals at this time. During some recent Midnight Mass telecasts the camera had panned lovingly over the gallery organ, the close-up shot unflatteringly revealing its pipes dulled and the carved wood of the case encrusted with decades of grime. Now more than sixty years old and in use every day of its life, the Kilgen was deteriorating to an extent that the St. Patrick's recital series, which had ground to a halt, hadn't been revived. Dumler and Davis had simply accustomed themselves to working around the parts of the organ that were dead or unreliable, a

---

* This didn't do much for the Cathedral Choir's reputation among some other New York church choirs, because it was construed as showing off. Even so, a few midtown churches followed suit.

situation that was brought home to Caprio one day when he pulled at a stop knob and it came off in his hand. Decades of alterations and make-do repairs under Courboin and Grady hadn't done much for the integrity of the instrument, and some experts and many kibitzers were advising that the entire installation be scrapped and replaced with an electronic instrument. However, consultant Nelson Bardon was brought in; he offered a trenchant assessment of the situation, enthusing that the Kilgen was "perfectly placed in a magnificent building," also that it was "built like a battleship and has proven itself over the last 80 years." He recommended unequivocally that it be restored, pointing out that much of the Kilgen's problem among the cognoscenti was not its condition but its name: "The builder is not 'famous' enough. Compared to a European builder, George Kilgen & Sons lacks charisma." And finally, "Amongst the small but highly vocal coterie of organ critics and aficionados, fashion wears out more organs than playing ever will." Whether or not the hyperbole had anything to do with it, the organ was earmarked for serious attention as part of a $10,000,000 Cathedral fundraising campaign. Robert M. Turner had been contracted to build new twin five-manual consoles for gallery and chancel organs (which for the first time would be linked—Davis and Dumler's idea—so that any part of gallery or chancel organ could be played from either console). Past that point, Caprio hadn't quite planned.

The other contractee came into the picture when Caprio ran into him at a concert in Newark. John Peragallo III was part of a three-generation dynasty of organ-builders, all of whom had ties to the Cathedral. His grandfather John Peragallo Sr. had first been brought to St. Patrick's by James Ungerer to tune the Jardine. Soon after that he was launched when he built an organ in Paterson that was dedicated by Pietro Yon. John Peragallo Jr. worked with his father and knew both Ungerer and Yon. As for John Peragallo III, not only had he taken his place in the family business, but in his younger days he had appeared in a Clifton production of *The Mikado* that had been conducted by . . . John-Michael Caprio. With such a pedigree, it was inevitable that the Peragallo Pipe Organ Company would become involved with the Cathedral project.

Peragallo remembered his initial walkthrough. "It was a disaster, as far as the condition went." The walls of the organ chambers were cracked and peeling, and "there were dead birds all over. . . . When an organ that big gets away from you, it's hard to get it back." But no one was daunted:

A forest of scaffolding obscured the gallery organ, a team of refinishers accomplished the job of bringing the case's woodwork back to life, and Peragallo and his crew set to work restoring the whole works, one pipe at a time.

In contrast to the intense press coverage that had surrounded the Kilgen's initial installation, there was virtually no media interest in its rebirth. Thus David Skoblow was surprised one late evening when, walking up Fifth Avenue, he spotted a large delivery truck backing up a ramp at the Cathedral's entrance. Workmen were readying the twin consoles, one being positioned in the narthex (where for several weeks it would be displayed to the public surrounded by a gigantic Plexiglas box, Caprio's tribute to the long-ago exhibition of the original console), the other to be hoisted by crane up to the gallery. The crew had already brought down the old console, or more accurately what was left of it: "There was the pedal board, standing with a heap of trash, ready to be demolished." Skoblow ran for a pay phone and got another chorister to grab a camera and hurry down to St. Patrick's in a taxi. By evening's end, he had as trophies not only a series of installation photos, but the pedal board, hauled home as a unique art piece.

What with installing each console, refurbishing each case, restoring each pipe, hooking up each part of the whole works, and making it usable, the restoration would take more than three years and would have to be done in increments so that some part of the organ, somewhere, would be playable at any given time. And because the Cathedral Choir shared the same spaces as the organ, there would be occasional collisions—such as the period when the work in the gallery forced the choir to sing from the ambulatory, ranged in front of the chancel pipes. The arrangement worked tolerably well, except for those Masses that involved a large procession. After each of those Masses, with the choir in the midst of a choral postlude, everyone would have to scramble out of the way, in mid-note, to avoid being trampled by returning clergy.

Even so, the music program continued its growth. Caprio offered the Fauré *Requiem* on Palm Sunday, then for the Christmas season a combination of the Poulenc *Four Motets* (sung by the Cathedral Schola) followed by the Saint-Saëns *Christmas Oratorio*. In between, Davis reinaugurated the recital series. And the new year began with 1994's Vespers of Epiphany on January 2, enhanced by new psalm settings commissioned from Charles Callahan.

Then, out of the blue, Caprio was approached by the BBC. The religious television series "Songs of Praise" was planning a program on the Irish in New York, and the producers felt that St. Patrick's would be the perfect setting. The only hitch was the program's format: "Songs of Praise" was famed for its swooping crane shots of a churchful of people, delivering hymns in beautifully accurate English style; and whether those people were congregants or guest choristers, a singing churchful wasn't usually the norm for a congregation at St. Patrick's. But an invitation to appear on the program, especially for the choir of an American church, was a mark of distinction. There was no question of turning down the invitation.

The Cathedral music department and the Archdiocesan Music Commission (meaning Caprio and Tranzillo) instantly sprang into action, with the first order of business that of finding 2,600 willing congregant-choristers. "We cashed in all our chips on this one," recalled Jessica Tranzillo. "It was a huge project, getting all the singers, making sure everyone had the music ahead of time, seating, programs, hiring the orchestra, getting the orchestral arrangements, rehearsal and taping." And all of it had to be done on short notice. "John-Michael had us call in all our friends for the audience"—who came from everywhere in the tri-state area. Finding people wasn't difficult: Cathedral regulars (whether or not they'd ever sung a note during a Mass) wanted to be a part of the show, and the clergy of St. Patrick's, including Cardinal O'Connor, were happy to attend. Seating was an issue, too: "Of course we had to have nuns in habits visible, and young people." In the chancel would be the Cathedral Choir, a full orchestra, and Caprio at the podium. Irish tenor Frank Patterson would be the guest soloist. The music would run the gamut from solid classics such as "The Battle Hymn of the Republic" and "Be Thou My Vision" to the contemporary "Here I Am, Lord."

A week before St. Patrick's Day, the whole company gathered at the Cathedral for a 7:00 P.M. taping—the music to be rehearsed with the orchestra and taped, all in three hours. However, "Songs of Praise" staff were well drilled in the finer points of getting huge groups to function as TV stars, and the session moved with precision.

The finished product was aired in the United Kingdom on March 20, and it made a fine impact. The "congregation" sang crisply. The Cathedral Choir, shoring up the sound, looked as soulfully intent as it needed to be. Beth Clayton, soloist for "The Battle Hymn of the Republic," was topnotch in voice and serene in delivery, as was Frank Patterson (supplying verses for "Here I Am, Lord," surely an example of caviar casting). The BBC camera, careering high above the heads of the congregation, made the Cathedral itself into a major player. Caprio, swaying on the podium, showed full authority. St. Patrick's had done itself proud. But the participants didn't get to enjoy it until the BBC sent videotapes to the United States. And even if it had aired in America, none of Caprio's singers would have been watching: The same night that "Songs of Praise" aired, the Cathedral Choir was occupied in performing the Mozart *Requiem*, its Lenten concert offering.

In a very pleasant way, things were starting to heat up for Caprio and his musicians. Father Shreenan remembered "a period when John-Michael was getting calls from just about everybody, interested in doing something with him or at the Cathedral"—including some discussions with representatives of *Phantom of the Opera* star Michael Crawford, who was considering the idea of making a recording with the Cathedral group.

Not every project moved smoothly, as was proved that summer with Young New York '94, "a two-day festival of faith" to take place in mid-August on the St. Joseph's Seminary grounds in the Westchester County city of Yonkers, drawing 20,000 visitors and set to feature as its climax a gigantic outdoor Mass. A large choir drawn from churches throughout the area was set to provide music; Caprio, as Archdiocesan music head, was slated to conduct. And it was a prime instance of everything going wrong at once.

The final day of the festival was dogged by ferocious weather, extraordinarily hot and muggy. Father Shreenan remembered, "It was hotter than blazes. Everyone had to go to Yonkers Raceway and then take a shuttle bus to the seminary to get there. I was going to sing in the choir . . . there were a couple of mobile trailers set up behind the stage. Then I saw an ambulance trundling along. . . . [T]urned out it was John-Michael." Indeed, Caprio had collapsed from the heat and had to be taken into a TV crew trailer to recuperate. Then, "this tremendous rainstorm came through the area—everyone went scattering." There was no way the outdoor Mass could take place. To salvage the day, Cardinal O'Connor contacted the owner of nearby Yonkers Raceway, who agreed to let the (remaining) attendees use his venue for the closing Mass. The shuttle buses carried the now-sopping crowds back to the Raceway, where they scrambled into the grandstand. Caprio—recovered—led the choir *a cappella* (the orchestra members, crammed in with the grandstand crowd, gave up the idea of playing). The Mass went resolutely forward. Father Shreenan said, "I decided, I'm going home."

Caprio made up for it during the Christmas season with the Vaughan Williams *Hodie*, a joint venture with the Princeton-based Choir of Trinity Church. It was his third time around conducting it, and the most lavishly budgeted conception to date (and the "suggested donation" was all of five dollars; Monsignor Dalla Villa made a point of acknowledging the Friends of Music during his welcome address, saying, "Because of that relationship, we have been able to do so many wonderful things here at the Cathedral"). The lavishness extended to the size of the audience, one of the largest to date for a Caprio concert, and for that matter it extended to the conductor's podium, a custom-built platform six feet wide that accommodated even Caprio's conductorial vigor. (This caused a few in-advertent chuckles during the final sequence as both choirmasters led their forces in view of the audience, emphasizing the contrast between the bounding athleticism of Caprio and the very English, precise-but-tiny beat pattern of Trinity Church's John Bertalot.) A week later, the year's experience was capped by a particularly glittering Midnight Mass, featuring Met star Renée Fleming.

However, some of the energy of the past year had been absorbed by the scheduling, then unscheduling, of a Papal visit. Now, much of the coming year would be taken up by the rescheduling of that visit, when Caprio's abilities would be tested to the limit.

The Pope Visits: Engineering Spontaneity

In March 1994, the Vatican had first announced plans for a Papal visit to the tri-state area in October. It was exciting news but, from a musical standpoint, harder work than usual for a man who was Archdiocesan Music Commissioner as well as Cathedral music director. Caprio called upon Father Shreenan, who had mastered the art of computer music engraving and would prove invaluable in helping to put together the im-mense amounts of music that a Papal visit would require. Everyone wanted to get in on the occasion—Father Shreenan recalled, "We had composers coming out of the woodwork." Caprio had an idea of what he wanted, however, and contacted a list of his current favorites. Among them would be Charles Callahan, commissioned to produce music for a first-time-ever Papal Vesper service to be held at the Cathedral; Richard Proulx, who crafted an anthem entitled "Follow Me"; and theater composer Michael Valenti, asked to write a march for the Pope's entrance into St. Patrick's.

But a month later the Pontiff fractured his thigh in a bathroom fall, requiring surgery to reconstruct the bone. News media covered his slow path to recovery, and in June the British publication *The Observer* reported that "while doctors say his fracture is mending well he needs continuing physiotherapy." By summer's end, reports were growing more and more doubtful as to the advisability of his making the grueling journey to the United States. As for Caprio, even during the work on the run-amok *Young New York* he had been obliged to continue his music plans. In mid-September, Father Shreenan received a package of Callahan's manuscript with a discouraged-sounding note from Caprio: "I thought you could at least get started."

Barely a week later, the *Times* announced POPE, CITING HEALTH, CALLS OFF VISIT TO NEW YORK. "In another sign of the Pope's physical frailty, the Vatican announced today that John Paul II was postponing a visit to the New York City area and Baltimore, which was planned for next month, because he has not fully recuperated."

Everyone in the Archdiocese—and the Cathedral, choir members included—had spent a good deal of the past six months in will-he-or-won't-he speculation. And all of the planning, fitting into a 1994 that had already been very crowded, was a definite strain. When the visit was cancelled, there was plenty of disappointment throughout the Archdiocesan offices. Caprio's reaction was different; he took a party to the Waldorf-Astoria for lunch.

The by-now-expected Vespers of Epiphany was the first large-scale musical event of 1995 (and a week later, St. Patrick's hosted the first of what would be annual concerts given by the Richard Tucker Music Foundation; the choir appeared with Ruth Ann Swenson and Hermann Prey). But before the next scheduled Vespers in the first week of March, the Vatican had made an announcement: "Catholics disappointed when Pope John Paul II canceled a visit to the New York region last year were heartened when the Vatican announced that the Pope would make a four-day trip to the United States in October." By April 27, *Catholic New York* scooped most other metropolitan papers when it announced that the Pope planned to say an outdoor Mass in Central Park. This locale could accommodate more than 100,000 worshipers and was so enormous that the finished design incorporated seven JumboTrons to give the crowd a view of what was actually happening.

The music would have to fit the scale of the event as well. While the planning period was twice as long as the three months John Grady had been given in 1979, everyone involved still felt it was important to hurry. Again, composers were coming out of the woodwork, and at the same time that Caprio chose classic choral pieces (the Bruckner "Ave Maria," "Panis Angelicus," even the "Hallelujah Chorus" for a big finish) he sorted through possibilities for new works. Proulx' "Follow Me" was ready and waiting. But Callahan's Vesper music would have to be scrapped, because the Papal Vesper service at St. Patrick's was going to be replaced with a Rosary. To make up for it, Caprio asked Callahan to write a psalm setting for the Central Park service. Bruce Saylor, composer of the opera *Orpheus Descending*, was set to write a "Hymn to Joy Fantasy" for the beginning of the Mass (it would include a tune that he named "Caprio") as well as "In Praise of Jerusalem," a setting of Psalm 122 for the Pope's entrance into St. Patrick's. However, Valenti's "Processional for a Pontiff," composed the year before to last two-and-a-half minutes (the time it would take for the Pope to walk down the Cathedral's aisle), would have to be expanded to eight minutes to allow for the much larger venue.

For orchestral arrangements of standard works such as the *Mass of Creation* and hymns, Caprio had the year before commissioned Johnnie Carl, the arranger/composer/musical director of the Crystal Cathedral (who as a bonus provided a new setting of "O Holy Night" for Renée Fleming's Midnight Mass visit). Because this would be a very large job and Carl was based in southern California, he was assisted by Father Shreenan, a continent away in New York. And they both were assisted by an electronic miracle that was still in its infancy—the Internet. " 'Immaculate Mary,' 'City of God'—he did the arrangements of all those pieces," remembered Father Shreenan. "We arranged it that he would email them to me as Finale music files. It was a whole new use of technology. I was learning on the fly. . . . I'd extract the parts, print them out and give them to John-Michael." At the time, the process of creating computer-generated sheet music was exotic enough that he told an interviewer, "Imagine—being able to pull these intricate scores out of cyberspace and have them land on the screen of my Macintosh in just seconds!" Even with this system, the work was so extensive that Caprio would receive the last of the orchestral parts only days before the orchestra rehearsal.*

With the arrangements underway, Caprio began to plan for the vocal personnel. Because of the vastness of Central Park's Great Lawn, there would be a quartet of cantors: Johanna Wiseman, Cori Ellison, Arn Prince, and new baritone Mark Heimbigner. For a choir, Caprio used the model of John Grady's multi-diocesan Papal choir, scaled more manageably to 225 singers who would perform from a grandstand behind the sanctuary. "It was an auditioned group," recalled Father Shreenan. "My sense is that he zeroed in on the choir directors he knew who could send decent singers to be part of it." Even so, when the Archdiocesan Festival Choir had its first rehearsals that summer at Archbishop Stepinac High School, it was a slow beginning. "We started with 'Joyful, Joyful'—it was awful. Over two or three months of rehearsals, once a week, throughout the summer, he took a large, ungainly group of singers and molded it into a very professional-sounding chorus."

At the same time, Caprio was coordinating a number of guest musicians who would entertain in the hours before the Mass—among them Roberta Flack, the Boys Choir of Harlem, and Natalie Cole. (This segment was irreverently called by everyone, even priests, the Pre-Game Show, just as it had been in 1979.) And there was the effort to nail down a guest to sing "Panis Angelicus" during Communion. (Jessica Tranzillo remembered, "Both New York and Brooklyn were vying for Placido Domingo. New York got him.") Less-classical music would be represented with Catholic pop diva Dana, offering "We Are One Body." Even nonvocal musicians were coming out of the woodwork. Father Shreenan said, "John-Michael called me up—'Listen to this! Listen to this!' There was a message on his machine saying, 'I have a portable carillon if you'd like to use it.'" They would, indeed. The carillon would be used during "Processional for a Pontiff" and would offer recessional music after the Mass.

By the end of the summer, the Papal agenda had been firmed up to include at least seven major events spread over three days, ranging from midtown Manhattan to Newark to East Rutherford (New Jersey) to Ozone Park (Queens) to Yonkers, then back to Manhattan. A strenuous schedule

---

* Even with this workload, Caprio asked Father Shreenan to handle the Papal programs, too.

for Pope and city alike, although the *Times* felt that "life in New York will not come to a virtual stop, as it did in 1979. . . . [T]he excitement has faded for a public familiar with papal visits." (As well as the fact that a great deal of media attention was being siphoned off at the same time by the recent verdict in O. J. Simpson's sensational murder trial. Most media didn't quite go so far as to compare the news value of the two stories, but the *Daily News* ran a cartoon depicting a reporter shoving a microphone into the Pontiff's face: "Sure, sure, all that church stuff is great, but how do *you* feel about O.J.?") Still, security this time around would be far tighter for a Pontiff who had survived an assassination attempt. As in 1979, every participant had to be screened and issued ID cards; but the increased level of security was brought uncomfortably home the day before the Mass when the Festival Choir came to the site for a work-through. Throughout the rehearsal, choir members could see police scuba divers, methodically searching through the pond at the end of the Great Lawn for explosives.

That rehearsal itself was a trial, with unseasonably warm weather, taking place on a Great Lawn that was a sea of mud because of a rainstorm the day before. Midway through the session, it was discovered that the choir's grandstand "needed reinforcement"; with the added repair time, they were there well into the evening. Meanwhile, there was agitation back at the Cathedral. Cardinal O'Connor had been unhappy with the quality of music at one of the recent Papal events and voiced sudden concern over Callahan's psalm setting for the next day's Mass. There was nothing to do but to snag Jessica Tranzillo (who'd had her own high-profile music experience earlier that day as cantor for the Papal Mass at Aqueduct Race Track in Queens but was now putting in overtime duty on Caprio's behalf) and Donald Dumler to make a quick demo cassette of "Song of Mary." Hearing the recording, the Cardinal was reassured.

In the hours before dawn the next day, Festival Choir members met at the Archdiocesan headquarters on First Avenue to board buses that would take them into Central Park, through metal detectors, and directly to the Mass site—an ironic jaunt for West Side residents like Cori Ellison who lived steps away from the park entrance. She said, "I remember watching the sunrise in Central Park . . . the first and *only* time I ever did that. Feeling chilled to the bone. And the endless sea of people out there." Early arrivals had begun to line up at 3:00 A.M., waiting for the site to open at 5:00 before the 9:00 A.M. Mass. In cool, rain-threatening weather, vendors went into action, hawking souvenir T-shirts, caps, and even bottled water printed with the Vatican coat of arms to an estimated 125,000 attendees.

As had been the case with previous Papal visits, the musical memories were made less of the planned moments than the accidental ones. Natalie Cole, soloist on "The Battle Hymn of the Republic" and backed by West Point cadets as well as the Harlem Boys Choir, went sky-high on her lyrics and inserted an extremely long pause in the music that lasted until conductor Walter Turnbull got her back on track. Father Shreenan, finished with his arranging and now part of the choir, recalled that the "Hymn to Joy Fantasy" proved to be slightly too long for the processional: As the penultimate verse was being sung, Cardinal O'Connor sent word that he wanted the music to end then and there. During the orchestral interlude, Caprio brought the whole thing to a halt, a single verse shy of completion, "and the choir were all standing there like, 'Huh?' "*

Otherwise, the Festival Choir performed smoothly and with enough security that they could assist Caprio as he influenced a bit of history. During the homily, the Pope began to speak of Christmas: "[I]t is because in less than five years we shall reach the end of the second millennium. . . ." And he began to sing the Polish carol "Wsrod Nocnej Ciszy."

At that moment, Alan Davis, organist for the Mass, remembered Caprio materializing next to him: "He said, 'If I give you the cue, go over to the choir and start them quietly on "Silent Night."' I thought, is he trying to set me up? But I went over, whispering 'pass it on' . . . the Pope had finished—John-Michael gave the cue, and they started singing 'Silent Night.' The whole congregation joined in.

"And the next day, it was reported that the whole congregation *spontaneously* broke into 'Silent Night.' "

The Pontiff apparently approved of the music, as well, stopping during the final hymn to greet each of the cantors—and then made a special trip

---

* Saylor would have to wait till the following year to hear his composition sung all the way through to the end; in April, it was (hastily) decided to hold a concert to commemorate a theological symposium, and Caprio needed a large work on short notice. Because the "Hymn to Joy Fantasy" was ready-rehearsed, it made perfect sense to use it as the evening's centerpiece.

to the Festival Choir and Caprio, as he was preparing to start the "Halle-lujah Chorus." The TV audience got to see Caprio in an unguarded moment, staggering off the podium in confusion, at which point the Pope smilingly gave him a "Don't mind me, please go on with what you were doing" wave. And he stayed to enjoy a good bit of the choir's Handel.

The Festival Choir was finished for the day, but the Cathedral Choir had to trot back to the buses and hurry downtown, escorted by police motorcade, over to the Helmsley Palace Hotel: to don choir robes, reenter the Cathedral (passing through metal detectors yet again), and take their places in the gallery. Donald Dumler was waiting at the organ, along with three brass quartets—one in the gallery and one positioned above each transept door, all of which would take part in Saylor's processional, "In Praise of Jerusalem." Once singers were in place, Caprio at the podium, Ellison at the cantor's desk (and Father Shreenan as Dumler's assistant, his final task of the day), they waited for the signal to begin Saylor's very energetic music with whatever energy they had left. "It was one of the most difficult pieces to perform," said Father Shreenan. "Extremely com-plicated choral writing. . . . God bless Donald for pulling it off. And the brass quartets—John-Michael had to conduct all three of them from the gallery. You couldn't even hear half of it, because there was so much cheering going on in the cathedral."

From a musical standpoint, the Rosary service disappointed no one. And after it was over, the Pontiff asked to meet Caprio at the Cardinal's residence, a singular honor. It had been a good day for the Cathedral's musicians.

Trying for the Big Time

No matter how often it appeared on television or how instantly famous it seemed, the Cathedral Choir was an anomaly, because in New York of the 1990s a church choir wasn't necessarily considered to be a *real* musical organization. The groups that won actual critical attention were those boasting sumptuous concert series, such as the Saint Thomas Choir, St. John the Divine's Music in a Great Space, and St. Ignatius of Loyola's Sacred Music in a Sacred Space—manned entirely by professional sing-ers, touted by professional publicists, extensively (and expensively) ad-vertised in print and broadcast media. But for the most part, New York critics no longer bothered to give print space to the efforts of church choirs,* and the St. Patrick's Cathedral Choir, a partly professional choir whose primary mission was liturgical, was lumped in with the bunch.

As for Caprio himself, it wasn't as if he lacked PR savvy: Still as friendly as ever with the *Times*, he had been interviewed in April for an article . . . about the inconvenience of Daylight Savings Time. *The American Organist* ran a two-page article, written by Caprio, in which he described the Cathedral's musical activities. And in the wake of 1995 and its Papal activities, he had been asked to participate in that year's "*Messiah* Sing-In" at Lincoln Center. But from a professional standpoint, Capiro's efforts weren't gaining much traction—not even the concerts of the Riverside Symphonia, as well respected as they were. When it came to quotes on his music-making from major publications, he was still relying on a blurb from the *Newark Star-Ledger*. At this point, he might have felt that it was time to break out, musically speaking.

Perhaps this was the underlying reason that Caprio's upcoming season would be the busiest yet. *CitySings* on December 19 was joined by the Vespers of Advent on December 3 and a Poulenc–Gounod concert (celebrating the fiftieth anniversary of Cardinal O'Connor's ordination) on December 17. In between the two, December 10 saw the first edition of a brand-new venture, in a brand-new venue.

While the Cathedral's Lady Chapel had always been known as a beautiful piece of architecture, no one had gone on record to mention the fact that it was a wonderful place in which to hear music. Singers at St. Patrick's had always known this; so had their congregations at the small-scale Masses, weddings, and funerals during which they heard them. Inconceivably, though, no one had used it as a concert setting.

Caprio inaugurated his new series, Our Lady's Chapel Concerts, with a performance of the Poulenc *Four Motets* (which had never absolutely worked when it was sung from the gallery), paired with the Britten *Ceremony of Carols*. It represented a departure from the Cathedral's usual music programs, exploring music that was too intimate for the Cathedral's

---

* One *Times* commentator, writing up Christmas music listings, went so far as to issue his own disclaimer-warning to potential attendees: "No critic would presume to know the exact quality of every church music program in the area, or to judge holiday programs in advance. This selection . . . was based on ambition of repertory, aspirations as a musical (as opposed to a strictly religious) event, scale and professionalism of forces. . . ."

space, or required a smaller ensemble, or was difficult enough to merit more highly trained singers (which for that first season would be the Cathedral Schola). As a bonus for those who preferred natural sound, Chapel Concerts would be the only choral performances at St. Patrick's to be given without amplification.

From the start, they were a decided success with audiences. Listeners responded to the smaller venue and the more intimate atmosphere, so much so that it became common to see extra rows of seats accommodating overflow crowds. As well, the basic format was flexible enough to be played around with (one Advent program was performed as a Candlelight Concert, a striking atmosphere to go with the music; another evening featured ARTEK, the resident orchestra of St. Francis of Assisi, along with their leading soprano—and it was impishly called *Jessica Tranzillo and 458 Strings*).

Still, the Cathedral's musical activity wasn't reported in the mainstream musical press, even in 1996, which would prove Caprio's liveliest year to date.

As he was lining up his schedule (the usual Vespers were slated, along with two *Requiem*s: Rutter for a March 7 Chapel Concert, Mozart three weeks later), Caprio was approached by representatives from the newspaper *Irish Echo*. Along with the Irish-American support group The Wild Geese (and with additional backing from communications giant MCI, as well as H. J. Heinz) they had commissioned composer Patrick Cassidy to craft a full-length work in commemoration of the 150th anniversary of Ireland's Great Hunger. And they wanted its premiere to take place at St. Patrick's, performed by the Cathedral Choir, with Caprio as conductor.

This was completely unexpected; it was also a potential windfall of public recognition. Patrick Cassidy was being dubbed "The Irish Mozart," with works that ranged from film scores to full-length choral works. His last major effort, *Children of Lir*, had been given an extravagant premiere by the London Symphony Orchestra. This piece (as yet unnamed) would be given its own sumptuous performance, paid for by outside sources. And the plans included a recording. Caprio didn't have to think very long before jettisoning his plans for the usual Irish Heritage Concert and scheduling Cassidy's work in its stead. *Irish Echo* started the ball rolling in its January 31 issue when it ran a full-page ad announcing a "Famine Symphony Concert."

Cassidy had been exploring a compositional style that he called "Narrative cantata," combining song with orchestral passages and speech, but arriving at a workable libretto hadn't been easy. He later told NPR,

> I think the original idea was for me to do . . . a chronological type of piece, based on what happened, and I wasn't very happy about that. . . . I had to go out and find a libretto myself. When I went to the National Library in Ireland to get poetry or texts from the period, I came across two poems that had been written by "Esperanza," that is, the mother of Oscar Wilde."

With those poems as the foundation of the work, he fashioned a text that contained passages in English, Gaelic, and Latin, scored for boy soprano, mezzo, and tenor soloists, narrator, chorus, and forty-piece orchestra (with a featured line for that specifically Irish instrument, the uilleann pipes, to ground the piece in national verity). And while the score was tonal, it was somber music. "It was a very particular sound, very sad, not uplifting or joyous," recalled Dolores Nolan, herself Dublin-born. "Haunting. So true to the sound of the lament." This was a departure from the usual cheerful sentimentality of the music performed at most Irish Heritage Concerts, and a number of choristers weren't taken with the music. Neither was Caprio, at first. Nevertheless, he scheduled extra rehearsals and everyone worked at top speed, with Peggy Breslin coaching Gaelic, to master the work in little over than a month.

In February the *Irish Echo* reported on the composer's arrival—"only the second time Cassidy will have visited New York"—to supervise the production. And the article provided details on *"Famine Remembrance,* which is what he's decided to call his new work for symphonic orchestra, choir, and vocal soloists." As the performance approached, the cast was announced: Met regional winner Emily Eyre, tenor Gregory Hostetler, boy soprano Terence Kelly . . . and the producers scored a coup when the incandescent Anjelica Huston agreed to narrate. The ink's-still-wet newness of the piece was emphasized when it was described as "an hour's length, or perhaps 70 minutes, and [Cassidy] admitted candidly that, at the time of the conversation, he had yet to add up the lengths of all the individual sections."

When *Famine Remembrance* was first announced, the mainstream media didn't cover the story, nor did they write about any other aspect of its production. But the *Irish Echo* had its own publicity machine along with its own built-in audience, connected to Irish lineage groups, and on the night of March 2 the Cathedral was packed with very enthusiastic listeners. Dolores Nolan remembered the night of the performance: "The Irish, they ate it up with a fork and spoon. Just great. Huge audience." (Father Shreenan, drafted for the chorus, had his own memory: "The best moment was standing in the chancel . . . and listening to the piper fill his bag with air. There was a lot of biting the inside of one's cheeks to keep from busting out laughing.") The *Irish Echo* made the performance a cover story, with a double-page color photo spread. But the major media neglected it completely.*

Caprio couldn't dwell on this; five days later came the Chapel Concert and the Rutter *Requiem*, preparation for which had been given short shrift because so much time had been devoted to *Famine Remembrance*. The Rutter performance hadn't gone as smoothly as past performances had. This might have been the reason that subsequent Chapel Concerts would be sung not by the Cathedral Schola but by the Chapel Choir—an all-professional group, comprising Caprio's paid singers along with whatever outside vocalists were needed. (Expert sight-reading skills were a must, as these concerts were put together in only two to three rehearsals and consisted of musically sophisticated works from modern composers, including Bruce Saylor, Stephen Paulus, Nancy Wertsch, Henryk Górecki and Herbert Howells.) At the other end of the spectrum, Caprio opened the major concerts to the outside community by creating the Cathedral Singers, supplementing the Cathedral Choir with extra personnel who wanted to participate but couldn't commit to the full liturgical schedule. What with the Chapel Singers, Cathedral Schola, Cathedral Choir, and Cathedral Singers, he was now juggling four choirs, four personnel lists,

---

* The media would neglect it once again, when Caprio and the Cathedral forces gave *Famine Remembrance* an encore performance at St. Patrick's the following year—even with the RTÉ Orchestra providing the accompaniment and film star Patrick Bergin narrating. In between those two performances, the Cathedral Choir recorded the piece in a hectic one-day session at St. George's Church. The resultant CD helped the work to gain its own fans, along with a place in the modern repertoire. Caprio wasn't one of those fans; he felt that the rushed schedule had prevented the choir from doing its best on the recording. Jessica Tranzillo remembered listening to a playback with him as he lamented, "Listen to that! We could do better than that!"

and four rehearsal schedules. But he wasn't alone in these efforts. Donald Dumler, as he always had, provided yeoman duty. John West, who had trained as a pianist and conductor before he had ever begun to sing, was becoming invaluable as a de facto assistant conductor.

And when Alan Davis decided to leave the Cathedral in order to continue his professional studies, Caprio hired up-and-coming concert organist Stephen Tharp as a replacement. Educated at Illinois College and Northwestern University, Tharp actually had first played the Cathedral organ as a fifteen-year-old (planning to visit New York with his parents, he wrote John Grady, who invited him to the gallery to try out the Kilgen). Answering an employment ad in *The American Organist*, Tharp was chosen from the applicants; but some of his first Cathedral moments took place during the Papal visit, not exactly business as usual. "John-Michael just said, 'Stand here and watch.' So I did." Tharp's duties involved his doing everything that Alan Davis had done, as well as playing the organ for *Famine Remembrance*, coordinating the organ recital series (stepped up as the organ renovation was being completed), and lining up instrumental musicians for yet another new series to take place in the Lady Chapel, Sunday Afternoons at the Cathedral.

At the same time, Donald Dumler was preparing—on very short notice—to record a CD. Years before, John Grady and the then-new Dumler had jointly recorded an LP (at the request of Monsignor Rigney, who thought it would be a good item for the Cathedral Gift Shop), but the result had been too cheaply produced to make for top-flight listening. Still, nothing had replaced it until after Grady's death, when Dumler was approached by Gothic Records president George Dickey to ask about his interest. (Dumler's characteristic comment: "I thought he was joking.") That idea lay fallow until the spring of 1996, when the American Guild of Organists (AGO) was planning its Centennial Convention, to be held that summer in New York. The opening event was set to take place at St. Patrick's, and Dickey had thought that a new CD, originating from the Cathedral, would be a good thing to have on sale. He wondered if Caprio could have the choir ready for recording in the spring. With everything that had been happening, Caprio demurred. Dickey then asked if it would be possible to revisit his original idea of an organ CD . . . but the recording date would have to be scheduled for only three weeks away. No problem. With Dumler playing from his core repertoire, the thirteen tracks of *The Great Organ of Saint Patrick's Cathedral* were recorded in a single evening. ("We had a couple of retakes the next night," he recalled. "A reed was out of tune.")

Signing Donald Dumler to record a CD was one of the smaller-scale preparations being made for the AGO convention. The July 7 convocation at St. Patrick's would feature a Vesper service, to be preceded by organists before and organists after; additional recitals would take place throughout the city; and as a high point, the overwhelming Berlioz *Te Deum* would be performed at the Cathedral of St. John the Divine. The Cathedral Choir would be responsible for the vocal music at the convocation, but because the convention was taking place smack in the midst of summer vacation (and because there would be very little rehearsal time to put together the Vesper music), Caprio decided to assemble the Cathedral Schola, reinforced with additional ringers. Stephen Tharp would accompany the choir, Jessica Tranzillo would attempt to play cantor to a cathedral full of organists—"The hardest thing I've ever done; everybody had their own idea of tempo"—and the homily was left to Father Shreenan, a very good decision because he knew his audience well.

But few people would remember much of the music that night. The NPR program "Pipedreams" was preparing to tape the service for broadcast; during their setup, technicians found that there were too many extraneous noises to get a clean recording . . . and one of those noises had been the sound of air passing through ductwork. Brutally hot though the day had been, there was no alternative but to shut off the air conditioning and close the doors. For three hours, a tightly packed crowd ("People were sitting in the aisles, on the floors," said Father Shreenan) sweated it out as best they could in near–hundred-degree heat.*

Principal organist of the Cathedral though he might be, Donald Dumler wasn't at the time a member of the AGO and hadn't been asked to participate in the convocation. Still, his CD had been released, and it would rapidly take off to become a commercial success.† Coincidentally or not, it was then that Caprio agreed to make the choir CD.

---

* The AGO Vespers were a joyous occasion, but tragedy struck less than two weeks later when TWA Flight 800 exploded in the air soon after leaving New York, killing everyone aboard. St. Patrick's made itself available to grieving family members, hosting nearly a dozen memorial services. With Donald Dumler out of town at the time, Stephen Tharp played every one of them—a sobering experience.

† At first, Cathedral authorities were so doubtful of its sales potential that the $1,000 production cost was deducted from Dumler's initial royalties.

As soon as the season began, the choir began rehearsing the twenty pieces that would make up the playlist, aiming for October recording sessions. But while Donald Dumler's recording experience had been calm and trouble-free, the choir had—as they had in 1959 and 1981—an unpleasant time of it.

This time, the blame was partly Caprio's. Chapel Concerts, Vespers, and the antiphonal moments of Tenebrae services (which had been sung from the ambulatory behind the main altar) had given him a fascination with the effect of voices coming from other places than the gallery, and he determined to get this sound onto disc. So the choir's first session (which began after Cathedral closing hours) was set up in the Lady Chapel. But while the narrow vaulted space added so much warmth to a live performance, it played havoc with the acoustics of recording. And the setup had been involved enough that Caprio began the evening in a state of tension that gradually communicated itself to everyone involved. "John-Michael had me sitting in the front row," said Dumler. "If I heard things going flat or wrong, I was supposed to give him a sign." (With singers now flustered enough that they were having intonation problems, this happened frequently.) To compound the situation, recording engineers were operating from the choir rehearsal room, a floor below. "From the start," said one singer, "John-Michael would conduct a piece, run downstairs, listen to the playback, run back up. . . ." Things went from bad to worse, until the exhausted and perspiring Caprio rounded on one of his tenors, publicly: "If you can't *blend in* next time, I'll cut your b—s off. Do you hear me?"

The microphones changed position, then the singers themselves, moving into the chancel in an attempt to improve the sound and the performances, as the session stretched into the small hours. That didn't help: Listening to the final result, Caprio realized that most of the evening's work was unusable. The next night found the choir reinstated in the gallery.

Editing the disc would take months.

Overshadowing all of this was the problem of the organ restoration, which had gone so far and no further. Both chancel and gallery organs had been put back into commission; in fact, John Peragallo had stepped up the work on the gallery organ during the previous year to have it ready for the Papal visit. But there was still work to be done—the echo organ had barely been touched—and $500,000 was still needed.

Caprio took a huge chance at this point. Realizing that there was no one on the horizon who could be asked for the full amount, he decided to ask a donor ("He never would tell who it was," said one insider) for somewhat less . . . and used the cash to take out a full-page ad, dominated by a photo of the gallery pipes, in the Arts Section of the December 8 *Times*. It was captioned:

The last thing we want this Christmas is a silent night.

The ad, which outlined the fundraising program and included an appeal for donations, apparently brought in enough additional money to revive the project. And on December 24, the *Times* itself helped by running a lengthy story on Caprio's efforts to fund the organ renovation, pointing out that "the cathedral has resorted to the unusual step of taking out advertisements, including a full page in The New York Times." (The *New York Post* carried the story, too, phrased in its own style: ST. PAT'S NEEDS ORGAN DONORS.)

That Christmas Eve was a particularly busy one even by Cathedral standards. Ireland's RTÉ Television was hoping to expand on the theme of the Irish in New York by broadcasting a Midnight Mass from St. Patrick's . . . live, to Ireland, at midnight Dublin time. Cardinal O'Connor agreed, although this would mean that clergy, staff—and musicians— would have to hold the Mass at 7:00 P.M. for RTÉ, and then repeat it at midnight for WPIX.*

A situation that could have resulted in two televised disasters came off without incident. Caprio had commissioned Bruce Saylor to write two pieces for Midnight Mass, one of which was a new setting of "O Holy Night" for the Met's Jennifer Larmore. The extra Mass meant that the piece could have a public dress rehearsal five hours before, with Frank Patterson supplying the solo line. (However, this meant that Saylor now had to produce vocal, choral, and orchestral scores in two keys, because Patterson was a tenor and Larmore a mezzo.) Both TV crews cooperated in the joint effort; WPIX contributed their usual camera platforms, and RTÉ contributed their robotic camera crane, set up in the gallery. (WPIX didn't own one of those at the time but apparently used RTÉ's that night

---

* WPIX may have been a local station, but by the late 1990s it was syndicating the program to a number of markets around the United States. And at least one source claimed that Midnight Mass from St. Patrick's had been seen in Tokyo.

with great enthusiasm: One chorister remembered that the Midnight Mass broadcast "looked like a roller-coaster.") The Mass went off perfectly for an overflow congregation who were glad of the opportunity to attend Midnight Mass at St. Patrick's, at whatever hour. Stephen Tharp, organist for the first service, had a fine time. "I hadn't played a Mass on live TV before—I was flying on adrenaline." Both Patterson (performing from memory) and Larmore sang beautifully. And the Cathedral Choir (reminded by Caprio to stay sharp for both Masses) took it all in stride, performing with unflagging zest. Both times.

In a year that had been chock-filled with accomplishments good and bad, it was something of a high point.

"Such a Weird Premonition"

Caprio's first duties of 1997 were involved with finding a replacement for Stephen Tharp. Because Tharp had been responsible for booking organ recitals and chamber concerts, many of the musicians involved would offer him recitals in return. And as he was first and foremost a concert artist, it was necessary for him to accept those invitations, which ultimately made it necessary for him to make a choice between the Cathedral and the larger music scene. Which made it necessary for Caprio to place another Help Wanted ad in *The American Organist.*

This time, the winning applicant was Memphis native Stanley Cox, Juilliard-educated and versed in the Catholic tradition from work at the Cathedral-Basilica of St. James in Brooklyn. His appeal may have been sartorial as well as musical; in a T-shirt world, Caprio had always believed in a coat-and-tie business style, and so did Cox. "I like the way you dress," Caprio said at their first interview. Soon after, when Cox was wearing a club tie from Phi Mu Alpha Sinfonia, Caprio asked, "Is that tie from your prep school?" Cox replied, "No, it's from my music fraternity in college, but we can pretend it's from my prep school if you like." They became fast friends.

(On the other hand, Caprio continually despaired over the wardrobe of his principal organist. Donald Dumler owned the necessary business clothing for the job, but none of it was a source of personal pride. And Caprio particularly remembered each Christmas Eve, which found Dumler decked out in the requisite tuxedo but ensuring the freedom of his arms by rolling his sleeves up beneath the jacket. At some point in the evening, Caprio would inevitably frown and mutter, "Where are your *cuffs?*")

As Donald Dumler had once been assigned to shadow Eddie Rivetti, Alan Davis had shadowed Donald Dumler, and Stephen Tharp had shadowed Alan Davis, Stanley Cox spent a couple of weeks shadowing Stephen Tharp. Then he jumped headlong into the business of Masses, concert scheduling, and choral accompaniment. Cox immediately proved that he was not only musically versed and as organized as a CPA but incapable of nervousness, a very highly prized trait at St. Patrick's. Some weeks later, out of nowhere Caprio praised him somewhat left-handedly: "Well, you must be doing something right. I usually get a lot of complaints by this time when there's a new organist."*

The Cathedral's music program was for the most part stable, wide-ranging, and well supported. Caprio was valued not only by his musicians but also by Cardinal O'Connor and other clergy around the Archdiocese. When asked to contribute an article to the Catholic music–publishing journal *GIA Quarterly*, he produced two pages in which he described the various musical attractions of St. Patrick's and their relationship to the liturgy, painting a glowing picture of the dedication shown by his crew: "Full attendance at rehearsals is a way of life. Performance at the concerts and at the liturgies constitutes a nourishment of the singers' spiritual life. Naturally, they enjoy each other's company." The choir CD, *O Come Let Us Sing*, had finally been issued to good sales and some industry buzz.

Still, music at the Cathedral constituted news rather than *musical* news, and Caprio, remembered Father Shreenan, "wanted to do it all." Thus he was very interested when organizers of the Palestrina Choir Competition invited the Cathedral Choir to inaugurate the opening of the competition in late 1998, also to sing at St. Peter's Basilica. On top of it, he was being asked to serve as a judge for the 1997 competition. This meant international recognition. Friends of Music began to discuss fund-raising options while Caprio took a sorely needed vacation, flying to Mexico in February.

When he returned, however, he felt ill. At first he ignored it—Caprio had always been averse to physicians—then he gave in and consulted a

---

* True enough. One music department employee remembered a Cathedral regular complaining about an (unidentified) organist, "Could you ask that bimbo who plays the nine o'clock to *shut up?!!*"

doctor, who assumed that he had picked up an intestinal problem on vacation and prescribed antibiotics. And he continued with Masses, Vespers, the Chapel Concert, the Irish Heritage Concert, Holy Week services, another concert . . . continuing to take antibiotics that didn't seem to be helping. Donald Dumler remembered one Sunday toward the end of the season when he stood with Caprio, watching a visiting choir in action. Suddenly Caprio bent in pain. "Oh, Donald," he whispered, "I don't know how much more of this I can bear."

Caprio was determined to celebrate his fiftieth birthday that July in high style, chartering a yacht for a party cruise around Manhattan. But there was more pain and more physical warning signals, and soon after he was alarmed by signs of internal bleeding. He finally consulted a specialist, who ordered a series of tests. The diagnosis: colon cancer.

Surgery took place at Manhattan's Lenox Hill Hospital, during which it was discovered that metastasis had already begun.

After a week in the hospital and three weeks at home, he returned to work. As he stepped off the elevator in the music office, Stanley Cox asked, "John-Michael, are you okay? Is there anything I can do?" Caprio replied, "I'm fine. Don't worry. I'm not going to die on you."

He proceeded as if nothing had changed, scheduling his usual summertime auditions (the *Times* audition ad had appeared, as it always did). At the same time, he was undergoing chemotherapy, which caused every remaining strand of hair to fall out; he lost even his trademark moustache. Cox remembered, "He had bought an expensive hairpiece to wear and he was nervous about his looks at the first rehearsal when the choir returned. I said, 'John-Michael, it looks great, and you look great. Everyone will be so glad that you're back. Don't worry about anything. And besides, you have your charisma.' He said, 'We'll see how long that lasts.'"

The news of Caprio's illness flashed around the Archdiocese as well as the Cathedral, occasioning a rush of support. Cori Ellison recalled, "I heard it before he spoke about it. He seemed very worried and frightened, but determined to fight—he put up a tremendous fight. Cardinal O'Connor was very pastoral to him at that time." There was additional validation when he was inducted into the Knights of the Holy Sepulchre in September. (This came about, somewhat inelegantly, when he ran into the regional lieutenant in the men's room of the Archdiocesan offices: "Why aren't you in the Order?" "I was never asked," replied Caprio. That took care of it.) The following month, the chemotherapy finished, he seemed to be improving to such an extent that a Mass of Thanksgiving was held at Holy Family, complete with after-party. As well, the Palestrina Competition was faxing him an itinerary for his mid-November trip to Rome. But by the beginning of November he learned that the chemotherapy had only slowed the progress of the cancer. His health was beginning to falter, and the trip would prove to be out of the question.

Father Shreenan remembered, "He always talked about what it would be like when he died—Timmy would be his chaplain at his bedside. I thought, why does he talk like this? It seemed like such a weird premonition." Nonetheless, it seemed to be coming true. All his energies were now saved for his work at the Cathedral, the 10:15 Masses and already-scheduled Vesper services. As one chorister put it, he would rally before conducting; and afterward, fade. A number of people were worried on his behalf, because the Christmas season, with its high-energy musical events, was approaching.

A Chapel Concert was scheduled for the evening of December 11, and Caprio arrived to conduct as usual. It was a frightening night for everyone. Jessica Tranzillo said, "He could barely focus. We were doing very difficult music. And we were singing a concert with a man who just couldn't conduct. . . ."

No one knew it then, but it would be the last time Caprio conducted at St. Patrick's.

Three days later, the choir was gathering before the Sunday 10:15 Mass when Caprio showed up. "He looked like a bag of bones in a suit," recalled James Poma. "Too weak to possibly conduct." John West, who had been handling some conducting duties since the onset of Caprio's illness, asked Poma to take him home. "He hugged the wall going up the stairs to the street. We got a taxi . . . he seemed half-asleep. Silent, all the way back." Poma took him to his apartment and settled him in an easy chair. "Go on back. I'll be fine," insisted Caprio. Later, it was learned that Caprio had returned to Lenox Hill Hospital and had suffered a seizure. From that point on he was no longer able to speak.

Family members, choir members, friends, and clergy made it a point to visit Caprio, who appeared to know they were there. Father Shreenan said, "His eyes seemed to be able to respond to people speaking to him . . . other than that, I suppose you could say that he was comatose." Stephen Tharp remembered, "You could hold his hand, say, 'John-Michael, it's Stephen,' and he'd squeeze your hand." Meanwhile,

Monsignor
Dalla Villa had performed the necessary task of coming before the choir
to say, "From here on in, John West is in charge."

December 24 was a bleak, rainy night. By the usual standards, it should
have been an exciting evening: Midnight Mass was reaching more viewers
than ever on cable via the Odyssey Network, and Met tenor Marcello
Giordani (who had sung before at the Cathedral, becoming friendly with
Caprio) was scheduled for "O Holy Night." The Cathedral was filled
with holiday-minded visitors for whom John-Michael Caprio was no
more than a name on the program—while others, particularly music department members, were trying merely to hold themselves together in
public. Cardinal O'Connor addressed Caprio's illness at the beginning of
the Mass, very calmly: "I was in to see him . . . he is indeed in very
critical condition . . . 1990 was the first Christmas Midnight Mass at
which he led this now-magnificent choir. We pray for him. . . ." Congregation and TV viewers saw nothing untoward. John West looked completely self-possessed at the conductor's podium, as did Cori Ellison at
the cantor's desk, and all the members of the choir. But a listener could
tell that the music was unsettled, with small vocal and instrumental mis-
fires scattered throughout the service. And Giordani (apparently learning
of Caprio's decline only when he showed up that evening) seemed obviously shaken, in appearance as well as in voice. The only other clue to
anyone's state of mind came in the final moments of the Mass—during
the recessional, when the Cardinal abruptly broke formation, strode over
to Cori Ellison in the midst of "Hark, the Herald Angels Sing," and
impulsively grasped her hand in a gesture of support. She started in surprise, but kept singing.

Less than two hours later, John-Michael Caprio died.

In the days following his death, Caprio was accorded a number of
tributes. For the viewing at Campbell's Funeral Home, his Holy Sepulchre gown was displayed behind his coffin. The morning of his funeral,
the Cardinal authorized him to lie in the Lady Chapel. By the time of the
funeral the Cathedral Choir had found its center once more, and they
acquitted themselves handsomely, singing Stanford, Fauré, and Rutter
under West's baton to a congregation of nearly a thousand. (Jessica Tranzillo couldn't take part; she sat in the congregation with her husband. "I
was too upset to sing.") Father Shreenan designed the program, complete
with Caprio's favorite picture of himself—the one he jokingly called "his

GQ shot"—on the cover. At the funeral itself, he read the Gospel. Cardinal O'Connor delivered a homily in which he eulogized Caprio, ending with something of a public private joke: "I suspect . . . that John-Michael Caprio will be leading the choir of angels. And he'll say, 'Hurry it up! Don't keep the Cardinal waiting. He gets mad.'"

Wanting to Do It All

John-Michael Caprio's legacy centered on two truths, diametrically opposed. One truth concerned Caprio himself. He was an organist who preferred not to play the organ, a conductor whose talents could be surpassed by a number of other conductors, a choral director who himself didn't sing. But he had distinguished himself with informed musical taste; a clear vision of the role that music could have in a church; the knowledge of when to trust his own abilities and when to employ the strengths of others; and the dynamic leadership to implement his vision. (One person recalled, "He could take a mediocre piece of music and turn it into an event.") And he achieved all of this in only seven years.

The other truth concerned the atmosphere in which he operated, which had made him arguably the most powerful figure in the Catholic music scene but not the most musically esteemed. In another time, Caprio's remarkable output would have marked St. Patrick's as a musical center. But Caprio was functioning in the 1990s, when the Catholic music scene had little need for history and correctness, and the commercial music scene had become so polished and glossy that it had little need for the efforts of the Cathedral Choir. Caprio was memorialized in *Catholic New York* and *The American Organist*. Nothing ran in the *Times*.

It was a no-win situation, and somewhere within him he knew it. Said Father Shreenan, "Wanting to do it all . . . I think 'wanting to do it all' is part of what killed John-Michael Caprio."

In his "GQ Shot,"
John-Michael Caprio.

Soon after being installed
as music director, Caprio
(*center*) posed with Donald
Dumler and Associate
Organist Alan Davis.
(*Chris Sheridan*)

Caprio and the Cathedral Choir in full cry during their first concert outing. (*Chris Sheridan*)

Consultant Nelson Bardon wrote that the gallery organ "is not a Rolls-Royce, it is an American-made Packard Touring Car." Behind the scaffolding, the Peragallo Organ Company performs some body work. (*James Poma*)

Central Park, 1995:
Enjoying the work of
John-Michael Caprio,
Pope John Paul II.
(*James Poma*)

Associate Organist Stanley Cox,
paying tribute to Caprio in pose
as well as wardrobe.

Jennifer Pascual, the first woman ever to hold an administrative position in the Cathedral's music department. (*Joe Vitacco*)

Associate Music Director Daniel Brondel at the gallery console. (*Steve Lawson*)

Pascual conducts the "Ode to Joy" at the close of the 2008 Papal Mass at Yankee Stadium—
a liturgy that paid homage to previous Cathedral music directors in its programming.
(*Robert Evers*)

Music loving in high places: Pascual and the Cathedral Choir meet President George W. Bush.
(*AP/Wide World Photos*)

Chapter 8

FOR THE FIRST TIME(S) IN CATHEDRAL
HISTORY (1998–)

> The higher the spire, the stranger the birds that crash into it.
>
> A liturgical musician

Whatever had befallen the music department of St. Patrick's, its members could point with pride to the fact that their music had been led by a succession of only six men in more than a century—a serene contrast to the erratic histories of the music in many other Manhattan churches. And in the sadness of John-Michael Caprio's farewell, as well as the death-vigil atmosphere that had overlaid Midnight Mass, members of the Cathedral Choir had nevertheless been able to find a measure of comfort. Their leadership was in the hands of a man who knew them personally, knew their routine, and whose competence was beyond question.

John Calvin West (throughout his career, the middle name came and went) had impeccable credentials, studying piano and voice at the Eastman School of Music, then moving on to advanced work at the Curtis Institute under famed baritone Martial Singher. As pianist or conducting assistant, and then as a singer, he had traveled an extensive circuit of national as well as international opera houses, including those of Santa Fe, Chicago, Dallas, and San Francisco, as well as City Opera, Las Palmas, and the Palacio de Bellas Artes, taking part in world premieres of works such as *The Aspern Papers* and Weisgall's *Esther*. Along with this had been a tidy amount of orchestra work, a teaching position at Juilliard, a longstanding solo stint at Temple Emanu-El . . . and St. Patrick's, with his own history stretching back to 1980 and John Grady. High-pressure events such as Midnight Mass and Caprio's funeral had demonstrated not only his abilities but his professional demeanor, as calm as Caprio's had been emotional. Cori Ellison remembered, "That was about the most comfortable transition we could have—here was this guy who was one of *us*. He understood and honored the culture of music at St. Patrick's, and he had no political agenda."

Yet the transition wasn't being engineered as a transition, and West wasn't campaigning for the job of music director. Monsignor Dalla Villa convened a meeting with West, Dumler, Jessica Tranzillo, and some of the members of Caprio's inner circle at which he offered West the post of interim music director. As well, he outlined plans for the formation of a search committee to solicit applications for a new music director. That settled, the season continued.

As one chorister remembered, West's time at the podium "felt very much like a caretaker year." West intended that Caprio's plans be carried out without interruption, and they were (except for Vesper services, which disappeared from the calendar). He programmed major concerts for the Lent (Mozart *Requiem*) and Advent (Saint-Saëns *Christmas Oratorio*) seasons, as well as a Chapel Concert (Britten *Ceremony of Carols*). *CitySings* was delivered without incident. Midnight Mass 1998 was a stress-free experience, in part because of its guest soloist, mezzo Susan Graham—a high-talent, low-maintenance performer who had achieved Met stardom but was also familiar to plenty of local singers from her own days working alongside them in Manhattan church choirs. She instantly endeared herself to Cathedral Choir members when she asked for a music folder, in order to follow along with the Mass parts; and when it came time for her to prepare for "O Holy Night," her unpretentiousness was apparent as she whispered to one chorister, "Now if you'll excuse me, I'll go and get into my Big Pink Dress."*

By early 1999, the search committee had received applications from more than seventy-five musicians, representing every level of talent. As interviews were scheduled, West began to consider the job for himself, an idea that might have been reinforced by Cardinal O'Connor's continued

---

* This was in marked contrast to some of the Cathedral's experiences with famous divas. One Met star was approached for Midnight Mass; as she had been wowing concert audiences that season with a particularly full and elaborate gown, she wanted to wear it at St. Patrick's and demanded, for her transportation, *two* limousines—one for her and one for the gown. Caprio's terse reply became famous among choir members: "St. Patrick's Cathedral does not send cars for dresses." (The lady never did sing at the Cathedral.)

support of the music department (public as well as private; he ended almost every service with thanks to the cantor, choirmaster, organist, and singers, and had written West to express his appreciation), as well as the fact that the search committee had asked him, more than once, for his résumé.

However, soon after that he was stopped in the hallway by a secretary. "Oh, you've saved me a stamp!" she announced. "Just wanted to let you know you're not one of the candidates." And she continued on her way.

John West continued in his post as interim music director and assisted the search committee in its efforts, until August. Monsignor Dalla Villa invited him to return to his position of bass soloist, but he thought it better to end his time at St. Patrick's.

Revolving Doors and Then Some

A sobering feature of liturgical music, no matter where it occurs or when, is that the liveliest and most painstakingly built program will last exactly as long as its director. Should that director leave his post, the program is at the mercy of his successor. John West had seen fit to honor the plans of John-Michael Caprio; but after West was gone, there was no guarantee that his musical vision would continue. It didn't.

The Cathedral now saw an unprecedented period: In only four years there were three musical directors, each with his own distinct musical style that differed markedly from those of the others. As the music at St. Patrick's veered from one extreme to another, liturgical music–watchers observed the scene with incredulous amusement. As one of them put it some time later, "You guys went from Caprio to Contempo to Gregorian to Baroque. How did you survive?"*

* During this period, the Irish Heritage Concert would be changed, occasionally cancelled, to the chagrin of its audience as well as that of its participants. But the real litmus test seemed to be *CitySings*, which was pulled about, sometimes in extreme fashion—depending on the year, it was a warmup to a performance by the American Boychoir; or it was partially supplanted by a complete Bach cantata, sung in German, with the Cathedral Choir restricted to singing carols with the congregation (and relegated to the gallery for the evening); or it was cancelled outright and replaced with a performance of *Messiah*. In every one of those cases, the Cathedral switchboard was bombarded the next day with angry phone calls.

First up was Robert Long, a Westminster Choir College alumnus who had previously served as choirmaster at the Cathedral of the Blessed Sacrament in Altoona, Pennsylvania, and who obviously believed in the cause of modern Catholic music. While he programmed occasional pieces from traditional composers such as Victoria, Tallis, and Mozart (the "Laudate Dominum" was apparently a Long favorite because it showed up frequently, on Sundays as well as for high occasions), those works were islands in a sea of current American composition. This programming created occasional tensions, demonstrated at one Mass as the choir was stationed in the gallery for a choral prelude, an anthem with a rock beat. In the middle of the piece, Monsignor Dalla Villa walked into the sanctuary and up to the microphone at the lectern, announcing to Long, the choir, and the entire congregation: "Would you stop that music now." The anthem ground to an instant, embarrassed halt. In the ensuing silence, Monsignor Dalla Villa calmly returned to the ambulatory to begin the procession.

During this period, no one was particularly obsessed with the state of music at St. Patrick's, a situation that was underlined by an incident at that year's Midnight Mass. Pop singer José Feliciano was part of the congregation; but a few minutes prior to the Mass, someone in authority decided that he should be a performer. Before anyone knew it, he was situated at the altar with a microphone and his guitar, delivering his own prelude with "Feliz Navidad." The congregation obligingly clapped along. And one priest, who hadn't been notified in advance, shrugged: "Par for the course."

The primary reason for this lack of concern was a sad one: Cardinal O'Connor had earlier that year been diagnosed with a brain tumor. Cathedral employees, along with people throughout the Archdiocese and beyond, spent the rest of 1999 watching as he underwent surgery, then radiation therapy, then a slow decline in his condition. When he died in May 2000, Long coordinated the music for six scheduled services, culminating in a funeral Mass. To grace a service that would take place in front of a congregation numbering some 3,000, among them President Bill Clinton, Vice President Al Gore, and ex-President George H.W. Bush, as well as millions of television viewers, the music chosen was a mix of timeless (the chant "Salve Regina") and traditional ("Morning Has Broken" at the reception of the body, and Frank Patterson's rendition of

"Ave Maria" at the funeral, both of them specific requests of the Cardinal). Those works were juxtaposed with a large selection of contemporary pieces, including moments from the Andrew Lloyd Webber *Requiem*. The music occasioned little comment from the media, except in the vaguest terms—"the choir in the loft above sang a full-throated series of amens."

Among the clergy in the congregation was Bishop Edward Egan, leader of the Diocese of Bridgeport, Connecticut. His thoughts on the music weren't recorded at the time, but when he was named to succeed Cardinal O'Connor and installed as Archbishop a month later, the *New York Post* had a field day with a front-page headline, SHAKEUPS LOOM AT ST. PAT'S. The three-page accompanying article bore, as a subhead, EVEN CHOIR ISN'T SAFE AS ARCHBISHOP MULLS LOPPING HEADS:

> Those who could fall out of favor include . . . anyone associated with the music programs at St. Patrick's Cathedral. . . .
>
> The well-educated priest, who plays classical piano, was clearly bristling at the brash music bouncing off St. Patrick's arched ceilings, and sources say he decided there and then to make big changes.

It may have been a throwback to the old days of newspapers' paying close critical attention to choral music in churches, but it was more unflattering attention than the Cathedral's music had received in years.

That Christmastime, Long was tendered the same compliment that had been given to Grady and Caprio when the National Choral Council invited him to be one of the guest conductors for the "*Messiah* Sing-In" at Lincoln Center. During the first months of 2001, the Cathedral's music avoided further media commentary as other events proved to be of greater interest—Archbishop Egan's elevation to Cardinal (and soon after that his choice of Monsignor Eugene Clark, pastor of St. Agnes Church, for Rector of the Cathedral, replacing Monsignor Dalla Villa, who was appointed pastor of St. Agnes).

By May, however, Robert Long was gone from St. Patrick's.

His replacement was Don Stefano Concordia, a forty-six-year-old Benedictine monk who had spent the previous eleven years in Italy at the Abbey of Montecassino. Born in Massachusetts, he had his initial training at the New England Conservatory of Music, then moved on to Rome and the Pontifical Institute of Sacred Music for diplomas in organ and Gregorian chant and degrees in philosophy and theology from Sant'Anselmo.

Invited by the Cardinal to lead the Cathedral Choir, he lived in the rectory for more than three months before he was asked, on less than a day's notice, to take over.

Father Concordia's musical style was a marked departure from that of the previous two years, centering on Gregorian chant, polyphony, and a number of classics that the Vatican itself would have sanctioned. He introduced the Cathedral's singers to composers of whom, by this time, most of them had never heard: Refice, Martorell, Perosi. And each Mass began with the day's introit, at the time something quite unusual for St. Patrick's. Under his direction, the choir sang through the month of May and broke for the summer recess, looking forward to the new season.

But by the beginning of September, they discovered that a new musical director had been installed.

That new director was Johannes Somary, a music teacher at the private Horace Mann School who for decades had conducted the semi-professional group Amor Artis, the Fairfield County (Connecticut) Chorale, and a succession of Manhattan church choirs. Somary's first professional move at St. Patrick's was reminiscent of Caprio's, as he announced that every singer would be auditioned privately. The result of those auditions came within days as some Cathedral Choir members (all of them volunteers) received phone messages to tell them that their services were no longer needed.

Barely a week later, the World Trade Center was destroyed in the September 11 attacks. As had been the case during other major tragedies in New York's history, people crowded into St. Patrick's for whatever comfort they could find; votive candles were being lit so frequently that the glass holders began to crack from the heat. In the days and weeks to come, St. Patrick's was a focus of the city's mourning. Cori Ellison remembered, "It went on until after Thanksgiving. . . . [T]here were endless, endless memorial Masses. We were a real epicenter. You genuinely felt you were doing a municipal service."*

The choir's involvement, however, was different. The night after the attack, choir members met for rehearsal, learning that there were to be

---

* At times it was wrenchingly difficult. This author remembers serving as cantor for the October 11 "Month's Mind" service. The idea of singing the 23rd Psalm at such an event was challenging enough; but the psalm was underscored by the sound of a woman, standing in the north aisle and bent nearly double with sobs.

back-to-back memorial services, attended by government officials and internationally televised, occurring within a few days. At the same time, they learned that Somary had made the decision to disinvite the Cathedral Choir (a few of whom worked in the World Trade Center and only by chance had been away from their offices at the time of the attack) from taking part in those services. Their place would be taken by Amor Artis.

Not only the personnel, but the music itself, would change during this time. Somary's taste leaned heavily toward a strict Early Music ideal, foreign to many Cathedral parishioners. (This was rammed home one Christmas Eve when the traditional pre–Midnight Mass carol service was cancelled, replaced with a rendering of the ultra-Baroque Schütz *Christmas Story*.) Concerts, though, tended to large-scale pieces such as the Mendelssohn *Lobgesang* and the Bruckner *Te Deum*, employing large choirs, extra choristers, and big orchestras. Unfortunately, none was able to draw a substantial audience.*

A small number of Manhattan churches had begun to take advantage of the growing historical-interest trend by scheduling Tridentine Masses, now permitted. Those Masses generated their own faithful congregations, some who came for the liturgy and some for the Gregorian chant, and may have been the reason that Somary drafted the men of the choir to form a schola for a weekly "Latin Mass." But it was a hybrid, with introits, antiphons, and Gregorian hymns shoehorned into the Cathedral's usual Mass format. Worse, it was scheduled for Sundays at 9:00 A.M., an hour when the congregation would be made up primarily of tourists rather than connoisseurs. To get those people to participate, laminated cards with the requisite music—printed in Gregorian notation—were placed in Cathedral pews. Most attendees didn't even pick them up.

And there was still the cantor problem, as Cathedral clergy continued to be dissatisfied with the level of congregational singing during Masses. Robert Long had tried to address the issue by adding to the roster cantors

---

* The Cathedral's daily Mass schedule meant that the physical task of setting up risers for these concerts usually had to be accomplished in something less than two hours—hard and thankless work for maintenance-crew members. They may have commented upon this one evening when they made the rounds of the Cathedral to scrape extinguished votive candles from their holders . . . during a concert. Throughout that performance, the music was accompanied by a clink-clink *obbligato*.

whose voices were more pop-oriented than the Cathedral had ever used before (including at one point Long himself, as well as his wife). But that didn't work. Somary reshuffled and reassigned cantors, to such an extent that Cori Ellison resigned at the end of 2001. He then attempted an idea allegedly used in a French cathedral, that of having auxiliary cantors stationed in front of the communion railing, singing along in order to exhort the congregation. That didn't work either. The cantors hated singing at such close quarters—and one of them remembered that some members of the congregation seemed to physically recoil from them. The idea ultimately devolved into that of a lone volunteer chorister, traipsing up and down the central aisle and waving her arms in time with the music.

By September 2003, there would be yet another new music director at St. Patrick's.

Coming out of the Chorus

Jennifer Pascual was born in Jacksonville, Florida, in 1971, daughter of parents who had come to the United States from Manila, and had started music lessons at an early age. Educated in the Catholic school system, she began her liturgical music career at Bishop Kenny Catholic High School. She recalled, "We used to have a 'Bishop's Mass' once a year. We turned our gym into 'Kenny Cathedral.' I started out playing for these Masses on piano; the organist graduated—and *I* wanted to play the organ." She did, and her wish got her drafted into playing at her local parish, St. Joseph's Church; as a college freshman at Jacksonville University, studying music education and piano performance, she added a third major with her first serious organ lessons.

In 1993, she moved to New York, enrolling at the Mannes School of Music for a master's degree in piano and advanced organ study with McNeil Robinson. To generate some income during her studies, she went through the Yellow Pages and wrote letters to a number of the city's Catholic churches, offering her services as an organist. This mailing got her some part-time work around town at St. Andrew's and Holy Name, and only months later she snagged a job as music director at the Church of St. Charles Borromeo, conducting two choirs and occasionally filling in as a music teacher at the church's school. In her spare time, she did some work as an accompanist-teacher for the Boys Choir of Harlem.

In 1995, she had a brush with the music of St. Patrick's when John-Michael Caprio advertised for choristers to sing at the upcoming Papal

Mass. Because of her musical skills (and her gift of perfect pitch), her sight-reading test at the audition was so good that it jolted Caprio—"Have you sung this before?" he asked her suspiciously—and earned her a spot in the soprano section of the Archdiocesan Festival Choir. "I couldn't be seen much on TV, except at the end of the Mass," she said. "During the 'Hallelujah Chorus,' I was the one taking pictures of the Pope instead of singing."

That would be her last taste of New York's liturgical music scene for a while, as the following year she relocated to Rochester, New York, and the Eastman School of Music for a doctorate in organ performance, studying with David Higgs, and a minor in church music. During that time, she worked at Rochester's Holy Cross Church, as interim music director for a year at Sacred Heart Cathedral, and with a group called the Latin Mass Community.

By 2000, doctorate in hand, she was back in New York with a position at St. Frances de Chantal, and the turn of events that brought her to that position proved that even the most casual acquaintanceships can bear fruit. The church hosted a congregation of Sisters of Life, whose choir was led by Father Richard Baker, who was impressed with Pascual's ability and asked her to serve as organist for the Sisters' upcoming profession of vows and other musical activities. In this manner their paths would cross and then diverge for two years.

By that time, Pascual had played on the St. Patrick's recital series; she also had been asked to come to Newark for an associate position at the Cathedral-Basilica of the Sacred Heart. In the meantime, back in New York Father Baker had been named Archdiocesan Music Commissioner. And Father Baker was in a dilemma. The Archdiocesan Festival Chorale (as opposed to the Festival Choir formed by John-Michael Caprio, this was a group that had been formed in the 1980s to sing at various Archdiocesan events) was scheduled to perform its 2002 holiday benefit concert at St. Joseph's Seminary but found itself without a conductor. Casting about for a substitute, Father Baker asked Pascual to lead the choir. Obligingly, she steered them through their program for an audience that included a number of high-level clergy—among them, Cardinal Egan. The Cardinal made a short speech after the performance, praising the musicians and the conductor, but nothing else was said at the time.

In early January, Pascual received a phone call from Monsignor Clark. "At first I thought, 'Maybe they want me to play a funeral?'" she recalled.

But this was different—he was seeking a face-to-face meeting. And at that meeting, he offered her the post of music director at St. Patrick's. He cryptically remarked, "You're highly recommended for this job."

As contract details were being worked out, Pascual went through a strange period during which she had little direct contact with the Cathedral but heard a great deal through other channels. Almost immediately after her meeting with Monsignor Clark, she attended that year's Conference of Roman Catholic Cathedral Musicians, where other attendees startled her by congratulating her on her appointment. She received phone calls from colleagues who had seen the latest issue of *The American Organist*, which contained a want ad for an associate music director to replace her at Sacred Heart. Getting very close to the bone, she was asked to conduct the Archdiocesan Choir when it sang for the upcoming ordination of priests . . . at St. Patrick's. And while her appointment was an open secret in New York, she was obliged to keep mum about the whole thing. By August, the situation reached near-comic levels—not having heard from Cathedral personnel for weeks, she was out of town when she received an unexpected phone call from Monsignor Clark's secretary: "Where were you? You were supposed to be here for today's meeting."

Finally, everything was signed and legal; but when she showed up at the Cathedral a few days shy of her September 1, 2003, starting date, a business person in the office told her firmly that she "wasn't supposed to be on premises until the beginning of the month." In order for her to start planning the choir season, Donald Dumler and Stanley Cox had to raid the music library for individual copies of whatever music the Cathedral owned. She carried it all home in shopping bags.

Thus Jennifer Pascual began work as the latest music director of St. Patrick's . . . and the first female music director there, ever. A sharp historian might have noted that her hiring had symbolically closed a circle, because she started work at the Cathedral almost exactly a century after the Papal *motu proprio* had banned women from its choir. But virtually no media picked up on her appointment. This didn't bother her. She had work to do.

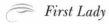 *First Lady*

Of Pascual, a Cathedral executive remarked to a chorister, "You guys don't have to worry. She's a mensch."

It was a casual assessment but a fortunate one, because Pascual had inherited a music department whose members were thoroughly upset from the rapid changes of the previous five years. Luckily, she was a musician who knew her own abilities but had no axe to grind. And her straightforward personality became evident as singers learned that she preferred to be addressed as "Jenny"; they learned as well that the Cathedral's new music director kept on her desk a supply of chocolates for the taking.

Pascual was a good choice for a number of other reasons. First, she would be working for possibly the most musically involved Archbishop in Cathedral history: Cardinal Egan was a trained cellist and pianist, as well as a dedicated opera buff who for his installation as Archbishop had asked Renée Fleming to sing two movements of the Mozart *Exsultate, Jubilate.* He knew his way around liturgical music, too, having sung as a boy in a Chicago choir that was conducted by the grandson of Cecilian composer John Singenberger. This gave him a wide-ranging knowledge of White List music, more complete than that of many choirmasters (so much so that he would later tell a radio interviewer of his wish to have the Perosi *Requiem* sung at his funeral). And his musical taste was expressed unequivocally—"I like *melody*." This might have been a problem for some previous Cathedral choirmasters, who hadn't hesitated to butt heads with clergy over musical matters, but Pascual thought that was nonsense. "You play the game as the clergy deals the cards to you," she said. "The key is keeping everything balanced." She was as good as her word: One of her first assignments was to conduct the Cathedral Choir in a 9/11 memorial Mass, for which Aprile Millo appeared as a guest soloist to deliver "Ave Maria." *CitySings* was restored to the schedule and sung to an overflow crowd. Midnight Mass returned to a more recognizable musical format.

While in bygone years soloists had been considered the "stars" of St. Patrick's, the imperatives of the Mass as well as the Cathedral's current musical style guaranteed that cantors, in their function as lay ministers, would now be the most visible and most important vocalists. Tenor John Des Marais was a prominent addition to that roster, cantoring a large number of important liturgies; but along with every other cantor on the roster, he would have to provide double duty in the choir during off-hours. As to the other members of the paid singing staff, impressive résumés were superfluous. Rather, musicianship was of prime importance, whether it came from very experienced professionals or fast-tracker undergraduates. And there would be more of them. One at a time, Pascual added singers until the St. Patrick's choir had a sixteen-member professional schola.

But beyond the notions of agreeable programming or choral sound, Pascual's vision encompassed a sense of the Cathedral's musical history and a determination to keep it alive. When St. Patrick's prepared for its 125th anniversary in May 2004, she decided to put together a concert that would highlight compositions of the Cathedral's past music directors. It wasn't an easy task; at the time, no one had a completely accurate list of the directors, let alone their compositions. Still, some persistent digging through the music library meant that *A Choral Concert Commemorating the 125th Anniversary of the Cathedral of St. Patrick* was able to feature works of Ungerer (his "O Salutaris," probably the piece's first hearing in more than eighty years), Yon, Courboin, and Grady. Grady's arrangements hadn't been performed for the previous two years; as far as the other composers went, no one had been aware of much more than "Gesù Bambino." This glimpse into the Cathedral's musical heritage intrigued choir members no less than the audience, and it became something of a game, for them as well as for Pascual, to unearth whatever additional bits of it they could find. More Ungerer was discovered in the Library of Congress, along with a handful of Pecher's works (among them "Ecce Sacerdos," lost to St. Patrick's for nearly a century). Yon's music was located in churches across the United States, as well as in unexplored file drawers at the Cathedral's music office.

Pascual had as well the ability to sense a good opportunity in an unusual circumstance—and she got to prove it, before the 125th anniversary concert had even reached performance. Out of nowhere came a call from a casting agent who was arranging the New York talent for *The Ballad of Bettie Page*, a film biography of the legendary 1950s pinup queen. On the surface it didn't seem to be the kind of entertainment that would feature liturgical music, but the agent was seeking fifteen choristers for the film's closing sequence, a scene during which the star walks into a Baptist church in Miami, drawn by the choir's singing, and Finds Religion. It was a great opportunity; as opposed to the low-money proposal initially made to singers during *The Godfather: Part III*, New Line Cinema began by offering SAG contracts to the participants. Also differing from *The Godfather* was the clear understanding, given the risqué nature of the story, that the Cathedral's name wouldn't be used in the film in any way. Still, before anything was put down in black and white, Pascual made sure to get permission for choir members to take part.

The schedule was tight enough that the agent had to observe the dress rehearsal of the anniversary concert in order to meet any interested singers. From that contact, a group was chosen, with Pascual as conductor; they reported the following week to St. Augustine's Episcopal Church on the Lower East Side (representing the Miami Baptist location) for costumes, sound recording of a single hymn, and an afternoon filming session . . . that lasted until 6:30 the next morning. An exhausting but very lucrative day's work. (The finished movie wouldn't show up in theaters for two years. When it finally hit the screen, renamed *The Notorious Bettie Page* and released to admiring reviews, choristers discovered the opposite situation that they had encountered when they saw *The Godfather* and heard, but didn't see, themselves. In *Bettie Page*, they were onscreen participants but their voices were gone; during post-production their singing had been overdubbed by that of another choir. Pascual was told that they had sounded "too good.")

As Pietro Yon had prodded the Cathedral toward radio, Pascual did her bit to help it into the Information Age. In years past, the Cathedral's use of the Internet had been halting at best, and in the late 1990s when website designer (and Cathedral Choir bass) Michael Boydston-White had volunteered his services to St. Patrick's, his offer wasn't accepted. But now the Cathedral was planning a website. And as Yon had understood radio's value, Pascual understood the value of the Internet; and she made sure that the St. Patrick's website would provide a comprehensive guide to the music department, complete with history and contact information. This made it easier than it ever had been for people anywhere in the world to familiarize themselves with the Cathedral's music—and to trade information; when new or rediscovered works were performed, said Pascual, "I'd get emails from all over the country."

She had yet another plan to expand the scope of the music department. But to handle that project, the right person would have to be found.

Working with New—and Old—Colleagues

It was only by a series of chance occurrences that Daniel Brondel became a professional organist, plying his trade in New York.

Born in France in 1970, he spent his childhood in Saint-Sylvestre-sur-Lot, attending a school run by Dominican nuns. By age eight, he had begun piano lessons with the local church organist—but didn't brave the organ itself until he was fifteen years old and tried to study with the organist of the Cathedral of Agen. That didn't work out. The man stopped the lessons after four sessions, "during which I learned nothing."

He came to the United States as a foreign exchange student, living with a Georgia family. By luck, they were involved with the Atlanta Symphony Chorus and invited him to participate. Not only did Brondel sing bass with the chorus, but he was eventually asked to coach the members in French diction. This enabled him to work directly with Robert Shaw, who proved to be a major influence on his musical formation: "Those were the most profoundly changing years of my musical life. I learned even more than I thought I had of the rigors musicians must abide by to create something worth listening to." In the meanwhile he had snagged a piano scholarship to Georgia State University and decided to give the organ another try.

In 1993, he went to the Eastman School for a master's degree in organ performance and literature, studying with David Higgs. After receiving his master's degree, he embarked on doctoral studies. While at Eastman, he won second prize in the 1996 National Young Artist Competition in Organ Playing, which brought him to New York (and to St. Patrick's for that memorably non-air-conditioned convocation, his first time visiting the Cathedral). In the audience to hear him compete was a fellow Higgs student, Jennifer Pascual. They met very soon afterward and developed a friendship based on mutual respect. "Wouldn't it be great to work to-gether someday?" she said.

He returned for further study and a long stint as choirmaster of Saint Anne Church. One Sunday, his alto soloist called in sick, and with no better option Brondel began to sing her part in falsetto, something he had never tried before. In the congregation was an Eastman faculty member, who was impressed. "You should develop that." Although Brondel hadn't thought of himself as a singer, he began to study as a countertenor and soon began to get solo jobs of his own in a number of venues. (One of those was a *St. John Passion* at the Cathedral of St. John the Divine, and while Brondel was in New York he scheduled an audition at St. Patrick's. He wasn't hired, but Johannes Somary complimented him, "Your French is quite good.")

By early 2004, he was ready to leave Rochester. Pascual came to Saint Anne Church to play a recital and to propose an idea. "Father Baker and I were talking about starting a high-caliber children's choir," she explained. "And . . . he's looking for a music director at St. Malachy's Church. Write him." Brondel did so and was auditioned, interviewed, and hired.

By that fall, he was in New York and conducting the choir of St. Malachy's; still, it took a year to assemble a board, come up with a name—the Cathedral of St. Patrick Young Singers, abbreviated "CSPYS"—and get the kids on board. Funding came from the Archdiocese, the local Department of Education, and private donations. Still, "it was from the ground up," remembered Brondel. "Finding children was definitely a challenge." Advertisements went out to Archdiocesan schools, and twelve children were recruited to meet weekly for training, starting in August 2005. By October, they were ready to sing for the Mass at St. Malachy's; the following week, they debuted at St. Patrick's and were an instant hit with clergy and congregation alike.

This was wonderful news to people with long memories, or to those who had heard of the days of choirboys singing at St. Patrick's, and the resulting interest helped board members of CSPYS as they plunged into the business of fundraising and development. But the regular Cathedral Choir was busy, too, with a jumble of extracurricular assignments. Some of these the choir would be executing on their own, some in collaboration with others, creating a "crunch time" that would last for years.

The crunch began in 2005 with an early Lenten season, which caused St. Patrick's Day to be followed only three days later by Palm Sunday and the first major concert of the season, a Mozart *Requiem*, which was followed by the seven choral services of Holy Week, which were supposed to be followed by a bit of downtime. But less than a week after Easter came the death of Pope John Paul II. The Cathedral responded quickly with a series of memorial Masses, some of them televised, all of them containing music.

Earlier in the year, the choir had agreed to collaborate with the Paderewski Festival Singers and the Wroclaw Philharmonic in a late-April performance of Wojciech Kilar's *Missa pro Pace*, which had been given before the Pontiff in the wake of 9/11 and was intended now as a Papal tribute. Now, with his death, it would be performed as a memorial. Along with its regular schedule, the choir had to add rehearsal time (some of it spent in hired-bus trips to Brooklyn) to work with the Festival Singers, and dress rehearsals were lengthy enough, with no seating provided, that some singers fainted during the performance. The *Times*, which hadn't as of late been paying much attention to the musical activities of the Cathedral, showed up to hear the work when it was given before a tightly packed audience: "'It is a very beautiful Mass,' the pope is reported to have said after hearing it. There will be no argument here." But in its review, only one sentence pertained to the Cathedral Choir:

> Rehearsal time with the combined St. Patrick's Cathedral Choir and Paderewski Festival Singers must have been limited; last-minute adjustments were still being made at the scheduled starting time.

While Pascual had nothing particular to do during the Kilar concert, she was the principal performer when JAV Recordings proposed that she record a CD. Stanley Cox had recorded for JAV in 2003, and Donald Dumler's recording was still enjoying brisk sales; producer Joe Vitacco naturally felt that the Cathedral's music director should have a disc of her own. The playlist would be composed of organ selections based on Gregorian chant; the men of the Cathedral's schola would do the singing. It was an ambitious project: seven major works, divided into forty-six tracks, half of the tracks played by Pascual and half sung by the men. Over three nights in October, Pascual recorded her half of the CD. The men showed up on the fourth night and made ready to record in the gallery.

But as usually was the case during Cathedral recording sessions, there were problems. This time, the problems were intensified by the fact that the men were singing completely without accompaniment, which seemed to magnify the slightest extraneous noise. And there were plenty of noises, as repairs at the corner of Fifth Avenue and 51st Street had turned the roadbed into a mosaic of uneven asphalt patches and steel plates. Take after take was ruined by *ch-chunk* noises generated by traffic. By 2:30 A.M., things deteriorated even further when a backhoe showed up, sent by the Department of Transportation to tear out more asphalt. (At that point this author was dispatched with John Des Marais to the worksite, where Des Marais asked the operator the perfectly reasonable, perfectly ridiculous question "Do you know when you'll be finished?")

Most of that was forgotten when *Organ Music and Gregorian Chant* was released the following year to critical assent. The *American Record Guide* wrote:

Pascual is a superb performer. She has no problem with the technical demands of this program. . . . There is no bravura here—simply subdued organ commentaries for each sung verse. All in all, a most satisfying recording. . . .

All of this attention seemed to give the Cathedral Choir a higher profile than it had enjoyed in quite a while, and *The New Yorker* referred to them as "[one] of the town's better choruses." It was welcome respect. But it tended to mean, more and more often, that the musicians of St. Patrick's would be collaborating with other groups on large-scale musical events. Or rather, large-scale events that involved music.

Along with the rest of New York, the Cathedral had been changed by the events of 9/11. Security checkpoints had been set up for all visitors; congregation members entering for Midnight Mass were sent through metal detectors; and more than one in-depth conversation had taken place between Pascual and her crew, dealing with the location of emergency flashlights and the specifics of quickly evacuating the gallery in case of "a problem." While no one liked those changes, everyone understood them.* And a change that involved not only all of New York but many world capitals as well was The September Concert. "A global day of music for peace," it was organized in 2002 and intended to be performed every September 11th, in every kind of locale, guaranteeing that audiences would hear "[a]ll music and all musicians . . . regardless of genre or background." By 2005 the organizers had arranged to feature St. Patrick's as one of their major New York venues. For that first Cathedral performance, the New York Choral Society and the Oratorio Society of New York combined with the Cathedral Choir for the centerpiece, the Bernstein *Chichester Psalms*, a suitably fitting work. But after the Bernstein was finished, the regardless-of-genre factor was satisfied by a pop harmony quartet from the Choral Society, singing a set of up tunes (including Gershwin's "Our Love Is Here to Stay").

The next day, the appropriateness of the quartet performance was reportedly questioned by an unidentified radio commentator. But no one

---

* A positive result of the increased security was the Cathedral's implementation, at last, of uniform photo ID cards for all of its employees and volunteers. Until then, identifying people who worked at St. Patrick's had been a chancy proposition. One soprano, arriving for a special service, couldn't convince security guards to let her in until she proved her identity by singing for them.

should have been surprised—New York had for a long time been turning into a society where liturgical music was of importance primarily to liturgical musicians. Subsequent editions of The September Concert would become ever more mixed-bag in their makeup, featuring compositions by ABBA and Harry Belafonte; trap sets and tambourines would be as ubiquitous as the organ. For Pascual's part, she understood the Cathedral Choir's job, which was to provide an emotional center to such evenings. And her programming hewed to a traditional line, presenting the choir in selections that were elegiac as well as nationalistic.

This dichotomy in musical styles would be discussed in the *Times* by the doyen of music critics, Bernard Holland, after he caught one September Concert performance. At first, he gave the evening a cursory writeup:

> The Cathedral of St. Patrick Choir, led by Jennifer Pascual, emphasized such themes, singing "America the Beautiful" and then underlining it with "God Bless America," one of Irving Berlin's perfectly shaped and uncluttered exercises in the melodic art.

But ten days later, Holland struck a more critical tone by putting The September Concert into a larger context.

> A ceremony at St. Patrick's Cathedral on Sept. 11 offered some patriotic music and a few dabs of the classics, but everything else made me wonder whether I should be listening as a critic or as a Christian. A lot of liturgical music these days asks you to choose between the two.
>
> With its hand-clapping, inspirational, just-folks character, how different this music is from a tradition that ran from plainchant through Josquin and Palestrina to Mozart and Beethoven, and finally to Messiaen and Britten. . . .

There was no easy answer to the question of pop-influenced liturgical music. But that discussion had been going on for years, was guaranteed to continue without interruption, and concerned many more venues than St. Patrick's alone.

If there was an unusual aspect of that article, it was probably the fact that it had appeared at all in a major newspaper. Most strident musical criticism had left mainstream print journals to go—not underground, but online. The blogosphere had begun its rise at about the time that Pascual had taken over the Cathedral Choir. Worldwide discussion forums on every subject were being created, and it was inevitable that along with discussion would come fanaticism. So when the topic of Catholic liturgical music came up, it became distressingly clear that the self-professed "experts" of a century ago, who had spent all that time writing furious letters to the papers about the sad state of sacred music, had plenty of emotional descendants.*

Radio Redux and Expanding Exposure

While the Cathedral's music was being discussed more frequently online, it was also receiving more opportunities to be heard. Where radio broadcasting of Cathedral services had once been a special thing, and television coverage even more so, twenty-first-century satellite technology made broadcasting easier (and more frequent) than it had ever been before. Midnight Mass was carried not only by WPIX but by a smattering of affiliates nationwide. Special events were newsworthy enough to be telecast, nationally and internationally, by major cable providers. Specialty carriers broadcast events of specific interest (such as Milan-based Radio Maria's coverage of the Cathedral's annual Columbus Day Mass, a service that was conducted largely in Italian and didn't receive much American coverage). And as it had been for years, an early-morning Mass was telecast in New York through a local-access cable provider who taped the service through the Cathedral's own A/V system.

This exposure was astonishingly expanded in May 2006 when the satellite radio network SIRIUS announced its impending launch of The Catholic Channel—and St. Patrick's was propelled into the high-tech broadcasting age. For a monthly fee (and the purchase of a specially designed receiver), listeners could now hear, as part of the twenty-four-hour program schedule, Cardinal Egan in his own series, "Conversations with the Cardinal"; or they could get the inside scoop on Catholic sacred music with Jennifer Pascual's weekly talk show, "Sounds from the Spires." Or they could tune in to the heaviest schedule of Mass broadcasts that St. Patrick's had ever attempted: every Sunday 10:15 Mass;

---

* An apt demonstration of this mindset was provided when a video clip of Renée Fleming, singing the Mozart "Alleluia" at Cardinal Egan's installation in 2000, found its way onto YouTube. One strikingly dense viewer left a comment: "And I thought Renée Fleming would be beyond doing crappy church gigs!"

every holiday; selected special services . . . and six days per week, an 8:00 A.M. Mass, with organ and cantor.

Because the Cathedral musicians hadn't been furnishing music for early-morning Masses (and most of them were frankly horrified by the prospect), the new 8:00 A.M. Mass prompted a jarring change in routine. There needed to be cantors, so a handful of the Cathedral's younger paid singers were promoted to cantor status, along with the obligation of being ready for the microphone first thing in the morning. There would have to be extra accompanists, as well: Daniel Brondel was brought on staff as an assistant organist, along with Christopher Berry, choirmaster of Holy Trinity Church. Any holes remaining in the schedule of the two men would be filled by Pascual herself.

The changeover went smoothly, and the only outward sign that the Cathedral was entering a new radio age was the replacement of the main altar's clock (a small brass timepiece that had stood in the same place for years) by a digital atomic clock, radio-linked to SIRIUS headquarters, calibrated to Coordinated Universal Time—and producing the spectacle, before even nonbroadcast Masses, of priest, lector, and cantor staring intently at the clock and counting down the seconds. Otherwise, most visitors had no idea that so many of the Cathedral services were being aired, and especially not to so many listeners; SIRIUS, which had started by covering North America, had now branched out into the field of Internet radio. Where the Cathedral Choir had once made news with a single shortwave broadcast, services and music from St. Patrick's were now available every day, to listeners anywhere in the world.

This schedule came with its own slight quirks. By agreement, time slots for regularly scheduled Masses were precise: Weekday Masses ran for a half hour, Sunday Masses for an hour and fifteen minutes. Should a Mass run overtime, it was cut off in mid-note; and if it finished ahead of time, the organist's job was to play additional postlude music until the broadcast time was finished. While all of the Cathedral's organists were able to play large chunks of repertoire from memory, Donald Dumler confessed that he had nightmares of sitting at the console, unable to decide what to play next, while someone in the background was shouting, "*No dead air!*"

Dumler's nightmares were happily unfounded. And, as in the days of Courboin, it was becoming apparent that the strength and variety of the St. Patrick's organ staff were giving it additional visibility. Pascual took advantage of this in 2006 with the introduction of the *Three Organists Spectacular!*, a triple recital that allowed Pascual, Cox, and Dumler to strut their stuff on the same evening. This format would make a point of including repertoire that was both on and off the beaten path (as it did that first evening when Cox and Pascual duetted on *The Stars and Stripes Forever*). The event was well-enough received to become an annual happening. The media liked it, too; the *New York Sun* simply nicknamed it DUELLING ORGANISTS.

Such goodwill was fortunate, because St. Patrick's was still responsible for occasional events that were often planned by people who didn't work for the music department . . . such as the Mass that was sung by the choir and conducted by Pascual, but whose organizers insisted on providing their own soloist. Because they knew that "the Cardinal liked opera," they booked a singer who they assumed was a reigning Italian diva. As it turned out, she was a diva—but a pop diva, a recording star who had never sung opera in her life but was delighted to have a crack at performing in St. Patrick's. During the Mass, the young woman belted out her own version of Schubert's "Ave Maria," *a cappella*. Complete with gestures.

"Everything Happens at Once"

The Bicentennial Year of the Archdiocese of New York was set to open on April 15, 2007, with a Sunday-afternoon liturgy that was meant to launch a year of additional Bicentennial events. The Mass would also mark the debut of the Archdiocesan Bicentennial Hymn, "By Our Faith in You, O Lord." This had been the winner of a nationwide competition; and even though the entries had gone through a blind judging, everyone was surprised when the winner turned out to be Deborah Jamini, a singer in the Cathedral Choir who was also an arranger and a theory instructor at the Mannes School.* The hymn would be sung as part of an elaborate musical service provided by the Cathedral Choir, the Festival Chorale, and the CSPYS. As well, the Met's Barbara Frittoli was on hand, along with a contingent of Knights of Columbus and representatives from every parish in the Archdiocese. The interest was evident in the hot-ticket nature of the Mass, guaranteed to be held before a packed Cathedral, a

* —and would become the Cathedral's first Composer-in-Residence, providing anthems and Mass settings for a number of occasions.

grand launch to a year of special events that would climax the following April with a grand Bicentennial Mass at Radio City Music Hall. Or so it was planned. Early in the day, rain began to fall, becoming only heavier as the time for the Mass neared, keeping away clergy, participants, and congregants and cutting attendance by nearly two-thirds. Still, *Catholic New York* philosophically labeled the weather as "[a]bout the only significant detail that did not work according to plan."

The Cathedral's music department had its own Bicentennial plans—an extensive series of nine concerts, covering a wide range of music from instrumental ensembles to organ recitals to an enormous Bicentennial Gala Concert. The season would be launched in the fall of 2007 with a recital by Vatican organist James E. Goettsche. During the planning, it was discovered that the organs had indeed been refurbished but never re-dedicated; Goettsche's recital provided a perfect opportunity. On the evening of September 15, aspergillium in hand, Monsignor Robert Ritchie (who had been named as Rector of the Cathedral upon the retirement of Monsignor Clark two years before) performed the Blessing of the Organ. Then the audience settled back to a program of Bach, Dubois, Reger, Franck, and Vierne.

While a bicentennial celebration happened once every two centuries, there was even bigger news on the horizon. Throughout the summer, rumors had been circulating from upper-echelon sources that "a visitor was coming." The story was confirmed in October: Pope Benedict XVI would visit Washington, then New York, in April. There would be a Mass at Yankee Stadium. And, for the first time ever, there would be a Papal Mass at St. Patrick's.

It was particularly exciting for musicians, especially those of the Cathedral. The Pontiff was a former choir director himself, a lover of classical music with a special affinity for Mozart. As well, only that July he had issued a *motu proprio* that had stunned some Catholics and thrilled others, *Summorum Pontificum*, officially permitting Tridentine Masses to be celebrated in virtually any parish (and making it no surprise that His Holiness had stated a desire for the increased use of Gregorian chant in churches). All of this provided more unmistakably clear direction than Courboin, Grady, or Caprio had received when planning the music for their Papal events, and it allowed for some great opportunities. Of that period, Pascual later remembered, "It took up six months of my life, working twelve to fourteen hours every day." And Cardinal Egan was as enthusiastic about the process as she was.

It began as they met in the Cardinal's residence, sitting down with a pile of recordings, a stack of scores, and a boom box, going through music to find just the right Mass setting. By the end of a three-hour session, they decided on the musical backbone for each service: at St. Patrick's, the Rheinberger *Mass in C*; at Yankee Stadium, the Victoria *Missa "O Magnum Mysterium."* The choice of the Victoria surprised Pascual: "Your Eminence . . . it's a Christmas Mass."

"Who's going to know?" replied the Cardinal. (He was right.)

After the initial session came weekly meetings at the Archdiocesan offices to fill in the rest of the programming and plan the logistics. It added up to a great deal of work for the Cathedral's musicians, who would not only sing for the Papal Mass at St. Patrick's on April 19 but would form the nucleus of the choir singing the next day at Yankee Stadium. The schedule promised to be exciting. It also promised to be wearing. This Papal visit would take in more music than the Cathedral Choir had been asked to prepare for any previous visit, and it was being put together with less notice than the Archdiocese had enjoyed in 1995. Even the liturgical calendar would make things difficult; the upcoming Easter would be the earliest since 1913, giving singers so little downtime between Epiphany and the beginning of Lent that St. Patrick's Day would fall on Monday of Holy Week.

The moment that news of the Papal visit was released, Pascual had the same experience as Caprio—composers started coming out of the woodwork. However, music for the two Masses would be very carefully chosen to reflect the Pontiff's taste. And with two full-scale Masses being planned, there would be a great deal of it. Complementing the Rheinberger and Victoria settings would be works classic (Gounod "Hymnus Pontificius," Palestrina "Sicut Cervus" and "Ego Sum Panis Vivus") and classically modern (Biebl "Ave Maria," Rutter "Jesus Is Risen," Kidd "Ubi Caritas"). There was a sprinkling of White List works that were very familiar around the Cathedral but would prove exotically unfamiliar to many listeners (Montani "Christus Vincit," Singenberger "Ecce Sacerdos," Perosi "O Sacrum Convivium"). For operatic starpower, the Met's Salvatore Licitra would offer the Rossini "Domine Deus" at St. Patrick's, while the next day Marcello Giordani would sing "Panis Angelicus." As a compliment to the Pope's heritage, Germanic composers were featured

(Brahms "How Lovely Is Thy Dwelling Place" Mozart "Ave Verum," and Beethoven "Hallelujah" from *Mount of Olives*). And there would be more Gregorian chant than had ever been used at previous Papal Masses.

As to custom-crafted Papal music, some was old and some was new. Bruce Saylor provided a section of his "Hymn to Joy Fantasy," along with a new arrangement of "Holy God, We Praise Thy Name." Carl MaultsBy contributed a setting of "Let Us Break Bread Together." Deborah Jamini wrote arrangements for the fifty-eight-piece orchestra that would accompany both Masses. Michael Valenti's "Procession for a Pontiff" was restored to its original shorter length for the Papal entrance into St. Patrick's. Pascual herself set the psalm for Yankee Stadium.

The Cathedral Choir set to work on the Papal music at the same time as the repertoire for holiday and Bicentennial events: *An Evening of Polish Music*, *CitySings*, Midnight Mass, and a late-January *Bicentennial Gala Concert* that would feature arias from five Metropolitan Opera singers, the Mozart *Vesperae Solennes de Confessore*, and the "Ode to Joy" from the Beethoven *Symphony No. 9*. It was a daunting assignment for everyone involved, made slightly easier by some judicious recycling work—the Rheinberger *Mass* would be used for Midnight Mass (which also gave it a built-in public dress rehearsal). Then it was decided to let the "Ode to Joy" perform double duty as the postlude to the Yankee Stadium Mass (and for that matter, concelebrants would enter to the first two movements of the *Symphony No. 9*).

Heavy as it was, this schedule was then made heavier. Daniel Brondel brought the CSPYS to the Cathedral to sing during Advent, which got them an invitation to sing at a Meeting with Young People Having Disabilities, taking place the same day as the St. Patrick's Mass in the chapel of St. Joseph's Seminary. (There would also be a youth rally that afternoon on the grounds of St. Joseph's, but its music was coming from other sources—notably "American Idol" pop queen Kelly Clarkson, announced to sing "Ave Maria.") And the evening before that Mass, the German-based St. Joseph's Church would host an ecumenical service, with the Bach *Lobet den Herrn* as its musical centerpiece; Cathedral Choir schola members would make up part of that choir.

Some preparations for the Papal visit and the Pontiff's eight public appearances were silly, such as the souvenir business: The *St. Petersburg Times* reported, "There are T-shirts, commemorative coins, miniature papal flags, buttons and a coffee mug, all with the pope's image. Unlicensed products include Pope's Cologne for $25.95 and a bobblehead Pope Benedict for $12.95." Some preparations were entertaining, such as the plan for distributing Communion at Yankee Stadium (530 priests and deacons, assigned by age and physical condition), or the seating plan and the reasons for it (other Papal visits had taken place in October, when Yankee officials didn't mind having Mass attendees trampling the playing field; but in April, they wanted their grass to remain intact . . . so a pattern of streamers was designed which would stretch over the field, guaranteeing that no one could even step on it).

Other preparations were carried out with some of the heaviest-level security ever extended for a public event. There would be few opportunities for casual observers to see the Pope in person, and chances to greet him were virtually nonexistent. Tickets for every event, even for the 5,000 people who would be admitted to stand on the steps of St. Patrick's and watch the Mass on a JumboTron, had been issued far in advance. Every person entering a security zone would go through a metal detector. Cathedral Choir members received color-coded ID cards for each event. Catering would be provided in each security zone, because no outside food or drink was allowed.

Not only the security was intense. There was far more media interest than there had been in 1995 concerning the music being prepared for the Papal visit to New York. A lot of it centered on Pascual, as a woman and a Filipino-American, and it showed up online, on television, and in print. MAKING JOYFUL NOISE AND LIVING A DREAM, wrote the *Daily News*. "At a rehearsal last Sunday, Pascual was animated, enthusiastic and exacting. At one point, she gently chided the members, 'You sound like amateur nuns at the convent!'" Even the Cardinal got in on the act during the last days, sending the choir a five-pound box of chocolates as a gesture of thanks (and an inducement to keep working).

There was even more interest in the music itself. The Papal visit to Washington, which ended the day before he arrived in New York, had showcased the choir of the National Shrine of the Immaculate Conception at a straightforward Vesper service; but the following day, there was a Papal Mass at Nationals Stadium. The music for that mass emphasized "Catholic multiculturalism"; as contemporary composer Father Michael Joncas put it, "The Washington program tried to be hospitable to the varying ethnicities making up this unique liturgical gathering." However, that music was roundly criticized by some broadcast commentators as well as some bloggers. "I have no problem with multicultural and multi-ethnic representation at any papal Mass," wrote one. "I only have a problem if the multiethnic music sounds like it came from a Disney movie." Cognoscenti far and wide were salivating at the prospect of comparing New York's music with Washington's.

The first afternoon of the Papal visit, schola members gathered at a central location, five hours ahead of time and with IDs at the ready. After a bus trip through blocked-off streets to St. Joseph's Church, they went through a security check and had a brief rehearsal with the Choir of St. Joseph's Church. Then the combined musical forces launched into a group of prelude selections—which, although it was being heard by high-ranking clergy of all denominations, was swamped by what sounded like a lively party. When Cathedral Choir soprano Ilya Speranza delivered the Mozart "Alleluia," it was drowned out by a solid babble of conversation. After the aria, she sat down with a slightly puzzled look, asking a few nearby choristers:

"Did I actually *sing* anything?"

The prelude continued, ignored by most of the attendees, until everyone was tipped off by a roar from the street, then a silence; the Pope had arrived. The cheering continued as the Pontiff entered the church and didn't stop until the Holy Father had reached the altar. Then the religious community of New York had its first meeting with Pope Benedict XVI. Happily, after the service, the Pontiff delivered his verdict to Cardinal Egan: "The music is marvelous here."

In pre-dawn darkness the following morning, choir members, orchestra members, clergy, and participants in the Papal Mass arrived for a 6:00 A.M. call at the Cathedral's back-door neighbor, the Palace Hotel (arriving on foot, because all streets surrounding the Cathedral had been closed to traffic), to be given coffee and a trip through metal detectors. Once the musicians were installed in the gallery and set up, they began another prelude program; and again, solo efforts by Laura Min, Adrienne Patino and Carla Wesby were obliterated by the enthusiastic congregation's talk.

Shortly after 9:00 A.M., there was a roar from the crowd on the Cathedral steps; Drew Santini made ready at the cantor's desk; and the Pontiff arrived. His entrance was greeted with cheers and shouts of "Viva Papa!" and blotted out the choir's "Christus Vincit." Other than that, the Mass went without a hitch. (One enthusiastic TV commentator blurted out,

"Now *this* is music!") Immediately afterward, though, Cathedral Choir members had to tear off robes, hurry downstairs, and head for waiting buses that would take them to Yankee Stadium for a final dress rehearsal with the Archdiocesan Festival Chorale and the upstate Ulster County Vicariate Choir. (As opposed to the Mass at the Cathedral, the dress rehearsal would go anything but smoothly. The choir, arranged behind home plate, didn't get to leave until 9:00 P.M., and Pascual's work wasn't finished until midnight.)

That afternoon, Daniel Brondel was preparing the CSPYS for the Meeting with Young People Having Disabilities. Arranged in the choir gallery at St. Joseph's Seminary, the children were ready with Couperin's "Christo Resurgenti" to greet the Pope as he entered the chapel. There was only one problem: The chapel had no windows, and Brondel would need a signal to begin. No one was available to act as lookout. He found a Secret Service agent and asked to be told when the Papal motorcade pulled up.

"The Pope's whereabouts are classified."

Brondel tried to explain to the man that he was trying to start an anthem rather than an uprising, and needed a cue.

"That's not possible."

It was nearly time for the Pope's arrival. Seeing a TV camera in the chapel, he seized upon an idea and phoned his mother—who was home in France, watching the Papal visit on CNN International. "Oh, yes, I see the outside of the building . . . now I see you!" (Brondel, along with the CSPYS, waved a hello to his mother. At the same time, an on-air commentator muttered in disbelief, "There's a guy up there talking on his cell phone!") "They say there's a car approaching . . . It's driving up . . . a circular driveway, is it? . . . he's getting out . . . he's speaking with some people . . . they're opening the doors . . . he's going in *now*."

At that point, Brondel thanked his mother, put down the phone, turned to the CSPYS, and began the anthem—precisely on time.

And after the music, the Pontiff waved his approval to the children.

The following day was the Mass at Yankee Stadium, the long-awaited Big Event. As had been the case in 1979 and 1995, there was a lengthy Pre-Game Show—the Concert of Hope—featuring a battery of entertainers, including Harry Connick Jr., Ronan Tynan, the Harlem Gospel Choir, José Feliciano, Dana, and the West Point Cadet Choir. This time, both the introductory "Hymnus Pontificius" and Mozart's "Dixit Dominus" were drowned out in the cheers of 57,000 attendees as the Popemobile slowly circled before the Pope took his place at the altar to begin the Mass.

Things went well enough until Communion, set to feature Marcello Giordani singing "Panis Angelicus." Pascual started the orchestra; but Giordani didn't appear. She stopped the orchestra and started it once again; Giordani didn't appear. There was a long moment of silence.

From his cantor's desk, roughly one hundred feet away, John Des Marais saw Pascual gesturing to him. Then she pointed. After a frightening instant of thinking that she wanted *him* to sing, he realized that she wanted him to find Giordani.

As casually as he could, he sprinted to the door of the artists' room and found some lounging men: "Cerco Marcello Giordiani?"

"Chi è?"

"Il cantatore."*

He got a blank look and fled back to the altar.

With nothing else to do, Pascual had the organ start the tune once again—and suddenly Giordani appeared. Because he was holding a microphone in one hand and his music in the other, turning pages proved to be a problem. Still, he made it through "Panis Angelicus." (And Cardinal Egan acknowledged the event at a post-Mass reception when he told the assembly that the *next* time, Signor Giordani would be placed right next to Dr. Pascual.)

The rest of the Mass was a breeze after that, even the "Ode to Joy" (much of which was drowned out, as the assemblage was occupied with screaming for the Pope during his final drive past them). After the service, the Vatican's Monsignor Guido Marini gave Pascual a Rosary with the Pope's compliments.†

---

* Loosely translated: "WHERE'S GIORDANI?" "Er . . . huh?" "THE SINGER!!"

† Pascual didn't actually meet the Holy Father until that summer, when she was planning a trip to Rome and Cardinal Egan got her admittance to a Papal audience. "Holy Father, I'm the one who prepared the music when you were in New York in April." "The music was wonderful!" replied the Pontiff. At which point he gave her another Rosary.

And the Pontiff gave her something else that December: membership in the Order of St. Gregory the Great.

While the Archdiocese had been forced to jettison its Bicentennial plans for that Mass at Radio City, the Bicentennial itself was finally given its due on April 24, with a black-tie fundraising dinner. "More than 700 guests traveled by ferry to the Ellis Island Immigration Museum," wrote *Catholic New York*. "The black-tie gathering attracted many of the archdiocese's major donors as well as clergy, religious and lay employees." Some of those lay employees were the Cathedral Choir, who shared the stage with Met soprano Maureen O'Flynn and tenor Matthew Polenzani. And *Catholic New York* concluded, "The ferry ride home on the beautiful spring night was highlighted by a spectacular fireworks display over New York Harbor."

Even Cathedral employees who hadn't attended the Bicentennial event were quite tired from the Papal preparations and glad to be moving slowly. So it was completely understandable that Donald Dumler would be annoyed to get a call, the day after the Bicentennial dinner, from a person who identified himself as calling from the White House.

He sighed, irritated that someone would consider playing a practical joke when everyone was exhausted. "All right, who is it, *really?*"

It was, indeed, the White House. May 1 was the National Day of Prayer. And President George W. Bush was inviting the Cathedral Choir to sing at the White House for the opening ceremony.

Pascual was in Lewiston, Maine, practicing for a recital that she would play the following evening. Unfortunately, both she and Dumler would discover—the hard way—that Lewiston had extremely poor cell phone service; they didn't connect until the following day. Some very hasty planning followed.

On Sunday morning, the choir met for its usual rehearsal, with Dumler at the keyboard. Uncharacteristically, the phone in the room rang. Dumler took the call and turned on the speaker. It was Pascual, calling the entire Cathedral Choir: "And when I said, 'We have an invitation to sing at the White House,'" she recalled, "there was this *scream* in the room."

The White House was asking the choir to sing only one selection; still, getting there meant an all-night drive to Washington. That was fine with choir members, who met for their usual Wednesday evening rehearsal, then left New York at 2:00 A.M. on a chartered bus. By the next morning, they were in the East Room of the White House, rehearsed, robed, and ready. After an introduction by the president, they offered the assemblage

"How Lovely Is Thy Dwelling Place." The adventure was topped off by a photo-op with the president, an hour's sightseeing, and a trip back to New York.

Not a bad ending for the choir's Bicentennial celebration.

New People, New Positions

Pascual's and Dumler's workloads during the past six months had increased when Stanley Cox left the Cathedral in late 2007 to take a position in Texas. Added to the Bicentennial and Papal preparations would be a search for a new organist.

Actually, more than an organist. Pascual was responsible for music at the Cathedral; but she also conducted the Archdiocesan Chorale, taught music to seminarians and deacons at St. Joseph's, and sat on several music boards. It wouldn't hurt to have an assistant with broader-based conductorial, and executive, powers. That decided, an ad was placed in *The American Organist*:

> Full-time *Associate Director of Music* for highly visible Roman Catholic Cathedral and seat of the Archbishop of New York. The associate director of music will collaborate with cathedral staff in continuing excellence and fostering growth in a very active and nationally recognized music department. Responsibilities include serving as organist for weekend and weekday liturgies, many of which are broadcast.

Everyone in the New York music community assumed that Daniel Brondel had already been offered the job, with the search making things publicly tidy—everyone except Daniel Brondel. Pascual was determined to keep things open and above board, and Brondel went through the same interviews and preliminary auditions as all of the other applicants. It was an odd period for him, because throughout the process he was asked to play not only his usual early-morning radio schedule but a number of extra services.

While all applicants had been informed that no decisions would be made until the Bicentennial had concluded, Brondel didn't hear anything until one evening at the end of May, when he was at a party. The phone rang at 11:00; it was Pascual. Because it had been six weeks since his final interview, he assumed he was being let down gently. That wasn't the case: he was being hired quickly.

"OK, I'm calling to offer you the position."

Another impending change at St. Patrick's concerned Cardinal Egan. In 2007, in accordance with canon law, he had submitted his resignation on his seventy-fifth birthday. By late 2008 it hadn't been accepted, but New Yorkers kept hearing whispers—during the Papal visit, rumors had been circulating that Archbishop Timothy Dolan of Milwaukee was a likely successor. Concerned sacred music lovers searched for clues to his musical taste, finding him to be the sort of Archbishop who allowed organists and choirmasters to work as they saw fit.

Amid the rumors, the Cathedral's business went on. That year's Midnight Mass featured as its guest soloist Angela Gheorghiu, billed as "the world's most glamorous opera star" and famed for her particularly independent spirit. While St. Patrick's had dealt with many idiosyncracies of opera singers (John-Michael Caprio had snapped at one diva who walked in unprepared, "I'll *vamp* 'til you're ready!"), Gheorghiu surprised everyone when she declined to sing "O Holy Night."* Instead, she offered to sing "Panis Angelicus" along with the Romanian carol "O, ce veste minunatâ." (Pascual shrugged and had the choir sing its own arrangement of "O Holy Night" at Communion.)

By February 2009, however, it was official: The Cardinal's resignation had been accepted, and Archbishop Dolan would be coming to New York. His first appearance before New Yorkers, completely unannounced, was at an 8:00 A.M. Mass, an absolute shock to clergy, congregation, Brondel, and cantor Michael Bodnyk.

True to the Cathedral's stack-one-thing-atop-the-other style, Easter would fall on April 12, the Vespers for the Archbishop's installation were set for April 14, and the Mass of Installation was set for the following day. Music department staff switched into high gear to assemble two large-scale services of music suitable to the occasions. They were helped by the Archbishop himself, as *Catholic New York* reported:

> Archbishop Dolan made requests for several hymns at the Mass of Installation: "Ave Maria," "Panis Angelicus" and "God, We Praise You." Famed Irish tenor Ronan Tynan will sing "Ave Maria" at the

---

* She also declined to sing from the choir gallery, preferring to sing from the cantor's desk. For her debut in the Cathedral chancel, she sported a bright red pants outfit trimmed with sequins.

offertory, and "Panis Angelicus" at Communion. The Cathedral Choir and the Archdiocesan Festival Chorale will perform, accompanied by the New York Symphonic Brass along with a flutist and harpist. Dr. Jennifer Pascual, director of music at St. Patrick's, will direct the music at the Mass.

The installation services were happy occasions, taking their cue from the Archbishop's own sense of humor. (TV reporters had a field day with the fact that the first service, the Reception of the Archbishop-Designate, required the Archbishop to knock at the Cathedral door in order to be admitted. This required a rehearsal, a test of various hammers to produce the right knock, and exact placement of a microphone to pick up the sound. The Archbishop was delighted with the whole process, as were viewers.)

And the services brought together a number of elements that intertwined the Cathedral's musical history with its future: Grady's arrangement of "Panis Angelicus," along with his beloved Strauss "Festival Entry"; Yon's *Missa Solemnis*, which the composer himself brought to St. Patrick's; the "Final" of Vierne's *Symphony No. 1*, which James Ungerer had so often played; and the "Hallelujah Chorus," which had given a surprise to John-Michael Caprio when Pope John Paul II stopped to enjoy it.

 EPILOGUE?

Most histories of ongoing institutions tend to wrap up with a somewhat lame ending of Where-We're-Going. In many ways (and especially for an institution like St. Patrick's, which like a barometer must always respond to happenings both in New York and the world beyond), this is impossible.

It's preferable, maybe, to end a history of music at the Cathedral by sitting in the Cathedral itself, quietly, looking hard at the surroundings. Trying to remember what it must have been like in the days when there were no movies, no television, no recordings, no amplification . . . when the mere sight of the Cathedral's interior would be an awe-inspiring experience. When a church organ was one of the most astonishing machines known, capable of roaring splendor or whispered lament. When human voices, unaided, would have to do the work of reaching the congregation's ears, and the congregation would have to do the work of actively—yet silently—listening to the music. This would have been easier in those days. Congregants were disposed to listen, and with no automobile traffic outside the Cathedral and no white noise of air-conditioning inside, the atmosphere would have a type of quiet that is foreign to modern-day New York.

Thinking of that quiet, it's a moving experience to imagine what it would have been like to hear those long-ago singers and organists. Or even longer ago, what it would have been like to hear those 106 boys and young men, processing slowly down the Cathedral's central aisle on a spring day in 1879, making the first music ever heard in the space of St. Patrick's, and hearing absolutely no sound other than their own voices in unison.

 NOTES

1. THE SUBSTITUTE CHOIRMASTER (MAY 25, 1879)

"a certain Miss Gibson succeeded": Allan Nevins and Milton Halsey Thomas, eds., *The Diary of George Templeton Strong*, abridged by Thomas J. Pressly (Seattle: University of Washington Press, 1988).

"the propriety of engaging a number of good, professional choristers": *Albion*, April 18, 1846.

"The choir of this church is undoubtedly . . . one of the most excellent in this city": *New York Herald*, May 16, 1859.

"this Church, unlike others": *New York Times*, March 10, 1871.

"at first sight it appears that the organ almost fills [the gallery] up": *New York Times*, May 18, 1879.

"He says, with much pride, that it is the most powerful organ in the world": *New York Times*, May 23, 1879.

"The procession moved down the central aisle of the building": *Frank Leslie's Illustrated Newspaper*, June 7, 1879.

2. MAMMON VS. CECILIANS (1879-1904)

"[A] burst of melody from the great organ": *New York Times*, May 26, 1879.

"This brilliant and effective music of Haydn's": *New York Tribune*, May 26, 1879.

"An exhibition of this organ was given last Thursday evening": Ibid.

"He was born in New York": *American Art Journal*, August 7, 1886.

"a Miss Mary Louise Clary, a young woman of Louisville": *New York Times*, April 9, 1893.

"Among the Roman Catholic choirs that of the Cathedral": *Werner's Magazine*, August 1897.

"The choir had been reinforced to some extent": *New York Times*, December 26, 1879.

"The music to the Tantum ergo belongs to the worldly style": File memo, January 28, 1886. Archdiocesan Archives of New York.

"I propose to organize a Choral Society": Lavelle to Corrigan, undated (1896). Archdiocesan Archives of New York.

"The beauty and solemnity of the mass at St. Patrick's Cathedral": *New York World*, December 15, 1895.

"Pope on Church Music": *New York Times*, December 29, 1903.

"Singers in church have a real liturgical office": *Tra le sollecitudini*

"The prelates of the Roman Catholic Church in this country": *New York Times*, April 26, 1904.

3. ONLY THE RIGHT MEN, ONLY THE WHITE LIST (1904-29)

"The Archbishop carries a letter from the American Archbishops": *New York Times*, February 4, 1904.

"It is a free recitation of the text": *New York Times,* March 20, 1904.

"'Do you mean that you will immediately dismiss all the women voices'": *New York Sun,* April 1, 1904.

"As there are two women soloists in each church besides the members of the chorus": *New York Herald,* April 3, 1904.

"Many in the large congregation were present": *New York Tribune,* April 4, 1904.

"The music was on the same splendid scale": *New York Times,* April 4, 1904.

"This was the last Sunday": Quoted in the *New York Tribune,* April 7, 1904.

"Upon Archbishop Farley's return from Rome": *New York Times,* April 25, 1904.

"[a] Diocesan Commission with a view of carrying out the instructions": *New York Times,* May 14, 1904.

"Each of the pieces approved is marked with a special seal": *New York World,* May 14, 1904.

"The Rev. Father James H. McGean, pastor of St. Peter's Church, the chairman of the commission, told a Tribune reporter": *New York Tribune,* June 21, 1904.

"[E]xcitement [anxiety] among the women choir singers of New York": *Kansas City Star,* June 12, 1904.

"Archbishop Farley of New York has directed": *Chicago Daily Tribune,* July 24, 1904.

"The authorities of the Catholic Church throughout Europe": *New York Times,* September 27, 1904.

"[the music of which] was sung by a picked choir of men and boys": *New York Times,* September 28, 1904.

"Some of the new rules": *New York Tribune,* October 24, 1904.

"The reform in church music struck the diocese of New York": John Talbot Smith, *The Catholic Church in New York: A History of the New York Diocese from its Establishment in 1808 to the Present Time: in 2 volumes, Vol. II* (n.p., 1905).

"There is always more or less difficulty": *New York Times,* October 22, 1905.

"[A] large portion of the old Easter glory is departed": *New York Tribune,* April 23, 1905.

"One of the questions asked of him was": *New York Tribune,* March 8, 1906.

"Mr. Ungerer's essential character was marked by a certain austerity": Program of *The Memorial Requiem Mass for Jacques-Cécilien Ungerer,* December 6, 1969. Private collection.

"All the above to show a stationary state of affairs": Ungerer to Rector and Trustees, August 26, 1898. Archdiocesan Archives of New York, C-1.

"The interpretation was German": *New York Times,* September 28, 1904.

"This is a return to a custom": *New York Times,* December 18, 1915.

"Jacques Cecelien Ungerer, for twenty-two years organist of St. Patrick's Cathedral": *The Catholic Choirmaster,* October 1915.

"At first he had a tiny studio": Ethel Peyser, *The House That Music Built: Carnegie Hall* (R. M. McBride & Company, 1936).

"He is an accomplished player": *New York Times,* March 25, 1914.

"Some might question whether there was not an excess": *New York Times,* March 24, 1915.

"[Martinelli] seemed a little comically out of place": *Toledo Blade,* September 4, 1917.

"[Yon's] high powers . . . as musician and as interpreter": *Chicago Daily Tribune*, March 2, 1920.

"The great gray pile at Fiftieth Street": *Musical America*, April 1919.

"[H]e played an interesting program and aroused the greatest enthusiasm": Ibid.

"[the appointment] has no precedent in the history of the Vatican": *New York Times*, January 2, 1922.

"it has been impossible, it is said, to make successful gramophone records": *Time*, April 28, 1923.

" 'The Catholic church requires of its parishioners actual physical attendance' ": *New York Times*, August 3, 1924.

"Mr. Yon has not appeared here in the past two years": *New York Times*, April 1, 1924.

"The boy choristers of the church": *Washington Post*, May 11, 1924.

" 'I came to your concert with a double purpose' ": Vera B. Hammann and Mario C. Yon, *The Heavens Heard Him* (Exposition Press, 1963).

"[Robert Hope-Jones] has been recently engaged in putting up in the cathedral loft a model": *New York Times*, March 26, 1905.

"The result of this trial has been [an] order by the authorities of the Cathedral of St. John": *New York Times*, March 7, 1906.

"The new organs jointly will cost $134,000": *New York Times*, June 26, 1927.

"An orchestra accompanied the choir": *New York Times*, April 18, 1927.

"Pietro A. Yon, organist and composer, has been elected organist of St. Patrick's Cathedral": *New York Herald Tribune*, April 17, 1927.

"The work of installing the first of the three new organs in St. Patrick's Cathedral": *New York Times*, November 26, 1927.

"A special feature of the service will be the rendering by Jacques Ungerer": *New York Times*, December 25, 1927.

"Beginning with the formal opening of the chancel organ in St. Patrick's Cathedral": *New York Times*, January 21, 1928.

"[T]here will be a concert": *New York Times*, January 28, 1928.

"Before the hour of service began": *The American Organist*, March 1928.

"Mr. Yon is the ideal organist for the Cathedral": Ibid.

"Under the direction of Pietro Yon": *New York Times*, April 9, 1928.

"My Dear Mr. Ungerer": Lavelle to Ungerer, August 4, 1928. Archdiocesan Archives of New York.

"After his retirement from Saint Patrick's in 1929": Program of *The Memorial Requiem Mass for Jacques-Cécilien Ungerer*.

4. "Professor" (1929–43)

"The average choirmaster in America is a musician who turns his mind": *New York Times*, September 28, 1930.

"an indubitably fine tenor voice": *New York Times*, September 21, 1920.

"Carl Schlegel, who in stature and rich timbre stands higher": *New York Times*, December 7, 1922.

"Carl Schlegel, formerly of the Metropolitan Opera Company, sang": *New York Times*, April 9, 1928.

"Two singers . . . are with him as chanters": *New York Herald Tribune*, October 3, 1932.

"The fine new instrument made by the Messrs. Kilgan": *New York Times*, June 10, 1928.

"[I]t was found that if the instrument was to be finished": *New York Times*, June 9, 1929.

"It is very much the same as light": *New York Times*, November 3, 1929.

"Please accept my sincerest thanks for Your most valuable prayers": Yon to Hayes, September 16, 1929. Archdiocesan Archives of New York, U-7.

"I wish to report now on the question of the radio": Yon to Lavelle, October 1, 1929. Archdiocesan Archives of New York, U-6.

"Cardinal Hayes and the lay trustees": *New York Times*, May 27, 1929.

"Announcement of the musical program": *New York World*, December 15, 1929.

"Dear Mr. Yon: Will you kindly": Sheen to Yon, undated. Private collection.

"On Tuesday evening, Feb. 11": *New York Times*, January 25, 1930.

"The several dozen police rather mismanaged the crowds": *The American Organist*, March 1930.

"There is only one organ in existence": *New York Evening World*, February 12, 1930.

"An exceedingly handsome program": *The American Organist*, March 1930.

"There is no timidity about the future of congregations": *The American Organist*, March 1930.

"Mr. Yon presented me with the libretto": Lavelle to Hayes, April 18, 1932. Archdiocesan Archives of New York, Q-24.

"It will take me many months to orchestrate it": *New York Herald Tribune*, October 3, 1932.

"A few days ago an invited audience heard": *New York Times*, November 4, 1933.

"Now he wants to insist that we should underwrite it": Lavelle to Hayes, February 10, 1934. Archdiocesan Archives of New York, U-18.

"We first behold the young Patrick": *New York Post*, May 1, 1934.

"Unfortunately the musical material was almost entirely undistinguished": *New York Times*, April 30, 1934.

"[A]s a rule, Mr. Yon is at his best": *New York Herald Tribune*, April 30, 1934.

"[L]et me make clear that this is not one of those contemporary pieces": *Musical America*, May 10, 1934.

"Mrs. McLaughlin is chairman of the patroness committee": *Chicago Daily Tribune*, January 18, 1936.

"[T]he first time in the history of the cathedral": *New York Times*, May 3, 1936.

"a fine composite of 'Laugh, Clown, Laugh' ": *Washington Post*, October 1, 1928.

"I beg Mr. Edward Rivetti to accept my sincere assurance": *Paterson Morning Call*, May 14, 1936.

"If he would put his mind to it he could probably beat me at my own game": *Extension*, April 1941.

"Pietro A. Yon, organist and musical director of St. Patrick's Cathedral, announced": *New York Times*, September 16, 1938.

"Circling my way round the eighth floor pandemonium": *Musical Digest*, April 1935.

"Worn only by the Pope and Archbishops": *New York Times*, March 13, 1940.

"International Station WCBX of the Columbia Broadcasting System presented": *The Diapason*, April 1940.

"He was one of the finest artists I ever knew": *Catholic News*, April 1940.

"a canvas pouch not unlike a carpenter's apron": *Time*, September 1, 1941.

"some of Paderewski's favorite music": *New York Times*, July 4, 1941.

"Once the clergy start a mass in the Catholic Church": *New York Times*, December 12, 1941.

"I am extremely sorry to disturb Your Excellency": Yon to Cicognani, February 22, 1942. Private collection.

"I have received your letter of February 22nd": Cicognani to Yon, February 27, 1942. Private collection.

"For the first time in more than fifteen years": *New York Times*, April 26, 1943.

"In the event that there be a vacancy": Giaquinto to Flannelly, May 2, 1943. Archdiocesan Archives of New York, C-18.

"At the conclusion of the mass, the choir sang": *New York Times*, November 27, 1943.

5. THE MORE THINGS CHANGE (1943-70)

"Extensive arrangements have been made": *New York Times*, April 29, 1945.

"Many were smiling, but others cried softly": *New York Times*, May 8, 1945.

"[H]e was again greeted with 'Ecce Sacerdos Magnus' ": *New York Times*, December 24, 1945.

"[P]ermit me to remind you": Flannelly to Courboin, April 10, 1947. Archdiocesan Archives of New York.

"It suddenly occurred to me that I was living in a twentieth century civilization": *New York Times*, February 15, 1948.

"An Easter Mass will be performed this Easter": Ibid.

"I have received your note suggesting an increase in salary": Flannelly to Courboin, June 7, 1948. Archives of St. Patrick's Cathedral.

"While the cost of living was increasing": Griffin to Flannelly, June 25, 1948. Archives of St. Patrick's Cathedral.

"I have given much consideration to the appeals": Flannelly to Courboin, October 28, 1948. Archives of St. Patrick's Cathedral.

"The midnight mass at St. Patrick's Cathedral . . . was televised": *New York Times*, December 25, 1948.

"The main point is the uncertainty": Courboin to Flannelly, June 25, 1953. Archives of St. Patrick's Cathedral.

"I applied for admission to the Walsh Home": Ungerer to Flannelly, March 17, 1953. Archdiocesan Archives of New York.

"Where it is impossible to have schools of singers": *Musicae sacrae disciplina*, encyclical of Pope Pius XII.

"The progress of the Choir": Concert program, dated December 13, 1960. Archdiocesan Archives of New York.

"Mabel Courboin was an attractive woman": "Charles Courboin, A Remembrance." *The American Organist*, September 1996.

"The monsignori and priests filed across Madison Avenue": *New York Times*, October 29, 1958.

"He lacked a complete choir": *New York Times*, August 10, 1959.

"The voice of the choir's soloist": *New York Times*, June 5, 1963.

"For a moment, there was not a whisper": *New York Times*, November 23, 1963.

"The high mass presents a special problem": *New York Times*, November 16, 1964.

"This was to encourage full participation": *New York Times*, May 16, 1966.

" 'We have to have certain pieces of music' ": *Wall Street Journal*, December 22, 1966.

"[the] ideal of exuberant, splashy, Great Master music": Thomas Day, *Why Catholics Can't Sing: The Culture of Catholicism and the Triumph of Bad Taste* (Crossroad Publishing Company, 1990).

"It is all in English now": *New York Times*, April 5, 1968.

"A few voices could be heard singing or humming quietly": *New York Times*, June 9, 1968.

"Protestant and Roman Catholic music": Ibid.

"A new musical era will begin in St. Patrick's Cathedral": *New York Times*, August 31, 1970.

6. BOYS AND GIRLS TOGETHER (1970–90)

"He was asked if he would hew to the line": *New York Times*, August 31, 1970.

"There should be a cantor or a choir director": *General Instruction of the Roman Missal*.

"Leopold Stokowski . . . conducted a tradition-shattering concert": *New York Times*, November 30, 1970.

" 'ecumenical' in its makeup": Ibid.

"a solemn but sometimes unchurchly work": Ibid.

"As an artistic event, this first program worked against large odds": Ibid.

"Donald Dumler has been appointed associate organist": *The Diapason*, January 1971.

"[I]t is certain that the amplification system was disadvantageous": *New York Times*, August 12, 1972.

"Bishop [Patrick V.] Ahern was principal celebrant": *New York Times*, March 18, 1973.

"Despite the overflow attendance": *New York Times*, February 19, 1975.

"long a champion of Mr. Hovhaness' music": *New York Times*, February 23, 1975.

"the first memorial Mass for a Jew": *New York Times*, October 15, 1975.

"a memorial concert honoring Arturo Toscanini": *New York Times*, November 24, 1977.

"You'll be there, red-cheeked and merry": *New York Times*, December 18, 1977.

"A highlight of the daylong program": *Catholic News*, November 9, 1978.

"Choirs from four parishes in the Archdiocese": *Catholic News*, May 17, 1979.

"For something nice and civilized to do tomorrow": *New York Times*, September 13, 1980.

"Beware of veristically minded prima donnas": *Los Angeles Times*, December 20, 1981.

"There have even been scalpers at St. Patrick's": *New York Times Magazine*, November 4, 1984.

7. THE TRASH TWIN OF FIFTH AVENUE (1990–97)

"We have to present music that reflects the liturgy": *New York Times*, December 24, 1996.

8. For the First Time(s) in Cathedral History (1998–)

"Those who could fall out of favor include": *New York Post*, July 3, 2000.

"Rehearsal time with the combined St. Patrick's Cathedral Choir": *New York Times*, April 26, 2005.

"Pascual is a superb performer": *American Record Guide*, July/August 2007.

"The Cathedral of St. Patrick Choir, led by Jennifer Pascual": *New York Times*, September 13, 2007.

"A ceremony at St. Patrick's Cathedral on Sept. 11": *New York Times*, September 23, 2007.

"Full-time *Associate Director of Music* for highly visible Roman Catholic Cathedral": *The American Organist*, December 2007.

"Archbishop Dolan made requests for several hymns": *Catholic New York*, April 8, 2009.

educational background, 251; as interim music director, 255–58; as Knight of the Holy Sepulchre, 289, 291; musical taste, 256, 259, 260, 261, 262, 266–67, 272, 279, 294; personality, 252, 253, 256, 257, 259, 265–66

Cardinal Hayes High School Band, 213

Cardinal Spellman High School Band, 180, 218

Carl, Johnnie, 274

Carlson, Stanley, 194–95, 195*n*

Carnegie Hall, 75, 77*n*, 79*n*, 87, 94, 99, 100–1, 103, 116, 117, 119, 120, 121, 122, 122*n*, 124, 126, 136, 142, 203

"Carol of the Bells," 170, 171

Caron, Gérard, 144, 147

Carreras, José, 229

Carroll Music, 220

Caruso, Enrico, xiii, 81

Cassidy, Claudia, 151*n*

Cassidy, Patrick, 280

Cathedral-Basilica of the Sacred Heart (Newark, N.J.), 301, 302

Cathedral-Basilica of St. James (Brooklyn, N.Y.), 287

Cathedral Basilica of St. Louis (St. Louis, Mo.), 92

Cathedral of Agen, 306

Cathedral of Annecy, 38

Cathedral Bells, 40

Cathedral of the Blessed Sacrament (Altoona, Pa.), 296

Cathedral of Breslau, 108

Cathedral Club, 69, 94, 131, 188

Cathedral College, 36, 69, 94, 131, 136, 143, 163, 172, 176

Cathedral of the Holy Cross (Boston, Mass.), 160

Cathedral of Notre Dame, 190, 242

Cathedral of St. John the Divine, 54*n*, 86, 196–97, 207, 215, 224, 240, 278, 284, 306

Cathedral of Sts. Peter and Paul (Philadelphia, Pa.), 217

Cathedral School, 61, 68, 94, 106, 120, 143

Catholic Charities, 84, 162

Catholic Choirmaster, The, 72, 76, 138

Catholic New York, 259, 273, 292, 314, 321, 323

Catholic News, 131, 146, 217, 219

Catholic Orphan Asylum, 4: as Boys' Orphan Asylum, 150

Catholic Theatre Movement, 69

Catholic University, 104

Cecilian Movement, 29–30, 35–36, 43, 48, 49*n*, 303. *See also* Society of St. Cecilia

Celebration of Irish Heritage, 232. *See also* Irish Heritage Concert

Chapel of Sts. Faith, Hope and Charity, 168

Chicago Daily Tribune, 56, 80, 151*n*, 185, 193

Children of Lir, 280

Chome, Victor (Mme.), 11

Choirs and choral societies: All City Concert Choir, 210; American Boychoir, 295*n*; American Musical Institute, 5; American Symphony Chorale, 207; Amor Artis, 298–99; Archdiocesan Festival Choir, 275, 301; Archdiocesan Festival Chorale, 301, 319, 324; Arion Singing Society, 121–22, 122*n*; Ars Nova Chorale and Orchestra, 251, 252, 253, 254; Atlanta Symphony Chorus, 306; Boys Choir of Harlem, 215, 275, 300; Cathedral College Choir, 131, 163; Catholic Oratorio Society, 59; The Chapel Chorale, 168–69; Choros Aristos, 234, 238, 242, 245, 248, 249; Chorus of St. Cecilia, 19, 29; Collegiate Chorale, 203; The Concert Chorale, 187, 235; Dessoff Choirs, 95; Fairfield County Chorale, 298; Fordham University Chorus, 207; Glee and Madrigal Society, 5; Harmonic Society, 5; Incarnation Choristers, 125; Mendelssohn Union, 5; Metropolitan Opera Chorus, 211; New Amsterdam Singers, 215, 237; New York Choral Society, 203, 309; New York Liederkranz,

157–59, 160, 160n, 162, 187, 198–99, 201, 206, 207, 208n, 211–12, 212n, 228, 235, 235n, 236, 240–41, 244, 257, 265, 267, 272, 274, 286–87, 286n, 291, 293, 294, 294n, 296, 299, 303, 309, 311, 316, 323; New Year's Eve, 41; at Sistine Chapel, 211

"Mighty Fortress Is Our God, A," 208

Millo, Aprile, 303

Min, Laura, 318

"Miserere," 21, 35, 129, 266

Mitterer, Ignaz Martin, 63

Moffo, Anna, 244–45

Moniz, Jeanne, 263

Montani, Nicola: "Christus Vincit," 315, 318

Monteverdi, Claudio, 239

Monti-Gorsey, Lola, 122

"Morning Has Broken," 296

Moro, Aldo (Prime Minister of Italy), 211

Morra, Antonio, 11

Moscona, Nicola, 132

Motley, John, 224

motu proprio: of 1903 (see also *Tra le sollecitudini*), 43–47, 48, 49, 49n, 51, 55, 56, 58, 59–60, 62, 65, 68, 73, 76, 113, 153, 167, 168, 302; of 2008 (see also *Summorum Pontificium*), 314

Mozart, Wolfgang Amadeus, 10, 24, 45, 55, 63, 167, 239, 310, 314: "Alleluia," 311, 318; "Ave Verum," 255, 316; "Dixit Dominus," 320; *Eine Kleine Nachtmusik*, 254; *Exsultate, Jubilate*, 254, 303, 307; "Lacrymosa," 255; "Laudate Dominum," 296; *Requiem*, 183, 224, 234, 271, 280, 294; *"Twelfth" Mass*, 7; *Vesperae Solennes de Confessore*, 316

Müller, Johann Immanuel: *St. Benedict Mass*, 157

Mundelein, George (Cardinal), 120–21

Murray, Matthew, 195n, 218, 223, 228

MUSIC/The AGO Magazine, 193, 205n

music copying, xiii, 25, 272, 274–75

Musicae sacrae disciplina, 167–68

Musical America, 73–74, 77, 80, 95, 118,

Musical Courier, 73, 76, 77, 81

Musical Digest, 126

Musical News and Herald, 140

Musicam Sacram, 191

Musicians' Union, 252

Mussolini, Benito, 130, 136

Naish, J. Carrol, 61n

Nardi, Claudia, 200n

Nassif, Lori, 263

National Association of Organists, 69

National Cathedral (Washington, D.C.), 236

National Choral Council, 297

National Day of Prayer, 321–22

National Shrine of the Immaculate Conception (Washington, D.C.), 251, 317

Nationals Stadium, 317

Nevison, Howard, 261

New England Conservatory of Music, 297

New England Magazine, 8

New Jersey Arts Council, 251

New Line Cinema, 304

New Music Review, 76, 86

New Year's Eve "Watch" service, 35, 111

New York American, 122

New York Civic Orchestra, 132

New York Daily News, 139, 218, 234, 276, 317

New York Freeman's Journal, The, 45, 48

New York Gregorian Club. *See* Gregorian Club

New York Herald, 7, 8, 51, 56

New York Herald Tribune, 87, 97, 104, 108, 113, 148, 178,

New York (magazine), 241

New York Philharmonic, 3, 6, 7, 11, 30, 32, 103, 117, 120, 153, 193, 193, 236: at St. Patrick's Cathedral, 19, 183, 184, 185, 250; with St. Patrick's Cathedral Choir, 235–36

New York Post, 117, 213, 286, 297

New York School of Liturgical Music, 252, 255, 256